Spiritual Friends

Spiritual Friends

A Methodology of
Soul Care and Spiritual Direction

Robert W. Kellemen, Ph.D.

RPM Books
PO Box 276
Taneytown, MD 21787

RPM Books exists to
equip the Body of Christ to change lives with Christ's changeless truth.

Visit *RPM Books* at www.rpmbooks.org on the Internet.

Contact *RPM Books* at publisher@rpmbooks.org.

The personal identities of the individuals described in this book
have been disguised in order to protect their privacy.

Publisher Publication Data

Kellemen, Robert W.
Spiritual friends: a methodology of soul care and spiritual direction / Robert W. Kellemen.
Includes bibliographical references.

ISBN: 0-9749066-4-6
Library of Congress Control Number: 2005904619

1. Pastoral counseling—Biblical teaching. 2. Spiritual life—Christianity. 3. Bible—Psychology.
253.5—dc 22

Printed in the United States of America

Contents

Acknowledgements

Partners on My Journey

As with *Soul Physicians*, my wife, Shirley, and my children, Josh and Marie, have been my primary partners on my journey—my life journey and my journey in writing *Spiritual Friends*. Shirley has been my spiritual friend for over a quarter-century as we have mutually enjoyed marital spiritual friendship—sustaining, healing, reconciling, and guiding each other's faith. Josh and Marie, 20 and 17 as I write, have openly and freely allowed me to be their spiritual friend, sustaining, healing, reconciling, and guiding their faith. Now as young adults, I'm enjoying a mutual spiritual friendship relationship with both of them.

My colleagues in the Master of Arts in Christian Counseling and Discipleship (MACCD) Department at Capital Bible Seminary have allowed me to relish a "David and Jonathan" relationship with each of them. What a privilege to work with a team, a family, of men and women committed to changing lives with Christ's changeless truth. Thank you Dwayne Bond, Chris Boucher, Susan Ellis, John Heater, Cindy Hunter, Shawn McBride, Doug McCracken, Terri Polm, Neva Powers, Mel Pride, Megumi Risden, Bob Rooney, David Swan, Jerry Teague, and Frankie Wright.

Fellow learners in our Discipleship Counseling II Labs have helped field-test these materials for the past decade. Without their open sharing, honest feedback, and dynamic relationships, *Spiritual Friends* would be a shell of itself.

My editorial team has sacrificed time and energy to shape *Spiritual Friends*. Thank you Carol Boucher, Chris Boucher, Kim Boucher, Susan Ellis, Nicole Joi, Marcia Neeley, Jim Nestle, Kim Nestle, Carl Strine, Robin Strine, and Lynn Vernon. Though any lingering faults are mine alone, without these individuals, *Spiritual Friends* would have been impossible.

Scott Ryser and I have shared a mutual spiritual friendship for nearly a decade now. He embodies the type of spiritual friend that I write about, and I hope that our relationship models the type of spiritual friendship that I teach. Thank you, Scott, for being my spiritual friend.

Two men, though viewed by many as occupying opposite poles of modern Christian counseling, have contributed to my theory and methodology of spiritual friendship: Drs. Larry Crabb and Jay Adams. From Dr. Crabb, I learned the *parakaletic* (encouraging) side of spiritual friendship—using "priestly presence" to sustain and heal those crushed by suffering. From Dr. Adams, I learned the *nouthetic* (exhorting) side of spiritual friendship—using "prophetic presentation" to reconcile and guide those overcome by besetting sins. They've taught me, like the Apostle Paul, that spiritual friendship involves speaking the truth in love through sharing soul *and* Scripture. They've modeled for me, like my "hero in the faith," Martin Luther, ministering, teaching, and writing from deeply held convictions. Like the Apostle Paul and Martin Luther before them, Larry Crabb and Jay Adams are pioneers. I salute their courage and creativity.

Introduction

Relating God's Truth to Human Relationships

> *"Man does not live on bread alone, but on every word that comes from the mouth of God"* (Matthew 4:4).

The Purpose of *Spiritual Friends*: Equipping You for the Personal Ministry of the Word

When people ponder the ministry of the Word, they often picture large and small group ministry—preaching from the pulpit, leading worship, teaching Sunday school classes, and facilitating small groups. When they consider personal ministry, they often picture "secular experts" who use "talk therapy" to heal the hurting and enlighten the confused.

How sad. Either we ignore the personal, one-to-one ministry of the Word altogether, or we surrender personal ministry to those who refuse to use the Word.

I've written *Spiritual Friends* to assist in the reversal of this trend. The purpose of *Spiritual Friends* is to provide a field-tested training manual that equips lay spiritual friends, pastoral soul physicians, and professional Christian counselors to master the personal ministry of the Word by implementing biblical and historical:

- Soul Care:

    - Sustaining: "It's normal to hurt."
    - Healing: "It's possible to hope."

- Spiritual Direction:

    - Reconciling: "It's horrible to sin, but wonderful to be forgiven."
    - Guiding: "It's supernatural to mature."

Please stop. Reread the preceding twenty-nine words (the bulleted section above). Befriend them. Memorize them. Roll them around on your tongue: soul care, spiritual direction, sustaining, healing, reconciling, guiding. "It's normal to hurt." "It's possible to hope." "It's horrible to sin, but wonderful to be forgiven." "It's supernatural to mature."

These concepts outline the difference between *Spiritual Friends* and other current approaches to the personal ministry of the Word. Everything in *Spiritual Friends* revolves around equipping you to become a skillful provider of the forgotten historic arts of soul care and spiritual direction through sustaining, healing, reconciling, and guiding.

Using these concepts, *Spiritual Friends* provides a biblically relevant and relationally practical model for relating God's truth to human relationships. Whether you're a loving lay person, a caring pastor, a competent professional Christian counselor, or an undergraduate/graduate student, you'll learn the personal ministry arts of biblical diagnosis and treatment intervention:

- Diagnosis: A *Diagnostic Spiritual Manual* (*DSM*) equipping spiritual friends with sixteen diagnostic indicators:

  - "Sufferology:" The eight unhealthy and healthy stages of response to suffering in sustaining and healing.
  - "Sancticology:" The eight unhealthy and healthy stages of response to sin in reconciling and guiding.

- Treatment Intervention: A workbook containing thousands of illustrative interactions and hundreds of skill-building exercises, for individual or group use, organized around twenty-two relational competencies using the acrostics:

  - *GRACE*: Sustaining
  - *RESTS*: Healing
  - *PEACEE*: Reconciling
  - *FAITHH*: Guiding

I've arranged *Spiritual Friends* in five sections. Section One explains what I mean by the term *spiritual friend*. It shares the relationships, résumé, roadmap, and roles of spiritual friends. Section Two equips you to practice the historic soul care art of sustaining as you learn how to implement sustaining diagnosis and treatment planning. Section Three trains you in the historic soul care art of healing, teaching you how to practice healing diagnosis and treatment planning. In Section Four, you'll learn how to put into practice the historic spiritual direction art of reconciling as you execute the skills of reconciling diagnosis and treatment planning. In Section Five, you'll master the historic spiritual direction art of guiding as you gain the relational competencies of guiding diagnosis and treatment planning.

How to Use *Spiritual Friends*: Active Engagement with the Material

To use *Spiritual Friends* effectively, you'll find it helpful to sense the relationship between it and *Soul Physicians*. As the respective subtitles suggest, *Soul Physicians* is a *theology* of soul care and spiritual direction, while *Spiritual Friends* is a *methodology* of soul care and spiritual direction.

Soul Physicians answers the "What?" question: "What is the nature of human nature?" It provides a biblical psychology—a theological understanding of image bearers as designed by God, depraved by sin, and redeemed by grace. It is the "why for" book focusing on biblical content and explaining the "science" of soul care and spiritual direction. Read it to enrich your counseling insight.

Spiritual Friends answers the "So what?" question: "So what do we do to biblically minister to image bearers?" It provides biblical therapy—a practical method for diagnosing and treating image bearers. It is the "how to" book focusing on relational competence and equipping you for the "art" of soul care and spiritual direction. Read it to master counseling competencies.

To benefit from *Spiritual Friends*, it is advantageous to read *Soul Physicians*. However, I've attempted to integrate just enough material from *Soul Physicians* into *Spiritual Friends* to assist those who have not read *Soul Physicians*, while refreshing the memories of those who have. Those of you familiar with *Soul Physicians* will notice charts, summaries, ideas, and quotes from that book. My intent has been to connect the two books without creating redundancy. I'm praying that you'll have many "aha experiences" where you will say, "So that's how you apply that truth!"

Whether new to the books or old friends, to profit from *Spiritual Friends* it's important that you view it as a *workbook*. I've designed it to encourage and assist active engagement rather than passive reading.

Every chapter provides content that explains how to diagnose or treat your spiritual friends using principles and practices of sustaining, healing, reconciling, or guiding. Further, every chapter provides at least one section called *Exploring Your Spiritual Journey*. These sections help you to relate spiritual friendship principles to *your* life. Whether using *Spiritual Friends* individually or in a group setting, I encourage you to complete these "assignments" before reading the subsequent materials. Having field-tested *Spiritual Friends* in churches, seminars, graduate schools, and seminaries for over two decades, trust me when I tell you that these personal application exercises are indispensable. Only those who walk the spiritual friendship journey with Christ, the ultimate Spiritual Friend, can offer spiritual friendship to others.

Additionally, every chapter provides at least one section (normally several sections) entitled *Maturing Your Spiritual Friendship Competency*. These sections equip you to relate spiritual friendship principles to *others*. They provide practice opportunities to develop the relational competencies necessary to be a biblically effective spiritual friend. Again, having field-tested *Spiritual Friends*, I can assure you that these competency exercises are essential for your training.

I've designed the book for either individual or group use. You'll notice this especially when using the *Maturing Your Spiritual Friendship Competency* sections. A number of your assignments/exercises in these sections offer you the opportunity either to write your responses to various situations, or to role-play with a partner providing spiritual friendship in those situations.

I've also planned *Spiritual Friends* for use with various people in a variety of settings. Whether you're a pastor, professional Christian counselor, or lay spiritual friend, you'll find this manual beneficial. You'll be able to use it in church settings training lay people, para-church settings training care givers, and in college, graduate, and seminary education settings equipping students for the personal ministry of the Word.

As you read *Spiritual Friends*, you'll note my use of various terms for personal ministry. Normally I choose terms like spiritual friend, spiritual friendship, soul care, and spiritual direction. At other times, when the context suggests it, I use other terms like pastoral counselor, Christian counselor, parishioner, client, and counselee. I use these terms interchangeably.

You'll be able to more effectively benefit from *Spiritual Friends* if you gain something of my heartbeat as I wrote it. Box I:1 portrays the mission, vision, passion, and commission of *Spiritual Friends*. You'll also find it helpful to keep the big picture in mind. Box I:2 summarizes the sixteen diagnostic indicators taught in *Spiritual Friends*. Box I:3 outlines the twenty-two relational competencies that you'll learn in *Spiritual Friends*. I pray that you'll enjoy your spiritual friendship journey as much as I have enjoyed writing about it.

Box I:1
Spiritual Friends MVP-C Statement

Mission Statement

My mission is to equip you to
sustain people so they experience the truth that *it's normal to hurt*,
heal people so they experience the truth that *it's possible to hope*,
reconcile people so they experience the twin truths that
it's horrible to sin, but wonderful to be forgiven, and
guide people so they experience the truth that *it's supernatural to mature*.

Vision Statement

It is my dream for you to
think biblically—diagnosis through biblical wisdom,
grow personally—ministry through maturity,
relate deeply—treatment through personal care,
and communicate skillfully—intervention through relational interaction.

Passion Statement

Relating God's truth to human relationships.

Commission Statement

You will become a soul care giver who
compassionately identifies with people in pain,
redirecting them to Christ and the Body of Christ to sustain and heal their faith,
so people experience communion with Christ and conformity to Christ as they
love God (exalt God by enjoying and trusting him) and love others.
You will become a spiritual director who understands spiritual dynamics,
discerns root causes of spiritual conflicts,
and provides loving wisdom to reconcile and guide faith,
so people experience communion with Christ and conformity to Christ as they
love God (exalt God by enjoying and trusting him) and love others.

Box I:2
Diagnosis/Diagnostic Indicators Overview

"Sufferology"
Diagnosing the Eight Unhealthy and Healthy Stages of Response to Suffering

Diagnosis in Sustaining: Sufferology Part I—"It's Normal to Hurt and Necessary to Grieve."

- **Diagnostic Indicator One**: Is My Spiritual Friend Practicing Denial or Candor?
- **Diagnostic Indicator Two**: Is My Spiritual Friend Practicing Anger or Complaint?
- **Diagnostic Indicator Three**: Is My Spiritual Friend Practicing Works or Cry?
- **Diagnostic Indicator Four**: Is My Spiritual Friend Practicing Depression/Alienation or Comfort?

Diagnosis in Healing: Sufferology Part II—"It's Possible to Hope in the Midst of Grief."

- **Diagnostic Indicator One**: Is My Spiritual Friend Practicing Regrouping or Waiting?
- **Diagnostic Indicator Two**: Is My Spiritual Friend Practicing Deadening or Wailing?
- **Diagnostic Indicator Three**: Is My Spiritual Friend Practicing Despairing or Weaving?
- **Diagnostic Indicator Four**: Is My Spiritual Friend Practicing Digging Cisterns or Worshipping?

"Sancticology"
Diagnosing the Eight Unhealthy and Healthy Stages of Response to Sin

Diagnosis in Reconciling: Sancticology Part I—"It's Wonderful to Receive Forgiveness by Grace."

- **Diagnostic Indicator One**: Is My Spiritual Friend Blind to Guilt or Aware of Guilt?
- **Diagnostic Indicator Two**: Is My Spiritual Friend Stubborn toward Sin or Acknowledging Sin?
- **Diagnostic Indicator Three**: Is My Spiritual Friend Working to Find Forgiveness or Accepting Grace?
- **Diagnostic Indicator Four**: Is My Spiritual Friend Stagnating Spiritually or Advancing in Growth?

Diagnosis in Guiding: Sancticology Part II—"It's Supernatural to Grow in Grace."

- **Diagnostic Indicator One**: Is My Spiritual Friend Practicing Sanctification by Law or by Grace?
- **Diagnostic Indicator Two**: Is My Spiritual Friend Practicing Sanctification by Works or by Faith?
- **Diagnostic Indicator Three**: Is My Spiritual Friend Practicing Sanctification by Temporal Focus or by Future Hope?
- **Diagnostic Indicator Four**: Is My Spiritual Friend Practicing Sanctification by Selfish Motivation or by Sacrificial Love?

Box I:3
Treatment Intervention/Relational Competencies Overview

Sustaining Relational Competencies: *GRACE*

G	Grace Connecting:	Committed Involvement
R	Rich Soul Empathizing:	Climbing in the Casket
A	Accurate/Active Spiritual Listening:	Faith-Drenched Alertness
C	Caring Spiritual Conversations:	Sustaining Theological Trialogues
E	Empathetic Scriptural Explorations:	Sustaining Biblical Trialogues

Healing Relational Competencies: *RESTS*

R	Relational Treatment Planning:	Mutuality in Hope Building
E	Encouraging Communication:	Hope-Based Interactions
S	Story Reinterpreting:	Co-Authoring Resurrection Narratives
T	Thirsts Spiritual Conversations:	Healing Theological Trialogues
S	Stretching Scriptural Explorations:	Healing Biblical Trialogues

Reconciling Relational Competencies: *PEACEE*

P	Probing Theologically:	Theory-Guided Awareness
E	Exposing through Confronting Wisely:	Disclosing Discrepancies
A	Active Softening of Stubbornness:	Loosening Resistance to Repentance
C	Connecting Intimately:	Relating in the Moment
E	Enlightening Spiritual Conversations:	Reconciling Theological Trialogues
E	Empowering Scriptural Explorations:	Reconciling Biblical Trialogues

Guiding Relational Competencies: *FAITHH*

F	Faith-Based Interventions:	New Covenant Living
A	Activating Envisioned Maturity:	Stirring Up God's Gifts
I	Insight-Oriented Treatment Planning:	Collaborative Spiritual Direction
T	Taking Action:	Homework That Works
H	Holiness Spiritual Conversations:	Guiding Theological Trialogues
H	Heroic Scriptural Explorations:	Guiding Biblical Trialogues

Chapter One

Portraits of Spiritual Friendship
The Relationships of Spiritual Friends

> *"Spiritual growth is concerned with companionship: first companionship with God, and second, companionship with our fellow human beings"* (Alan Jones, *Exploring Spiritual Direction: An Essay on Christian Friendship*, p. 1).

The Art of Arts

A church member knocks on her pastor's door early Monday morning. She's in tears over her teenage son's suicide attempt. Her pastor greets her with a loving, gentle welcome, ushers her into his office, and opens in prayer. Together they're ready to engage in the art of arts: spiritual friendship.

A young man firmly grips the hand of his new friend, a graduate-counseling student serving as his mentor. By this point in their relationship they're oblivious to the required videotaping, as they enter the "Counseling Center." Together they're ready to engage in the art of arts: spiritual friendship.

A client arrives for his scheduled appointment with his professional Christian counselor. He's hopeful that he'll finally find help to break the hold that rage has on his heart and relationships. Together they're ready to engage in the art of arts: spiritual friendship.

A young woman hugs her female lay encourager as they enter the "Encouragement Center" for their seventh meeting. They both experience a close connection and a calm confidence that Christ will continue his good work in and through them. Together they're ready to engage in the art of arts: spiritual friendship.

Two friends sitting in the corner of an almost empty local diner sip coffee as they talk. For two years this has been their "sacred place" where they meet to bear one another's burdens. Together they're ready to engage in the art of arts: spiritual friendship.

The settings are almost limitless and the individuals so very diverse. Yet, the art is the same—the art of spiritual friendship.

The titles seem almost endless as well: spiritual friend, physician of the soul, soul care giver, spiritual director, sacred friend, soul friend, spiritual companion, companions in hope, pastoral counselor, lay counselor, biblical counselor, Christian counselor, discipleship counselor, discipler, mentor, elder, pastor, shepherd, and encourager.

The concept seems equally bottomless: spiritual direction, care of souls, soul care giving, the art of

Exploring Your Spiritual Journey

1. What impact are you hoping *Spiritual Friends* will have on you personally?

2. What impact are you hoping *Spiritual Friends* will have on how you minister to others? How do you long to use this equipping in other people's lives?

3. Share some of your fears and apprehensions as it hits you, "I'm going to 'counsel' people!?"

4. Share some of your joy and anticipation as it hits you, "I'm going to 'counsel' people!!"

soul keeping, the practice of Christian spirituality, discipling, mentoring, encouraging, coming along side to help, comforting, confronting, sharing, shepherding, pastoring, and befriending.

All these settings, titles, and concepts paint portraits of the art of arts, portraits of spiritual friendship. Each pictures something of what it means to be a spiritual friend. But what exactly is a spiritual friend? What does a spiritual friend "look like"? How do spiritual friends relate?

Stories of Spiritual Friendship

You're reading this book because you want to learn how to become a more effective spiritual friend. I'm writing this chapter because I long to turn your *want to* into a *have to*. By the time you complete this chapter, I pray that your heart cries out, "I *have to* be a spiritual friend." By the time you finish reading these stories, vignettes, illustrations, and biblical examples of spiritual friendship, I'm wanting you to say, "Father, I *have to* engage others, regardless of the setting, regardless of my paid position, in the art of arts, in spiritual friendship."

Join me as we picture in our imaginations and experience in our souls what it means to be a spiritual friend. Eavesdrop on some personal stories of spiritual friendship.

Lisa Beamer's Story of Spiritual Friendship

Recently my daughter and I have been reading *Let's Roll!*, Lisa Beamer's account of her husband, and 9-11 hero, Todd Beamer. Lisa writes:

September 11, 2001, began like any other normal day. Yet it was a day we'll never forget. The ringing of an alarm clock dragged me reluctantly from a deep sleep at 5:45 AM on Tuesday, September 11. My husband, Todd, rolled over and silenced the annoying noise. I roused slightly, peeking out from under the covers only long enough to notice it was still dark outside (Beamer, *Let's Roll!*, p. 1).

Some three hours later, Lisa's friend Elaine called.

"Hi, Lisa. I know Todd is traveling today . . . and I was just calling to check on him . . . Do you have your television turned on? Have you seen what's happening?" "Elaine, what are you talking about?" "Turn the TV on," Elaine instructed. "There's been a plane crash at the World Trade Center" (Beamer, *Let's Roll!*, p. 4).

There would be four plane crashes that day. The United Airlines Flight en route from Newark to San Francisco that shattered upon impact in the fields of Pennsylvania farm country, shattered Lisa Beamer's life.

"No!" I screamed helplessly at the television. Without a shred of hard evidence, I knew intuitively that Todd was on that flight. Suddenly I felt as though my body weighed a million pounds; it seemed my heart might explode. I fell to my hands and knees and gasped again, "No!" (Beamer, *Let's Roll!*, p. 10).

In a chapter Lisa entitles *Inside the Nightmare*, she describes the clash of realities that we all face when tragedy ruptures our existence.

As I sat on the bed that Tuesday morning, September 11, my world had suddenly come to a halt. For a long time after I saw the crash site on TV and heard the news that it was a United flight that had crashed in Pennsylvania, I stared blankly at the field outside our window, trying to make sense of it. Just a few short hours earlier, Todd had been lying beside me. Now I was certain he was dead. My day had started out so . . . *ordinary*—with a shower, breakfast, laundry. And then the phone call had come. My mind somehow couldn't reconcile the two realities (Beamer, *Let's Roll!*, p. 163).

Lisa raised the question that we all wonder. "What do you do when your whole world is suddenly turned upside down?" (Beamer, *Let's Roll!*, p. 164*).*

What did Lisa Beamer need at this point? What would spiritual friendship have looked like?

David's Story of Spiritual Struggle and Spiritual Friendship

God calls shepherd-boy David to shepherd all Israel. Called, David serves. Serving, David suffers. When the chorus line of the day sings out, "Saul has slain his thousands, and David his tens of thousands" (1 Samuel 18:7), Saul becomes enraged. The refrain galls him. From that time on, Saul keeps a jealous eye on David. An evil eye.

The more success David enjoys, the more fear Saul endures. When Saul realizes that the Lord is with David and that his daughter, Michal, loves David, Saul becomes still more afraid. He remains David's enemy the rest of his days.

Plotting to kill David, Saul even enlists his son, Jonathan. Jonathan, very fond of David, spills the beans, not only warning David of impending danger, but also spying on his own father on David's behalf.

Exasperated, Saul expels a torrent of rage toward the harp-playing David, attempting to pin him to the wall, through the heart, with his spear. David eludes him and makes good his escape.

The plot thickens. Saul assembles his death squad to hunt down and execute David. David hides out in the cave of Adullam, surrounded by a rag-tag bunch described by the biblical author as, "all those who were in distress or in debt or discontented" (1 Samuel 22:2). Sounds like an ancient version of *The Bad News Bears*.

Day after day, Saul pursues David, forcing him to move his band of brothers from place to place. Camping in the wilderness like vagabonds, David learns that once again Saul has come to take his life (1 Samuel 23:15).

What did David need at this point? What would spiritual friendship have looked like?

Your Story of Spiritual Friendship

What about you? You've been there. We've all experienced a "dark night of the soul."

Think for a moment about one of the darkest times in your life: the death of a loved one, a dashed dream, a work termination, the illness of a child, the failure to overcome a besetting sin, a prodigal child, betrayal by a trusted friend, the affair, a divorce, a church split, unresolved conflict, depression, anxiety, your teenager's eating disorder, a rape, childhood sexual abuse, a robbery, the car accident, the fire . . .

What did your soul need at this point? What would spiritual friendship have looked like? What help do we need when we are suffering or sinning?

The Rest of the Story of Spiritual Friendship

Paul Harvey has always been one of my favorite radio personalities. I love his signature closing in his distinctive voice, "This is Paul Harvey. Good day." I enjoy the stories that he tells and how he tells them. "Page two," he'll say as he moves along in his story telling. Then, after the obligatory commercial break, he returns with his famous words said famously, "And now, the rest of the story."

To you, I say, "And now, the rest of the story." We've considered three stories of spiritual struggle: Lisa Beamer's, David's, and yours. Now let's hear the rest of the story of spiritual struggles endured through spiritual friendship.

The Rest of Lisa Beamer's Story of Spiritual Friendship

Lisa Beamer, who is a committed Christian, writes in her book what she needed and received. Having received official confirmation from United Airlines that her husband had indeed died in the crash of Flight 93, Lisa's spiritual friends swarmed to her side. "Rev. Bob Cushman, Todd's and my pastor, was among the first to arrive, along with Dr. Al Hickok, the professional counselor at our church. They came upstairs and prayed with me" (Beamer, *Let's Roll!*, p. 168).

However, it wasn't only the "professionals" who came alongside Lisa. "Members of our Care Circle and others from the community and church brought in food all day long, feeding the many people who gathered at our home, cleaning up messes, running errands, and taking care of the children" (Beamer, *Let's Roll!*, p. 168).

Lisa highlighted one particular spiritual friend.

At one point, in the middle of the day, during a lull in the activity in my room, I was staring blankly into space. I looked across Todd's and my bed, and there was Jan Pittas, one of our more quiet-natured friends, just sitting on the opposite corner of the bed, quietly praying for me, not talking aloud. Not talking at all. I didn't want to talk; I wasn't able to talk, and with her sweet, gentle spirit, Jan knew better than to try to talk to me. But her presence in the room was comforting. *Thank you, God, for sending Jan,* I prayed (Beamer, *Let's Roll!*, p. 170).

"But her presence in the room was comforting." What did Lisa need? She needed *human* love to keep her open to faith in *Divine* love. People like Jan Pittas and others enabled Lisa to remember the goodness of God. "In those days following the crash, this truth became even more real to me: God knows exactly *what* we need *when* we need it" (Beamer, *Let's Roll!*, p. 170).

Throughout the remaining pages of *Let's Roll!*, Lisa shares the quiet, natural way others helped her to see her human tragedy from God's perspective—through prayer, interaction, listening, and exploring Scriptures like Psalm 23; Isaiah 40:30-31; Romans 11:33-36; and 1 Thessalonians 4:17.

In an appropriately titled chapter *The Big Picture*, Lisa shares how these human messengers, her spiritual friends, helped her to hear God's message. "God has whispered two words to me over and over again: *Look up . . . Look up.* Through that quiet voice I'm reminded to look beyond my own little life to the Creator of the universe and what I know of his perspective. Without fail, looking up brings peace to my soul" (Beamer, *Let's Roll!*, p. 297).

What did Lisa Beamer need? Lisa Beamer needed:

- ◆ *Human* love to remind her of *God's* love.
- ◆ *Human companionship* to remind her of her *Divine Companion's* goodness.
- ◆ *Compassionate discernment* to reconnect her to God by reminding her of God's grace.
- ◆ *Community* to invite her to *communion* with Christ.

Lisa Beamer needed spiritual friends—ordinary people helping her to connect to her extraordinary God.

The Rest of David's Story of Spiritual Friendship

And what about David, the innocent fugitive hunted by the insane king? In David's desperate setting, we learn the source of his strength. "And Saul's son Jonathan went to David at Horesh and helped him find strength (*hazaq*) in God" (1 Samuel 23:16).

Finding strength (*hazaq*) pictures binding together, girding, and uniting. The Old Testament uses it for strengthening, encouraging, instilling courage in another, and aiding. The core idea emphasizes strengthening another person's grip by joining hands in support (Carl Weber, *Theological Wordbook of the Old Testament*, Vol. 1, p. 276).

We're made firmer and stronger when we bind ourselves together with one another. When we're losing our grip, we need to be gripped by others. In spiritual struggle, we need spiritual friendship.

As illustrative as this is, we've pondered only a portion of David's story of spiritual struggle and spiritual friendship. As David's spiritual journey continues, Saul pursues. David evades. Saul is vulnerable. David spares Saul's life, not once, but twice.

David battles victoriously for Yahweh. Returning from Yahweh-battle, David and his men experience Yahweh-mystery. The evil Amalekites have raided their camp at Ziklag where the wives and children of David and his men resided. Returning to Ziklag, "they found it destroyed by fire and their wives and sons and daughters taken captive" (1 Samuel 30:3). Grieving greatly, "David and his men wept aloud until they had no strength left to weep" (1 Samuel 30:4).

We would say that they're "wiped." Exhausted. Shattered. Overwhelmed.

David is no exception. "David was greatly distressed because the men were talking of stoning him; each one was bitter in spirit because of his sons and daughters" (1 Samuel 30:6a). If my wife and children had been taken hostage while I was away ministering for God, I would be distressed, too. If all those who worked for me were so bitter that they wanted to kill me, I would be distressed, too.

David's narrative begs for the intervening voice of Paul Harvey saying, "And now, the rest of the story." Here it is. "But David found strength (*hazaq*) in the LORD his God" (1 Samuel 30:6b).

Strength is the identical Hebrew word we examined in 1 Samuel 23:16—*hazaq*. David's previous *connection* with Jonathan empowers him to experience *communion* with Yahweh. Having *a* spiritual friend in his life to strengthen him, equips and empowers David to connect with *the* Spiritual Friend.

> **We need spiritual friends—Christians,**
> **and we need the Spiritual Friend—Christ.**
>
> **Spiritual friends—the Christian community—**
> **point us to our ultimate Spiritual Friend—Christ.**

From whence cometh David's help? Who do we need when we are suffering or sinning? What do we need along our spiritual journey when we face spiritual struggles? We need spiritual friends—Christians, and we need the Spiritual Friend—Christ.

Spiritual friends—the Christian community—point us to our ultimate Spiritual Friend—Christ. God has designed us to find communion and closeness with him—our true source of all help—through community and connection with one another. Spiritual friendship is our greatest hope for connecting to God's help.

The Rest of Your Story of Spiritual Friendship

From whence cometh your help? What did you need and receive during your dark night of the soul? Think about it. Reflect. Remember. Ponder.

How did God touch you? Who did he touch you through? How did you experience his love? What enabled you to live based upon his truth? Which spiritual friend comes to mind as you ponder how God empowered you to victoriously confront your spiritual battle? How did your *connection* with your human spiritual friend encourage you to *commune* with your Divine Spiritual Friend?

God's Art Gallery of Spiritual Friendship

In the midst of spiritual crisis, we need spiritual connection—spiritual friendship. But just what does spiritual friendship look like? Would we know it if we saw it?

Allow me to guide you on a tour through God's art gallery filled with walls lined with pictures of spiritual friendship. View pictures of spiritual friendship as:

- Sacred Companionship
- Voice and Touch
- Christ Incarnated in Christians

Art Gallery Portrait One: Spiritual Friendship as Sacred Companionship

Spiritual friends are *sacred companions*. I'm convinced that one of the primary reasons that we fail to experience Christ's power is because we fail to take our friendships seriously enough.

Our close friendships are sacred. They're holy and sanctified, committed and consecrated, serious and mysterious, beautiful and blessed by God.

A sacred companion dares to enter the holy place of your soul—the messy rooms filled with fear, darkness, chaos, and confusion. She also thrills to enter the redeemed core of your soul—that central room touched by God, yet rarely tapped into or stirred up by the mere acquaintance. A sacred companion is someone who cares about you so much and knows you so well, that he helps you to taste God's goodness and grace where others only see suffering and sin.

Even more, your sacred companions courageously encourage you to enter the Holy of Holies of your soul—to live face-to-face with God in intimate integrity. No wonder the author of Hebrews directly links bold entrance into God's presence (Hebrews 10:19-23) with the bold encouragement shared between brothers and sisters in Christ (Hebrews 10:24-25).

Art Gallery Portrait Two: Spiritual Friendship as Voice and Touch

Spiritual friends connect *voice and touch*. In the prologue to *Leadership Jazz*, Max DePree writes about his granddaughter, Zoe:

Zoe was born prematurely and weighed one pound, seven ounces, so small that my wedding ring could slide up her arm to her shoulder. The neonatologist who first examined her told us that she had a 5 to 10 percent chance of living three days. When Esther and I saw Zoe in her isolette in the neonatal intensive care unit, she had two IVs in her navel, one in her foot, a monitor on each side of her chest, and a respirator tube and a feeding tube in her mouth. To complicate matters, Zoe's biological father had jumped ship the month before Zoe was born. Realizing this, a wise and caring nurse named Ruth gave me my instructions. "For the next several months, at least, you're the surrogate father. I want you to come to the hospital every day to visit Zoe, and when you come, I want you to rub her body and her legs and arms with the tip of your finger. While you're caressing her, you should tell her over and over how much you love her, because she has to be able to connect your voice to your touch" (DePree, *Leadership Jazz*, p. 1).

DePree concludes with these insightful words. "God knew that we also needed both His voice and His touch. So He gave us His Word (His Son) and also His Body (the Church). God's voice and touch say, 'I love you'" (Depree, *Leadership Jazz*, p. 2).

God's Word is his voice speaking to you. God's people are his touch speaking his Word into your soul.

Art Gallery Portrait Three: Spiritual Friendship as Christ Incarnated in Christians

Spiritual friendship is *Christ incarnated in Christians*. Dave is one of my best friends from seminary days. One night when his daughter, Kristen, was about five or six, she awoke from a bad dream. Hearing her cries and whimperings, Dave got out of bed to comfort Kristen. He hugged her, and she was still. Then they prayed together. His prayer was meant to reassure her that Jesus was watching over her. But when Dave finished praying and was about to leave Kristen, her whimperings began again. Dave reminded her again, "You know that Jesus is watching over you."

Kristen responded, "I know, but I need Jesus with some skin on him!"

That's what God calls us to be for each other: *Jesus with skin on him*. Spiritual friends give each other small tastes, samples now, of how good and gracious Jesus is.

Spiritual friendship is a human relational bridge that reconnects our soul to God. We are more than professionals, or practitioners, or pastors; we are fellow pilgrims. We journey with one another through the valley of the shadow of death. Then we lay down our lives for each other, forming a bridge from the valley of death to the oasis of hope—the oasis of God's goodness and grace.

The Power for Spiritual Friendship: Grace Alone

Having enjoyed stories of spiritual friends and portraits of the nature of spiritual friendship, now we need to ponder how we practice spiritual friendship. By "how," I do not mean what we do—we'll learn and experience that throughout *Spiritual Friends*. By "how," I mean by *what power* for *what purpose* and in *what manner* do we perform the art of arts?

The Priority of Spiritual Friendship: Grace

Spiritual friends are dispensers of Christ's grace. Why grace? Because only two things have ever changed the human soul: *sin* and *grace*.

Sin, spread like a cancer by Satan, changed us from lovers of God to prodigal spouses. Grace, dispensed as the cure by Christ, returns our hearts home. Grace enables us to envision God once again as our *Pursuing Father*, Christ once again as our *Worthy Groom*, and the Holy Spirit once again as our *Inspiring Mentor*. Grace enlightens us to envision the Trinity as *a Divine Community of Lovers* who long to welcome us into their eternal, perfect circle of unbroken love.

God commissions us to connect one another to Christ's grace. As ambassadors of reconciliation, we understand that Christ's gospel of grace heals the evils we have suffered and the sins we have committed.

The Purpose of Spiritual Friendship: Grace Glorification

Let's start big. Huge. Why are we here? What is the purpose of life on planet Earth? Why hasn't Jesus brought us home to heaven yet? Our primary purpose while we remain on planet Earth is to experience *communion* with Christ, *conformity* to Christ, and *connection* with Christians, while fulfilling our *commission* to call others to enjoy and exalt Christ.

In Philippians 3, Paul counts everything else in life dung (camel manure) compared to knowing Christ intimately (communion), being conformed to Christ's likeness (conformity), and calling others to Christ's family (connection and commission). That's our goal as spiritual friends: to *interdependently* help each other to move toward *intimacy* with Christ and *imitation* of Christ that *increases* the glory brought to Christ.

In other words, ultimately spiritual friendship is not about us. Spiritual friendship is about our ultimate Spiritual Friend.

The Process of Spiritual Friendship: Grace Relationships

How do we know him and make him known? It may be simpler than we suspect: by knowing one another. The purpose of the Church is to be a community of lightbearers who make Jesus known through grace relationships.

God unleashes his power to be like Christ in Christian community. The ability to know Christ is nourished as we connect to Christ's children. "I pray that you, being rooted and established in love, may have power, *together with all the saints*, to grasp how wide and long and high and deep is the love of Christ" (Ephesians 3:17b-18, emphasis added).

Since living face-to-face with God by grace alone is central to biblical Christianity, then grace relationships are the key to Christian maturity. We need gospel communities where we truly touch soul-to-soul with the grace to recognize and delight in the goodness God has created in each other.

The issue is not, "Can I listen? Can I diagnose?" It's, "Can I relate? Can I share tastes of grace?"

In Colossians 1:27-2:3, Paul pictures the life of Christ in him being poured into his disciples. He explains how this occurs in 1 Thessalonians 2:8. "So being affectionately desirous of you, we were willing to have imparted unto you, not the gospel of God only, but also our own souls, because you were dear unto us" (KJV). Paul shares his *soul* and the *Scriptures*. Paul believes in *intervention* through *interaction* and *insight* because he believes that relationships are God's channel of grace. He practices spiritual friendship, modeling the nature of all true spiritual friendships:

- Spiritual friendship helps us to pay attention to God.
- Spiritual friendship provides company along a tough but extremely important journey.
- Spiritual friendship opens us increasingly to Christ's resurrection power.
- Spiritual friendship brings spirituality and sacredness to relationships.

Spiritual friends are *conductors of Christ's resurrection power and dispensers of Christ's grace*. The communication of wisdom takes many forms, the most intimate and powerful being friendship. "I have called you friends, for everything that I have learned from my Father I have made known to you" (John 15:15). Some of my dreams for you as a spiritual friend are:

- To possess and present compassionate discernment.
- To share the wisdom of God in the context of spiritual friendship.
- To participate in the art of caring engagement.
- To share spiritual theology where truth deeply impacts relationships.

The Pattern of Spiritual Friendship: Grace Narratives

We are called to live a "grace narrative." Our lives are Christ's epistle. Our purpose is to dispatch love letters to the world that read, "God is good. He's beautiful. Awesome. He's your Worthy Groom. Come home to his good heart."

In what manner do we dispatch love letters in spiritual friendship? This question reminds me of another question that people often ask me, "Is spiritual friendship non-directive or directive?"

My answer?

"Neither. It is *collaborative*."

Directive spiritual friendship is like a *monologue* where one person talks *at* another. Non-directive spiritual friendship is like a *dialogue* where two people share together. Collaborative spiritual friendship is a *trialogue* where three people share—two spiritual friends and the ultimate Spiritual Friend—Jesus.

Some approaches to spiritual friendship and counseling focus on *monologue*. There is a declaration of truth, but it is given apart from an intimate relationship. Still other spiritual friendship and counseling models highlight *dialogue*. There is a discussion, but God is relatively absent from it. True biblical counseling and spiritual friendship is a *trialogue*. We invite God into the core of our lives. His Word communicates to us piercing both our hearts. "Where two or three are gathered together in my name, there am I in the midst of them" (Matthew 18:20, KJV).

Effective spiritual friends *exegete souls* and *Scripture*. We combine truth and love. Christianity is an invitation into a drama, a love story. Our spiritual meaning and mission is given to us in story form. As spiritual friends, we enter others' journeys helping them to remember their part in God's drama. We help them to see that God is good even when life is bad, and that God is gracious even when they are sinful.

Biblical counseling is Emmaus Road Counseling (compare Luke 24:13-35 and see a parable based upon this passage in Box 1:1). As traveling companions, we unveil the hidden Christ to hungry and hurting people.

Where We've Been and Where We're Headed

How's your *want to*? Is God moving it to a *have to*?

We've entered Lisa's, David's, and your story of spiritual friendship in the midst of spiritual crisis. We've browsed God's art gallery of spiritual friendship seeing pictures of sacred companions, voice and touch, and Christ incarnated in Christians ("Jesus with skin on him"). We've pondered the priority, purpose, process, and pattern of spiritual friendship, detecting that *grace* claims ground zero in each case.

What is God stirring in your heart? Are you leaving the same as you came?

On second thought, don't leave just yet. On your own, with a spiritual friend, or in a spiritual friendship small group, spend time further developing your spiritual friendship competency of grace-based spiritual friendship by completing the two pages following Box 1:1.

Then, return for Chapter Two: The Qualifications for Spiritual Friendship. Here we'll view the spiritual friend's résumé.

Box 1:1
Emmaus Road Counseling

Once upon a time, two discouraged middle-aged men endured a seven-mile walk. Talking as they walked, they dialogued about the events of the past week.

"Not how I expected it to end," said the first man, Cleopas.

"Nope. Not at all," concurred his friend, Jacob.

"Kinda' like that time I ran the marathon," Cleopas continued. "I was way ahead at the twenty-mile mark. Got my hopes up. Thought I might finally win something. Pictured the victor's crown placed on my head by the Emperor. The cheers of the crowd. The pride of my son. The joy in my heart. But those last few miles killed me. Seemed like the whole world was passing me by. I said then that I'd never dream again about anything. But Messiah started me dreamin' again."

"Boy can I relate. When my ship sunk in that storm—right after I had the best fishing season of my career, I said the same thing: 'Don't hope—ever!' But Messiah, he made me hope. Wish he hadn't. Wish I hadn't."

About then a stranger sauntered upon them. "What are you talking about, men?"

Cleopas, head down, heartbroken, responded. "You have to be the only person on the face of planet Earth who knows nothing about what happened this past week!"

"Tell me," the stranger urged.

"Messiah of Nazareth came. A great prophet. Powerful in every way. We had hoped that he was the one who was going to bring us life. But he only brought death. His death. The death of our dreams."

"Fools!" Stranger shouted. "Blind. Slow. Didn't your Scriptures teach you anything? Nothing about death before life? Winter before Spring? Suffering before resurrection?"

For the next several miles, Stranger trialogued with them from Scripture. Opening their eyes to himself.

Reaching their destination, they invited Stranger to their home for dinner. It was then, when Stranger prayed, that their blind eyes saw.

*They asked each other, "Weren't our hearts on fire inside us while he talked to us on the road? While he **trialogued** with us, bringing compassion and discernment into our dialogue?"*

Jacob added, "No one ever talked to me like that. With such passion. Such power. So personal. Truth and love kissing, soul and Scripture mingling. Cleopas, you are my best friend in all the world. I've known you for over four decades. We've shared so much together. Yet, we've never shared like Messiah just shared with us. What does that say about our relationship?"

"Hmm." Thoughtful. Stroking his beard as he leaned away from the table, Cleopas finally replied. "Guess it means that we could go deeper. Oh, I love swapping war stories. Talking about work, the weather, the kids. Love walking to the synagogue with you. Yet, when our hearts were discouraged, neither of us talked the way Messiah talked. Neither of us connected with Jehovah Elohim deeply enough that his words spilled over into ours, that his encouragement empowered us to encourage and empower each other."

*"Cleopas," Jacob interrupted, "I want to be different. I want **us** to be different. From now on, let's invite Messiah into the center of every conversation."*

"Jacob, I couldn't agree more," Cleopas concurred. "I want to commune with God so I can connect with you. I want our relationship to strengthen each other so we can find strength in God."

Then off they raced to trialogue with others about Messiah.

Maturing Your Spiritual Friendship Competency
Becoming a Grace-Based Spiritual Friend

1. Describe one of your best friendships as a child. What would your life have been like without that friendship?

2. Share about one of your best friendships now. What would be missing from your life without this friendship?

3. During one of your dark nights of the soul when you felt God's seeming absence:

   a. What did you need? In your situation, what met your need? What helped you?

   b. How did God touch you? Who did he touch you through? How did you experience his love? What enabled you to live based upon his truth?

4. Who is "Jesus with skin on him" for you? How?

5. For whom are you "Jesus with skin on him"? How?

6. As a spiritual friend, is your tendency more toward:

    ♦ Interaction: Sharing Your Soul   Love   Grace Relationships?
    ♦ Insight: Sharing Scripture   Truth   Grace Narratives?

    a. Where did you learn your tendency?

    b. What might it look like for you to better integrate these:

        ♦ Intervention through Interaction *and* Insight?
        ♦ Sharing Your Soul *and* Scripture?
        ♦ Grace Relationships *and* Grace Narratives?

7. What do you think needs to occur in your soul for you to grow as a spiritual friend?

8. Share a recent time when:

    a. You were involved in a *monologue* conversation. What impact did it have on you?

    b. You were involved in a *dialogue* conversation. What impact did it have on you?

    c. You were involved in a *trialogue* conversation. What impact did it have on you?

Chapter Two

Qualifications for Spiritual Friendship
The Résumé of Spiritual Friends

> *"If you have sought a spiritual companion before, you know the ambivalence it can involve. Whom can I really trust with this most intimate dimension of my being? Will he or she be able to understand me? Dare I really bare my soul with someone else?"* (Tilden Edwards, *Spiritual Friend*, p. 105).

Competent to Counsel

While I was working on my Ph.D., an article published in a major counseling journal sent shock waves through the counseling community. Its results, summarized below, called into question the efficacy of professional counseling training, while also distilling basic elements that qualify an individual to be an effective people helper.

The article traced the history of modern research into counselor effectiveness beginning with J. Durlak's landmark work examining the results of 42 studies which compared the effectiveness of professional helpers to paraprofessionals (lay helpers, spiritual friends). The data from the study indicated that lay helpers equaled or surpassed the effectiveness of the professional therapists (Durlak, *Comparative Effectiveness of Paraprofessional and Professional Helpers*).

J. Hattie, C. Sharpley, and H. Rogers attempted to refute those findings by combining the results of 46 studies. Their data, however, supported Durlak's conclusions. Clients of lay helpers consistently achieved more positive outcomes than did clients of the professionally educated and experienced counselors (Hattie, *Comparative Effectiveness of Professional and Paraprofessional Helpers*).

J. Berman and N. Norton reanalyzed Hattie's study. Their reanalysis indicated that lay counselors were equally effective as professional counselors in promoting positive change. They concluded that no research currently supported the notion that professional training, knowledge, or experience improved therapist effectiveness (Berman, *Does Professional Training Make a Therapist More Effective?*).

K. Herman, in his review of these studies, indicated that research suggested that professional training was not the primary means for developing competence in helping people. Rather, the personal characteristics of the helper were the greatest factors leading to competence as a counselor. In other words, the studies demonstrated that maturity, love, genuine concern, empathy, humility, and vulnerability were more important than professional training (Herman, *Reassessing Predictors of Therapist Competence*).

Exploring Your Spiritual Journey

1. What advantages might a lay spiritual friend have over a "professional" friend (psychologist, professional counselor, etc.)?

2. What advantages might a professional friend have over a lay spiritual friend?

3. Research evidence is clear. The more people train to counsel, the less effective they become.

   a. Why do you think this is true?

   b. What can spiritual friends do to avoid such a horrible scenario?

4. If you were looking for someone to talk to about issues in your life, what qualifications would you look for?

The research perspective of the world has turned upside down the notion that an M.A., Ph.D., or professional license truly qualifies someone to claim the mantle of "counselor." It has called into question the résumé qualifications of an effective people helper.

Since I train pastoral and professional counselors for a living and since I equip lay counselors in churches across the country, I have no fundamental bias for or against pastoral, professional, or lay counselors. My purpose is not to demean the counseling profession. Rather, I want to raise to the surface the issue of counseling competency.

More than that, I want to raise your level of confidence in your Christ-instilled competence to counsel. In Chapter One, my goal was to move you from an attitude of *want to*, to *have to*. "I don't just *want to* be a spiritual friend; I *have to* be a spiritual friend!" Now, in Chapter Two, my purpose is to create in you an attitude of *can do*. "In Christ, I *can do* the ministry of spiritual friendship!"

The Divine Counselor's Résumé Qualifications

Imagine that you are forwarding your résumé to the Holy Spirit, the Divine Counselor. What items would you highlight to demonstrate your eligibility to enter the ranks of soul physicians? What do the Scriptures say? What qualifies a person for the art of spiritual friendship? What qualities make you eligible to claim the mantle of soul care giver and spiritual friend?

Fortunately, for those of us who desire to be people helpers, the Apostle Paul already completed our résumé. "I myself am convinced, my brothers, that you yourselves are full of goodness, complete in knowledge and competent to instruct one another" (Romans 15:14). In this verse and the surrounding context, we discover the résumé of a spiritual friend:

- Character: "Full of Goodness"
- Content/Conviction: "Complete in Knowledge"
- Competence: "Competent to Instruct One Another"
- Community: "Brothers"

Consider who Paul is addressing by his phrase, "brothers." Are these pastors, elders, deacons, deaconesses, or former Jewish priests? Have they graduated from Bible college, seminary, or graduate school? Do they have degrees in psychology or counseling? Are they members of a mega-church or a church with a counseling center?

No. They are "average, ordinary" Christians in Rome. "Brothers" was the common designation of a believer regardless of gender, status, position, or rank. Based upon the surrounding context (Romans 16:1-16), Paul's addressees are members of small house churches spread throughout the city and dotting the countryside of Rome. These men and women, converted Jews and Greeks, slaves and free, Paul considers competent to counsel.

Based upon Paul's language, I conclude that Paul knew that his readers would be skeptical about their ability to disciple one another. I imagine them thinking, "Now Paul, perhaps you, a super Apostle, you are competent to counsel. Perhaps the other Apostles, also. Perhaps the great philosophers of the Roman Empire. But not us!"

Paul is quite emphatic in his language. The NIV accurately translates his emphasis, "I myself." "You yourselves." Paul's addition of the personal pronoun to the verb produces emphasis by redundancy. Paul wants no mistakes. He's positive that they're powerful. "I, I myself. Inspired by the Divine Counselor; I'm telling you that I am absolutely confident in you, you yourselves. Yes, you lay believers, men and women. You yourselves are competent to counsel one another."

Paul's not making an assumption here. He says that he's "convinced" (*pepeismai*). He's confident in them, trusts them, and knows that he can count on them to competently counsel one another. He has faith in their spiritual ability, being inwardly certain because of external evidence. The evidence he offers provides the biblical prescription for soul physicians, the biblical résumé for spiritual friends.

Character: Loving Like Jesus—Reflecting Christ
"Full of Goodness"

Is Paul saying that Christians who are far from Christ and unable to relate their way out of a paper bag are powerful spiritual friends? Of course not. Powerful spiritual friends have résumés with "full of goodness" as the first qualification, the first piece of evidence, that Paul accentuates.

"Goodness" (*agathos*) is the same word Paul uses in Galatians 5:22-23 as one of the nine aspects of the fruit of the Spirit. When I first read Romans 15:14, I wondered why Paul would pick the fruit of goodness. Why not love, joy, peace, or any other fruit of the Spirit?

So, I explored goodness. The Old Testament highlights the basic confession that God *is* good because his love endures forever (1 Chronicles 16:34). It also emphasizes that our good God *does* good (Exodus 18:9). That is, he displays his goodness in active social relationships. Further, I noted Christ's statement that only God is good (Matthew 19:17). Then I noticed the equation of goodness and godliness with god-like-ness—with Christlikeness (Matthew 5:43-48; Ephesians 2:10; Colossians 1:10). In each of these passages, goodness displays itself in active, grace-oriented relationships, as when our good Father causes his sun to shine upon and his rain to fall on the righteous and the unrighteous.

William Hendriksen, in his commentary on Galatians, explains that goodness is a virtue that reveals itself in social relationships, in our various contacts and connections with others (Hendriksen, *Galatians and Ephesians*, pp. 224-225). Theologian and linguist Walter Gundmann demonstrates that biblical goodness always reveals itself in relational contexts through undeserved kindness (Gundmann, *Theological Dictionary of the New Testament*, pp. 3-4).

> ## The powerful spiritual friend reflects the ultimate Spiritual Friend, Jesus.

Thus, in Romans 15:14, Paul is talking about *Christlike character* that relates with grace. The powerful spiritual friend reflects the ultimate Spiritual Friend, Jesus. We are powerful to the degree that we love like Jesus. Paul's teaching us that the powerful minister is the person who relates well, who connects deeply, who is compassionate, and who has the ability to develop intimate, grace relationships.

In discussing goodness, Paul uses the modifier "full" (*mestoi*). "Full" pictures a net that breaks due to the stress and tension of too much weight and a cup that is so full that its contents spill over. Paul pictures mature love and godly character flowing through Christ to us, then spilling over from us into our spiritual friend's life.

To the degree that you and I relate more and more like Jesus Christ, to the degree that we love like Jesus loves, to the degree that our relationships are as lovely as Christ's were, to that degree we will be powerful spiritual friends. The person who is good at relating, is the person whose words and actions have powerful impact.

Character Counts: Maturity Precedes Ministry

Lack of character development explains why typical counseling training can hinder rather than help. Typical training in "people helping" is harmful because theory and skill are emphasized over character.

Such training focuses on skills and techniques rather than on relationships, resulting in counselors who are technocrats—mechanical, soulless, and artless.

A generation ago, Eugene Kennedy and Victor Heckler performed a research study of priests that now seems prescient. They found priests severely underdeveloped in interpersonal relationship abilities. Their training was highly cognitive, although they were being trained for a calling that is extremely relational—demanding a great variety of practical skills and relational competencies. Yet, they received practically no training in human relations skills (Kennedy, *The Catholic Priest in the United States: Psychological Investigations*).

The same is true today of typical graduate training in counseling. Students receive cognitive and technological training (information and techniques), but little equipping in character and care. Many graduates in helping fields, for this very reason, become less capable of helping (see R. Carkhuff, *The Art of Helping*; D. Goleman, *Emotional Intelligence*; J. Kottler, *On Being a Therapist*; and M. McMinn, *Psychology, Theology, and Spirituality in Christian Counseling*). Overly cognitive training, run by educators who themselves lack basic helping competencies, is a devastating combination.

Of course, we don't have to rely upon research to form our conclusions. Instead, we can turn to passages like those in Box 2:1 that insist that character counts and that maturity must precede ministry.

Character Development Required: Internal Fruit Precedes Ministry Fruitfulness

We already have some indication concerning *what* character counts—the Christlike character of relational goodness. Though Paul accents this one fruit of the Spirit in Romans 15:14, it's clear from Galatians 5:22-6:10 that it requires all the Spirit's fruit to express the fullness of Christlike character. Following his discussion of the nine-fold fruit of the Spirit, Paul instructs those who are "spiritual" to be restorers. Who is qualified for the task of spiritual direction? The person who increasingly reflects the Christlike characteristics of love, joy, peace, patience, kindness, goodness, faithfulness, gentleness, and self-control.

This is why biblical spiritual friendship training integrates the cultivation of the fruit of the Spirit. We want to grow not only in relational competence, but also in spiritual intelligence. Box 2:2 overviews the relationship between the fruit of the Spirit and the four primary components of spiritual friendship: sustaining, healing, reconciling, and guiding.

Through the New Covenant, God has implanted in us a new heart filled with the Spirit's fruit. However, as Peter reminds us, we must cultivate the Spirit's fruit.

His divine power *has given us* everything we need for life and godliness through our knowledge of him who called us by his own glory and goodness. Through these he has given us his very great and precious promises, so that through them you may participate in the divine nature and escape the corruption in the world caused by evil desires. For this very reason, *make every effort* to add to your faith goodness; and to goodness, knowledge; and to knowledge, self-control; and to self-control, perseverance; and to perseverance, godliness; and to godliness, brotherly kindness; and to brotherly kindness, love. For if you possess these qualities *in increasing measure*, they will keep you from being ineffective and unproductive in your knowledge of our Lord Jesus Christ. But if anyone does not have them, he is nearsighted and blind, and has forgotten that he has been cleansed from his past sins (2 Peter 1:3-9, emphasis added).

God calls us to diligently discipline ourselves so that in humble cooperation with the Holy Spirit the implanted fruit grows. The blossoming of these character traits guarantees that we will be fruitful in our spiritual friendship ministry.

Box 2:1
Why Character Counts

- Matthew 7:3-5—Personal duplicity and hypocrisy prevent ministry integrity and efficacy.
- Matthew 11:28-30—Only the restful of heart can bring rest to restless souls.
- Matthew 22:35-40—The purpose of life and the goal of Scripture is love.
- Matthew 23:23-28—The more important matters are matters of the heart.
- Luke 10:25-37—The true minister fulfills the law of love from a heart of love.
- John 1:1-18; 17:1-26—Reality is relational.
- Romans 12:1-8; 1 Corinthians 12:1-14:25; 1 Peter 4:8-11—The Bible associates the giftedness of the Body of Christ with the love of the Spirit.
- Romans 13:8-10; James 2:8—Love is the summation of the entire law and the royal law of life.
- 1 Corinthians 13:1-13—Loveless and characterless ministry is worthless and useless.
- Galatians 5:22-6:10—The spiritual director must reflect the Spirit's fruit.
- Ephesians 4:11-16—The goal of ministry is growth in maturity, not simply increase in ability.
- Ephesians 4:15—Love is the context for speaking the truth.
- Philippians 1:9-11—The true source of ministry power is love abounding in knowledge.
- Colossians 1:24-2:2—Biblical encouragement flows from loving personal commitment.
- 1 Thessalonians 1:3—Personal ministry must be prompted by relational intimacy.
- 1 Thessalonians 2:8—Personal ministry shares Scripture and soul.
- 1 Timothy 1:5—The goal of truth is love.
- 1 Timothy 3:1-7; Titus 1:5-9—God's shepherding qualifications highlight inner heart character.
- 1 Timothy 4:12-16—Personal maturity and biblical purity are equally important ministry credentials.
- 2 Timothy 2:1-2—Relationships are the best context for learning to love.
- 2 Timothy 2:22-26—The one who confronts others must do so out of a pure heart.
- 2 Peter 1:3-11—Ministry is unfruitful when the implanted Spirit's fruit remains uncultivated.

Box 2:2
What Character Counts

Love:	Loving Compassion	Meta-Fruit
Joy:	Joyful Celebration	Guiding Fruit
Peace:	Peaceful Integrity	Sustaining Fruit
Patience/Longsuffering:	Longsuffering Resilience	Healing Fruit
Kindness/Gentleness:	Nourishing Kindness	Reconciling Fruit
Goodness:	Relational Goodness	Guiding Fruit
Faithfulness/Faith:	Grace-Focused Faith	Sustaining Fruit
Gentleness/Meekness:	Courageous Meekness	Reconciling Fruit
Self-Control:	Hope-Based Self-Control	Healing Fruit

Content/Conviction: Thinking Like Jesus—Renewed in Christ
"Complete in Knowledge"

Is Paul implying that the best spiritual friend is the "touchy-feely" person who never dedicates himself or herself to serious study of the Scripture? Not at all. Remember that God calls us to love him with our minds, with our brains. That's why Paul lists "complete in knowledge" as the second qualification on the spiritual friend's résumé.

"Complete" does not mean that we're walking biblical encyclopedias with absolute knowledge of all theological truth. Only God has encyclopedic knowledge of all things actual and possible. Instead, by "complete" Paul means that we're so filled with God's Word that it claims our entire being and stamps our whole life, conduct, attitude, and relationships. We're captured by God's truth.

What sort of knowledge does Paul emphasize? He could have chosen any of several words that highlight content or factual knowledge alone. However, Paul chooses a word for knowledge (*gnoseos*) that highlights the combination of fact and implication. Paul's word focuses upon insight and wisdom— the wisdom to relate truth to relationships.

Powerful spiritual friends apply God's Word first to their own relationships. They also have the insight to see how God's Word relates to their friend's relationships. Additionally, they have the biblical vision to see how God is relating to their friend. They have discernment to see life from God's perspective.

In Philippians 1:9-11, Paul develops his philosophy of gospel ministry.

And this is my prayer: that your love may abound more and more in knowledge and depth of insight, so that you may be able to discern what is best and may be pure and blameless until the day of Christ, filled with the fruit of righteousness that comes through Jesus Christ—to the glory and praise of God.

Notice Paul's coupling of truth and love. For him, ministry is never either/or—either we are loving, touchy-feely, heart people, or we are scholarly, academic, head people. Rather, ministry is both/and— we unite head and heart, love and truth in our personal ministry of the Word. Truth and love kiss.

When our love abounds more and more in knowledge, the result is insight—the ability to help our spiritual friends to discern not simply what is good, but what is best in their situation. This kissing of love and truth flows through us when we are people of character, and it develops deepened Christlike character in those to whom we minister.

In *Signs*, Mel Gibson plays a minister, Graham Hess, who has lost his faith. As the movie unfolds, we slowly learn why. His wife was killed while taking a late-night stroll along a country road near their farm. Called to the scene, the police chief informs Graham that his wife has only minutes to live. Leaning close to her mangled body that's trapped between a truck and a tree, he hears her whisper final words—words about both their children, about him, and about his brother, Merrill. Concerning Merrill she utters the cryptic phrase, "Tell him to swing away."

Turning from church and God, Graham tells Merrill, "'Swing away' was nothing more than the chance collision of random synapses bringing to mind a stored memory of your failed baseball career." Graham's cynicism only worsens as the plot thickens. Signs—crop circles—mysteriously appear on his farm. Inexplicably they begin to appear all around the world.

When foreboding ships hover over major cities across the globe, Merrill asks Graham for words of consolation and hope. The best Graham can do, at this point, is explain two possible ways to view life. "You can look at any sign either as some plan laid out and purposed by God, finding hope in the mysterious, seeing what others cannot see, trusting that God is active. Or, you can see signs simply as the hand that fate dealt you, deal with it, run from it, whatever. But it is nothing but chance."

In the fitting finale, aliens invade Graham's home. No weapon in sight, Graham remembers the prophecy given by his wife, "Tell Merrill to swing away." Looking just beyond Merrill's shoulder, Graham sees Merrill's baseball bat, a trophy from his batting championship. "Swing away, Merrill. Swing away!" Graham yells. Merrill does. The alien falls. Water—water from cups left by Graham's daughter who was afraid of contamination—spills on the creature, killing it, contaminated by life-giving water. Yet another sign shared by Graham's wife.

Biblical counselors read the signs—not cryptic signs from a movie, but God's perspective from inspired Scripture. They discern the activity of God in their spiritual friend's life. They understand something of God's behind-the-scenes activity. They are able to relate the mystery of Christ's gospel of grace to the minutia of daily life.

Spiritual friends read the signs because they read the Scriptures. They are filled with the conviction that God knows what he's talking about. They're convinced that God's Word is sufficient for human needs. They're filled with biblical content about people, problems, and solutions—from God's perspective.

This aspect of spiritual friendship is so vital, so foundational, that I devoted an entire book—*Soul Physicians*—to a detailed exploration and explanation of God's truth about life. *Spiritual Friends* builds upon the groundwork laid in *Soul Physicians*.

Competence: Serving Like Jesus—Reproducing Christ
"Competent to Instruct One Another"

Typical Christians in Rome with character and conviction are qualified to do what? Paul says they're competent to "instruct." The word "competent" (*dunamenoi*) means to have the power to accomplish a mission. It reminds me of Engineer Scotty on *Star Trek* crying out to Captain Kirk, "Captin' Kirrrk. We ainta' got da poworr! Our dilithium crystal, she's breakin' up!" Competence is the dilithium crystal, the warp drive, the fuel, the power, the dynamite necessary to fulfill God's call on our lives.

Competence also means to have the ability, capability, resources, and strength to function and relate well. Paul's saying that he's confident that believers are capable and competent in Christ.

Powerfully competent to do what? Powerful to "instruct" (*nouthetein*). Jay Adams, founder of the National Association of Nouthetic Counselors (NANC), describes nouthetic counseling as confronting for change out of concern (see Adams, *Competent to Counseling*, *The Christian Counselor's Manual*, and *More than Redemption: A Theology of Christian Counseling*). *Noutheteo* contains this nuance, especially when the proposed change emphasizes inner heart change leading to relational change.

The foundational meaning of *noutheteo* comes from the root *noeo* meaning to direct one's mind, to perceive, and from *nous*—the mind, heart, seat of spiritual, rational, and moral insight and action. The mind is the place of practical reason leading to moral action. The stress is not merely on the intellect, but also the will and disposition (J. Behm, *Theological Dictionary of the New Testament*, pp. 636-646). *Noutheteo* means to impart understanding, to set right, to lay on the heart. Nouthetic impartation of truth can take the form of admonition, teaching, reminding, advising, and spurring on.

Paul uses *noutheteo* in Colossians 1:20-29 to describe one aspect of his pastoral ministry. God commissioned him to present Christ's gospel of grace to people (1:20-25), infusing them with the hope of who they are in Christ (1:26-27), with the goal of presenting them mature in Christ (1:28), through personal, passionate, persistent involvement in their lives (1:28-29), by Christ's resurrection power (1:29). Believers who possess Christlike goodness (character) plus Christlike insight (conviction) are competent to disciple one another toward communion with Christ and conformity to Christ through the personal ministry of the Word.

Paul never intended Romans 15:14 to be the final or only word on the nature of personal ministry. Nor did he use *noutheteo* as the only or even the primary concept to describe personal ministry. For instance, in 1 Thessalonians 5:14, Paul uses five distinct words for soul care and spiritual direction. "And we urge (*parakaleo*) you, brothers, warn (*noutheteo*) those who are idle, encourage (*paramutheomai*) the timid, help (*antechomai*) the weak, be patient with (*makrothumeo*) everyone."

Among the many New Testament words for spiritual care, *parakaleo* predominates. Whereas *noutheteo* occurs eleven times in the New Testament, *parakaleo* (comfort, encourage, console) appears 109 times (Tim Clinton and George Ohlschlager, *Competent Christian Counseling*, p. 58).

In 2 Corinthians 1:3-11, Paul informs us that we are competent to comfort (*parakaleo*) one another. Those who have humbly received God's comfort, God equips to offer comfort to others.

The word *parakaleo* emphasizes personal presence (one called alongside to help) and suffering with another person. It seeks to turn desolation into consolation through hope in God. The duty of comfort, in Old and New Testament thinking, fell not upon professional helpers, but upon close relatives, neighbors, friends, and colleagues (G. Stahlin, *Theological Dictionary of the New Testament*, pp. 779-782). Comforters come alongside to help struggling, suffering people through personal presence coupled with scriptural insight.

When Christ ascended, he sent the Holy Spirit to be our *Parakletos*—our Comforter and Advocate called alongside to encourage and help in times of suffering, trouble, grief, injustice, and hardship (Stahlin, *Theological Dictionary of the New Testament*, pp. 778-779). The Spirit performs his ministry by being in us and by revealing truth to us (John 14:16-17). As the Spirit of Truth, his ministry is the exact opposite of Satan who is the father of lies (John 8.44). Satan's name is "the Accuser" (Revelation 12:10) and his core strategy is to speak lying words of condemnation to us. The Spirit's name is "Encourager" and "Advocate" and his strategy is to speak the truth in love about our justification and acceptance in Christ.

Think about what Paul is saying to *you*. You don't have to have a Ph.D. in counseling to be a biblical counselor or a spiritual friend. You have the Resource planted within you—the *Parakletos*, the Holy Spirit. You also have the resources planted within you—the ability to be a competent *parathetic* (combining *parakaleo* and *noutheteo*) counselor/spiritual friend who provides:

- ◆ Soul care through *parakaleo*: Coming alongside hurting people in their victimization and grief, suffering with them while offering hope to them through your personal presence coupled with scriptural insight—sustaining them so that they know that it's normal to hurt and healing them so that they know that it's possible to hope.
- ◆ Spiritual direction through *noutheteo*: Engaging struggling people in their personal walk with Christ through passionate, persistent, personal involvement in their lives in which you assist them to see the hope of who they are in Christ and help them to live out their lives in communion with and conformity to Christ—reconciling them so that they know that it's horrible to sin, but wonderful to be forgiven and guiding them so that they know that it's supernatural to mature.

You are competent to serve like Christ. You are equipped to reproduce Christlikeness in your spiritual friends. If the passages we've discussed so far are insufficient to convince you, then I challenge you to explore the extensive sampling of additional passages on one anothering presented in Box 2:3.

Community: Connecting in Jesus—Related in Christ
"Brothers"

Have you noticed Paul's plural address? He addresses "brothers" plural. The effective spiritual friend is no "Lone Ranger" believer.

Have you noticed the context for Paul's address? In Romans 12:3-8, he talks of using gifts in the context of the members (plural) of the Body of Christ.

Box 2:3
One Anothering: A Sampler

- Matthew 18:15-19—Restore one another.
- Matthew 22:35-40—Love one another.
- Matthew 23:23-26—Practice justice, mercy, and faithfulness with one another.
- Matthew 28:18-20—Disciple one another.
- Mark 9:50—Be at peace with one another.
- Luke 10:25-37—Love one another.
- John 13:14—Serve one another.
- John 13:34-35—Love one another.
- John 15:12-13, 17—Love one another.
- John 17:20-26—United with one another.
- Acts 2:42-47—Learn, share, and worship with one another.
- Acts 4:32-37—United in heart with one another.
- Acts 6:1-7—Care for one another.
- Acts 11:22-26—Encourage one another.
- Romans 1:11-12—Mutually encourage one another.
- Romans 12:3-8—Members one of another.
- Romans 12:10—Devoted to one another in brotherly love.
- Romans 12:10—Honor one another.
- Romans 12:15—Rejoice with one another.
- Romans 12:15—Weep with one another.
- Romans 12:16—Live in harmony with one another.
- Romans 13:8-10—Love one another.
- Romans 14:13—Stop passing judgment on one another.
- Romans 14:19—Edify one another.
- Romans 15:1—Bear with one another.
- Romans 15:2—Please one another.
- Romans 15:2—Build up one another.
- Romans 15:5—United with one another.
- Romans 15:7—Accept one another.
- Romans 15:14—Instruct one another.
- Romans 16:16—Greet one another with a holy kiss.
- 1 Corinthians 1:10—Agree with one another.
- 1 Corinthians 4:6—Do not take pride in one person over another.
- 1 Corinthians 10:24—Seek the good of one another.
- 1 Corinthians 12:4-27—Members one of another.
- 1 Corinthians 12:25—Equal concern for one another.
- 1 Corinthians 12:26—Suffer with one another.
- 1 Corinthians 12:26—Rejoice with one another.
- 1 Corinthians 13:1-8—Love one another.
- 1 Corinthians 14:1-3—Strengthen, encourage, and comfort one another.
- 1 Corinthians 16:20—Greet one another with a holy kiss.
- 2 Corinthians 1:3-11—Comfort one another.

Box 2:3
One Anothering: A Sampler, Continued

- 2 Corinthians 2:7-11—Forgive one another and reaffirm your love for one another.
- 2 Corinthians 5:14-21—Live for one another.
- 2 Corinthians 13:12—Greet one another with a holy kiss.
- Galatians 5:13—Serve one another in love.
- Galatians 5:15—Stop biting and devouring one another.
- Galatians 5:26—Stop provoking and envying one another.
- Galatians 6:1-3—Restore one another.
- Galatians 6:1-3—Carry each other's burdens.
- Ephesians 4:1-7—Bear with one another in love.
- Ephesians 4:11-16—Equip one another through speaking the truth in love.
- Ephesians 4:25—Speak truthfully to one another.
- Ephesians 4:29—Speak words that build up one another.
- Ephesians 4:32—Be kind and compassionate to one another.
- Ephesians 4:32—Forgive each other.
- Ephesians 5:19—Speak to one another in psalms, hymns, and spiritual songs.
- Ephesians 5:21—Submit to one another.
- Philippians 2:1-5—Consider others better than self.
- Philippians 2:1-5—Look out for the interests of others.
- Philippians 4:2—Agree with each other in the Lord.
- Colossians 1:25-2:2—Admonish, and teach one another.
- Colossians 3:9—Do not lie to one another.
- Colossians 3:12-14—Bear with one another.
- Colossians 3:12-14—Forgive one another.
- Colossians 3:15-17—Teach and admonish one another with all wisdom.
- 1 Thessalonians 2:12—Encourage, comfort, and urge one another.
- 1 Thessalonians 3:12—Increase in overflowing love for one another.
- 1 Thessalonians 4:9—Love each other.
- 1 Thessalonians 4:18—Encourage each other.
- 1 Thessalonians 5:11—Encourage one another.
- 1 Thessalonians 5:11—Build up each other.
- 1 Thessalonians 5:13—Live in peace with one another.
- 1 Thessalonians 5:14—Urge, warn, encourage, help, and be patient with one another.
- 1 Thessalonians 5:15—Be kind to each other.
- 2 Thessalonians 1:3—Love one another.
- 2 Thessalonians 3:15—Warn one another as brothers.
- 1 Timothy 5:20—Rebuke one another.
- 2 Timothy 2:2—Disciple and teach one another.
- 2 Timothy 2:22-26—Gently instruct one another in kindness.
- 2 Timothy 3:16-17—Teach, rebuke, correct, and train one another.
- 2 Timothy 4:1-8—Preach, correct, rebuke, encourage, and carefully instruct one another.
- Titus 1:6-11—Encourage one another by sound doctrine.
- Titus 2:1-15—Mentor one another.

Box 2:3
One Anothering: A Sampler, Continued

♦ Hebrews 3:7-19—Encourage one another daily.
♦ Hebrews 10:24—Consider how to spur one another on toward love and good deeds.
♦ Hebrews 10:25—Do not give up meeting with one another.
♦ Hebrews 10:25—Encourage one another.
♦ Hebrews 13:1—Keep on loving each other as brothers.
♦ James 2:8—Love one another.
♦ James 4:11—Do not slander one another.
♦ James 5:9—Do not grumble against one another.
♦ James 5:13-16—Pray for one another.
♦ James 5:16—Confess your sins to one another.
♦ 1 Peter 1:22—Love one another deeply from the heart.
♦ 1 Peter 3:8—Live in harmony with one another.
♦ 1 Peter 4:8—Above all, love each other deeply.
♦ 1 Peter 4:9—Offer hospitality to one another without grumbling.
♦ 1 Peter 4:10—Use all gifts to serve one another faithfully.
♦ 1 Peter 5:5—Clothe yourselves with humility toward one another.
♦ 1 Peter 5:14—Greet one another with a kiss of love.
♦ 1 John 1:7—Have fellowship with one another.
♦ 1 John 2:7-17—Love one another.
♦ 1 John 3:11-15—Love one another.
♦ 1 John 3:16-18—Lay down your life for one another.
♦ 1 John 4:7-21—Love one another.
♦ 2 John 5—Love one another.

In Romans 12:9-21, the context reflects one anothering. Be devoted to one another in love. Honor one another above self. Share with one another. Practice hospitality with one another. Rejoice with one another. Weep with one another. Live in harmony with one another.

In Romans 13, the context is love: "Whatever other commandments there may be, are summed up in this one rule: 'Love your neighbor as yourself.' Love does no harm to its neighbor. Therefore love is the fulfillment of the law" (13:9-10).

Paul continues his one anothering theme in Romans 14:1-15:13. Don't judge one another, instead mutually edify each other. Bear with one another. Please one another. Build up one another. Be united with one another. Encourage one another. Accept one another. Worship with one another.

In Romans 16, Paul writes about meeting together with one another in house churches where believers connect intimately. Connecting in community is the context, before and after Romans 15:14.

In the seminary program that I chair, we have lab courses where we learn and experience spiritual friendship. A core course requirement pairs students as spiritual friends/encouragement partners. These relationships blossom into some of the most meaningful aspects of our counseling training. For example, the pairing of Debbie, a mid-30s Caucasian woman, and Linda, an early-50s African-American woman, developed into a deep, lasting friendship. Never having met before September, they became so close that by December of that year, Linda asked Debbie to be her Matron of Honor at her May wedding. Not surprisingly, both Debbie and Linda are effective biblical counselors. They know how to connect.

One-to-one connection is vital, but so is small group community, which is another distinctive of our spiritual friendship labs. We not only develop relational competencies and cultivate Christlike character, we also connect as a caring community. As one of our professors likes to put it, "We get raw and real!" In the context of a nurturing small group environment, we become transparent and vulnerable. We weep with those who weep and rejoice with those who rejoice. Effective spiritual friends add another important line to their résumé: connection and community. Spiritual friends relate and connect in Christ.

Confident Competency in Christ

My friends, don't take a backseat to anyone! Spiritual friends, I'm confident that your maturing character, increasing content/conviction, and deepening communion/community makes you competent to counsel. Paul is likewise confident. Most importantly, God is confident because your competence comes from Christ. For your confidence in your Christ-instilled competency to grow, continue to develop Paul's spiritual friendship résumé:

- Character:
  - Loving Like Jesus—Reflecting Christ
  - ". . . Full of Goodness . . ."
- Content/Conviction:
  - Thinking Like Jesus—Renewed in Christ
  - ". . . Complete in Knowledge . . ."
- Competence:
  - Serving Like Jesus—Reproducing Christ
  - " . . . Competent to Instruct One Another . . ."
- Community:
  - Connecting in Jesus—Related in Christ
  - " . . . Brothers . . ."

The following pages further picture the spiritual friendship résumé qualifications found in Romans 15:14. Box 2:4 (*The Job Interview*) portrays what *not* to do—what *not* to prioritize in counseling training, in spiritual friendship preparation. Box 2:5 (*The Résumé of a Spiritual Friend*) illustrates what *to* do—what *to* emphasize in counseling preparation to become a qualified *parathetic* spiritual friend.

Where We've Been and Where We're Headed

How's your *can do*? Is God increasing your confidence in your Christ-instilled competence? Do you have a clearer picture of the qualities to focus on and develop to become a more equipped spiritual friend?

Thus far we've moved from *want to*, to *have to*, to *can do*. Now we head to *how to*.

We begin our *how to* section by exploring God's roadmap for spiritual friendship. We'll overview the nature of *parathetic* spiritual friendship through soul care and spiritual direction, and we'll outline the four biblical and historical aspects of *parathetic* spiritual friendship: sustaining, healing, reconciling, and guiding. Consider it our GPS—Global Positioning System—showing us *how to* offer personal ministry God's way.

Box 2:4
The Job Interview

Once upon a time, a spiffed up, nails-polished, hair-combed, twenty-something young woman shifted impatiently in her chair. Her first interview loomed with the **Bethlehem Counseling and Discipleship Center** *(BCDC). This was, she hoped, the entryway into her dream job, her dream vocation of being a Christian counselor.*

"I hope I have everything in order," Liz thought to herself. "Let's see, what is it I want to emphasize? Oh, yeah, my credentials, the great schools I've attended, the fine professors I've learned under . . ."

Just then, the Administrative Assistant beckoned Liz into another room.

Seated there was a man clad in a long flowing robe. A confident, yet humble look on his face. Weathered, but gentle.

"Welcome, Liz! Jim, who spoke with you on the phone, was called away on another matter. He asked me to pinch hit for him. I hope you don't mind."

"Oh, no. Not at all. Um. What should I call you?"

"Call me Josh. Well, I'd like to ask you a few questions about your potential qualifications for being a spiritual friend."

"Uh. I don't mean to interrupt, Josh, but the job position I was thinking about was 'Christian counselor,' not exactly 'spiritual friend.'"

"I understand Liz. Humor an old man. What character qualities do you believe equip you to be a competent spiritual, er, Christian counselor?"

Hemming while she hawed, Liz cleared her throat in the wild hope that such an act would clear her mind. She wanted to reply, "I've been told that such personal questions may be grounds for an employer harassment charge," but somehow she just couldn't see Josh ever being guilty of such.

"Well," she replied instead, "I received an A, almost an A+, in my course on Ethics. I completely understand the professional distance that a counselor must keep, the boundaries that I must maintain between my clients and myself."

Liz noted Josh's penetrating eyes and surmised that her answer was not quite what he desired.

"Okay, Liz. Thank you. A second question. What relational competence will you bring to your work as a spiritual friend, er, Christian counselor?"

Scratching her head while hoping something would penetrate her brain, Liz again was caught off guard. "Relational competence," she muttered under her breath, "he must mean what techniques and skills I have."

So she replied, "I took two lab courses where my grades were excellent. I learned the meta-skills model . . ." Her voice trailed off as she detected a sadness emanating from Josh.

"Liz, tell me some about your community connections . . ."

Before Josh could finish, Liz assumed she understood his meaning. "Oh, I think I have contacts with a number of social agencies and large churches so that developing a client base would not be difficult at all."

"Well," Josh interjected, "I was thinking of your faith community, of how your connections with your brothers and sisters in Christ will empower and encourage you in your ministry to others. But let me ask my final question. Tell me about the content you bring to your ministry of spiritual friendship."

Box 2:4
The Job Interview, Continued

"Finally," Liz thought to herself, "a question concerning what I actually know about counseling." Looking hopefully into Josh's eyes, Liz expounded the theories she had learned and the concepts she had gleaned from her years of education. But even now she was detecting that somehow she missed the mark. "Perhaps he was asking more about my deeply held personal convictions about Christ, Christianity, and Christian living . . ."

"Liz," Josh said compassionately, "I wonder if we could talk for a while about what we here at BCDC believe truly qualifies someone to be a Christian counselor, to be a spiritual friend . . ."

Box 2:5
The Résumé of a Spiritual Friend

Position Desired:
Spiritual Friend: Soul Care Giver and Spiritual Director

I'm applying for the position of *spiritual friend*. I want to minister as a *soul care giver* who compassionately identifies with people in pain and redirects them to Christ and the Body of Christ to sustain and heal their faith so they experience communion with Christ and conformity to Christ as they love God (exalt God by enjoying and trusting him) and love others.

I also want to serve as a *spiritual director* who understands spiritual dynamics and discerns root causes of spiritual conflicts, providing loving wisdom that reconciles and guides souls so they experience communion with Christ and conformity to Christ as they love God (exalt God by enjoying and trusting him) and love others.

Educational Values:
Being, Knowing, Doing, and Connecting

I commit to remaining on the cutting edge of ministry preparedness by following Christ's disciple-making model of intentionally and continually educating my whole person—my heart (being), my head (knowing), and my hands (doing), in the context of God's home/community (connecting).

Biblical Qualifications:
Heart, Head, Hands, and Home

My qualifications for this position include the following four areas of personal and professional development and preparation: heart, head, hands, and home.

1. An Enriched Heart to Manifest Godly Love: Being

Love: Spiritual Goal—Equipped to Be ("Full of Goodness")

- **Character: Christlike Love**
- **A Soft Heart for Godliness: Spiritual Maturity**
- **Spiritual Formation: Maturity through Intimacy with Christ and His Ministers**

Since personal maturity is the foundation for powerful spiritual ministry, as a Christlike disciple-maker I have been and am being enriched to be "full of goodness"—to love more like Jesus (**reflecting** Christ).

Box 2:5
The Résumé of a Spiritual Friend, Continued

2. An Educated Head to Understand God's Truth: Knowing

Truth: Educational Goal—Equipped to Know ("Complete in Knowledge")

- **Content/Conviction: Christlike Thinking**
- **A Sharp Mind for Biblical Truth: Biblical Wisdom**
- **Spiritual Foundation: Biblical Ministry by Changing Lives with Christ's Changeless Truth**

Since powerful ministry requires biblical wisdom, as a Christlike disciple-maker I have been and continue to be educated to know God's Word deeply—"complete in knowledge"—to think more like Jesus (**renewed** in Christ).

3. Empowered Hands to Serve God's People: Doing

Service: Ministry Goal—Equipped to Do ("Competent to Instruct")

- **Competence: Christlike Ministry**
- **Serving Hands That Impact Lives: Relational Skillfulness**
- **Spiritual Friendship: Personal Ministry by Relating God's Truth to Human Relationships**

Since relational ministry requires relating Christ's grace to human hurts, as a Christlike disciple-maker I have been and continue to be empowered to skillfully do—"competent to instruct"—to serve more like Jesus (**reaching** others for Christ).

4. Equipping God's House to Become a Home: Connecting

Community: Relational Goal—Equipped to Connect ("Brothers")

- **Connecting: Christlike Relationships**
- **A Sensitive Home That Connects People: Biblical Community**
- **Spiritual Fellowship: Maturity through In-Depth Relationships with Christians**

Since effective ministry requires Christian community, as a Christlike disciple-maker I have been and continue to be equipped to encourage the Christian community to meaningfully, powerfully, and confidently address the needs of people in the great tradition of soul care and spiritual direction where discipleship, counseling, and Christian community are united—"brothers"—to build community in Jesus (**reconnected** through Christ).

Maturing Your Spiritual Friendship Competency
Becoming a "4 C" Spiritual Friend

1. Picturing spiritual friendship as a combination of character, content, competence, and community:

   a. Rate the relative importance of each component. For instance, is character "worth" 15%, content 50%, competence 10%, and community 25%? What is *your* rating and why?

   b. Consider current models of secular and Christian counseling. In what "percentages" do various models emphasize character, content, competence, and/or community?

2. To become a more powerful spiritual friend, what area do you feel you want to most develop? Why? How will you go about this?

   a. Character

   b. Content

   c. Competence

   d. Community

3. Having overviewed spiritual friendship training, what parts are you most anticipating and excited about? Why?

4. What are you already doing to restore spiritual friendship (soul care and spiritual direction) to your church?

5. Dream a bit.

    a. A year from now, what would demonstrate that you had caught God's vision of yourself as a competent spiritual friend?

    b. A year from now, what would demonstrate that your church had caught the vision of the power of spiritual friendship?

    c. What would you see your church doing differently? How would you see them relating to one another?

Chapter Three

Lenses in Spiritual Friendship
The Roadmap for Spiritual Friends

"The ministry of the cure of souls, or pastoral care, consists of helping acts, done by representative Christian persons, directed toward the healing, sustaining, guiding, and reconciling of troubled persons whose troubles arise in the context of ultimate meaning and concern" (William Clebsch and Charles Jaekle, *Pastoral Care in Historical Perspective*, p. 4).

Spiritual Map Quest

Two recent interviews with prospective faculty members reminded me of Frank Lake's insight. "The maladies of the human spirit in its *deprivation* and its *depravity* are matters of common pastoral concern" (Lake, *Clinical Theology*, p. 37, emphasis added).

The first interviewee saw deprivation or suffering as the core issue addressed in Christian counseling. "We have to focus on healing the hurts in human hearts," he contended. The second interviewee perceived depravity or sin to be the core issue that biblical counselors must face. "God calls us to expend our energy on confronting hard hearts," he insisted.

Which is it? Do we follow the counseling roadmap marked *deprivation, suffering, hurts, healing, and parakaleo*? Or, do we travel the route marked *depravity, sinning, hardness, confronting, and noutheteo?* Or, like Frank Lake, do we see deprivation *and* depravity as matters of common spiritual friendship, pastoral care, and professional counseling concern?

Of course, there's a more fundamental issue. "Do we even need a roadmap?" Some say, "I don't have a counseling model. I just do what comes naturally." Still others claim, "I don't follow a model of counseling. I simply use the Bible."

Realize it or not, we all have *some* counseling "model." We all approach personal ministry from some perspective and practice our approach according to some pattern.

Tilden Edwards (*Spiritual Friend*) notes that every person approaches spirituality and spiritual care out of some particular framework. The value of a model, according to Edwards, is that it makes explicit the already implicit framework.

Further, it's evident that we either develop a biblical approach to counseling or we borrow a secular model of counseling. Speaking about what happens when we lack a well thought-out Christian model of care, William Clebsch and Charles Jaekle explain:

Exploring Your Spiritual Journey

1. Describe your typical approach to helping people, your normal way of discipling and counseling.

2. Where were you recruited into your model? Did you learn it "officially" from some class or training? Did you develop it from your own study? Or, did it just "happen"?

3. On a scale of 1 to 10 (1 being unwilling and 10 being very willing), evaluate your willingness to learn a new approach, a new model of counseling/spiritual friendship. Explain your evaluation.

4. It's been said that, "In preaching/teaching we minister God's Word to many people's lives in a large group setting, while in counseling/spiritual friendship we minister God's Word to an individual's life in a one-to-one setting."

   a. What do you think of this comparison?

   b. To what extent does this comparison help or not help you to grapple with the differences and similarities between "pulpit ministry" and "personal ministry"?

The unfortunate result of this circumstance is that the pastoral profession sorely lacks any up-to-date vocabulary of spiritual debilities and strengths that takes seriously man's intense personal and social aspirations and anguishes. Faced with an urgency for some system by which to conceptualize the human condition and to deal with the modern grandeurs and terrors of the human spirit, theoreticians of the cure of souls have too readily adopted the leading academic psychologies. Having no pastoral theology to inform our psychology or even to identify the cure of souls as a mode of human helping, we have allowed psychoanalytic thought, for example, to dominate the vocabulary of the spirit. The flat, biologically based syntax of Freudian thought has colored pastoral care, perhaps more than many would care to admit, but in so doing it has restricted both the depths and heights of which the human spirit under Christian formation is capable (Clebsch and Jaekle, *Pastoral Care in Historical Perspective*, p. xii).

Edwards concurs with Clebsch and Jaekle when he speaks of the price we pay for not following a biblical and historical model of Christian care.

The price has been a tragic Western categorization of the truth into bits and pieces that never seem to weave a single cloth. In the mainline churches, for example, theologians offer broadscale analysis. Helping a person with the integral appropriation of the truth to which theology points, however, is left to "practical people," especially pastoral clergy. Unable to adequately translate their theological training into the nitty-gritty of the personal crisis and developmental help asked of them by people, and goaded by the lack of perceived spiritual concern on the part of many people coming for help, they usually turn to the empirical sciences for assistance (Edwards, *Spiritual Friend*, p. 31).

Urgent concerns plus no Christian model equals acceptance of secular psychology as the only hope.

Someone enters your office saying, "My son has been diagnosed with schizophrenia. You have to help us. Please meet with him tomorrow."

What do you do? Does your Bible concordance have a notation for "schizophrenia"? Since it doesn't, you and I are tempted to rush to the self-help shelf of the local bookstore. When faced with the complexity of the human soul, we turn to secular models *if* we have no thought-out Christian model.

Edwards proposes that Christian and secular thinking have always co-existed. However, in past generations Christians had a historical biblical model to follow and were able to evaluate and transform current approaches in light of Christian tradition. Edwards sounds a dire warning concerning what is happening in post-modern Christianity due to our lack of a time-tested, traditional, Christian model of care.

But if there is no deep awareness of the experiential, developmental anthropology of the tradition, then there is no real mutation, just a whole-hog graft. If the graft takes, it tends to take over. Sooner or later then the Church loses its unique experiential wisdom for society; it finds itself more and more absorbed as an expedient base for someone else's "revelation," unqualified by its own (Edwards, *Spiritual Friend*, pp. 32-33).

Without a theological foundation and a historical Christian model, we reject biblical revelation in favor of human reasoning.

Wayne Oates joins his voice to the chorus of concern. Speaking specifically of Protestants, he notes:

Protestants tend to start over from scratch every three or four generations. We do not adequately consolidate the communal wisdom of the centuries because of our antipathy for tradition. Therefore, we have accrued less capital in the form of proverbs, manuals of church discipline, etc. We have been, furthermore, in closer contact with the distinctly empirical dimensions of pastoral counseling by reason of our greater dependence upon secular forms of education. At the same time, as Protestants we have tended to draw our theoretical presuppositions for pastoral counseling from the scientific sources that are extrinsic to the theology of the church (Oates, *Protestant Pastoral Care*, p. 11).

We all follow some model in our people helping, and our approach is either Christian or non-Christian. We surrender our approach to the prevailing secular theories unless we follow some roadmap, some model of Christian care based upon biblical theology and Church history.

God's Treasure Map

Since God does not play games with us, he hasn't hidden his treasure map from us. Through the pages of Scripture and the halls of Church history, we find our way. The Church has always been about the business of soul care and spiritual direction. God's people have always provided soul care through sustaining and healing hurting people in the midst of suffering (*parakaleo* for deprivation). Spiritual friends have always offered spiritual direction through reconciling and guiding hardened people struggling against sin (*noutheteo* for depravity). The role of the Church has always been to train soul physicians who work in concert with the Holy Spirit to diagnose the condition of the soul, and from there proceed to the personal work of sustaining, healing, reconciling, and guiding souls toward communion with Christ and conformity to Christ.

> **The Church has always been about the business of soul care and spiritual direction.**

I can still recall the summer almost two decades ago when I first began to uncover this treasury of wisdom about the history of Christian counseling. I remember saying to myself, "I knew it! The Church has always helped people who are suffering *and* sinning." My initial excitement has blossomed as I've seen this model confirmed in the Scriptures and practiced throughout Church history.

Mapping Soul Care and Spiritual Direction

Experts examining the history of pastoral care have consistently identified the twin historical themes of soul care and spiritual direction. John T. McNeil's *A History of the Cure of Souls* traced the art of soul care throughout history and various cultures. He summarized the entire New Testament period and highlighted the Apostle Paul's teaching:

Lying deep in the experience and culture of the early Christian communities are the closely related practices of mutual edification (*aedificatio mutua*) and fraternal correction (*correptio fraterna*) . . . In such passages we cannot fail to see the Apostle's design to create an atmosphere in which the intimate exchange of spiritual help, the mutual guidance of souls, would be a normal feature of Christian behavior (McNeil, *A History of the Cure of Souls*, p. 85).

Throughout his historical survey, McNeil spotlighted the twin concepts of mutual edification and fraternal correction. Mutual edification involved the care of souls through the provision of sustaining (consolation, support, and comfort) and healing. Fraternal correction included the direction of souls through the provision of reconciliation (discipline, confession, absolution) and guidance (direction and counsel). McNeil observed in Jesus the convergence of these two aspects and understood Jesus to be both physician of the soul (soul care) and spiritual counselor (spiritual direction).

Seward Hiltner, a leading figure in the pastoral theology movement of the 1940s and 1950s, based his pastoral theology on a historical study of shepherding. In his work *Preface to Pastoral Theology*, he traced a model of soul care and spiritual direction from early writings to modern times. He found that the German phrase *seelsorge* (shepherd, pastor) provided a foundation for outlining the history of pastoral care. A. H. Becker (*Luther as Seeslsorger*) built upon Hiltner's work by delineating two broad classifications from the concept of the pastor as *seelsorger*. The first category was *fur die Seele sorgen* which means to care for souls, to be concerned for souls—soul care. The second category was *die Seele weiden* which means to guide souls, to tend to their direction and condition—spiritual direction.

H. Ivarsson (*The Principles of Pastoral Care According to Martin Luther*) proposed a very similar breakdown. He used the two categories of soul care and spiritual direction while also describing the use of these pastoral functions both with individuals and the entire congregation.

> **Pastoral care is defective unless it can deal thoroughly both with these evils we have suffered as well as with the sins we have committed.**

Lake (*Clinical Theology*) advanced an analysis of historical Christian care in which soul care dealt with suffering, while spiritual direction treated sin. He summarized his breakdown when he explained that "pastoral care is defective unless it can deal thoroughly both with these evils we have suffered as well as with the sins we have committed" (p. 21).

Mapping Sustaining, Healing, Reconciling, and Guiding

Church historians who have studied the history of soul care and spiritual direction have identified four common themes running throughout Christian spiritual care, labeling them: *sustaining, healing, reconciling,* and *guiding.* Using these four motifs, often called "the four tasks," they created a profile of historic pastoral care according to the following framework:

- ◆ Soul Care: *Parakaletic* Comfort for Suffering

    - ◆ Sustaining
    - ◆ Healing

- ◆ Spiritual Direction: *Nouthetic* Concern for Sinning

    - ◆ Reconciling
    - ◆ Guiding

Plotting the Map of Sustaining, Healing, Reconciling, and Guiding

Few contemporary descriptions of the inner life of the Christian congregation during the first three centuries have been preserved. Therefore, Church historians attach special interest and influence to the *Didascalia Apostolorum* (c. 225/1903). A major portion of this work is a treatise on the office and pastoral function of the bishop or presbyter. The *Didascalia Apostolorum* sets forth four analogies for understanding the character and duty of the chief minister of pastoral care. The bishop is to be:

◆ A shepherd who sustains by partaking of the suffering of the flock—sustaining.
◆ A physician who heals by mending the wounds of the patient—healing.
◆ A judge who reconciles relationships by providing discerning rulings—reconciling.
◆ A parent who guides by giving parent-like direction to the young in the faith—guiding.

Reflecting on these four concepts, Clebsch and Jaekle noted that:

Thus the pastoral office, even as early as the third century, was seen as consisting of the four functions of guiding, sustaining, reconciling, and healing. The far-reaching influence of this early analysis of pastoral care can be measured by reference to modern writings on the subject (Clebsch and Jaekle, *Pastoral Care in Historical Perspective*, p. 103).

Clebsch and Jaekle further stated that pastoral care or the cure of souls has historically involved "helping acts, done by representative Christian persons, directed toward the healing, sustaining, guiding, and reconciling of troubled persons whose troubles arise in the context of ultimate meanings and concerns" (Clebsch and Jaekle, *Pastoral Care in Historical Perspective*, p. 4).

Kenneth Leech (*Soul Friend*), writing from an Anglican background, asserted that Clebsch and Jaekle's definition had become the standard definition for pastoral care and counseling. Leech supported his contention with the observation that the Association for Pastoral Care and Counseling had adopted the definition into their constitution.

Edwards (*Spiritual Friend*), writing from an Episcopalian background about Catholic and Eastern Orthodox spiritual direction, explained that St. Anthony of Egypt, in the fourth century, was one of the early pioneers of spiritual direction. According to Edwards, St. Anthony's soul care involved comforting/sustaining, healing, reconciling, and guiding.

C. Schieler (*Theory and Practice of the Confessional*) wrote a prominent Roman Catholic treatise that followed these four areas of sustaining, healing, reconciling, and guiding. He asserted that the confessor must be a judge to hear the person's confession (reconciling), must act the part of the shepherd (sustaining), the physician (healing), and a father (guiding).

Hiltner (*Preface to Pastoral Theology*) discussed six themes in the history of pastoral care that he combined into four core areas. The six themes were discipline, comfort, edification, healing, sustaining, and guiding. Edification and guiding he combined into the guiding function; comfort and sustaining he combined into the sustaining function; healing he maintained as a separate category; and discipline Hiltner saw as the reconciling and purifying function of the pastor with the congregation.

Hiltner defined these four areas from a historical perspective and believed that all these functions were needed to do justice to the full dimensions of the shepherding perspective viewed historically. He identified sustaining as the relationship between pastor and people where the pastor comforts and upholds an individual, standing with that person in suffering even if that situation cannot be altered except perhaps by a change in the person's attitude. Healing historically expressed the relationship between pastor and people as the pastor binds up the wounds of the individual. Hiltner saw discipline or reconciling as the relationship between pastor and people in which the purity of the entire congregation's relationship to God is the priority. He saw guiding as the relationship between pastor and people in which a pastor helps an individual to find direction when the person has sought such help.

Hiltner identified Martin Bucer as one of the first Protestant ministers to systematically structure the ministry. Bucer, a follower of Martin Luther, wrote a pastoral care manual called *On the True Cure of Souls* (1538/1950). Bucer's systemization contained the categories of sustaining (strengthening weak Christians), healing (restoring sickly Christians), reconciling (drawing to Christ the alienated), and guiding (preserving Christians who are whole and strong, urging them forward in all good).

Charles F. Kemp's *Physicians of the Soul: A History of Pastoral Counseling* attested to the same categories of care. He affirmed that there had apparently never been a time or a place where individuals did not seek out religious leaders for personal help for: sustaining comfort, healing for spiritual health, reconciliation through forgiveness and assurance, and guidance and counsel.

He traced this process from the Old Testament to Christ and the Apostles in the New Testament, to the early Church, the Medieval Church, and from the Reformation to his own day. Kemp viewed physicians of the soul as those who were concerned both with soul care and spiritual direction. They were guides and counselors (spiritual direction) and soul physicians (soul care). His terms for these two roles, which encompass the four tasks, were: physician of the soul and spiritual adviser.

R. Kolb (*Luther: The Master Pastor*) studied the work of Conrad Porta. In the generation after Luther's death, Porta compiled a textbook on pastoral theology that consisted largely of quotations from Luther's works. Porta's purpose was to organize Luther's insights into an easily usable form for young pastors of the 1580s. Kolb proposed that Porta apprehended the breadth and depth of Luther's pastoral care by identifying four primary categories: healing, sustaining, guiding, and reconciling.

M. Begalke (*An Introduction to Luther's Theology of Pastoral Care*) wrote a doctoral dissertation on the theological foundation behind Luther's pastoral care. His study of the history of pastoral care identified the same four themes of sustaining, healing, reconciling, and guiding. Begalke commented that "certainly in Luther's pastoral care, we will discover all four of these functions" (p. 10).

E. Brooks Holifield (*A History of Pastoral Care in America*) outlined the model followed by Richard Baxter, the great English Puritan pastor and teacher of future pastors. Baxter believed the pastor's "task was to glorify God through the traditional range of healing, sustaining, guiding, and reconciling activities that characterized the work in a local congregation" (p. 37).

Gary Collins (*Evangelical Pastoral Care*) outlined the history of evangelical pastoral care explaining that "like other believers, evangelical care givers have long been involved in the 'four pastoral functions' of healing, sustaining, guiding, and reconciling" (p. 373). J. R. Burck and R. J. Hunter (*Protestant Pastoral Theology*), in their study of pastoral theology, commented that sustaining, healing, reconciling, and guiding are terms that have become standard in American pastoral care (p. 869).

As Church historians have probed the history of personal ministry, they have categorized all "people-ministry" using the four tasks of sustaining, healing, reconciling, and guiding. Though different terms were used in different epochs, these historians have found consistent categories, definitions, and descriptions. Historically, holistic care of people involved the twin functions of soul care and spiritual direction and the four tasks of sustaining, healing, reconciling, and guiding.

The two functions and four tasks are not the only way to organize historic pastoral care. However, as this section demonstrates, the suggested model encompasses Evangelical, mainline Protestant, Eastern Orthodox, and Roman Catholic faith traditions. The pattern of soul care (sustaining and healing) and spiritual direction (reconciling and guiding) does represent a breadth of vision and scope of perspective under which we might subsume various approaches (Collins, *Evangelical Pastoral Care*).

Thomas Oden (*Care of Souls in the Classic Tradition*) suggested that the four tasks "try to absorb and work seriously with a wide variety of confessional and denominational viewpoints on ministry" (p. 10). They try to "reasonably bring all these voices into a centric, historically sensitive integration, with special attention to historical consensus" (p. 10).

The framework of the two functions and four tasks provides a perspective—a historical way of viewing and thinking about spiritual friendship, pastoral care, and professional Christian counseling. It is one way to systematically organize what Christians have done throughout Church history to care for people. It offers us the lenses for spiritual friendship through which we will view and develop a biblical methodology of soul care and spiritual direction.

Boxes 3:1 and 3:2 sketch pictures of spiritual friendship. Together they portray the historical and biblical methodology of *parathetic* spiritual friendship through soul care (sustaining and healing) and spiritual direction (reconciling and guiding). Consider them two maps to one location.

God's Roadmap Marker Number One: Soul Care

Whether we label it biblical counseling, Christian counseling, or pastoral counseling, spiritual friendship has always dealt with the evils we have suffered *and* the sins we have committed. God's roadmap, our treasure map, provides the two primary directional markers or lenses of soul care and spiritual direction. We begin our spiritual friendship journey looking through the lens of soul care.

Parakaleo: "The Evils We Have Suffered"

Soul care recognizes that not all suffering is due to personal sin (compare Job 1-2 and John 9). Therefore, not all counseling focuses upon confrontation of the sins we have committed (spiritual direction).

Parakaletic spiritual friends gladly assume the role of encouragers coming alongside to help a friend upon whom the fallen world has fallen. As the Good Samaritan crossed over to the other side and bloodied himself to care for a stranger's suffering body, so soul care givers move near to enter the mess and muck of a friend's suffering soul.

Spiritual friends *compassionately identify with people in pain*. We reject the shallow pretense that denies suffering. Like Jeremiah, we lament. Like Paul, we groan for home. We're out of the nest. East of Eden. We're not home yet. We join our hurting spiritual friend in admitting that *life is bad*.

We also insist that *God is good*. Therefore, we don't direct people to us. We eschew their becoming dependent upon us, or needing "life-long counseling sessions." Instead, we redirect people to Christ and the Body of Christ. We point suffering friends to their suffering Savior. We remind them what a Friend they have in Jesus. We also equip them to avail themselves of all the resources of the Body of Christ through discipleship, worship, fellowship, stewardship, and ambassadorship.

As we participate with the Holy Spirit in the sustaining and healing of their faith, we have God's greater purposes in mind. Our map provides our soul care mission on behalf of our spiritual friends: experiencing communion with Christ and conformity to Christ as they love God (exalt God by enjoying and entrusting him) and love others. Symptom relief is *not* our primal goal. Whether our spiritual friends find cure or not, whether their symptoms are alleviated or not, we want to help them to find God (communion) in the midst of their suffering.

Finding God, we long for them to love Christ and love like Christ. We want them to see that God is good even when life is bad, so that they *exalt* God (worship, glorify, praise, and honor him) by *enjoying* God (seeking, desiring, thirsting for, and drawing near to him) and by *entrusting* themselves to him (clinging to, living for, obeying, serving, and surrendering to him). Empowered by their deepened connection to Christ, they love others more deeply.

Satan wants suffering to crush us. God uses suffering to soften us. Satan wants suffering to defeat us. God uses suffering to defeat Satan by transforming us into better lovers. Becoming a better lover—that's the goal of soul care for suffering.

Box 3:1
Soul Care and Spiritual Direction
Sustaining, Healing, Reconciling, and Guiding

Soul Care: The Evils We Have Suffered

"God Is Good Even When Life Is Bad"

*Soul care givers compassionately identify with people in pain
and redirect them to Christ and the Body of Christ
to sustain and heal their faith so they experience
communion with Christ and conformity to Christ
as they love God (exalt God by enjoying and trusting him) and love others.*

Sustaining: *"It's Normal to Hurt"*

Sense Your Spiritual Friend's Earthly Story of Despair

Empathize with and Embrace Your Spiritual Friend

Healing: *"It's Possible to Hope"*

Stretch Your Spiritual Friend to God's Eternal Story of Hope

Encourage Your Spiritual Friend to Embrace God

Spiritual Direction: The Sins We Have Committed

"God Is Gracious Even When I Am Sinful"

*Spiritual directors understand spiritual dynamics
and discern root causes of spiritual conflicts,
providing loving wisdom that reconciles and guides people so they experience
communion with Christ and conformity to Christ
as they love God (exalt God by enjoying and trusting him) and love others.*

Reconciling: *"It's Horrible to Sin, but Wonderful to Be Forgiven"*

Strip Your Spiritual Friend's Enslaving Story of Death

Expose Your Spiritual Friend's Sin and God's Grace

Guiding: *"It's Supernatural to Mature"*

Strengthen Your Spiritual Friend with Christ's Empowering Story of Life

Equip and Empower Your Spiritual Friend to Love

Box 3:2
Parathetic Spiritual Friendship

Parakaleo	*Noutheteo*
Soul Care	**Spiritual Direction**
"The Evils We Have Suffered"	"The Sins We Have Committed"
Encouragers	Disciplers
Mutual Edification	Fraternal Correction
Aedificatio Mutua	*Correptio Fraterna*

Sustaining	**Healing**	**Reconciling**	**Guiding**
Anthropology Soul	Sufferology Suffering	Hamartiology Sin	Soteriology Sanctification
"It's Normal to Hurt"	"It's Possible to Hope"	"It's Horrible to Sin, but Wonderful to Be Forgiven"	"It's Supernatural to Mature"
Desert	Thirst	Cistern	Spring
Fellowship of Suffering	Power of Resurrection	Friend of Sinner	Power of Sainthood
"Climb in the Casket"	"Celebrate the Empty Tomb"	"Speak the Truth in Love"	"Stir Up the Gift of God"
Hurting	Hoping	Hardening	Holy Living
Comfort	Courage	Confront	Challenge
Empathizing/ Engaging	Encouraging/ Extending	Exhorting/ Exposing	Empowering/ Equipping
Sense Their Earthly Stories of Despair	Stretch Them to God's Eternal Story of Hope	Strip Them of Their Enslaving Stories of Death	Strengthen Them by Christ's Empowering Story of Life
"Life Is Bad"	"God Is Good"	"I Am Sinful"	"God Is Gracious"

Soul Care through Sustaining: *"It's Normal to Hurt"*

Knowing that life lived in a fallen world can be raw, we communicate to one another, *"It's normal to hurt."* We weep with those who weep, refusing to blame people for hurting or shame them for feeling pain. We join them in the fellowship of their suffering. Created for Paradise, our hurting spiritual friends now live in a desolate desert. Our first calling is to sense their earthly story of suffering. We empathize with their agony, engaging them in their despair.

How? We offer *compassionate commiseration*, a term flowing through the pages of Church history. Co-passion feels another's passion, shares a friend's suffering. Co-misery becomes a partner in our spiritual friend's misery and woe. Such empathy is not simply understanding with someone's pain, but sharing in and experiencing his or her pain.

Shared sorrow is endurable sorrow. As Jonathan with David, the binding of our hearts together exponentially and miraculously enables us to endure what otherwise would overwhelm. Ponder Paul's words.

Praise be to the God and Father of our Lord Jesus Christ, the Father of compassion and the God of all comfort, who comforts us in *all* our troubles, so that we can comfort those in *any* trouble with the comfort we ourselves have received from God. For just as the sufferings of Christ flow over into our lives, so also *through Christ our comfort overflows*. If we are distressed, it is for your comfort and salvation; if we are comforted, it is for your comfort, which produces in you patient *endurance* of the same suffering we suffer. And our hope for you is firm, because we know that just as you *share in* our sufferings, so also you *share in* our comfort (2 Corinthians 1:3-7, emphasis added).

In order to provide compassionate commiseration, we need to practice *dual listening*: listening to our friend's earthly story while listening to God's eternal story. Spiritual friends tune into their friend's smaller story that communicates *"Life is bad"* (sustaining). Spiritual friends also tune into God's larger story that communicates *"God is good"* (healing).

In sustaining, our empathy promotes our spiritual friend's grieving. Paul commands us to grieve within the context of hope (1 Thessalonians 4:13). Without hope, grieving terrifies. Faced with what appears to be nothing but a black hole of unending pain, we back away. We deaden ourselves; deny. We refuse to grieve and groan. Often to start the "chain of grieving" we must grieve for our spiritual friends before they can grieve for themselves. Our weeping allows them to weep. Grieving is the bridge toward healing. When we grieve and groan we admit that we are not God, that we cannot control life, and that we need God (Romans 8:18-27).

We have to climb in the casket with our spiritual friends.

Spiritual friends understand the essential principle for sustaining faith in the goodness of God: *we have to climb in the casket with our spiritual friends*. Life is a series of multiple deaths, daily crucifixions. We need the courageous compassion to climb in the casket with our friends in the throes of death, in the valley of the shadow of death. When they sense us there with them, when they see our courageous hope, then they're encouraged to face death so that they can face life again. As Paul wrote to his friends in Corinth:

We do not want you to be uninformed, brothers, about the hardships we suffered in the province of Asia. We were under great pressure, far beyond our ability to endure, so *that we despaired even of life*. Indeed, in our hearts *we felt the sentence of death* (2 Corinthians 1:8-9a emphasis added).

Let's not be ignorant of our friends' earthly stories of suffering. Let's not miss their hearts. When we do, we tend to cram God in. Instead, we want to encourage them to invite God into the casket with them.

Soul Care through Healing: *"It's Possible to Hope"*

Neither should we be ignorant of God's larger story of hope. When we are, then we allow Satan's lying story to win the day. His story proclaims, "Curse God and die." His story reads, "Life is bad and so is God. Life is bad because God doesn't care about you." Before our friends buy the lie, they need healing.

What if our friends do buy the lie? What if we leave them in the casket? They know we care, but that's all they know. Sustaining faith is an awesome starting point, but an awful finish line. Notice how Paul moved from the casket of despair to the resurrection of hope. "But this happened that we might not rely on ourselves but on God, who raises the dead" (2 Corinthians 1:9b). Like Paul, in healing we're sharing the power of Christ's resurrection.

We need to stretch our spiritual friends to God's eternal story of hope. They need to know that "it's possible to hope because God is good, even when life is bad." We encourage our spiritual friends in the biblical sense of that word—to stir up courage to face life with God and for God.

We encourage through *extensio animi ad magna*—stretching the soul to great things. Soul stretching is necessary in the midst of suffering because when life stinks, our perspective shrinks. Created for Paradise, we find ourselves in a desert. Naturally, we're parched, thirsty. In our thirst, Satan tempts us to forget to remember God (Job 1-2). We feel as though Father has skipped town, abandoned us to this evil world, and left us orphans.

When life stinks, our perspective shrinks.

So, we need spiritual eyes to see life from God's eternal perspective.

Therefore we do not lose heart. Though outwardly we are wasting away, yet inwardly we are being renewed day by day. For our light and momentary troubles are achieving for us an eternal glory that far outweighs them all. So we fix our eyes not on what is seen, but on what is unseen. For what is seen is temporary, but what is unseen is eternal (2 Corinthians 4:16-18).

Spiritual friends learn how to perform spiritual laser surgery on their friends by engaging in spiritual conversations that invite God back into the picture. They create a greater God awareness by developing a spiritual curiosity. "I wonder where God is in this? I wonder what he's up to? I know he always has a plan. He amazes me how he works stuff out. Where do you see him at work even in this?"

Their spiritual curiosity causes them to see what others might miss and pursue what others might ignore. They scope out and share ways their spiritual friend is already connecting to God. "Jim, how in the world have you been able to cooperate with God to survive and thrive like you have? It's amazing to me what a loving, together man you are. God sure has been doing a great work of healing in your life over the years."

When we're at the end of our rope, there's less of us and more of God. When we embrace and face our suffering, then we can embrace and face our need for God. As in Paul's soul, so in ours: "This happened that we might not rely on ourselves but on God, who raises the dead" (2 Corinthians 1:9).

During the dark night of the soul, as we trudge through the valley of the shadow of death, God is present. He does care. He comforts. He heals and delivers—in his time and in his way—but he always heals. "He has delivered us from such a deadly peril, and he will deliver us. On him we have set our hope that he will continue to deliver us" (2 Corinthians 1:10). Paul knows that God has a good heart.

Did you notice *who* Paul hopes in? *"God who raises the dead"* (2 Corinthians 1:9, emphasis added). In sustaining, our calling is to climb in the casket. In healing, our joy is to celebrate the empty tomb!

> **In sustaining, our calling is to climb in the casket.**
> **In healing, our joy is to celebrate the empty tomb!**

In his excellent book *Mourning into Dancing*, Walter Wangerin teaches us to embrace our daily deaths so that we can experience daily resurrections. Death is always experienced as separation. So every event of separation (divorce, job loss, empty nest, fractured relationships, illness, etc.) is a "mini-death." When we invite God into the casket of our mini-deaths, then we can experience daily resurrection. Every day is Easter when we hope in God. Again, as Paul reminds us: "Indeed, in our hearts we felt the *sentence of death*. But this happened so that *we might not rely on ourselves but on God, who raises the dead*" (2 Corinthians 1:9, emphasis added).

God's Roadmap Marker Number Two: Spiritual Direction

Recall that God's roadmap, our treasure map, provides two directional markers: soul care *and* spiritual direction. The absence of either lens leaves our counseling out of focus, distorted. We continue our spiritual friendship journey looking now through the lens of spiritual direction.

Noutheteo: "The Sins We Have Committed"

Some Christian counselors focus only on the evils we have suffered: the damage done to us. They tend to ignore or minimize the sins we have committed: the damage we have done. Spiritual directors, on the other hand, focus on the truth that *"God is gracious even when I am sinful."* They are disciplers who practice the ancient art of fraternal correction—concerned confrontation and challenge creating core change.

Spiritual directors understand spiritual dynamics and discern root causes of spiritual conflicts. They understand anthropology—God's original design for the soul. They also grasp sufferology—the effect of being sinned against in a fallen, hurtful world. Additionally, spiritual directors comprehend hamartiology—sin, our fallen nature, and the horrors of personal sin against God and others. Furthermore, they apprehend soteriology—salvation, sanctification, and the process of growth in grace.

Spiritual directors use their discernment to provide loving wisdom that reconciles and guides people. Their reconciliation and guiding emphasizes the same ultimate purpose of sustaining and healing—

communion with Christ and conformity to Christ. They want to empower and equip people to fulfill the great commandment of loving God and loving others.

Spiritual Direction through Reconciling: *"It's Horrible to Sin, but Wonderful to Be Forgiven"*

Some Christian counselors who focus on sin fail to focus on grace. They are quick to quip, "It's horrible to sin." But slow to grasp, "It's wonderful to be forgiven." We must focus on both.

Satan loves to foul and fool us. Even as regenerate believers with a new heart, Satan dupes us into believing that we are his slaves. He tempts us to curse God, condemn others, and experience contempt for ourselves. It requires tremendous biblical wisdom and personal discernment to sort through his pack of lies and cling to God's Word of truth.

The truth is, it *is* horrible to sin. Sin alienates us from God, separates us from each other, and disintegrates us from our own selves (Romans 1:18-32; Ephesians 2:1-3; 2:11-19; 4:17-32). Due to sin's deceitfulness (Romans 7:11; 2 Corinthians 4:4; Ephesians 4:17-20; Hebrews 3:13) we need spiritual friends. We need spiritual directors who can ask and answer the question raised in James 4:1. "What causes fights and quarrels among you?" Only spiritual directors like these can fulfill the ministry description provided in Hebrews 3:12-13.

See to it, brothers, that none of you has a sinful, unbelieving heart that turns away from the living God. But encourage one another daily, as long as it is called Today, so that none of you may be hardened by sin's deceitfulness.

We also need spiritual directors who can use the living Word of God to expose the thoughts and attitudes of the heart (Hebrews 4:12-13), and to teach, rebuke, correct, and train in righteousness so that God's people are equipped for every good work (2 Timothy 3:16-17).

As spiritual directors, we are like the Puritans who practiced the art of *loading the conscience with guilt.* Like them, we know that to break the habitual web of sin's deceit, people need to experience the horrors of their sin against God and others.

We also need to be like the Puritan spiritual directors in practicing the art of *lightening the conscience with grace.* How sad that many Christian counselors de-emphasize grace. It *is* wonderful to be forgiven. Forgiveness by grace is the dynamic God uses not only to cleanse our lives, but also to change our love. Christ woos us back to God by grace (Romans 2:4; 3:1-5:21; 1 John 4:7-20).

> **Grace is God's medicine of choice for suffering and sin.**
> **Grace is God's prescription for our disgrace.**

Christ calls spiritual directors to be dispensers of grace meeting human guilt with God's grace and forgiveness. Grace is God's medicine of choice for suffering and sin. Grace is God's prescription for our disgrace.

Notice how the author of Hebrews exposes grace in the context of exposing sin. After exposing sin in Hebrews 3:12-13, he shifts to grace in 3:14. "We have come to share in Christ if we hold firmly till the end the confidence we had at first." We detect the same pattern in Hebrews 4:12-16. After discussing the power of the Word to expose evil in 4:12-13, he immediately focuses on grace in 4:14-16.

Therefore, since we have a great high priest who has gone through the heavens, Jesus the Son of God, let us hold firmly to the faith we profess. For we do not have a high priest who is unable to sympathize with our weaknesses, but we have one who has been tempted in every way, just as we are—yet was without sin. Let us then approach the throne *of grace* with confidence, so that we may receive *mercy and find grace* to help us in our time of need (emphasis added).

We expose our spiritual friends' sins *and* Christ's grace. We speak the truth in love to them, softening their hardened hearts. We invite them to drink from Jesus their Spring of Living Water who is the Friend of sinners—even of sinners who dig broken cisterns that can hold no water.

Spiritual Direction through Guiding: *"It's Supernatural to Mature"*

Spiritual directors also have the privilege of guiding believers to realize that it's supernatural to mature. Our task is to guide faith by strengthening our spiritual friends to understand, depend upon, and apply Christ's resurrection power.

We start the process by understanding new life in Christ—our new nature (regeneration) and our new nurture (reconciliation). We look inside our struggling spiritual friends and see the power of sainthood—a new creation in Christ, and the presence of sonship—a new relationship to God.

We enlighten our spiritual friends to the truth that God's grace not only saved them for all eternity, but also changed them for life *now*. In Christ, they have everything necessary to live a godly life (2 Peter 1:3). Thus it is neither impossible to mature, nor is it natural to mature. Maturity is the *supernatural* work of God implanted in us at salvation and growing daily in sanctification (2 Corinthians 3:18; 2 Peter 1:3-11; 3:18). We grow in grace by grace because God is gracious.

We grow in grace by grace because God is gracious.

We continue the guiding process by envisioning the work of God within our spiritual friends (2 Timothy 1:5-7; Hebrews 10:24-25). Paul realizes that he does not need to *create* spiritual power, love, and wisdom within his disciples. All he has to do is stir it up. Provoke it. Fan it into flame.

For this reason I remind you to *fan into flame* the gift of God, which is in you through the laying on of my hands. For God did not give us a spirit of timidity, but a spirit of *power*, of *love* and of *self-discipline* (a sound mind, wisdom) (2 Timothy 1:6-7, emphasis and parenthesis added).

In fact, according to the author of Hebrews, one of the prime directives for Church life is mutual provocation.

And let us consider how we may *spur* (provoke) one another on toward love and good deeds. Let us not give up meeting together, as some are in the habit of doing, but let us encourage one another—and all the more as you see the Day approaching (Hebrews 10:24-25, emphasis and parenthesis added).

We draw out what God has already placed within.

Notice what we draw out—love. The goal of guiding is not to make life easier. The purpose of spiritual direction is not to change circumstances. The focus is to equip and empower our spiritual friends to love—holy living through Christlike loving.

Created for Paradise, our friends find themselves in a desert of suffering. Tempted to dig broken cisterns (self-sufficient idols of the heart and false lovers of the soul), they repent and receive Christ's grace. Turning to God, they drink from the Spring of Living Water. Streams of living water overflow into the lives of others (John 7:37-39). Empowered by the Holy Spirit, our spiritual friends become shepherds in a jungle. In the jungle of fallen life in a fallen world, they exalt God by loving him and loving others.

Where We've Been and Where We're Headed

God really has left us his roadmap, our treasure map. Discovering it, we uncover his *how to*—his plan for offering soul care and spiritual direction through sustaining, healing, reconciling, and guiding.

How to, of course, does not imply *easy to*. It does not suggest a one-size-fits-all, mechanical, soulless process.

Consider sustaining, healing, reconciling, and guiding like the four points on a compass. They inform you what direction you are heading and what direction to head. However, there's still the journey. The dance. The art of soul care and spiritual direction.

Chapter Four introduces two core components in the artistry of spiritual friendship:

♦ Great Soul Lovers	Compassion	Relationship	Soul
♦ Great Soul Readers	Discernment	Truth	Scripture

We'll meet again there to continue our journey toward becoming soulful spiritual friends.

Maturing Your Spiritual Friendship Competency
Becoming a *Parathetic* Spiritual Friend

1. Think about the person who has been the greatest help to you during those times of suffering in your life—who has been there for you to comfort and encourage you. What is it about this person that makes her or him so helpful (so powerful in your life)?

2. Think about the person who has been the greatest help to you in your Christian walk—who has helped you to find victory over sin, strengthened you, discipled you. What is it about this person that makes her or him so helpful (so powerful in your life)?

3. Share about a person who helped you to sense that *it's normal to hurt*. Who has climbed in the casket with you?

4. Share about a person who helped you to sense that *it's possible to hope*. Who has stretched you to God? Who has sensed God's goodness and grace when all you could see were suffering and sin?

5. Share about a person who helped you to sense that *it's horrible to sin, but wonderful to be forgiven*. Who has met your guilt with God's grace? Who has dispensed God's grace as the prescription for your disgrace?

6. Share about a person who helped you to sense that *it's supernatural to mature*. Who has known you so well that she or he saw a vision of Christ being formed in you?

7. Of soul care and spiritual direction, which do you more naturally tend toward? Are you more likely to focus on the pain of someone suffering or the sin of someone moving away from God and others?

    a. Why do you suppose that is?

    b. What implications might this have for you as a spiritual friend?

8. Of sustaining, healing, reconciling, and guiding, which one do you more naturally tend toward? Are you more inclined toward helping people to know that *it's normal to hurt*, or that *it's possible to hope*, or that *it's horrible to sin, but wonderful to be forgiven*, or that *it's supernatural to mature*?

   a. Why do you suppose that is?

   b. What implications might this have for you as a spiritual friend?

♦ If you are working through this material individually, then instead of role-playing, use the space after each scenario to write your responses to each situation.

9. You're a lay spiritual friend in your local church. You're in a first meeting with a parent whose teenage son was crippled last month in a car accident. Role-play how you would climb in the casket with this hurting parent. After you complete your role-play, provide each other with feedback.

10. You're a professional Christian counselor. In your third meeting, your client tells you that he/she has been having an affair. Role-play how you would probe the truth that *it's horrible to sin, but wonderful to be forgiven*.

Chapter Four

Compassionate Discernment in Spiritual Friendship
The Roles of Spiritual Friends

"Discernment comes from 'sapiens'—to be wise. It is so named from sapor (savor), because just as the taste is quick to distinguish between savors of meats, so is a wise man in discerning things and causes. Unwisdom is contrary to wisdom because it lacks the savor of discretion and sense" (Thomas Aquinas, *Summa Theologica*, Part II-III, Q. 46, Art. 1, Vol. II, p. 1384).

Open the Eyes of My Heart, Lord

Veteran pastoral counselors as well as rookie lay care givers experience sweaty palms because of it. Seasoned professional counselors and novice spiritual friends fight anxiety concerning it. Believers from the halls of Church history as well as Christians in church hallways have ruminated over it. "As I engage my spiritual friend, where do I start, how do I proceed, and how do I do it lovingly?"

As we connect with our spiritual friends, how do we soulfully clarify the issues and interpret the change process? How do we practice artful and accurate diagnosis and treatment planning?

Some answer that it takes truth alone—head knowledge, biblical content. "All we need to do is understand people, problems, and solutions." These doctrinaire models focus almost entirely on information and insight, neglecting interaction and engagement.

Others state that it takes skill only—heart connection, relational competence. "Master the skills and techniques of people-helping." These eclectic approaches focus almost exclusively on skills and techniques, neglecting theory and theology.

I'd answer that it's not either/or, but both/and. We need both biblical truth and relational competency. Theology and methodology. Theory and practice. Head and heart. Discernment and compassion. We must derive our methodology from our theology and apply it relationally.

This is why Paul prayed that our love (compassion) would abound more and more in knowledge and depth of insight (discernment) (Philippians 1:9-11). It is why throughout Church history believers summarized the practice of spiritual friendship with the phrase "compassionate discernment."

Compassionate discernment is *the mind of Christ meeting the secrets of the heart*. We tune our ears to hear the song of God and the groaning of creation; to prize what is lovely and to suffer over what is corrupt; to ponder these things and to struggle to understand them and God's redeeming way with them. Compassionate discernment is becoming alert in my awareness of God, thus increasing my mindfulness of God's children.

Exploring Your Spiritual Journey

♦ Social awareness (compassionate discernment of others) begins with self-awareness. We can't expect to know others well, if we know ourselves poorly. Self-awareness begins with spiritual awareness—with insight into who we are in Christ and who Christ is to us. Use the questions below to deepen your awareness of your relationship to Christ.

1. I first came to know Christ personally through:

2. My "first love for Christ" (the time of my deepest love for Jesus) occurred when:

3. My "first love for Christ" (my time of deepest love for Jesus) felt like:

4. I am closest to Christ when:

5. My deepest thirsts for and longings from Christ are:

People considered the wise person of old, like Solomon, a *sapor*—one quick to savor and appreciate the good and beautiful. Sapors have the compassionate discernment to discriminate between the good and the bad, the healthy and the spoiled, the beautiful and the ugly. Wise spiritual friends have a palate for fine spiritual goodness. They're connoisseurs of the heart.

Our new nature includes our new ability to perceive, desire, appreciate, and be attracted to the beauty of God—his excellence, holiness, and love. We love him because we come to realize how loveable and lovely he is. We apprehend the supreme good in God and love him for his own sake, for his intrinsic worth. We become enraptured with him. Thus, the first requirement for wisdom is a deep spiritual relationship with God—our soul's ability to appreciate God's beauty.

The great Puritan soul physician, Jonathan Edwards, understood the connection between perceiving God's beauty and perceiving the state of the soul. Those who are wise toward God are wise toward image bearers. When God's beauty is discovered, a new perspective is uncovered.

Those who are wise toward God are wise toward image bearers.

As Edwards states it:

When the true beauty and attraction of the holiness found in divine things is discovered by the soul, a new world of perspectives is opened. The glory of all the perfections of God and of everything that pertains to Him is revealed. It shows the glory of all God's works both in creation and in providence. The glorifying of God's moral perfections is a special end of all creation. A sense of the moral beauty of divine things enables us to understand the sufficiency of Christ as Mediator. In this way the believer is led into the knowledge of the excellency of Christ's person. The saints are then made aware of the preciousness of Christ's blood and of its sufficiency to atone for sin. Thus all true experiential religion comes from this sense of spiritual beauty. For whoever does not see the beauty of holiness cannot appreciate the graces of God's Spirit. Without this there is ignorance of the whole spiritual world (Edwards, *Religious Affections*, p. 109).

When we appreciate God, then we more insightfully understand everything that pertains to him. What pertains to God more than those created in his image?

Edwards continues:

Whoever has a musical ear knows whether a sound is in true harmony; he does not need the reasonings of a mathematician to consider the proportion of the notes. Whoever has a taste for gourmet food does not need reasoning in order to know good food. Likewise, if an unworthy or unholy action is suggested to the spiritually discerning, a sanctified eye sees no beauty in it nor is it pleased with it. Sanctified taste will only be nauseated by it. In this way a holy person is led by the Spirit by having a holy taste and disposition of heart (Edwards, *Religious Affections*, p. 113).

In other words, if we "get God right," then we don't need the *Diagnostic and Statistical Manual* in order to "get people right." When we have a "taste for God," then we gain a "taste for God's children." As we counsel our spiritual friends, we intuitively sense whether their affections, mindsets, purposes/pathways, and mood states are pleasing or nauseating, both to us and to God.

Edwards concludes:

To have a sense of taste is to give things their real value and not to be dazzled with false lusters or be deceived in any way. In judging actions by spiritual taste, true saints do not have specific recourse to definite rules in God's Word with respect to every word and action that they have to communicate. Yet their taste itself is generally subject to the rule of God's Word and is tested and tried by it (Edwards, *Religious Affections*, pp. 113-114).

At first glance, Edwards' statement might concern us. It need not. Yes, God's Word gives us clear rights and wrongs in many specific areas. However, many are the gray areas (consider Romans 14-15). We use wisdom to apply God's biblical principles for daily living in specific, real-life relationships and situations. Soul physicians who are enthralled by God will be best equipped to "taste" whether their spiritual friend's love life, thought life, will life, and emotional life is palatable to God.

Compassionate: Great Soul Lovers

Biblically aware and relationally competent spiritual friends skillfully practice the art of grace-based compassionate discernment. They develop spiritual friendships that assist others to wisely live their lives face-to-face with God in Christ. Spiritual friends are neither soul scientists nor calculating technicians. Instead, through their personal encounter with Christ's grace, they become:

- Great Soul Lovers: Compassionate
- Great Soul Readers: Discernment

Interpersonal competence is left to chance in our society. Our culture teaches what worldly culture has always taught. How to hide from God, ourselves, and others (Genesis 3). How to remain superficial (Matthew 23). How to promote self-interest (Philippians 2). How to downplay risk in relationships (the opposite of death-to-self). How to manipulate and retaliate against others (James 4).

Instead of remaining interpersonally incompetent, spiritual friends become relationally competent. Instead of relying on technical skills, spiritual friends become "Proverb-Skilled"—successful in human relationships. Spiritual friends understand that counseling skills do not produce personal maturity. Rather, human contact and interaction encourages others to grow in Christ. Spiritual friends realize that the meta-skill or meta-competence that they need is connection through communion: co-passion.

Compassion is the passion in your new heart as you engage with your spiritual friend that allows you to speak grace words (Colossians 4:5-6). Compassion is a one-word description of the relational competencies that flow out of your soul into your spiritual friend's soul because you've received compassion from your ultimate Spiritual Friend (2 Corinthians 1:3-7).

> **Practicing skills alone is like one corpse performing cosmetic surgery on another corpse.**

Recall that typical clinical training actually impedes and handicaps spiritual friends because it tends to breed a clinical, managerial, one-up attitude. Since the Spirit is the Healer-Sanctifier, spiritual friendship is gift, not technique. It is sharing as equals, not giving as an expert. Practicing skills alone is like one corpse performing cosmetic surgery on another corpse (Matthew 23:3-29). Mental health is really a theological issue since it is about our relationship to God and one another.

Discernment: Great Soul Readers

Spiritual friends don't stop here. Yes, they are great soul lovers filled with Christ-like compassion. However, they are also great soul readers filled with Christ-like discernment.

Discernment or diagnosis literally means "to see through." Diagnosis sees through to what a person needs for his or her unique spiritual nurture.

Discernment is both gift and work, both art and knowledge. As art, Church historians have called it the gift of reading hearts and the diagnosis of interior mental movements. It includes discrimination, or the ability to know what's going on in me, in you, and *between us*, and how that relates to what *God* is up to in *your* life.

As gift, it requires the ability to discern the movements of grace in your spiritual friend's soul. "What is God doing in her life?" "Where do I detect signs of grace in his walk?"

In order to develop the gift of discernment, we must be in touch with ourselves (not consumed with self). It means that we are self-aware—aware of who we are in Christ, aware of what we are experiencing as we counsel, and why we're experiencing those longings, thoughts, goals, and feelings.

Discernment also requires work and knowledge. We base biblical discernment upon biblical categories from *Soul Physicians* such as:

♦ God's Eternal Story and the Earthly Story
♦ Satan's Lying/Works Narrative and Christ's Truth/Grace Narrative
♦ Creation, Fall, and Redemption
♦ People, Problems, and Solutions
♦ Relational Romancers and Affections, Rational Dreamers and Mindsets, Volitional Creators and Purposes/Pathways, Emotional Singers and Mood States, and Physical Actors and Habituated Tendencies

We enter spiritual friendship "encounters" armed with biblical truth in the form of categories for thinking deeply about life. We pray for the ability to understand our spiritual friends and for the capacity to discriminate between where they are believing Satan's lies and where they are accepting Christ's truth. We pray for the discernment to know whether our spiritual friends are living according to false lovers or grace lovers, foolish mindsets or wise mindsets, self-centered purposes or other-centered purposes, and ungoverned mood states or managed mood states.

We use *theology* to propose *biblical categories* (Romancers, Dreamers, Creators, Singers) and then we use *compassionate discernment* (the ability to "taste beauty") to *diagnose* how maturely or immaturely our spiritual friends are loving God and others.

If spiritual friendship encompasses soul care for suffering *and* spiritual direction for sinning, then how do we know where to focus? How do we diagnose whether our spiritual friends have a greater present need for soul care or spiritual direction? How do we discern whether the most pressing concern is sustaining, healing, reconciling, or guiding? As we interact, how do we determine the root issues? How do we ascertain the nature of our spiritual friends as relational, rational, volitional, and emotional beings? These are the questions addressed by compassionate discernment.

Learning to Be Discerning

Discernment is an art based upon an understanding. Therefore, it requires the intersection of truth learned in *Soul Physicians* with relational skillfulness developed in *Spiritual Friends*.

Discernment is the art of applying biblical truth to daily living, of applying biblical theology about people, problems, and solutions to real life image bearers who are relational, rational, volitional, emotional, and physical beings. It is the artistry of applying truth wisely as we discern how our spiritual friends are moving along their journey from desert, thirst, cistern, and spring.

In order to learn to discern, I'll introduce now, and explore throughout the rest of *Spiritual Friends*, how to perform dual diagnosis: diagnosing how image bearers are facing level one and level two suffering:

- Diagnosis of Level One Suffering: Learning to be discerning about your spiritual friend's *external life situations*.
- Diagnosis of Level Two Suffering: Learning to be discerning about your spiritual friend's *internal life responses*.

Diagnosis of Level One Suffering: Gathering Situational Data

Martin Luther first introduced me to the idea of two levels of suffering. Level one suffering is what happens *to* me. It involves losses and crosses that I experience as I live in a fallen world that often falls on me. Level one suffering includes all those external life situations that cause me pain, especially the pain of lost connection and lost contribution.

The pain of lost connection includes external events such as a prodigal child, a divorce, an argument with a close friend, the nest emptying, the death of a loved one, best friends moving away, being criticized, feeling rejected, abandoned, betrayed, being abused, and the like. The pain of lost contribution includes external events such as losing a job, being demoted, not being accepted into the college of your choice, being told your ministry is ineffective—anything that calls into question your sense of making a difference, of making an impact.

> **We need to know the *S*cript (Scriptures—God's universal story)
> and the *s*cript (our friends' individual stories).**

When spiritual friends come to us, our first task is to listen well to their external stories of level one suffering. We want to hear what it is that they are experiencing. What life losses have they endured? We need to know the *S*cript (Scriptures—God's universal story) and the *s*cript (our friends' individual stories). We learn about our friends' unique stories by exploring their life contexts—their personal "table of contents." We can compassionately discern their life stories through:

- Probing Trialogues
- Tracking Trialogues
- Gathering Situational Data: Initial Intakes, Spiritual Friendship Information Forms, Personal Information Forms, and Release of Information Forms

Probing Trialogues

Picture your spiritual friend coming over for coffee, arranging an appointment in your professional counseling practice, or dropping by your pastoral office. You know he or she has a concern. How do you explore it with compassion and discernment? Some basic probing trialogues are most helpful.

- *What is your goal in talking today?*
- *How did you get the idea of coming to counseling?*
  - *When did you get the idea?*
  - *Why now?*
- *How will you know that our counseling has been successful, helpful?*
- *How will you know that you no longer need to come for counseling?*
- *What will be different in your life when counseling is successful?*
- *How will you be relating differently after successful counseling?*
- *How will you be thinking differently after successful counseling?*
- *What will you be doing differently after successful counseling?*
- *How will you be feeling differently after successful counseling?*
- *Have you had other situations similar to this?*
  - *What have you learned from these situations that might be helpful to you now?*
- *What are things like when you are not having this problem?*
  - *What are you doing differently when you do not have this problem?*
- *So how will you and God keep these times of victory going?*
- *What would you like to change about this situation?*
- *What do you dream would be different about this situation?*

Interactions like these not only tune your ear to your spiritual friends' situations, they also encourage your spiritual friends to focus, to be specific about their situations and their concerns.

Tracking Trialogues

We often approach life from "passengerhood." We don't feel like "more than conquerors." Tracking the influence of situations helps your spiritual friends to clarify their level one suffering. It also helps them to see that "the giant out there, the monster hiding under the bed of life," is something tangible, relational, and through Christ, "conquerable."

Tracking the Influence of the Problem

Once you've used probing trialogues to clarify the situational issues, then you can use tracking trialogues to map the influence of the problem on your spiritual friend.

- Label the Problem:

  - *What is the nature of your loss, of your suffering?*
  - *What theme or title can you give your loss/suffering that summarizes its essence?*
  - *What is the nature of your sin, of your sanctification struggle?*
  - *What theme or title can you give your sanctification struggle that summarizes its essence?*

- Trace the Problems:

  - *Tell me about the history of the problem.*
  - *Tell me when the problem first began.*
  - *Where were you recruited into the problem?*
  - *What might happen if this problem vanished?*

- Track the Influence of the Problem:

  - *How does it affect you?*
  - *Who else does it affect?*
  - *How is this problem depleting you?*
  - *How is this problem depleting your relationships? To God? To others?*

- Explore the Life Support System of the Problem:

  - *How might you be feeding this problem?*
  - *Are there any ways you're prolonging it?*
  - *Are there any ways you're contributing to its ongoing existence?*

Tracking the Influence of Your Spiritual Friend Over the Problem

Once you track the influence of the problem on your spiritual friend, then you can track your spiritual friend's influence over the problem.

- Track the Person's Influence Over the Issue:

  - *When is the problem a little bit less?*
  - *Imagine into the future. How do you see this problem being defeated?*
  - *Tell me about the time before this stuff ever started . . .*

- Grace Interpretations (Alternative Stories):

  - *Could we explore any other ways of looking at this?*

- Desired Interpretations (Preferred Outcomes):

  - *What would you like to see happen instead?*

- Answered Prayer Questions:

  - *Imagine that whatever you prayed about this issue, God would grant your request.*
    - *How would you pray?*
    - *What would you pray?*
    - *How would you know that God had answered your prayer?*
    - *How would others know that God had answered your prayer?*
    - *What would be different?*
    - *What would you be doing differently?*
  - *Suppose that one night, while you were asleep, there was a miracle and this problem was solved.*
    - *How would you know?*
    - *How would others know?*
    - *What would be different?*
    - *What would you be doing differently?*

Gathering Situational Data: The Initial Intake, The Spiritual Friendship Information Form, The Personal Information Form, and The Release of Information Forms

Even before your face-to-face interactions with your spiritual friend, you can gather vital information. Pages 67-74 offer *sample* forms that you can use to gather data before an initial counseling appointment or spiritual friendship meeting. Feel free to alter these forms to fit your situation. I offer them so that you will not have to "reinvent the wheel."

The Spiritual Friendship Initial Intake Form

You, or an administrative assistant, can use the *Spiritual Friendship Initial Intake Form* (see page 67) as your introductory screening. It helps you to organize contacts, collect basic personal information, summarize the purposes of the meeting(s), assess who the person should meet with, and has a place to record initial homework.

The Spiritual Friendship Information Form

Clients, parishioners, and spiritual friends can complete the *Spiritual Friendship Information Form* (see page 68) before the first meeting, or they can complete it with you as part of your first session together. This form is more "user friendly," hope-focused, and simpler than the *Personal Information Form* described below. Depending upon your setting and your client, you may use one or the other, or both.

The Personal Information Form

You would want to ask your clients, parishioners, and spiritual friends to arrive thirty minutes before their first meeting in order to complete the *Personal Information Form* (see pages 69-72). This more detailed data collection form provides the type of information useful in "professional" settings (and is worded accordingly). However, it is useful for all settings.

The Release of Information Forms

Good diagnosis seeks to collect all possible helpful information. Therefore, at times you will want to receive permission to share information with other "people helpers." Through the *Authorization for Release of Information Form* (see page 73), you receive written permission to request information *from* others about your spiritual friend. Through the *Authorization to Release Information Form* (see page 74), you receive written permission to give information *to* others about your spiritual friend.

Spiritual Friendship Initial Intake

Personal Information

Name: _____ Date: _____ Time: _____

Address: _____

Home Phone: _____ E-mail: _____ Age: _____ Gender: _____

Church Membership/Attending: _____

Work Schedule: _____ Work Phone: _____

Marital Status: _____ Referred by: _____

Open to Lay Spiritual Friendship: Yes: _____ No: _____

Brief Summary of Why the Person Desires Spiritual Friendship

Assessment

_____ 1. Referred to _____ because/for:

_____.

_____ 2. Scheduled with _____ for one immediate session on

_____.

_____ 3. Appointment scheduled to complete forms and have initial meeting with

_____ on _____.

Homework Assignment

Provide a brief description of the homework assignment given to complete before the first meeting.

Spiritual Friendship Information Form

1. How did you get the idea of coming for spiritual friendship meetings? When did you get the idea? Why now?

2. How will you know that your spiritual friendship meetings have been helpful? How will you know that you no longer need to meet?

3. Suppose that one night while you were asleep, there was a miracle and this problem was solved. How would you know?

4. What will be different in your life when your spiritual friendship meetings are successful?

5. Have you had other situations similar to this? What have you learned from these situations that might be helpful to you now?

6. What are things like when you are not having this problem? What are you doing differently when you do not have this problem?

7. How will you and God keep these times of victory going?

Personal Information Form

Identification Information:

Name: _____ Home Phone: _____

Address: _____

E-mail: _____ Birth Date: _____ Gender: _____

Education in Years: _____ Occupation: _____ Work Phone: _____

Marital Status: Single: _____   Married: _____   Separated: _____

                   Divorced: _____   Widowed: _____   Engaged: _____

Referred Here By: _____

Reason for Seeking Counseling:

Why do you desire to meet with a counselor? _____

_____

_____

How long has this issue existed? _____

Were there any significant events occurring in your life/your family's life when this issue began?

_____

_____

What have you done about this issue? _____

_____

_____

How would things be different for you if the issue were remedied? _____

_____

_____

What results are you expecting in coming here for counseling? _____

_____

_____

Marriage and Family Information:

Spouse's Name: _____ Home Phone: _____

Spouse's Address: _____

Spouse's E-mail: _____ Birth Date: _____ Gender: _____

Spouse's Education in Years: _____ Occupation: _____ Work Phone: _____

Date of Marriage: _____ Age When Married: Husband: _____ Wife: _____

Is your spouse willing to come for counseling? Yes: _____ No: _____ Uncertain: _____

Give brief information about any previous marriages: _____

_____

Information About Children:

PM*	Name	Age	Sex	Education (Grade)	Marital Status

*Check this column if child is by previous marriage.

What type of instruction in Christian living is given in your home and by whom? _____

_____

Who does the disciplining in your home? _____

For what behaviors are your children disciplined? _____

What methods of discipline are currently being used? _____

_____

How do you and your family members communicate that you love each other? _____

_____

How much time do you spend with your family members each week?

Spouse: _____

Children: _____

Personality Data:

Circle any of the following words that best describe you now:

Active	Shy	Hardworking	Leader	Compulsive
Nervous	Likeable	Impulsive	Follower	Excitable
Impatient	Self-conscious	Often-blue	Sarcastic	Serious
Moody	Jealous	Calm	Self-confident	Easy-going
Imaginative	Ambitious	Good-natured	Persistent	Quiet
Introverted	Extroverted	Fearful	Loner	Stubborn

Others: _____

Complete the following sentences:

People that know me think that I am: _____

_____

If they knew the "real me" they would know that I am: _____

_____

What I desire more than anything else in life is: _____

_____

What I fear most in life is: _____

_____

The person I admire most in life is: _____

Because: _____

Is there any other information that you would like us to know? _____

_____

_____

_____

Health Information:

Rate your health: Very Good: _____   Good: _____   Average: _____   Poor: _____

Weight changes recently: None: _____   Lost: _____   Gained: _____

List all important present or past illnesses, injuries, or disabilities: _____

_____

_____

Date of last medical exam: _____   Report: _____

_____

Physician's name: _____   Address: _____

Are you presently taking medication? Yes: _____   No: _____   Type: _____

_____

Have you used drugs for other than medical purposes? Yes: _____   No: _____

If yes, explain: _____

Have you ever had any counseling before? Yes: _____   No: _____   When: _____

For: _____

Are you willing to sign a release so that your counselor may write for medical or counseling reports?

Yes: _____   No: _____

Religious Background:

What church do you attend? _____

How often do you attend church? _____

Are you saved? Yes: _____   No: _____   Not sure what you mean: _____

What ministries/activities are you involved in at church? _____

_____

How often do you read the Bible? _____

Describe your prayer life: _____

_____

Authorization for Release of Information

To: Pastor Jonathan R. Smith, Ph.D., LCPC
Grace Fellowship Church
321 Hope Lane
Union Bridge, MD 21777
Phone: 410-555-7000
pastorjrs@gfc.net

Name/Address of Facility/Counselor: **Counselee's Address at Time of Service:**

_____   _____

_____   _____

_____   _____

_____   _____

Re: Name: _____

DOB: _____

SS #: _____

This signed release authorizes you to furnish Pastor Jonathan R. Smith the following:

_____

_____

Please forward the requested information to Pastor Smith at the address listed above. It is understood that this is confidential information and that it will not be released without the written permission of the counselee or guardian.

I understand that I may revoke this authorization, except for the action already taken, at any time. Expiration date, event, or condition after which consent is no longer valid:

_____

_____   _____
(Signature of Counselee or Guardian)   (Date)

_____
(Witness)

Authorization to Release Information

From: Pastor Jonathan R. Smith, Ph.D., LCPC
Grace Fellowship Church
321 Hope Lane
Union Bridge, MD 21777
Phone: 410-555-7000
pastorjrs@gfc.net

To:

Name/Address of Facility/Counselor: Counselee's Address at Time of Service:

_____   _____

_____   _____

_____   _____

_____   _____

Re: **Name:** _____

     DOB: _____

     SS #: _____

This signed release authorizes Pastor Jonathan R. Smith to furnish the following:

_____

_____

The requested information will be forwarded to the address listed above. It is understood that this is confidential information and that it will not be released without the written permission of the counselee or guardian.

I understand that I may revoke this authorization, except for the action already taken, at any time. Expiration date, event, or condition after which consent is no longer valid:

_____

_____   _____
(Signature of Counselee or Guardian)   (Date)

_____
(Witness)

Maturing Your Spiritual Friendship Competency
Diagnosis of Level One Suffering: Gathering Situational Data

♦ If you are working through this material individually, then instead of role-playing, use the space after each scenario to write your responses to each situation.

1. You're a lay spiritual friend in your local church. A friend drops by your home after work. They tell you that they were just fired. With a partner, role-play using probing trialogues to explore your spiritual friend's level one suffering. After you complete your role-play, provide each other with feedback.

2. You're a minister in a local church. You're ready to start your first session with a parishioner whose spouse is having an affair. With a partner, role-play using tracking trialogues to explore your parishioner's level one suffering. After you complete your role-play, provide each other with feedback.

3. You're a professional Christian counselor. You're beginning your first session with a new client. Your client's daughter has run away from home. With a partner, role-play using the *Spiritual Friendship Information Form* to explore a client's level one suffering. After you complete your role-play, provide each other with feedback.

Diagnosis of Level Two Suffering: Gathering Personal Data

In diagnosing level two suffering, you learn to discern your spiritual friends' *internal life responses*. How are they reacting *to* what is happening to them?

The approach to personal diagnosis that you'll learn is not the only approach. I can summarize the various approaches into four basic diagnostic models:

- ♦ The Medical Model
- ♦ The Personality Model
- ♦ The Psychodynamic Model
- ♦ The *Imago Dei* Model

The Medical Model

In the medical model, the therapist asks, "What disease does my client have?" Note the word "dis-ease." What lack of ease, what dysfunction of normal functioning does my client have?

The medical model is the foundation behind the *Diagnostic and Statistical Manual IV TR (DSM)*—the psychological "bible" used by medical doctors, psychiatrists, psychologists, professional counselors, social workers, the legal system, and insurance agencies. The *DSM* clusters symptoms together and then provides a label—nomenclature—so that therapists can clearly communicate what "disease" they have diagnosed. Intake and diagnosis in this model is somewhat structured. As therapists interview clients, they look for a grouping of common symptoms.

The "cure" in the medical model involves the attempted removal of the symptoms of the disease. Contributing factors are certainly considered and root issues are analyzed, however, "health" becomes the removal of the "dis-ease"—the removal or at least management of the symptom cluster.

Though there certainly are some benefits to this model, not the least of which is the ability to think and communicate clearly about a cluster of symptoms, there are also drawbacks.

- ♦ *Pathology-Based*: It looks only, or at least predominantly, at the person through the grid of disorder.
- ♦ *Victim-Focused*: It tends to result in clients seeing themselves as helpless victims overwhelmed and overcome by an outside force.
- ♦ *Solution-Focused*: It tends to focus on symptom relief and short-term remedies rather than heart issues and the long-term, even eternal, goal of maturity.
- ♦ *Reifies*: To reify is to become one's label. "I am no longer a person who might struggle against depressive thoughts, *I am a depressed person*." The label can become a self-fulfilling prophecy.
- ♦ *Psychologizes Society*: Life is viewed through the lens of a humanistic way of thinking about people, problems, and solutions. As the litany of psychological categories grows, everyone is seen as and sees themselves as having some dysfunction.
- ♦ *Fluctuating Categories*: The labels change and grow over time, as evidenced by the exponential growth in the size and scope of the *DSM* with each new edition.
- ♦ *Non-standardized Treatment*: Even once the diagnosis is given, there is no agreement on the care, cure, and treatment of the disorder.

The Personality Model

Others diagnose according to a personality model. "What personality type is my parishioner?" Extroverted or introverted? Sanguine, choleric, phlegmatic, or melancholy? Assessment involves figuring out the personality type or traits. Treatment highlights exposing the weak aspects of the personality and changing them. "Balance" is the goal.

The weaknesses of this diagnostic model include the lack of scientific validity or research. The various systems of personality tend to be more proverbial (observations about how people tend to relate), than actual. Further, these types are simply labels. They, too, can reify.

Perhaps most importantly, the model of maturity tends to lack biblical depth. It is difficult to prove biblically that "balance" is the scriptural norm. Was Jeremiah "balanced"? Was John the Baptist? Paul?

Additionally, biblical study and psychological research indicate that personality is a rather fixed spectrum of reactions to life, unique to each person from birth. These personality traits become rather established early in life and endure for the rest of life (Psalm 139, Jeremiah 1). Certainly, God calls us to maturely develop our unique personality. However, an overemphasis on personality types and changing them may be somewhat futile and may counter God's creative genius in making each of us unique.

The Psychodynamic Model

Following Freudian theory, the counselor asks, "What is my counselee's controlling unconscious like?" What are the hidden, repressed issues that underlie the surface symptoms? Diagnosis in this model involves the complex process of psychodynamic therapy. There's a search to uncover the hidden thinking about the past that is hindering the present.

This model seeks to move beyond surface issues to deeper factors. This approach attempts to explore root problems instead of contenting itself with symptom reduction.

However, there's a root problem with this search for a root problem. Psychodynamic understanding of people, problems, and solutions is humanistic. It is unapologetically *coram anthropos*—it studies humanity only from the perspectives and insights of humanity, all apart from Deity. The creature is examined and understood apart from the Creator. The id, ego, and superego, for instance, though fascinating concepts, were simply the creation of Sigmund Freud as he tried to understand, apart from Scripture, the complexities of the human soul.

The *Imago Dei* Model

The diagnostic approach that I'm presenting is the *imago Dei* model. The soul physician asks, "How maturely or immaturely is my spiritual friend living life as an image bearer who is a relational, rational, volitional, emotional, and physical being?" As a Romancer, Dreamer, Creator, Singer, and Actor, is he or she Christlike or fleshly? What is the nature of his or her characteristic affections, mindsets, purposes/pathways, mood states, and habituated tendencies? How's my spiritual friend's love life, thought life, volitional life, emotional life, and physical life? How's his or her soul, heart, mind, will, emotions, and body? Box 4:1 overviews a spiritual anatomy of the soul that serves as the foundation for the *imago Dei* model of diagnosis.

Cure in the *imago Dei* model is actually not cure, but *care*. God alone heals, cures. You care. Through connecting with your spiritual friends, you encourage them to connect to God. As they connect to God, they grow in conformity to Christ.

The greatest benefit of the *imago Dei* model is its biblical foundation. It's built upon a biblical understanding of people (Creation), problems (Fall), and solutions (Redemption). It focuses upon the process of sanctification—growing to reflect increasingly the relational, rational, volitional, and emotional image of Christ. Its goal is clear: *the inner life of your spiritual friend is to look more and more like the inner life of Christ.* Further, the issues diagnosed are real-life categories, not simply labels. How we love, think, choose, and feel are topics that reflect the rawness of life as we live it each day.

Box 4:1
A Spiritual Anatomy of the Soul

1. **Relational Beings: Romancers Loving Passionately—Affections**

   a. **Spiritual Beings:**   **Communion**

   b. **Social Beings:**   **Community/Connected**

   c. **Self-Aware Beings:**   **Conscience**

2. **Rational Beings: Dreamers Thinking Imaginatively—Mindsets**

3. **Volitional Beings: Creators Choosing Courageously—Purposes/Pathways**

4. **Emotional Beings: Singers Experiencing Deeply—Mood States**

5. **Physical Beings: Actors Living Fully—Habituated Tendencies**

Imago Dei Personal Diagnosis

Wisdom is foundational to *imago Dei* personal assessment. No chart, map, model, or diagram can analyze the soul. You need compassionate discernment to love and understand image bearers. How do you develop it?

You need scriptural insight gleaned from God's Word applied to human relationships. This provides the categories for your thinking. *Soul Physicians* labels these universal life themes:

- *Affections*: Lovers, thirsts, longings, desires, idols. What affections reign in my spiritual friend's soul?
- *Mindsets*: Characteristic ways of thinking, patterns of believing, core images, routes and ruts in the mind and brain. What mindsets reign in my spiritual friend's heart?
- *Purposes/Pathways*: Patterns, styles of relating, habituated responses to life, consistently pursued goals, chosen purposes. What purposes/pathways reign in my spiritual friend's will?
- *Mood States*: Controlling emotions, governing feelings, dominating moods. What mood states reign in my spiritual friend's emotions?
- *Habituated Tendencies*: Characteristic patterns of yielding the members of the body, disciplined or undisciplined habituated responses to life. What habituated tendencies reign in my spiritual friend's physical body?

The Process of *Imago Dei* Personal Diagnosis

In each section on sustaining, healing, reconciling, and guiding, you'll learn specific strategies for gathering data that provides information for an accurate personal diagnosis. In summary, *you diagnose the state of the soul in the world*. Thus, you ponder two diagnostic categories:

- ◆ *The State of the Soul: Relational Image Bearers*—How's my spiritual friend doing as a Relational Romancer (affections), Rational Dreamer (mindsets), Volitional Creator (purposes), Emotional Singer (mood states) and Physical Actor (habituated tendencies)?
- ◆ *The Soul in the World: Relational Life Events*—How's my spiritual friend handling his/her desert (sustaining), thirst (healing), cistern (reconciling), and spring (guiding) journey?

Resist becoming bogged down in the terminology. Keep it simple. People long, think, choose, feel, and act as relational, rational, volitional, emotional, and physical beings (*the state of the soul*). People experience deprivation, doubt, depravity, and development to which they respond with disappointment, despair, distance, and devotion (*the soul in the world*). (For a review of these concepts and their theological foundation, you will find *Soul Physicians* helpful.) Personal diagnosis makes practical use of these categories, using them as probes to gather personal data to diagnose level two suffering.

The Probes Used in *Imago Dei* Personal Diagnosis

Picture Katy. Last year her husband left her for another woman. She's suffered in silence for months. Finally, she's come to you for help, telling you her soul story of level one suffering. Now you're probing for level two suffering. What's going on *inside* Katy as she wrestles with her husband's abandonment and betrayal? *Imago Dei* personal diagnosis suggests that you ponder the state of her soul in her world.

Who is Katy relationally, rationally, volitionally, emotionally, and physically as she faces issues related to desert, thirst, cistern, and spring? For sustaining, you probe Katy's inner life responses (relationally, rationally, volitionally, emotionally, and physically) to *disappointing* life events in her desert of suffering. In healing, you explore her despairing inner life responses in her thirsty groanings for heaven. With reconciling, you examine Katy's inner life responses in which she distances herself through cistern digging. In guiding, you stir up her inner life responses in which she devotes herself to spiritual growth through God her Spring of Living Water.

1. *Sustaining* and *Deprivation*: Exploring *Disappointing* Life Responses—*Desert*

   a. *Relationally (Affections)*: Where is Katy experiencing the greatest relational disappointment? How is she handling her hurt? How's she responding in her soul to the loss of her deep social connection with her husband? How is hope deferred making her heart sick? What affections, longings, desires, and wants are going unmet?
   b. *Rationally (Mindsets)*: Where is Katy enduring the greatest mental anguish? What lying story is Satan hissing at her? What mindsets control her evaluations of her loss? What disappointing images pervade her perspective?
   c. *Volitionally (Purposes)*: How is Katy responding and reacting in her will to her situation? Is she withdrawing, lashing out, pretending, self-protecting? Where's her "courage meter"—on all-time low, half-empty/half-full, ready to despair, to give up?
   d. *Emotionally (Mood States)*: How is Katy responding and reacting in her emotions to her loss? What is she feeling? How aware is she of her moods? How in control of her moods does she feel/seem? What's the hurt like for her? What's her EQ: Emotional Quotient?

e. *Physically (Habituated Tendencies)*: How are Katy's inner life responses impacting her physically? Is she depleted? Exhausted? Resting in God? Connecting to Christ's resurrection power? Is her disappointment motivating her to discipline her life and offer the members of her body to Christ's service, or is it motivating her to surrender to the lusts of the flesh and habituated fleshly tendencies?

2. *Healing* and *Doubt*: Exploring *Despairing* Life Responses—*Thirst*

   a. *Relationally (Affections)*: Where is Katy experiencing the greatest relational despair? Where is she enduring the greatest "groaning?" What are the unmet thirsts of her soul? In her thirsts, who is she turning to? In what ways is she drinking from her Spring of Living Water? What is her agony like? Where do I see glimpses of hope? Evidences of grace?

   b. *Rationally (Mindsets)*: Where is Katy enduring the greatest mental battles? What is the battle like in her mind between Satan's lying narrative and Christ's grace narrative? What is it like to "be in her head"? How is she sorting out questions about God's goodness?

   c. *Volitionally (Purposes)*: What evidence do I see of Katy re-engaging the battle? What would it look like for her to respond courageously even as she feels deeply? What does the "way of the fool" look like in her response? What does the "way of the godly" look like in her response? Is she worshipping and ministering?

   d. *Emotionally (Mood States)*: How well is Katy managing her moods? Is she self-aware? Is she gaining self-control? What would joy in the midst of sorrow be like for her? Is she crying out to God? Suffering *coram Deo*?

   e. *Physically (Habituated Tendencies)*: How are Katy's despairing life responses impacting her physically? How can I use her "physical energy meter" as a diagnostic tool to assess whether she is hoping in God or despairing of hope? What spiritual disciplines would assist her to connect to Christ's resurrection power and thus empower her to yield the members of her body to Christ's service even while experiencing deep thirsts? What spiritual disciplines would help her to better quench her thirsts in Christ?

3. *Reconciling* and *Depravity*: Exploring *Distancing* Life Responses—*Cistern*

   a. *Relationally (Affections)*: Where is Katy experiencing the greatest separation in her relationships? What idols of the heart is she pursuing? In what ways is she alienated from God? In what ways is she separated from others? In what ways is she dis-integrated in her own soul? What would relational repentance and return look like for Katy? What are the horrors of her sinful response to her suffering? How can God's grace impact her soul? What will soulful godliness look like in her relationships? What old impure affections should she put off? What new purified affections should Katy put on?

   b. *Rationally (Mindsets)*: Where is Katy losing the battle for her mind? What evidence do I detect of her buying Satan's lie? What fleshly mindsets prevail in her heart? What would repentance as a change of mind look like in Katy's heart? What would mind renewal look like in her situation? What new images of Christ, herself, and her situation could she put on? What old mindsets should she discard?

   c. *Volitionally (Purposes)*: What evidence do I see of Katy following purposes/pathways of the world, the flesh, and the Devil? What sinful patterns might she need to put off? What would the putting off process entail in Katy's life? What evidence do I see of Katy following pathways of the Word, the Spirit, and Christ? What godly patterns might she need to put on? What would the putting on process look like in Katy's life? How could God's grace empower her to respond courageously?

d. *Emotionally (Mood States)*: How poorly is Katy managing her moods? Is she failing to be self-aware? Is she lacking self-control? What would repentance look like in this area? How could she soothe her soul in her Savior?

e. *Physically (Habituated Tendencies)*: How are Katy's distancing life responses impacting her physically? How can I use her "physical energy meter" as a diagnostic tool to assess whether she is living wisely or foolishly? What spiritual disciplines would assist her to put off old ways and put on new ways?

4. *Guiding* and *Development*: Exploring *Devoted* Life Responses—*Spring*

a. *Relationally (Affections)*: Where is Katy most passionately loving God and others? Where is she freely offering herself to others? How can I stir up, draw out, and strengthen her to offer more, to risk more, to love more, to sacrifice more? How is she captured and captivated by her Worthy Groom? What would mature relating look like in her soul in this situation? What new grace lovers, new affections is she putting on?

b. *Rationally (Mindsets)*: Where is Katy winning the battle for her mind? What evidence do I detect of her defeating Satan's lie? What spiritual mindsets prevail in her heart? What new beliefs and images is Katy putting on? How can I stir up the mind renewal already occurring in her heart? What will ongoing sanctification look like for her mentally? What resurrection power multipliers could Katy tap into? What new dreams is God stirring in her soul?

c. *Volitionally (Purposes)*: What evidence do I see of Katy following pathways of the Word, the Spirit, and Christ and how can I stir these up? What godly patterns can I encourage her to put on? How can she respond like a courageous creator? As a maturing feminine soul, what would godliness look like in her relationships?

d. *Emotionally (Mood States)*: How can Katy mature as a singer who experiences life fully, deeply, honestly? What does emotional maturity look like in her situation? How can she spread her joy to others? How fully open is Katy to the Lover of her soul?

e. *Physically (Habituated Tendencies)*: How are Katy's devoted life responses empowering her physically? How can I use her "physical energy meter" as a diagnostic tool to assess how well she is putting off old patterns and putting on new ones? What will it look like for her when she connects to Christ's resurrection power and begins to live for others? What will it look like for her to habituate her tendencies toward godliness by yielding the members of her body to Christ?

By implementing these "probes" with compassionate discernment, you'll connect and resonate with your spiritual friends. You'll be able to engage your spiritual friends in their level two suffering, diagnosing the condition of their souls.

Where We've Been and Where We're Headed

Section One (Understanding the Art of Spiritual Friendship) comes to a close. We've examined the roles, résumé, roadmap, and relationships of spiritual friends.

These aspects of spiritual friendship provide the foundation we need to implement sustaining and healing soul care as well as reconciling and guiding spiritual direction. That process begins in Section Two (Maturing the Art of Sustaining Spiritual Friendship). Chapter Five explains sustaining diagnosis, while Chapters Six and Seven teach sustaining treatment and intervention.

Maturing Your Spiritual Friendship Competency
Diagnosis of Level Two Suffering: Gathering Personal Data

♦ If you are working through this material individually, then instead of role-playing, use the space after each scenario to write your responses to each situation.

1. With a partner, role-play intervening with Katy in *sustaining* by exploring her *disappointing* life responses. After you complete your role-play, provide each other with feedback.

2. With a partner, role-play intervening with Katy in *healing* by exploring her *despairing* life responses. After you complete your role-play, provide each other with feedback.

3. With a partner, role-play intervening with Katy in *reconciling* by exploring her *distancing* life responses. After you complete your role-play, provide each other with feedback.

4. With a partner, role-play intervening with Katy in *guiding* by exploring her *devoted* life responses. After you complete your role-play, provide each other with feedback.

Chapter Five

Sustaining Diagnosis
Compassionate Discernment in Sustaining

> *"I'm willing to be with you in your moment of pain. This is the embrace of God, his kiss of life. That is the embrace of his mission, and of our intercession. And the Holy Spirit is the force in the straining muscles of an arm, the film of sweat between pressed cheeks, the mingled wetness on the backs of clasped hands. He is as close and as unobtrusive as that, and as irresistibly strong"* (John V. Taylor, *The Go-Between God*, p. 27).

A Biblical Model of Sustaining

Chapter Four explained that *imago Dei* personal diagnosis seeks to discern *the state of the soul in the world*. Spiritual friends seek to understand how image bearers are handling *internally* what they're facing *externally*.

In Chapter Five, we focus upon compassionate discernment of our spiritual friends' relational, rational, volitional, and emotional responses to life in the desert of suffering—the black hole of deprivation. We will learn how to sustain their faith in a good God while living in a bad world.

Recall that the biblical focus of sustaining says, "It's normal to hurt." Life is bad. Our fallen world often falls on our spiritual friends. When it does, what do we do? How do we sustain them? Consider two descriptions of sustaining, one technical and one personal.

- Sustaining—Technical Definition: We sustain our spiritual friends during *spiritual despondency* by aiding them to experience *spiritual security* through facing suffering with *spiritual integrity*.
- Sustaining—Personal Picture: *Coram Deo* suffering—suffering face-to-face with God.

The temptation when bad things happen *to* us is for despair to creep *into* us. When caught in the slough of despair, in the desert of despondency, we need *spiritual security*. We need to know that God is good even when life is bad. Such faith develops only when we face suffering face-to-face with God.

In the presence of suffering, Satan tempts us to turn away from the presence of God. We doubt the goodness of God and then feel guilty about our doubting. In our despair and guilt, we position our backs to God. Instead, we must turn our faces to God to find grace to help in our time of need. We don't necessarily find answers, but we do find God. *Coram Deo* suffering brings our agony into the presence of Deity.

Exploring Your Spiritual Journey

1. One of my worst casket experiences (times of defeat and despair like the Apostle Paul's in 2 Corinthians 1:3-10) was:

2. Read Psalm 13 and/or Psalm 88.

    a. During your casket time, if you had written your own Psalm 13 or Psalm 88, how would it have sounded?

    b. In writing your Psalm of Lament, what honest emotions would you have shared with God?

3. What is it like for you to invite God into your casket?

    a. Do you find it hard or easy to share honestly with God your pain, anger, disappointment, etc.?

    b. Why do you suppose that is?

4. During your "casket time," did anyone, trying to be helpful, dismiss your pain, not really listen to your hurt, and quickly share how God would make it all better ("Christian clichés")?

   a. What did that feel like? How did that short-circuit your grieving and healing process?

   b. What would you have wanted instead?

5. During your "casket time," did anyone hear your pain, but then leave you there? They listened, nodded, even cried, but never moved with you at your pace to a place of hope?

   a. What did that feel like?

   b. What would you have wanted instead?

The Biblical Focus of Sustaining: "It's Normal to Hurt"

In sustaining, you pray that your suffering spiritual friends will experience the security of turning back to their Security Blanket. You want to help them to say from deep within their being, "Life is bad, but I can face it with Christ because he is good. Surely, God is good to me. He has a good heart."

In sustaining, you're seeking to help *faith survive* the onslaught of spiritual doubt. Standing shoulder to shoulder, you draw a line in the sand resisting further retreat. You encourage your spiritual friends to turn to the presence of God in the presence of suffering—neither denying the reality of evil, nor the goodness of God. You climb in the casket with them, waiting for the day when you can celebrate the empty tomb together.

As you enter their casket, you join with them, connect with them. You embrace them so they can face and embrace their suffering. (In healing, they face and are embraced by God.) You want them to be like Christ in suffering when he cried out, "My God, My God! Why hast thou forsaken me?" Jesus faced suffering *coram Deo*—face-to-face with God. Such integrity frees your spiritual friends to experience the truth that it's normal to hurt.

Knowing this removes the shame of Satan's condemning narrative, freeing your spiritual friends to face the truth that life is bad. God uses this awareness, as he uses all the desert experiences of life (Deuteronomy 8:1-5), to create hunger for him and the realization that "Man does not live on bread alone, but on every word (every sustaining breath of grace) that comes from the mouth of God" (Matthew 4:4, parenthesis added). *Candor* with God and self about the "badness" of life is the first stage on the journey toward the sustaining truth that God is good.

The Biblical Theology of Sustaining: "I Believe in the Fellowship of Christ's Suffering"

Imagine if your church statement of faith included the line: "I believe in the fellowship of Christ's suffering." This belief was central to Paul's personal process of sanctification, of becoming like Christ. "I want to know Christ and the power of his resurrection and the *fellowship of sharing in his sufferings*, becoming like him in his death" (Philippians 3:10, emphasis added).

Christ is a man of sorrows, intimately acquainted with grief. Paul was a man of sorrows intimately acquainted with groaning (Romans 8:18-27; 2 Corinthians 1:3-10). Paul not only wants to be like Christ in his exaltation, he wants to be like Christ in his humiliation. More than that, Paul is willing to join others in their humiliation, in their suffering, in their casket.

Biblical Sufferology in Sustaining: Trials of Faith

If we're to be like Paul as he imitates our suffering Savior, then we need to have the mind of Christ and the mind of Paul regarding suffering. We need a biblical sufferology.

We experience suffering as *a trial of faith*. Martin Luther, as I've noted, conceptualized the trial of faith on two levels:

- *Level One Suffering*: What happens *to* us and around us. What we are facing. This is the external stuff of life to which we respond internally. We lose a job, our child is ill, we face criticism, and the like. Level one suffering involves our situation and our circumstances—what happens to us.
- *Level Two Suffering*: What happens *in* us. How we face what we are facing. Level two suffering is the suffering of the mind that gives rise to fear and doubt as we reflect on our external suffering. It is what happens in us as we face our circumstances. Do we doubt, fear, or run? Or, do we trust, cling, and face our suffering by facing God *coram Deo*? How do we respond internally to our external situations?

Luther called the level two trial of faith *anfechtungen*—spiritual depression. I call it *spiritual separation anxiety*—the terror of a felt sense of abandonment. Satan incites terror when he whispers, "Life is bad. God controls life. He must be bad, also. How can you trust his heart? He has left you all alone. Again . . ."

Spiritual depression and anxiety result from our internal responses to external events. They are satanic temptations to doubt God, spiritual terrors, restlessness, despair, doubt, pangs, panic, desolation, and desperation. The absence of faith in God in the presence of external suffering leads to a terrified conscience which perceives God to be angry and evil instead of loving and good. These doubts lead to a potential hemorrhage in our experience of relationship to God, others, and self.

To counter the trial of faith we need *the perspective of faith*, which is the Divine perspective on life from which we can erect a platform to respond to suffering. *Coram Deo* faith perceives the presence of God in the presence of suffering. Since God's heart is good beyond question, we don't have to live in denial. Like Paul, we can groan over how horrible our world is (Romans 8:17-27). To truly sense the depths of God's goodness, we must face the pit of life's "badness." As Joseph models, "you intended to harm me, but God intended it for good" (Genesis 50:20).

> ### *Coram Deo* faith perceives the presence of God in the presence of suffering.

In desert suffering, Satan says, "Give up on yourself, God, and others. Curse God and die. God is bad. Grieve without hope. Minimize God. Shrink life. Doubt God's goodness." If we succumb to his deceits, then we enter the casket of caskets. "We do not want you to be uninformed, brothers, about the hardships we suffered in the province of Asia. We were under great pressure (*level one suffering*), far beyond our ability to endure, so that we despaired even of life (*level two suffering*). Indeed, in our hearts (*level two suffering*) we felt the sentence of death (*level two suffering*)" (2 Corinthians 1:8-9a, parenthesis added).

The casket is the potential hemorrhage in our triune relationships:

1. Spiritual Abandonment: "I feel forsaken by God."   Alienation
2. Social Betrayal: "I feel betrayed by others."   Separation
3. Self Contempt: "I feel dead in my soul."   Dis-integration

Loss frequently provokes disequilibrium and doubt. Yet, many people fear openly discussing their doubts. How sad. How un-Job-like. Suffering has the potential to cause us to reflect on issues of ultimate meaning—relational meaning.

You can offer wise pilotage to your suffering friends—wise pilotage for souls in danger of floundering in inner doubt, distress, and darkness. God calls you to encourage—to stand alongside to lend support when the situation cannot be changed, at least not immediately, to carry on a ministry of sustenance as long as circumstances preclude healing.

This is *comfort* in the original sense of *with courage*, upholding or standing with one who suffers even if the situation cannot be altered except perhaps by a change in the person's attitude. You enhearten your spiritual friends to find courage to face the difficulties of life. When they encounter experiences driving them headlong away from what they long for, then they need shared strength to mobilize their resources to meet the crisis with creative energy.

Maturing Your Spiritual Friendship Competency
Sufferology in Sustaining

1. Ponder some of your most recent experiences of "level one suffering." Did you experience any "level two suffering"—feelings of abandonment, betrayal, doubt, and despair? If not, how did you manage to avoid such thoughts? If so, how did you manage those thoughts?

2. Reflect on the last time one of your friends, family members, parishioners, counselees, or clients shared about suffering.

   a. What level two issues did they face?

   b. Did they appear to face those issues alone or *coram Deo* (honestly and openly with God)?

   c. What did you do, or could you have done, to "climb in the casket with them," to embrace them in their suffering?

Biblically Diagnosing Suffering: Stages of Sustaining

When people come to you in the midst of suffering, one of your first callings is to compassionately discern how they're handling their suffering. Before you can assist them to handle suffering well, you must determine how well or poorly they're currently facing their pain. To do so, you need to discern the process of suffering.

Students of human grief have developed various models that track typical stages of grief. One model uses the acronym TEAR:

- *T*: To accept the reality of the loss.
- *E*: Experience the pain of the loss.
- *A*: Adjust to the new environment without the lost object.
- *R*: Reinvest in the new reality (Jane Bissler, *Counseling for Loss and Life Changes*).

Swiss-born psychiatrist Elisabeth Kubler-Ross, in her book *On Death and Dying*, popularized a five-stage model of grieving based upon her research into how terminally-ill persons respond to the news of their terminal illness. Her five stages, which have since been used to describe all grief responses, are:

- *Denial*: This is the shock reaction. "It can't be true." "No, not me." We refuse to believe what happened.
- *Anger*: Resentment grows. "Why me?" "Why my child?" "This isn't fair!" We direct blame toward God, others, and ourselves. We feel agitated, moody, on edge.
- *Bargaining*: We try to make a deal, insisting that things be the way they used to be. "God, if you heal my little girl, I'll never drink again." We call a temporary truce with God.
- *Depression*: Now we say, "Yes, me." The courage to admit our loss brings sadness and depression.
- *Acceptance*: Now we face our loss calmly. It is a time of silent reflection and regrouping. "Life has to go on. How? What do I do now?"

These various stages in the grief process record what *typically occurs*. They do not attempt to assess if this is what is *best to occur*, or if it is *God's process for hurting and hoping*. My study of sufferology suggests an eight-stage process. The first four stages concern sustaining in suffering, which I present in this chapter, while the second four stages relate to healing in suffering, which I describe in Chapter Eight. Box 5:1 overviews these stages under the heading of "Biblical Sufferology."

In sustaining, you use these stages to diagnose how your spiritual friends are responding to suffering. How are they living in the desert east of Eden, outside Paradise? You contrast unhealthy handling of desert suffering with healthy handling of it. Specifically, you want to diagnose whether your spiritual friends are experiencing and practicing denial *or* candor, anger *or* complaint, bargaining *or* cry, depression *or* comfort.

Stage	Unhealthy Desert Suffering	Healthy Desert Suffering
Stage One	Denial/Isolation	Candor: Honest with Self
Stage Two	Anger/Resentment	Complaint: Honest to God
Stage Three	Bargaining/Works	Cry: Asking God for Help
Stage Four	Depression/Alienation	Comfort: Receiving God's Help

Box 5:1
Biblical Sufferology

Levels of Suffering

Level One Suffering: External Suffering

- Circumstances: What Happens *to* Us—Separation
- Theological Reality: Our World Is Fallen and It Falls on Us

Level Two Suffering: Internal Suffering

- Condemnation: What Happens *in* Us—Spiritual Depression
- Experiential Reality: Our World Is a Mess and It Messes with Our Minds

Sustaining in Suffering
"It's Normal to Hurt and Necessary to Grieve."

- Stage One: Candor—Honest with Self
- Stage Two: Complaint—Honest to God
- Stage Three: Cry—Asking God for Help
- Stage Four: Comfort—Receiving God's Help

Healing in Suffering
"It's Possible to Hope in the Midst of Grief."

- Stage One: Waiting—Trusting with Faith
- Stage Two: Wailing—Groaning with Hope
- Stage Three: Weaving—Perceiving with Grace
- Stage Four: Worshipping—Engaging with Love

Stage One: Candor—Honest with Self Rather Than Denial and Isolation

Candor contrasts with the typical first stage of grieving—denial. The Apostle Paul does not tell us not to grieve; he tells us not to grieve *without hope* (1 Thessalonians 4:13). Paul uses the word *lupesthe* meaning to feel sorrow, distress, grief, pain, heaviness, and inner affliction. The only person who can truly dare to grieve, bear to grieve, is the person with a future hope that things will eventually be better.

Candor is courageous truth telling about life *to ourselves* in which we come face-to-face with suffering. Candor requires integrity (*aletheia*/truthfulness) and faith (*pistis*/trust). When we trust God's good heart, then we trust him no matter what. Refusing to pretend, we face and embrace life's mysteries.

When level one suffering first hits; when we first hear the news of the unexpected death of a loved one; when we are told without warning that we have been fired; we respond with shock. We can't believe it. Life seems unreal. I believe that this initial response is a grace of God allowing our bodies and physical brains to catch up, to adjust. Grief is the grace of recovery because mourning slows us down to face life. No grieving; no healing. Know grieving; know healing.

However, after a necessary period, long-term denial becomes counter-productive. More than that, it is counter to faith because true faith faces all of life *coram Deo*.

Candor or denial. The choice is a turning point. It is a line drawn in the sand of life, a hurdle to confront. Faith crosses the line. Trust leaps the hurdle. We face reality and embrace truth, sad as it is. If facing suffering is wrestling face-to-face with God, then candor is our decision to step on the mat.

Candor is truthing: courageous honesty about experience in the context of intense encounter with God. Solomon is full of candor in Ecclesiastes. He contrasts under the *sun* candor with under the *Son* candor. Life lived under the sun (based purely on reason) leads to cursing. Life lived under the Son (based upon reason redeemed by grace/faith) leads to candor, which leads to complaint.

Stage Two: Complaint—Honest to God Rather Than Anger and Resentment

Stage one seeks to discern whether spiritual friends are in denial *or* practicing candor. Stage two tries to determine whether spiritual friends are experiencing unproductive anger *or* practicing productive complaint.

In candor, we're honest with ourselves; in complaint, we're *honest to God*. We needlessly react against the word "complaint." Complaints are faith-based acts of persistent trust. Complaint is vulnerable truth telling about life to God and others. It is one of the many moods of faith. Psalm 91's exuberant trust is one faith mood, while Psalm 88's dark despair is another faith mood. A mood of faith is simply trusting God enough to bring everything about us to him. Unlike Adam-the-Hider, in complaint we hide nothing from God because we trust his good heart.

Satan is the master masquerader (2 Corinthians 11:13-15). His counterfeit for biblical complaint is unhealthy, destructive anger. He substitutes cursing for complaint. Cursing God demeans him, seeing him as a lightweight, as a dark desert, and a land of great darkness (Jeremiah 2). Cursing others blames them (Genesis 3). Cursing self condemns self, denying the image of God within. Cursing separates. Complaint connects. Complaint draws us toward God; hatred and anger push us away from God.

The genre of complaint expresses honesty about the reality of life experience that is incongruent with the character of Yahweh. It is a hopeful, trusting expression that Yahweh will mobilize himself on our behalf. Complaint is an act of truth-telling faith, not unfaith. "Trust in him at all times, O people; pour out your hearts to him, for God is our refuge" (Psalm 62:8).

Psalm 73 presents a perfect example of complaint. Asaph begins, "Surely God is good to Israel" (Psalm 73:1). He continues with a litany of apparent evidence to the contrary. But Asaph concludes, "But as for me, it is good to be near God" (Psalm 73:28).

In complaint, we come to God with a sense of abandonment, divorce, being orphaned, forgotten, forsaken (Isaiah 49:14; 54:7-8; Lamentations 5:20). Complaint lives in the real world candidly, refusing to ignore what is occurring. In Job 42:7-8, God honors Job's candid complaint because Job spoke right about life and God. God prizes complaint and rejects all deceiving denial and simplistic closure, preferring candid complexity.

In complaint, there is a courageous yet humble cross-examination. It is not a cross-examination of God, but a cross-examination and a refuting of the earth-bound reality. In Jeremiah 20:7, Jeremiah complains that God appears, by reason alone, to be an unprincipled, abusive Bully. God responds to Jeremiah's rehearsal of life's incongruity. God acts on voiced pain. Complaint is a rehearsal of the bad allowed by the Good. It is radical trust in God's reliability in the midst of real life.

To deny or diminish suffering is to arrogantly refuse to be humbled. It is to reject dependence upon God. Consider how God chastises his people in Deuteronomy 8:1-10 for forgetting their past suffering.

God wants us to remember our suffering, remember our need for him in our suffering, and rehearse our suffering before him.

Stage Three: Cry—Asking God for Help Rather Than Bargaining and Works

Stage one evaluates whether the sufferer is in denial *or* practicing candor, stage two assesses whether the sufferer is angry *or* practicing complaint, and stage three appraises whether the sufferer is involved in bargaining and works *or* crying out to God for help. Cry is a faith-based plea for mobilization. Psalm 72:12 assures us, "For he shall deliver the needy when he crieth" (KJV). Psalm 34 reminds us, "The righteous cry out, and the LORD hears them; he delivers them from all their troubles. The LORD is close to the brokenhearted and saves those who are crushed in spirit" (Psalm 34:17-18).

We pray our tears and God collects them in his bottle (Psalms 56:8). Crying out to God, lamenting, is a testimony that God is responsive, while the idols are non-responsive (1 Samuel 12:20-24).

Crying empties us, so there is more room in us for God. David wept until he had no strength left, but then he found strength in the Lord (1 Samuel 30). His cry summoned Yahweh into action. God's good heart goes out, especially, to the humble needy. Cry is the core theme of life in a fallen world. Stop crying; stop hoping. As long as we can cry, we can hope.

> **Crying empties us, so there is more room in us for God.**

When we cry out, we entreat God to help. Never be docile nor indifferent because God is never like that. Crying out is the piety of vigorous embrace in suffering. Take the initiative to call on God because expressed neediness compels God's very character to act. Prayer is a relational transaction that moves God; he wants us to call him to action on our behalf. He will not force himself on his lover; however, he'll never disappoint his pleading lover.

The opposite of cry is arrogance. It is the tough, stoic, self-made lone ranger who needs no one, especially not God. The last thing Satan wants us to do is to cry out to God for help. Imagine if Eve and Adam had cried out to God in the garden. Satan wants works. Self-effort. Self-sufficiency. Toughness. Independence.

Suffering is God's *opus alienum*—God's dominant way of destroying our self-reliance and complacency. He uses suffering to gain our attention. As C. S. Lewis reminded us, "God whispers to us in our suffering, but shouts to us in our pain." Once he has our attention, then God uses suffering to produce child-like trust—cry.

Stage Four: Comfort—Receiving God's Help Rather Than Depression and Alienation

Stage one probes whether the sufferer is in denial *or* candid, stage two whether angry *or* biblically complaining, stage three whether bargaining/works *or* crying out, and stage four whether experiencing depression due to alienation *or* finding comfort due to communion. Through *candor*, we choose to step on the mat with God. With *complaint*, the match begins. With *cry*, we cry, "Uncle." We say, "I'm pinned. I'm helpless. You win. Now I win, too." *Comfort* is the crippling touch of God bringing healing.

In comfort and communion, the God we cried out to, comes. We are embraced; we are encountered face-to-face. "So Jacob called the place Peniel, saying, 'It is because I saw God face-to-face, and yet my life was spared'" (Genesis 32:30). Tenacious wrestling with God, Jacob shows us, results in painful yet profitable *coram Deo* connection.

Satan longs to use (misuse) suffering to cause us to curse God and die (Job 2). God longs to use suffering to cause us to embrace him and live. Every problem is an opportunity to know God better, and our primary battle is to know God well. Thus, an essential soul care question is always, "How are these problems influencing your relationship to God?" Suffering can either shove us far from God into the land of despair, or drag us kicking and screaming closer to him into the solid soil of comfort.

Our comfort is three-fold—with God, with others, and with self. First, we gain comfort through *communion* with *God*. As I've noted, faith perceives the presence of God in the presence of suffering. In fact, faith believes that "in all their distress he too was distressed" (Isaiah 63:9). Faith perceives that God feels our pain, joins us in our pain, and even shares our pain. Faith does not demand the removal of suffering, but desires endurance in suffering. Faith understands that what can't be cured, can be endured.

According to Psalm 73:21-28, suffering is an opportunity for God to divulge more of himself. When Asaph's heart was grieved, and his spirit embittered, God brought him to his senses. "Whom have I in heaven but you? And earth has nothing I desire besides you. My flesh and my heart may fail, but God is the strength of my heart and my portion forever" (Psalm 73:25-26).

We also find comfort through connection with *others* through *compassionate commiseration*. Think about those words. Co-passion: shared passion and pathos. Co-misery: shared misery. Shared sorrow is vital because we always experience suffering as separation and betrayal.

As a spiritual friend, you provide human comfort through grace relationships where you climb in the casket with others as they face daily deaths. You also offer human comfort through grace narratives: spiritual eyes, reason redeemed by grace/faith, and the perspective of faith. You assist your suffering spiritual friends to erect a platform of faith from which to respond to suffering—the Divine perspective. You help them to contemplate their suffering from a new, Divine viewpoint. They reshape their interpretation of life in light of their image of God. You nurture in them alternative ways to view life. This does not eradicate their pain, fear, or misery, but it robs them of their hopelessness. The Christ of the Cross becomes their ultimate interpretive context.

We also find comfort through *contentment* in Christ as *self-aware* beings. Paul encourages us when he teaches that contentment is *learned*. We can acquire and recite the ABCs of contentment in any situation. How? According to Philippians 4:13-20, by rooting our sense of self in who God is and who we are *in* Christ and *to* Christ.

Sustaining Intervention: Preparation and Preservation

After compassionately discerning the stages of suffering, you need to provide sustaining for suffering. In the next two chapters, you'll learn and practice many specific sustaining relational competencies. In the remainder of this chapter, you're asking and answering the broader question, "Who do I need to be and what do I need to do to sustain my spiritual friend's faith?"

What you're wondering in sustaining is, "What will keep my spiritual friend from dying in the casket, from shriveling up in the desert? What will keep my spiritual friend from staying in the desert and turning to mirages (broken cisterns, false lovers, idols of the heart, the sinful world, Satan)?"

To sustain your spiritual friend, you must remember the warfare between Christ's grace narrative and Satan's lying narrative. God and Satan work with the same material—the story of our lives. Satan, the scoundrel that he is, lies about the nature of our life story, telling us that it is a murderous story full of death and despair. God, the Lover that he is, tells us the truth about our life story, reminding us that even in death-like events, he is the resurrection and the life.

Maturing Your Spiritual Friendship Competency
Diagnosis of Healthy or Unhealthy Responses to Suffering

1. A spiritual friend tells you that he/she has just discovered that his/her teenage son is using drugs.

   a. Paraphrase what your spiritual friend would say if in denial.

   b. Paraphrase what your spiritual friend might say if practicing candor—honesty with self.

2. In your second meeting, your spiritual friend has moved to stage two.

   a. Paraphrase what your spiritual friend would say if consumed by anger.

   b. Paraphrase what your spiritual friend might say if practicing complaint—honesty with God.

3. In your third meeting, your spiritual friend has moved to stage three.

   a. Paraphrase what your spiritual friend would say if practicing works and bargaining.

   b. Paraphrase what your spiritual friend might say if practicing cry—asking God for help.

4. In your fourth meeting, your spiritual friend has moved to stage four.

   a. Paraphrase what your spiritual friend would say if experiencing alienation and depression.

   b. Paraphrase what your spiritual friend might say if experiencing comfort—receiving God's help.

Concerning the *earthly* story, as a spiritual friend, you tune into your friends' stories of suffering, promoting the acknowledgement that "life is bad." You embrace them so they can embrace their pain. Concerning the *eternal* story, as a spiritual friend, you help your friends tune into God's larger story of healing, encouraging the confession that "God is good." They embrace their pain in order to embrace God in their pain and be embraced by God who feels their pain.

First, you help them face reality and admit pain, helping them to learn that it's normal to hurt. Second, you help them endure their pain, experiencing the truth that shared sorrow is endurable sorrow. Through your connection with them, they're able to hold the line against further retreat. You connect by climbing in the casket with them, refusing to remain ignorant of their suffering. If you do ignore their pain, then you tend to force God in by telling them God's story before you listen to their stories.

Once they face their pain, then you help them to invite God into the casket with them. Your connection (climbing in their casket) leads them to communion (inviting God into their casket). You help them to remember God's story because ignoring God's story allows Satan's lying story to win the day.

The Apostle Paul writes his own autobiography of a suffering child of God in 2 Corinthians 1:3-10. In verse 8, he teaches that suffering people long to be known, not ignored and certainly not analyzed. Paul does not want his friends to be *ignorant* of his intense external affliction nor of his intense internal despair. He communicates, "If you want to know *me*, then you must know my intense suffering and my raw soul." Image bearers cannot be analyzed, dissected, examined, or studied. They can only be known, experienced, and loved. Do not analyze suffering friends; know them soul-to-soul.

Image bearers cannot be analyzed, dissected, examined, or studied. They can only be known, experienced, and loved.

In verses 3-5, Paul demonstrates that powerful spiritual friends must face their suffering face-to-face with God. Paul lays it on the line with God, telling God and his spiritual friends exactly what he's experiencing and feeling. He is wounded, but has found healing in Christ.

Are you a *wounded healer* or an *unhealed wounder*? Unhealed wounders have never faced life face-to-face with God as suffering image bearers. Therefore, try as they might, they love without passion, think without imagination, choose without courage, and feel without depth.

You become a wounded healer by turning to God with your hurts. *Only comfort-receivers spill over and overflow into comfort-givers.* That is the simple, yet profound message of 2 Corinthians 1:3-10. Healed wounded healers, heal others. Because God is infinite, you do not need to experience the same situation or soul pain as your spiritual friend; you only need to have experienced the same God.

Once you become the type of person who turns to God, then you can become the type of person who tunes into others. Once you become this type of spiritual friend, then you can sustain your spiritual friend through preparation and preservation.

- ♦ Preparation: How to Explore Your Spiritual Friend's Casket (Proverbs 18:13)
    - ♦ Entering Your Spiritual Friend's Earthly Story of Suffering
    - ♦ Awareness of Affliction and Despair
- ♦ Preservation: How to Climb in the Casket with Your Spiritual Friend (Romans 12:15)
    - ♦ Embracing Your Spiritual Friend in His/Her Earthly Story of Suffering
    - ♦ Weeping with Those Who Weep

Preparation: How to Explore Your Spiritual Friend's Casket

Picture the following scenario. Becky comes to "chat" with you. While talking, you "diagnose" that she is "a suffering image bearer in need of sustaining." Being a wise spiritual friend, you don't want to cram a one-size-fits-all approach/response into her soul. You want to know what's up. You long to know *her soul*. However, you also realize that you must first know *her situation*. "He who answers before listening—that is his folly and his shame" (Proverbs 18:13).

Using the analogy of life as a story, you want to *read Becky's life situation.* It is like gaining some understanding of what an author was experiencing when she wrote her novel. It is similar to the research that must be done by an author before she can write a historical novel.

What are you listening for? How do you explore Becky's casket? You need to practice "theory-guided listening" or what I call "theological exploration." Knowing that life is a three-act play (Creation, Fall, and Redemption), and knowing what you know about the actors in the play (Romancers, Dreamers, Creators, and Singers), there are certain concepts that you tune into, certain issues that catch your attention. So in sustaining you:

- Listen for *Relational* Interactions That Provoke *Disappointment*
- Listen for *Rational* Interpretations That Provoke *Doubt*
- Listen for *Volitional* Decisions That Provoke *Dis-Integration*
- Listen for *Emotional* Reactions That Provoke *Despair*

Listen for Relational Interactions That Provoke Disappointment: Engage Your Spiritual Friend's Story of Suffering as a Relational Romancer

Since reality is relational, the greatest disappointments in life are *relational disappointments*. Since relationships are triune (people relate to God, others, and self), you want to read Becky's story of:

- Disappointing *Social* Interactions: Relationships with Others That Evidence a Sense of Betrayal and Loss
  - Listen for a Sense of Betrayal of Connection: Acceptance/Love/Relationship
  - Listen for a Sense of Betrayal of Contribution: Respect/Purpose/Impact
- Disappointing *Self-Aware* Interactions: Relationship with Self That Evidences a Sense of Contempt
- Disappointing *Spiritual* Interactions: Relationships with God That Are Perceived As a Sense of Abandonment

Disappointing Social Interactions: Relationships with Others That Evidence a Sense of Betrayal and Loss

I find it most helpful to start with social relationships. Few people are deeply aware of their spiritual "state" or of their own "sense of self." What they are aware of is their own pain, especially pain related to the betrayal of relationship (connection) and the loss of impact (contribution).

Therefore, you want to listen for a *sense of betrayal of connection—of acceptance, love, and relationship*. Becky tells you that her boss "made a pass at her." He claims to be a believer. He claims to be a good friend to Becky's husband, Jim. Becky and Jim have been betrayed. When Becky talks about this subject, tune in to her sense of betrayal by her boss (Bill).

Out of loving curiosity, in the back of your mind you might also be thinking, "I wonder how Jim has come through for Becky. Is he supportive, accusatory, indifferent? Has Becky even told him? If not, what do I make of that?"

You also want to listen for a *sense of betrayal of contribution—respect, purpose, and impact.* Becky happens to love her work. She feels fulfilled, has been able to witness on the job, and her career feels like much more than a job. It feels like a calling. Now that, too, is in jeopardy. What fears rise within her soul at the thought of losing her calling in her company?

Disappointing Self-Aware Interactions: Relationship with Self That Evidences a Sense of Contempt

You also are wondering about how all of this is leading Becky to think about herself. What narrative is she buying into? Satan's narrative of shame, "Serves you right, you are such a flirt!" Satan's narrative of works, "If you had only been praying harder, this would have never happened." Satan's cursing narrative, "God must see you as a prostitute."

Disappointing Spiritual Interactions: Relationships with God That Are Perceived As a Sense of Abandonment

You're wondering, "As Becky faces this, what's her orientation to God? Is she face-to-face, running scared, running in circles, going downhill? Does she feel protected, abandoned, cared for, wanted, rejected, neglected? Has she believed Satan's lie that life is bad because God is bad?"

As you listen to Becky with loving curiosity, you're wondering, "Of all of this, what is most disappointing to Becky? Where is she most deeply being failed relationally? Feeling failed relationally?"

Listen for Rational Interpretations That Provoke Doubt: Hear Your Spiritual Friend's Story of Suffering as a Dreamer

Remember that suffering always has two levels—what happens to us and what happens in us. Listen now for level two suffering. In particular, listen for false interpretations—perceptions filled with doubt.

Every story has a theme, a plot. Listen to Becky's story. Not just what she says, but what she leaves out, and how she says it. Our mind does not simply store events, we also "story" events in our imagination (the Hebrew is *yeser* in Genesis 6:5). We are "meaning-makers." We want to make sense of our lives. We hate confusion.

Becky can interpret her situation using reason apart from faith. By this perspective, she may devise a theme that says, "No one can be trusted." She may determine never to get close to anyone again.

Alternatively, interpreting this event from reason redeemed by faith, Becky may be saying to herself, "This stinks. It hurts. I'm shocked. Confused. Terrified. If not for the Cross, I don't know that I could even face God. Talk to God. But he does care. 'For God so loved the world that he gave his only begotten Son that whosoever believes on him should never perish, but have everlasting life.' Oh, Father. Help me . . ."

Diagnosis involves determining which narrative reigns. Thus, you want to hear how Becky is seeing and defining her suffering. You do this by:

- Listening for Clues to Satan's Smaller, Lying Theme
- Listening for Clues to Christ's Larger, Loving Theme

Listen for Clues to Satan's Smaller, Lying Theme

What is Becky "buying into"? Where is she being duped? Where do you see a works mentality? Shamed-based thinking? Self-sufficiency? Covering? Hiding? Blaming? Contempt? Doubt? Despair? Deceit?

Listen for Clues to Christ's Larger, Loving Theme

Where can Becky and you find glimpses of grace? What is God up to in all of this? Where do you sense Becky thinking grace thoughts like forgiveness, God's goodness, eternal purposes, delayed gratification, trust, hope, persistence, God-sufficiency?

Listen for Volitional Decisions That Provoke Dis-Integration: Watch Your Spiritual Friend's Unfolding Story of Suffering as a Creator

We are relational, rational, and volitional. Suffering affects us in all three arenas.

Volitionally, listen for the pathways that Becky is choosing to follow. What decisions is she making in her heart? What goals and purposes is she now pursuing? Are her responses courageous ones of bold love? Or, is she moving along the path of dis-integration—feeling weak, overpowered, helpless, hopeless, and overwhelmed?

Listen and watch for patterns. What are her typical responses to disappointing events? Does she play the martyr? The stoic? The good girl? The tough girl? Does she push people away, you away, God away?

Perceive purposes. How does she relate to God, others, and to you in light of these situations and why? What does it "do for her" to play the role of the helpless victim? What is her agenda in choosing the response of the stiff warrior? What might motivate her dis-integration—separation and distancing in her relationship to God, others, and herself?

Listen for Emotional Reactions That Provoke Despair: Experience Your Spiritual Friend's Sad Story of Suffering as a Singer

We're relational, rational, volitional, and emotional. Suffering is most easily "tasted" emotionally. Many of us tend to "wear our feelings on our sleeves." What emotional "clothing" is Becky wearing? Is she self-aware or in denial? Is she managing her moods or totally ungoverned in her reactions? What is Becky experiencing because of her boss's sexual harassment?

Assess her emotional quotient. Is she emotionally honest with herself, God, and others? In her emotional honesty with others, is she handling her expression of her emotions maturely or immaturely?

Taste Becky's despair. Where is she about to give up hope? Where is she overwhelmed? Drowning?

Before you can climb in Becky's casket, you must help her to lift the lid. Together you peer inside. It's not a pretty sight. It's cold. Smells of death. But then, that's what desert living is all about. And that's what sustaining is all about—the sorrow of daily deaths.

Before you can help Becky to open her casket, you need to understand, based upon God's Word, what's inside her casket. That's where the preceding theory-guided explorations assist you. Uncover the casketed remains of relational disappointment, rational doubt, volitional disintegration, and emotional despair. These are "markers," "handles," "clues," or "guides" that remind you where to look because you know what to look for.

Maturing Your Spiritual Friendship Competency
Exploring Your Spiritual Friend's Casket

♦ With a partner, role-play Becky's story. The "counselor" needs to draw out Becky's story. No advice. No exhortation. No Scripture yet. By the time you're done, you should be able to write a half-page summary of Becky's suffering.

♦ If you are working through this material individually, then instead of role-playing, use the space after each scenario to write your responses to each situation.

1. Listen for Becky's *relational disappointments*. Write what you hear.

2. Listen for Becky's *rational doubts*. Write what you hear.

3. Listen for Becky's *volitional dis-integration*. Write what you hear.

4.   Listen for Becky's *emotional despair*. Write what you hear.

5.   Write your summary of Becky's suffering. Don't just repeat what you've written under questions 1-4. Turn it into a "soul story." Weave together themes. Make her story come alive—she is, after all, alive.

Preservation: How to Climb into Your Spiritual Friend's Casket (Romans 12:15)

Once you've opened the casket lid, what in the world do you do next? What does it actually look like and feel like to climb in the casket? What's the point?

Preservation is *compassionate commiseration*. Becky's misery becomes your misery. Becky's passion (literally from *paschal* lamb for suffering) is your passionate suffering. God calls you to sympathize with Becky in her suffering, to actually feel what she feels and have it hurt you also. "So that there should be no division in the body, but that its parts should have equal concern for each other. *If one part suffers, every part suffers with it*; if one part is honored, every part rejoices with it" (1 Corinthians 12:25-26, emphasis added).

When Becky's clobbered with the double blow of external disappointment and internal doubts, she's ready to go down for the count. She wants to throw in the towel. Without strength, she needs an infusion of spiritual power that comes through shared suffering.

Preservation involves making suffering endurable by sharing it. In it, your goal is to maintain a troubled person like Becky in her situation with as little loss as possible. Help Becky to hold the line against excessive retreat. Together (Becky, you, and God) create the line drawn in the sand of the soul which finds a stopping place against a full retreat.

How do you "get there from here?" Follow four aspects of casket climbing:

♦ Personal Suffering: "I Have Wrestled with Suffering." Embracing Your Own Suffering
♦ Participation in Suffering: "I Suffer with You." Embracing Your Spiritual Friend
♦ Permission to Grieve in Suffering: "I Respect Your Struggle in Suffering." Empowering Your Spiritual Friend
♦ Person to Turn to in Suffering: "I Speak to God about My Suffering." Your Spiritual Friend Embraces God

Personal Suffering: "I Have Wrestled with Suffering." Embracing Your Own Suffering

By personal suffering, I'm referring to the *counselor's suffering*, the counselor's courageous choice to be the type of person who dares to suffer. Personal suffering says, "I feel." It's the integrity to face your own suffering *coram Deo*. Such integrity is the prerequisite to helping others with their suffering.

What does it look like? It looks like the Psalms.

Is your life a psalm? I don't mean only a praise psalm. Psalms sing to God. Psalms are love poetry to the Worthy Groom. Is your life an open book? An open love letter to God? In all areas, including in suffering?

M. V. Begalke, speaking of how Luther learned his theology and his pastoral care from his own struggles with suffering, notes that "Luther gained a tremendous awareness and acceptance of the human condition. Troubled persons could sense in him, a humble fellow-sojourner who experienced many of the same depressive anxieties as they did" (Begalke, *Luther's Anfechtungen*, p. 15).

After his father's death, Luther wrote of his own deep grief.

This death has cast me into mourning. Although it is consoling to me that, as he writes, my father fell asleep softly and strong in his faith in Christ, yet his kindness and the memory of his pleasant conversation have caused so deep a wound in my heart that I have scarcely ever held death in such low esteem (G. Tappert, *Luther: Letters of Spiritual Counsel*, p. 30).

Luther faced suffering with integrity. He viewed this as a prerequisite to helping others walk through their suffering journey. Facing suffering *coram Deo* is imperative for anyone who wants to offer spiritual care.

Participation in Suffering: "I Suffer with You." Embracing Your Spiritual Friend

Christ calls you to participate in suffering with others to the point of experiencing their pain. It is not just, "I understand your pain," or "I feel your pain," but "I connect with you in experiencing your pain."

Take a walk with Becky in the desert. Experience the heat, the sand, the winds, the thirst, the pain, and the confusion. Come alongside Becky. Allow Becky to know that you know her pain. Help her experience the feeling of your feeling her pain.

Place yourself in the role as a lead character in Becky's story. Write a synopsis of what life might be like for you if you were living her story.

Get away to the "desert." Retreat to a quiet place where you have space to reflect on Becky's shattered dreams, alienation, anxiety, and darkness. You need the silent attentiveness, quiet time, and solitude—the space and time where you're conscious of needing Christ—to truly feel what Becky needs.

Permission to Grieve in Suffering: "I Respect Your Struggle in Suffering." Empowering Your Spiritual Friend

Permission to grieve in suffering says to Becky, "I will grieve for you first so you can then allow yourself to grieve." What might this look like? It might look like you literally flying up out of your chair when Becky first tells you that her boss made a pass at her. "What! He did what!" Or, it might look like a tear trickling down your cheek as Becky shares her story. However it looks, Becky feels your feelings for her. She feels embraced by you.

This requires an insightful personal awareness of the groanings of living in a fallen world. It requires that you become a Romancer who loves passionately and a Singer who feels deeply. The purpose of giving permission to grieve is to promote an awareness of deeper affections, thirsts, and longings. You want to help Becky face her relational experience—with candor.

Once you think that you may have "captured" what it might be like to be Becky, then you share your sense of the theme of Becky's disappointing relational events/experiences. "Becky, from some of the things you've shared, it seems to me that you feel really let down by Jim. Kind'a like you wish he had gone in there and ripped your boss's head off. Thinking about it, I'm surprised that Jim has been so passive. I don't know. Is this just me? How does this connect with you?"

Or, you might use some probing interactions:

◆ Spiritual Conversations Granting Permission to Grieve: Drawing Out Becky's Suffering

   ◆ *If you knew that God would say, "Yes," to your prayers about this, what would you pray for?*
   ◆ *If God immediately answered, "Yes," how would you respond? How would things be different? What would you be doing differently?*
   ◆ *What do you think the Bible teaches about feeling anger or disappointment toward God?*
   ◆ *What do you think about expressing your feelings (anger, disappointment, complaint) toward God?*
   ◆ *Have you come across any verses that illustrate how God's people have talked to God when they felt that he was not hearing their cry?*
   ◆ *If you were to write a Psalm 13 (or any Psalm of Lament or Psalm of Complaint to God), how would it sound?*

- *If you painted a picture of God right now, what would you paint?*
- *In what ways have you sensed that God has not heard the cry of your soul?*
- *In what ways have you sensed that God has heard the cry of your soul?*
- *What is it like for you when God seems deaf to your cry?*
- *Sometimes my soul seems to shout, "God, where are you now?" And yet my mind reminds me that God is always faithful, always with me. When you have those conflicting thoughts, how do you go about choosing which to believe?*

- Social Conversations Granting Permission to Grieve: Drawing Out Becky's Suffering

  - *To have your employer, a friend, a Christian no less, do this to you . . . It has to hurt deeply.*
  - *How is your situation affecting your relationships?*
  - *How are others handling this?*
  - *What does Jim think about all this?*
  - *Makes me wonder what others are feeling.*
  - *When else have you experienced betrayal similar to this? What did you learn about God in that situation? Tell me what you would repeat and what you would change about your response back then.*
  - *Jim not talking to you, not saying much to you. What is this like for you?*

- Self-Aware Conversations Granting Permission to Grieve: Drawing Out Becky's Suffering

  - *Have you ever faced anything like this before? How did you feel then?*
  - *How is this impacting how you see yourself? Feel about yourself?*
  - *If you painted a picture of yourself now, what would it look like?*
  - *When have you felt similarly about yourself?*
  - *What's it like to go through all of this?*
  - *For me, this would be _____. How does that connect for you?*
  - *I can only imagine that you might _____. What do you think?*
  - *I would guess (bet) that you feel _____. Am I close?*
  - *As you speak, I picture you seeing yourself as _____ (put in suffering identity). How does that compare to how you see yourself now? Have you ever seen yourself like this before? How do you normally see yourself?*

Person to Turn to in Suffering: "I Speak to God about My Suffering." Your Spiritual Friend Embraces God

In the right time and the right way, you encourage Becky to take all her pain and complaint to the Lord who knows all. Psalm 120:1 teaches who to turn to. "In my distress I cried unto the LORD, and he heard me" (KJV). Luther's exposition of this verse explains the truth that we must come face-to-face with God when we face suffering.

The first verse teaches us where we should turn when misfortune comes upon us—not to the emperor, not to the sword, not to our own devices and wisdom, but to the Lord, who is our only real help in time of need. "I cried unto the Lord in my distress," he says. That we should do this confidently, cheerfully, and without fail he makes clear when he says, "And he heard me." It is as if he would say, "The Lord is pleased to have us turn to him in our distress and is glad to hear and help us" (Tappert, *Luther: Letters of Spiritual Counsel*, p. 204).

Luther had a house full of guests every evening at the main meal. Many of their lively discussions were transcribed. Veit Dietrich wrote of one conversation he and Luther had concerning what a Christian was free to share with Christ.

When I asked him about the passage in which Jeremiah cursed the day in which he had been born, and when I suggested that such impatience was sin; Martin replied, "Sometimes one has to wake up our Lord God with such words. Otherwise, he doesn't hear. It is a case of real murmuring on the part of Jeremiah. Christ spoke in this way, also. 'How long am I to be with you?' (Mark 9:19). Moses went so far as to throw his keys at our Lord God's feet when he asked, 'Did I conceive all these people?' (Numbers 11:12)" (Luther, *Luther's Works*, Vol. 54, p. 30).

The ongoing dialogue is fascinating. Luther continues by saying that everyone feels and thinks such things, so those who say that Christians should not express them to God are unrealistic. "Accordingly it is only speculative theologians who condemn such impatience and recommend patience. If they get down to the realm of practice, they will be aware of this" (Luther, *Luther's Works*, Vol. 54, pp. 30-31).

Perhaps Luther would have used spiritual conversations, such as the following, to point people to God.

- ◆ Spiritual Conversations Pointing People to God: Encouraging Becky's *Coram Deo* Candor

    - ◆ *What are you doing with God in your suffering?*
    - ◆ *If you were not a believer, what do you think you would feel? Think? Do? Say?*
    - ◆ *What Scripture could you turn to in order to understand God's perspective on what you're going through?*
    - ◆ *What Scripture have you turned to, to understand God's perspective on what you're going through?*
    - ◆ *What passages have you found helpful in gaining a new perspective on your situation?*
    - ◆ *What passages have you found helpful in comforting you in this?*
    - ◆ *If you didn't have the Scriptures to turn to, how would your perspective on this be different?*
    - ◆ *If you didn't have Christ/God/the Holy Spirit to turn to, how would your perspective on this be different?*

Where We've Been and Where We're Headed

Spiritual friendship starts with *people*: a biblical *understanding* of image bearers. It continues with *problems*: a biblical *diagnosis* of what's wrong. It commences with *solutions*: biblical *treatment and intervention*. Chapters Six and Seven will equip you to implement a five-phase sustaining treatment and intervention plan using the acrostic *GRACE*.

- ◆ *G*   Grace Connecting: Proverbs 27:6
- ◆ *R*   Rich Soul Empathizing: Romans 12:15
- ◆ *A*   Accurate/Active Spiritual Listening: John 2:23-4:43
- ◆ *C*   Caring Spiritual Conversations: Ephesians 4:29
- ◆ *E*   Empathetic Scriptural Explorations: Isaiah 61:1-3

Maturing Your Spiritual Friendship Competency
Climbing in the Casket with Your Spiritual Friend

1. Evaluate your personal suffering level.

    a. Use the following 1-10 scale to rate and explain your personal suffering level. One: "I refuse to face my own suffering." Ten: "My suffering is an open psalm that I experience face-to-face with God."

    b. What could you do to increase your level of integrity/honesty with your own suffering?

    c. What difference would it make in your ministry of spiritual friendship if you grew more mature in wrestling with and embracing your own suffering?

2. Evaluate your participation in the suffering of others.

    a. Use the following 1-10 scale to rate and explain your level of participating in others' suffering. One: "Your hurt does not touch me." Ten: "Your hurt is my hurt. I weep with your weeping."

    b. What could you do to increase your ability to suffer with others, embracing them in their suffering?

    c. What difference would it make in your ministry of spiritual friendship if you grew more mature in connecting with others in their pain?

♦ If you are working through this material individually, then instead of role-playing, use the space after each scenario to write your responses to each situation.

3. Partner Role-Play # 1: Use *spiritual conversations* granting permission to grieve to draw out Becky's suffering.

4. Partner Role-Play # 2: Use *social conversations* granting permission to grieve to draw out Becky's suffering.

5. Partner Role-Play # 3: Use *self-aware conversations* granting permission to grieve to draw out Becky's suffering.

6. Partner Role-Play # 4: Use *spiritual conversations* pointing people to God to encourage Becky's *coram Deo* candor.

Chapter Six

Sustaining Treatment and Intervention
GRACE Relational Competencies, Part I

"Incompetent spiritual directors know no way with souls but to hammer and batter them like a blacksmith" (Saint John of the Cross).

Bedside Manners

You sit silently at Alonzo's bedside. He doesn't even know you're there yet. His wife, Therese, just called you with the news concerning his liver biopsy—cancer. Anesthetized in the recovery room, within the hour he'll awake with groggy head and blurry eyes to see you and his wife.

Waiting, you picture his "firstborn," Stefan, the always-energized nine-year-old who loves Daddy's high-fives and hugs. You picture "the middle child," Marcie, a six-year-old bundle of joy who's always holding Daddy's hand in church. You picture "the baby of the family," Joseph, just three, and you wonder how many memories he will have of Daddy.

Fighting back tears, you silently pray, "Lord, what do I say? What do I do? How do I help? Help me to be here for Alonzo, Therese, and the kids. Keep me from trite platitudes. Don't let me babble. What would Jesus do? What would Jesus say? How would he relate?"

Your mind drifts to Jesus and Lazarus. "Jesus loved Martha and her sister and Lazarus" (John 11:5), you recall. "Jesus loved . . . Help me to love, Lord."

"This sickness will not end in death. No, it is for God's glory so that God's Son may be glorified through it" (John 11:4). You know that you don't have a promise that *this* sickness will not end in *physical* death. You do know that Alonzo's sickness will not end in spiritual death. You smile, remembering burly, bike-riding Alonzo reluctantly attending Stefan's baptism two years ago. Who would have thought that two weeks later Alonzo would be baptized, publicly expressing his newfound faith in Jesus. "Lord, be glorified."

"A short while ago the Jews tried to stone you, yet you are going back there?" (John 11:8). Pondering the ever-impetuous disciples and their warning to their Master, you pray again. "Father, this death and dying stuff terrifies me. I hate it. I loathe hospitals. I despise funerals. Give me a nice chair, a functional computer, a terrific biblical library, and let me prepare sermons. Bedside manners? They didn't teach that in seminary. They couldn't. How do you teach this stuff? Help me to face my fears so I can help Alonzo to face his."

Exploring Your Spiritual Journey

1. Describe how someone has touched you through grace relationships (acceptance, loving, listening, caring, empathy, connecting deeply, understanding, sacrifice, giving, other-centered loving, etc.).

2. Share how God has helped you to touch someone through grace relationships (acceptance, loving, listening, caring, empathy, connecting deeply, understanding, sacrifice, giving, other-centered loving, etc.).

3. Share about one grace relationship that you're in that encourages you and the other person to go through the unpleasant, difficult, hard, strenuous, and painful process toward growth.

4. Evaluate your "bedside manner." Not simply how well or poorly you handle a crisis in a hospital, but how well or poorly you connect with the emotionally hurting. Use the following 1-10 scale to evaluate and explain your empathy level or connection quotient. One: "I believe in pulling yourself up by your bootstraps. Wipe your nose. Don't navel-gaze, don't whine. Don't worry; be happy." Ten: "I weep with those who weep. I make their pain my pain. Like Jesus, I resonate with the hurting."

"Our friend Lazarus has fallen asleep; but I am going there to wake him up" (John 11:11). "Let me be Alonzo's *friend*, Lord. His spiritual friend. His Jesus-like friend. What does that mean? Look like?"

"When Jesus saw her weeping, and the Jews who had come along with her also weeping, he was deeply moved in spirit and troubled" (John 11:33). Interesting, you think to yourself. Jesus knew the outcome. "Your brother will rise again" (John 11:23). He knew God would be glorified. Yet, he was still deeply moved and troubled. "Father, help me to feel before I preach. To sustain before I heal. Don't let my awareness of your final victory minimize my hatred of the final enemy—Death! Don't let my confidence in your capability to weave all things together for good depreciate my groaning in this messed up world."

"Jesus wept" (John 11:35). And your tears flow. Unashamed. Unbridled.

"See how he loved him!" (John 11:36). "Help me to love Alonzo," you pray.

Therese enters. Seeing your tears, she hugs you as you stand. "Thank you for being here. Thank you for loving Alonzo," she shares.

Relational Competencies

Perhaps now it becomes clear why words like "skill" and "technique" are far too shallow for what spiritual friendship is all about. "Relational competence" still doesn't fully grab me, but it's a better phrase, especially when carefully defined. Relational competence is our ability—given by grace and cultivated by spiritual discipline—to express the character of Christ in our relationships with people so they experience our love and are changed by God's grace.

> **Relational competence is our ability—given by grace and cultivated by spiritual discipline—to express the character of Christ in our relationships with people so they experience our love and are changed by God's grace.**

We relate deeply to others only if we are already relating deeply to Christ. "If you have any encouragement from being united with Christ, if any comfort from his love, if any fellowship with the Spirit, if any tenderness and compassion" (Philippians 2:1). When we are nourishing our souls in Christ, then our souls can spill over to others.

Then, like Christ, we will be other-centered in our relationships. "Do nothing out of selfish ambition or vain conceit, but in humility consider others better than yourselves. Each of you should look not only to your own interests, but also to the interests of others" (Philippians 2:3-4).

Our attitude (motivation, passion, mindset, conviction) will then be like Christ, "Who, being in very nature God, did not consider equality with God something to be grasped, but made himself nothing, taking the very nature of a servant, being made in human likeness" (Philippians 2:6-7).

Like Paul, who was like Christ, we offer our own souls, our very selves, to our spiritual friends. "We loved you so much that we were delighted to share with you not only the gospel of God but our lives as well, because you had become so dear to us" (1 Thessalonians 2:8).

Paul did not become this mature without effort. Instead, he followed a lifestyle of spiritual discipline, of spiritual formation, that allowed him to so connect to Christ that Christ's goodness flowed out of him into others.

We proclaim him, admonishing and teaching everyone with all wisdom so that we may present everyone perfect in Christ. To this end I labor, struggling with all his energy, which so powerfully works in me. I want you to know how much I am struggling for you and for those at Laodicea, and for all who have not met me personally. My purpose is that they may be encouraged in heart and united in love, so that they may have the full riches of complete understanding, in order that they may know the mystery of God, namely, Christ (Colossians 1:28-2:2).

Spiritual friendship is grueling. Agonizing. Exhausting. It's work that results in the release of grace.

Pastoral ministry, professional Christian counseling, lay spiritual friendship, they all require biblical content, Christlike character, *and* relational competence in the context of Christian community. Let's not simply become more skillful. Let's get on track toward becoming better encouraged, enlightened, and empowered to give tastes of grace. I call these tastes of grace "relational competencies."

Sustaining Relational Competencies: *GRACE*

The concept we're probing is easy to state, but takes a lifetime to develop. "How can my spiritual friends and I engage in grace relationships that sustain their faith?"

This question begs another. "What is a grace relationship?" Throughout this chapter and the next, we'll learn that grace relationships involve five relational competencies that I summarize using the acronym *GRACE*:

- ◆ *G*   Grace Connecting: Proverbs 27:6
- ◆ *R*   Rich Soul Empathizing: Romans 12:15
- ◆ *A*   Accurate/Active Spiritual Listening: John 2:23-4:43
- ◆ *C*   Caring Spiritual Conversations: Ephesians 4:29
- ◆ *E*   Empathetic Scriptural Explorations: Isaiah 61:1-3

Whenever you think of the essence of sustaining, think, "grace." Picture grace that helps others in their time of need.

Therefore, since we have a great high priest who has gone through the heavens, Jesus the Son of God, let us hold firmly to the faith we profess. For we do not have a high priest who is unable to sympathize with our weakness, but we have one who has been tempted in every way, just as we are—yet was without sin. Let us then approach the throne of grace with confidence, so that we may receive mercy and find grace to help us in our time of need (Hebrews 4:14-16).

What a perfect picture of sustaining relational competency, of grace relating. Jesus is not aloof, distant, or removed. In his incarnation, he went through the heavens to earth sharing in our humanity, becoming like us, so that he might help us (Hebrews 2:14-18). Jesus is not unsympathetic. He is touched with the feelings of our infirmities. He's able to suffer with and be affected similarly to us. He has the same pathos, shares the same experience, has fellow feelings, endures a mutual participation, and partakes of a full acquaintance with us (W. Michaelis, *Theological Dictionary of the New Testament*, pp. 801-803). He offers grace to help in our time of need—well-timed help, help in the nick of time, words aptly spoken in season and seasoned with grace (A. T. Robertson, *Word Pictures in the New Testament*, p. 565).

We can become Jesus with skin on him. In sustaining, we do so by expressing *GRACE* relational competencies. The first of which is aptly called: "Grace Connecting."

Grace Connecting: Committed Involvement—Proverbs 27:6

Grace connecting involves *communion through communication*. You have love in your heart for your spiritual friends. Do they know that? Can they feel it? Do they experience you? Grace connecting allows your passionate love to powerfully touch your spiritual friend.

Connecting is the foundational competency in the art of relationships. Spouses need it. So do parents, co-workers, teammates, friends, church members, and neighbors. We all need to become *competent connectors*. If we were, all professional helpers (social workers, counselors, and psychologists) would be superfluous, extra, excess, fluff.

Putting "grace" before connecting, reflects:

- *The Source of True Connection—Christ's Mercy:* Christ's generous, undeserved love for us is the spring from which our generous, often mutual, sometimes undeserved, love flows to one another.
- *The Nature of True Connection—The Spirit's Generous Sharing:* The Spirit's fruit in us is the nourishment we offer others in their time of deprivation/suffering. Connection is gift-giving; giving away the fruit the Spirit grows in us. We want to be friendly neighbors who perform all the hard work of mulching, fertilizing, tilling, weeding, watering, and harvesting; and then freely share our bumper crop of ripe, delicious fruit with all our neighbors.
- *The Power of Connecting—Father's Influence*: The grace of God teaches us to say, "No!" to ungodliness and, "Yes!" to Father. When we freely share the attractive fruit of the Spirit, then others are influenced for Christ. "So that in every way they will make the teaching about God our Savior *attractive*. For the *grace* of God that brings salvation has appeared to all men. It teaches us to say, 'No' to ungodliness and worldly passions, and to live self-controlled, upright and godly lives" (Titus 2:10-12, emphasis added).

The Need for Grace Connecting

There's plenty of potential pain in spiritual friendship. Ponder what it's like for you when another person becomes aware of the grief in your soul or the sin in your heart. Risk. Vulnerability. Exposure. Consider:

- How unpleasant it is when you experience and acknowledge devastating emotions (Psalm 42, Psalm 88) (emotional).
- How shameful it feels to admit your sinful motivations and actions, and to feel too weak to do anything about them (Romans 7, James 4-5, Hebrews 3) (volitional).
- How embarrassing it is to confess your mental confusion and sub-biblical images and beliefs about God, others, yourself, and life (Romans 8, 12, Ephesians 4) (rational).
- How vulnerable you feel when you open up about emptiness and thirsts in your soul (Romans 8:18-27) (relational).
- What it's like to feel like your hurt is abnormal (sustaining).
- What it's like to believe that it's impossible to hope (healing).
- What it's like to experience the horrors of your sin without understanding the wonders of God's grace (reconciling).
- What it's like to sense that you'll never mature (guiding).

These emotional, volitional, rational, and relational matters form the core of spiritual friendship through sustaining, healing, reconciling, and guiding. Therefore, when people share about these issues, they need a trustworthy friend. They need grace relationships offered through grace connecting.

Defining Grace Connecting: Proverbs 27:6; 20:30

What is grace connecting? I don't know about you, but I often learn best by opposites, by poor examples. Let's start with what grace connecting is not.

Grace Connecting Is *Not*

The following would not make the pain, risk, and vulnerability of spiritual friendship bearable.

- *A Warm Feeling*: "Boy, I feel neat when I'm with you." Spiritual friendship is not always a pleasant experience.
- *Sweetness*: Stereotypical Rogerian counseling. Merely reflecting and mirroring whatever your spiritual friend says. Non-directive acceptance of everything, including sin.
- *A Stage in Counseling*: "We'll do connecting today and then drop it."
- *A Technique in Counseling*: "Crying 101." "Three steps to really caring."

What Grace Connecting *Is*: Incarnation

Grace connection is personal involvement with a deep commitment to the maturity of another person. "Faithful are the wounds of a friend," Solomon teaches in Proverbs 27:6 (KJV). "Wounds" are a splitting apart as a doctor does for surgery, an exposure. You enter the ER and say, "Doctor, my chest and the right side of my body are killing me!" You don't want him to simply be sweet. "That must be really hard for you." You want him to be skillful, competent—able to diagnose and treat your ailment. So, too, with spiritual friendship. You want to be able to compassionately diagnose heart issues, pulling open the soul and peering deeply inside.

"Faithful" means to support, to bear, to be trustworthy. Alonzo, facing the diagnosis of inoperable cancer, wants to be able to say about you, "I trust you with my soul." "Faithful" also means to be strong, stable. Alonzo wants to know that his words will not overwhelm you. Touch you deeply, yes. Overwhelm you, no. As his wounds are opened, he wants to know that they will not make you faint, that you will not think less of him.

"Friend" literally means "one who loves you, lover." The Scriptures use the same word in 2 Chronicles 20:7, calling Abraham God's "forever friend." Think of God's grace relationship with Abraham—encounter, intimacy, fellowship, accountability, fidelity, stability—and you will picture grace connecting.

Proverbs 20:30 speaks of deep commitment to maturity. "Blows and wounds cleanse away evil, and beatings purge the inmost being." "Cleanse" means to rub, to polish, to grind and buff repeatedly. Picture waxing your car, cleaning your silver. That's hard work requiring time, effort, and commitment. Alonzo wants to know that you will use all your resources to help him in his time of need. Connection means that you are committed to Alonzo's growth even when it hurts him and you.

What Grace Connecting Requires: Romans 5:6-8

Grace connection requires exposure without rejection, truth with relationship, curiosity rather than analysis, and face-to-face relating instead of back-to-back professionalism. Christ models *exposure without rejection* in Romans 5:6-8. "While we were yet sinners" (exposure). "Christ died for us" (acceptance). Grace connection communicates, "I see you warts and all, and I still love you, accept you, like you, and move toward you."

Paul models *truth with relationship* in Ephesians 4:15. He tells us that the essence of pastoral care involves speaking and living out the truth in love. Consider possible ways to do ministry:

- Truth Minus Relationship: Intimidation/Compliance
- Relationship Minus Truth: Indecision/Confusion
- Truth Plus Relationship: Internalization/Conformity to Christ

Jesus models *curiosity versus analysis*. At the end of John 2, John notes that Jesus knew all people universally and deeply. Yet, he did not allow his full knowledge to blind him to the uniqueness of individuals. Following John 2, Jesus engages two of the most diverse individuals imaginable: the Jewish male moral religious leader and the Samaritan female immoral irreligious follower. Reread both accounts and you'll see his respect for each. His probing curiosity. His unique interactions and involvement.

Analysis views your spiritual friend as "a specimen" to be dissected, analyzed, and studied. Curiosity sees your spiritual friend as an image bearer to be experienced, a mystery to enter, and a soul to know.

We would all do well to tape the following prayer somewhere in our "counseling" office. Or better, somewhere in our soul.

The Spiritual Friend's Prayer:

"Dear Lord,

Help me to approach every relationship
as an audience with an eternally valuable human being."

In John 3-4, Jesus *models face-to-face relating instead of back-to-back professionalism*. He enters their individual worlds. He goes where they are, both geographically and soulfully. He becomes a cartographer of their soul, exploring their personal terrain.

With the woman at the well, in particular, he exposes his humanness. He's authentic, open, vulnerable, and honest. He connects, touches, and moves toward. He's anything but surface, fake, phony, uncaring, and distancing.

Building a Connected Spiritual Friendship: Galatians 6:1

How do you develop connected relationships? Exploring how *not* to develop grace relationships begins to answer that question.

*How **Not** to Build Grace Connections: Job 16:2*

Job accused his "friends" of being "miserable comforters." The word "miserable" means troublesome, vexing, and sorrow-causing. They were the opposite of "comforters"—they were not consoling, sympathetic; they did not feel deeply Job's hurt. They never said or conveyed in any way, "It's normal to hurt."

Instead of grace connecting, they practiced *condemning distancing*. Read the verses below and notice examples of their poor relational abilities flowing out of their poor theology (Job 42:7) and their cold hearts:

1. Superiority: Job 5:8; 8:2; 11:2-12; 12:1-3; 15:7-17

    "We're better than you. You're inferior to us."

2. Judgmentalism: Job 4:4-9; 15:2-6

    "It's *not* normal to hurt! Your suffering is due to your sinning!"

3. Advice without Insight/Discernment: Job 5:8; 8:5-6; 11:13-20; 42:7

    "Here's what I would do if I were you." "Do this and life's complexities will melt away." "I have the secret that will fix your situation." They offered quick, trite advice. They were rescuers, answer men, and cliché makers.

*How **to** Build Grace Connections: Galatians 6:1-3*

Remember that connecting is a commitment to love another person. It is *compassionate discernment in action*. It is not a technique to be mastered, but a way of life to be nurtured by personal communion with Christ. Communion with Christ leads to connection with others.

Galatians 6:1-3, in the context of Paul's discussion of the fruit of the Spirit in Galatians 5, exposes how *to* build grace relationships.

1. Loving Motivation: "You who are spiritual."

    The fruit of the Spirit characterizes effective spiritual friends. The Holy Spirit is the Comforter who comes alongside to help in time of need. In the Spirit's power, you are to be a friend acting in the best interest of your friend. You're a friend acting on behalf of another, interceding for, defending, and advocating. You're an encourager standing up for, standing behind, standing with, and standing back-to-back and alongside your spiritual friend. The "spiritual" person is like a *coach* who has been in the game, lost, struck out, but has some game experience that sure does help.

2. Intimate Friendship/Knowledge: "Brothers."

    Spiritual friendship requires intimate family relationship. "A friend loves at all times, and a brother is born for adversity" (Proverbs 17:17). "A man of many companions may come to ruin, but there is a friend who sticks closer than a brother" (Proverbs 18:24). Picture *best friends* hiking a mountain. One has been there before, so she's the *guide* who has found a few good routes and gladly shares them with her best friend.

Evaluation forms from folks who have been "counseled" by lay encouragers express this sense of intimate friendship. "Even though we had never met before, our times were like two friends walking together." "I could feel your concern; we were on the same level." "You accepted me. You didn't scold me like a Mom, but were honest like a friend."

3. Communicating Equality: "But watch yourself or you also may be tempted." "Restore gently."

Gentleness looks like a tamed stallion, strength under control, firm compassion, mature self-control, and power and love mingled through wisdom. Christ labels himself "gentle" in Matthew 11:29, saying that unlike the Pharisees who were sin-spotters and burden-givers, he was Rest-Giver and Sin-Bearer.

"Watch" (Galatians 6:1) is the Greek word *skopon* from which we gain our word "scope." Put yourself under the microscope before examining your spiritual friend. As a grace connector, maintain a strong mental attention to your own potential temptability. Remain humble in spirit.

4. Demonstrated Commitment: "Restore." "Carry each other's burden."

Paul places "restore" in the present, continual tense. Maintain a patient persistence in mending, furnishing, equipping, and setting the dislocated member of the body back in place. Picture the marathon runner. "I love you for the long haul. I'm in this relationship for a lifetime." Picture the physical therapist who brings her patient back to the place of health by pushing without being pushy.

Paul also describes the spiritual friend as a committed burden-bearer. "Carry each other's burden" (Galatians 6:2). God calls you to pick up and help carry the weight that overwhelms your friend. "Weight" means anything pressing on people physically, emotionally, or spiritually that makes a demand on their resources. When your friend's platelets are low, become a spiritual blood transfusion of grace. When your friend's RPMs are slowing, become their energy conduit.

> **Carrying each other's burdens is not optional, nor the domain of a few.**

Carrying each other's burdens is not optional, nor the domain of a few. "Carry each other's burdens, and in this way you will fulfill the law of Christ" (Galatians 6:2). Pastors can't say, "I just want to preach from the pulpit," not if they intend on fulfilling Christ's law. Lay people can't say, "That's the pastor's job," not if they intend on obeying Christ's law. Professional counselors can't say, "I must maintain a professional distance," not if they intend on living Christ's law.

Verbal Grace Connecting

The preceding principles, in large measure, focus upon your *attitude* as you interact. The following principles focus upon your *actual interactions*—what you say and how you communicate—verbal grace connecting. Consider wrong and right ways to communicate grace connecting.

Wrong Ways to Communicate Grace Connecting: Works Disconnecting—Matthew 23:1-4

Pharisaical counselors communicate works, not grace. That is, they put on heavy burdens, but refuse to lift a finger or say a word to help carry that load. They use:

- *Attacks*: Cutting remarks, sarcasm, subtle distancing (Matthew 23:1-4).
- *Defensive Words*: Any interaction designed to make them look good and to make another person look bad (Matthew 23:5-10).
- *Corrections*: Not accepting feelings, direction without insight, "You shoulds" (Matthew 23:1-4, 11-24).
- *Apologies*: Quick apologies that avoid intimacy and maintain a safe distance (Matthew 23:20-26).
- *Premature Advice*: Talking before understanding the issue (Matthew 23:8-22).

Effective Ways to Communicate Grace Connecting: Nurturing Wisdom—Proverbs 27:6

"Friends mean well even when they confront you. But when enemies put their arm around your shoulder—watch out!" (Proverbs 27:6, author's paraphrase). Those who are meek like Jesus give others rest. They become a place of nurture and safety. Consider Becky from Chapter Five and possible grace interactions through:

- *Reflection*: Putting Her Words into Your Own:

  - Becky says, *"I have **no idea** what to do next."*
  - You respond, *"I'd be **baffled** too."*

- *Clarification*: Reflection with a Stated or Implied Question:

  - Becky tells you, *"I can imagine what will happen if I take this to HR. My boss will say, 'Oh, you misunderstood. I'm sorry.' But that won't end it. There will be an investigation. People will say it was all my fault. Jim will get involved. What a mess."*
  - You respond, *"You kinda' see it as a no-win situation?"*

- *Exploration*: Direct Open-Ended Questions Designed to Elicit More Details:

  - Becky continues, *"Yeah. More than anything, I wish I could count on Jim coming through for me in this."*
  - You continue, *"Tell me a little bit about what 'coming through' might look like."*

- *Intimate Interaction*: Conveying the Courage to Talk Seriously and Offering to Go Further/Deeper:

  - Becky says, *"Well, not making light of it. He never seems to take me seriously."*
  - You say, *"I can tell that Jim's lack of responsiveness really hurts you. And it would me, too. What's it like for you when Jim doesn't come through for you?"*

- *Silence*: Listening, Waiting, Verbal "Clues" Like "Uh-huh," or Nods:

  - Becky shares a bit. As she does, she starts to cry. First a few tears. Then sobs.
  - You lean forward and wait. Silence in the room except Becky's crying.

Maturing Your Spiritual Friendship Competency
Grace Connecting

♦ If you are working through this material individually, then instead of role-playing, use the space after each scenario to write your responses to each situation.

1. Your spiritual friend says to you, "I'm about ready to give up on my marriage."

   a. Role-play *doing it wrong*. Use distancing responses that disconnect you from your friend. Examples: sweetness, "Crying 101," non-involvement, lack of commitment/energy, shallow relationship, rejection, analysis, surface relating, fake, phony, uncaring.

   b. Role-play *connecting with grace*. Use grace connecting responses to move toward your friend. Examples: strength, stability, courage, intimacy, effort, acceptance, relationship, curiosity, risk, respect, vulnerability, authenticity.

2. Your spiritual friend says, "I'm not getting this spiritual friendship stuff that we're supposed to be learning!"

   a. Role-play responses that might communicate superiority, judgmentalism, and advice without discernment.

   b. Role-play responses that might communicate loving motivation, intimate friendship, communicating equality, and demonstrated commitment.

3. Becky has just told you about her boss's unwanted advances. You know of her past trust in him as a good Christian friend. You know something of Becky's fear, her sense of betrayal, her concerns about telling her husband Jim (who also is a good friend to her boss). Role-play connecting with Becky with grace through:

   a. Loving Motivation: Coming alongside as a caring coach.

   b. Intimate Friendship/Knowledge: Walking alongside as a mature best friend.

   c. Communicated Equality: Humility, meekness, and rest-giving.

   d. Demonstrated Commitment: Staying for the long haul like a marathon runner and like a patient physical therapist who longs to see a return to wholeness.

4. It's a week after you first visited Alonzo in the hospital. While talking with him, he expresses doubts and frustrations toward God and exasperation about how relationships are going in his family since "the news."

   a. Role-play wrong ways of communicating grace connecting:

      ♦ Defensive Words:

      ♦ Attacks:

♦   Corrections:

♦   Quick Apologies:

♦   Premature Advice:

b. Role-play effective ways of communicating grace connecting:

♦   Reflection: Putting his words into your own:

♦   Clarification: Reflection with a stated or implied question:

♦   Exploration: Direct open-ended questions designed to elicit more details:

♦   Intimate Interaction: Conveying the courage to talk seriously and offering to go deeper:

Rich Soul Empathizing: Climbing in the Casket—Romans 12:15

Soul empathy is the ability to sense your spiritual friend's level two suffering and communicate that "it's normal to hurt." Picture soul empathy with the phrase "climbing in the casket." Many biblical passages urge rich soul empathizing:

- Rejoice with those who rejoice; mourn with those who mourn (Romans 12:15).
- If one part suffers, every part suffers with it (1 Corinthians 12:26).
- . . . who comforts us in all our troubles, so that we can comfort those in any trouble with the comfort we ourselves have received from God (2 Corinthians 1:4).
- Because he himself suffered when he was tempted, he is able to help those who are being tempted (Hebrews 2:18).
- For we do not have a high priest who is unable to sympathize with our weaknesses, but we have one who has been tempted in every way, just as we are—yet without sin. Let us then approach the throne of grace with confidence, so that we may receive mercy and find grace to help us in our time of need (Hebrews 4:15-16).
- In the same way, the Spirit helps us in our weakness. We do not know what we ought to pray for, but the Spirit himself intercedes for us with groans that words cannot express. And he who searches our hearts knows the mind of the Spirit, because the Spirit intercedes for the saints in accordance with God's will (Romans 8:26-27).

Empathy, like connecting, is *incarnational*. Jesus entered our story (Hebrews 2; John 1). He is not only the Author of our story; he is in our story.

Empathy means to suffer along with another, to suffer in the soul of another. It involves feeling yourself into or participating in the inner world of another person while remaining yourself. Through empathy, you see your spiritual friends' world through their eyes as if their world was your own. You seek to understand their inner and outer world from their perspective.

Using the "narrative motif," you can picture empathy as placing yourself in the role as *a* lead character in Becky and Alonzo's stories. They are *the* lead characters in their stories; you are their friend, their protagonist. You are no longer simply a reader *of* their stories; you participate with them *in* their stories.

How *Not* to Empathize with the Soul: Slamming the Casket Shut—Job's Miserable Counselors, Part II

If empathizing is climbing in the casket, then slamming the casket shut pictures its opposite. A return to Job's miserable "comforters" pictures how *not* to practice soul empathy.

Eliphaz (Job 4-5, 15, and 22) is the master of discouragement and dismay. He provides Job with conditional love while he curses God. Eliphaz teaches that God is good to the good, but bad to the bad. He does not know grace. He does know works: "You can manipulate God into being good to you by being good to him." What a petty God Eliphaz worships. Eliphaz says to Job, "Don't live *coram Deo*. Don't tell God your heart. Be surface." He misinterprets Job's words as venting rage at God rather than soul-sharing with God.

Bildad (Job 8, 18, and 25) has a somewhat right theology with very wrong application. "The issue is your sin!" Seeing only sin, he is wrong in Job's case. For God, the issue was Job's response to him in his suffering. The issue was Job's privileged opportunity to be a universal witness to God's goodness. The issue was not Job's sinfulness. Bildad does not know the man he calls "friend." He labels (and libels) Job "the evil man who knows not God."

Zophar (Job 11 and 20) also presents a works righteousness. He believes that good works can cover shame.

How does Job view their counsel? He longs for the devotion of his friends (6:14), which they aren't. He calls them undependable brothers (6:15), which they are. They can't handle Job's doubts, treating the words of a despairing man as wind (6:26). He feels they say, "Forget it! Smile!" However, "Don't worry; be happy," does not cut it for Job. His dread remains. "If I say, 'I will forget my complaint, I will change my expression, and smile,' I still dread all my sufferings, for I know you will not hold me innocent" (Job 9:27-28). He experiences their total lack of empathy. "Men at ease have contempt for misfortunate" (Job 12:5).

Miserable comforters (Job 16:2) they are. Rather than communicating that "it's normal to hurt," they increase Job's hurt. Having no compassionate discernment, they claim that his wounds are self-inflicted. "How we will hound him, since the root of the trouble lies in him" (Job 19:28). They crush Job's spirit through their long-winded speeches, argumentative nature, lack of empathy and encouragement, failure to bring relief/comfort, and their closed-minded, arrogant, superior, hostile attitudes based upon wrong motives and a condemning spirit (Job 17:1-5).

Of them, Job concludes, "These men turn night into day; in the face of darkness they say, 'Light is near'" (Job 17:12). They are like the counselor who says, "Don't talk about your problems, don't think about your suffering, and don't remember your past hurts. Forget those things which are behind!" They have no night vision, no 20/20 spiritual vision, and no long-distance vision; so they have to call the darkness light. Job, however, has long-distance vision. His heart yearns for God and he knows that he will see God (Job 19:25-27).

Job feels no rapport with them. "They torment me, crush me with words. I sense their reproach as they shame me. They exalt themselves. I feel so alone when I am with them. So alienated and forgotten. Here's how my 'spiritual friends' make me feel: alienated, estranged, forgotten, offensive, loathsome. All my intimate friends detest me; they have turned against me, having no pity on me" (author's paraphrase of Job 19).

They are unwise. They offer nonsense answers because they're not paying attention to life, not learning life's lessons. "You have not wisely paid attention to how things work in the real world. Your academic knowledge, your theologizing, is out to lunch. How can you console/comfort me with your vain nonsense, since your answers are falsehood? You are wrong about life, about me, and about God!" (author's paraphrase of Job 21).

They are "sin-spotters." They know confrontation only. Thus, they become co-conspirators with Satan the accuser who condemns men and curses God.

> **Our greatest failure in counseling arises
> when we speak wrongly of God while we speak to one another.**

What was God's view of their counsel? After speaking to Job, Yahweh says to Eliphaz. "I am angry with you and your two friends because you have not spoken of me what is right as my servant Job has" (Job 42:7). They failed to speak of God's generous goodness and grace. Their God was a tit-for-tat God who could be easily manipulated by and impressed with works. Our greatest failure in counseling arises when we speak wrongly of God while we speak to one another.

How *to* Empathize with the Soul: Climbing in the Casket—Hebrews 4:15-16

Soul empathy involves your capacity for "as if" relating. Ambrose wrote, "Show compassion for those who suffer. Suffer with those who are in trouble *as if* being in trouble with them" (Thomas Oden, *Classical Pastoral Care*, Vol. 3, p. 8, emphasis added).

Soul empathy requires *compassionate imagination*. You need to imagine what it is like for your friends to experience their life stories. To understand others with intimate knowledge, you must read into their experiences asking, "What is it like to experience and perceive the world through their stories?"

Hebrews 2:14-18 and 4:15-16 teach that empathy is not less than, but more than, intellectual. It is also experiential. Biblical, Christ-like empathy shares the experiences of another, connecting through common inner experiences. Such soul sharing occurs by way of incarnation—entering another's world and worldview.

As a spiritual friend, the more human you are, the more real, the more fully alive and passionate, the more you will tune into others. Then you'll experience a sympathetic resonance no matter the melody, dirge, minor or major key, or discordant note.

Empathy, however, does not come from sharing the same experience, situation, or suffering. No two people experience a situation identically, nor do they share the identical experience. *Empathy comes from sharing the same dependency upon God.* The God of all comfort, comforts you in your *specific* trouble so that you can comfort those in *any* trouble with the *infinite* comfort you receive from the God of *all* comfort. I derive a core spiritual friendship principle from these concepts: You will be empathetic with others to the degree that you are facing your struggles face-to-face with God.

> **You will be empathetic with others to the degree that you are facing your struggles face-to-face with God.**

When your soul is attuned to others, then you "pick up their radio waves, the vibes of their inner reactions." Having accomplished this, you need to go the distance. You need to communicate to your spiritual friends in a way that helps them to "have empathy with your empathy." They need to feel that you feel with them. Otherwise, their sorrow is not shared, it is simply "understood." When both your "soul radios" are tuned to the same frequency, then you can share your soul friends' experiences. You share their sorrows by climbing in the casket with them, and they know you are there.

While death is separation; shared sorrow is connection. It is the stitch connecting the wound. It is the healing balm. However, shared sorrow must never be a healing replacement. It must not replace grief. Shared sorrow does not purpose to eliminate sorrow, to rescue, or to cheer up. Shared sorrow purposes to help another to face and embrace sorrow.

Effective soul empathy includes several "levels."

1. Level One Empathy: "How would that affect an image bearer?" Here you understand your spiritual friend through God's eyes. A foundational level of empathy, it builds upon a *universal* understanding of people (a biblical Creation, Fall, and Redemption understanding of Romancers, Dreamers, Creators, Singers, and Actors).

2. Level Two Empathy: "How would that affect an image bearer like me?" Here you understand your spiritual friend through your eyes. A filtering level, you use your life as a filter through which you relate God's truth to your friend's life.

3. Level Three Empathy: "How would that affect an image bearer like him/her?" Here you understand your spiritual friend through his or her eyes. You move from *universal* to *unique* empathy. In this final, deepest level of soul empathy you need to:

   a. Adopt Your Spiritual Friend's Viewpoint: Replace your internal frame of reference with his. Neither condone nor condemn, agree or disagree, at this point. Simply seek to see what it is like to be him—to be his character through his mindset and frame of reference.

   b. Express Your Spiritual Friend's Viewpoint: Express in your own words what you sense that she has said, felt, and thought about the situation. Then seek clarification.

   c. Encourage Your Spiritual Friend to Accept His/Her Viewpoint: Nudge him to acknowledge his own storied experience. Help him to verbalize how he sees things and to accept his own perspective.

   d. Help Your Spiritual Friend to Evaluate His/Her Viewpoint: She needs to begin to assess how near or far her viewpoint is from reality.

You can also gain soul empathy by asking your spiritual friends to examine their own souls, especially their thirsts. Box 6:1 provides the sample form—*Understanding My Soul Thirsts*—that you can use to help your spiritual friends to better understand their own souls. It also helps you to better understand the depths of their souls. You can assign it as homework or you can work through the sheet together when you meet.

Where We've Been and Where We're Headed

The relational competencies of *Grace Connecting* and *Rich Soul Empathizing* provide the first two sustaining "skills" necessary to help your spiritual friend's faith survive the onslaught of levels one and two suffering. Through them, you build a trusting, mutual, caring relationship.

Having done so, what next? In particular, how do you use the Scriptures to skillfully discuss and explore applications specific to your spiritual friend? Chapter Seven addresses that question through the other three sustaining relational competencies:

   ♦ *A*   Accurate/Active Spiritual Listening: John 2:23-4:43
   ♦ *C*   Caring Spiritual Conversations: Ephesians 4:29
   ♦ *E*   Empathetic Scriptural Explorations: Isaiah 61:1-3

Box 6:1
Understanding My Soul Thirsts

1. Describe some of the most fulfilling moments of your life.

2. I experience great joy when:

3. Some of my biggest fears are:

4. Some of the things that I avoid are:

5. Some of my most commonly recurring desires are:

6. Some of my most commonly recurring disappointments are:

7. Reread your answers. Ponder. Reflect. What themes or patterns do you sense developing?

Maturing Your Spiritual Friendship Competency
Rich Soul Empathizing

♦ If you are working through this material individually, then instead of role-playing, use the space after each scenario to write your responses to each situation.

1. Role-play with a partner how *not* to empathize with a soul. Each of you "make up" a life situation. Take turns sharing and take turns being the "miserable comforter." As your partner shares, respond like Job's counselors: conditional love, discouraging, surface interaction, labeling and libeling, being a sin-spotter, expressing contempt, crushing with words, being arrogant, long-winded, close-minded, reproaching, and shaming.

   a. When you're done, even though this was a "made up" role-play, share how you felt when you were treated (mistreated) like this.

   b. When you're done, share what you learned about what *not* to do.

2. Role-play with a partner how *to* empathize with a soul. Each of you share a real life event/situation from the past week or month. Interact with the goal of trying to understand how your partner/spiritual friend experienced this event—what happened, how he/she felt, what he/she did, what he/she thought, how his/her longings were impacted.

   a. When you're done, your partner/spiritual friend will share with you his/her honest evaluation of your level of empathy.

   b. When you're done, your partner/spiritual friend will share with you his/her honest evaluation of where and how you connected and empathized deeply at a soul level.

   c. When you're done, your partner/spiritual friend will share with you his/her honest evaluation of how you could better communicate soul empathy.

3. Complete Box 6:1 (*Understanding My Soul Thirsts*) as a way to tap into your own thirsts. After completing questions 1-6, be sure to complete question 7 about pondering themes and patterns.

Chapter Seven

Sustaining Treatment and Intervention
GRACE Relational Competencies, Part II

"Clinical pastoral care has, as its introduction, the task of listening to a story of human conflict and need. To the extent that our listening uncovers a situation which borders the abyss or lies broken within it, we are nearer to the place where the Cross of Christ is the only adequate interpretive concept" (Frank Lake, *Clinical Theology*, pp. 18-19).

Biblical Caring

In the process of equipping hundreds of lay spiritual friends, pastors, and professional Christian counselors, I've detected a consistent theme. People want to know how to move from caring connection to competent intervention. "I'm not too bad at caring, if caring means connecting and empathizing with my spiritual friend. I can feel people's pain. However, I feel lost to know what to do next. I can nod. I can listen. Yet even with listening, what do I listen for and why? Once I'm done listening, then what? What do I say? How do I share? Where do the Scriptures enter? How do I use them artfully? There must be something more to sustaining than a heart-felt hug and a promise to pray."

Caring people want to know how to care biblically. They want guidance that addresses the question raised in Chapters Six and Seven: "How can my spiritual friend and I engage in a grace relationship that sustains his or her faith?" The two relational competencies probed in Chapter Six equip spiritual friends to more effectively communicate the compassion they feel. The three relational competencies examined in this chapter equip spiritual friends to help others to live *coram Deo*—to find God in the midst of their suffering.

The acronym *GRACE* summarizes these five sustaining relational competencies:

- ♦ *G* Grace Connecting: Proverbs 27:6
- ♦ *R* Rich Soul Empathizing: Romans 12:15
- ♦ *A* Accurate/Active Spiritual Listening: John 2:23-4:43
- ♦ *C* Caring Spiritual Conversations: Ephesians 4:29
- ♦ *E* Empathetic Scriptural Explorations: Isaiah 61:1-3

Exploring Your Spiritual Journey

1. Think about a current area of suffering/loss. Explore your loss.

    a. What is this loss like for you? What are you feeling right now?

    b. What do you wish were happening instead of what you're experiencing?

    c. Have you ever faced a loss like this before? Has your hurt ever been this deep before?

    d. What has been robbed from your life due to this? What is missing? What are you grieving over the most? What hurts the most in this situation?

    e. What do you fear the most in this situation? What if that happened? What's the worst-case scenario? What if that happened?

2. While still thinking about this current area of suffering/loss, face God in your loss.

    a. What are you doing with God in your suffering?

    b. Where is God in all this?

    c. What might God be up to in all of this?

    d. Have you been able to share your heart with God? What have you said?

    e. What are you sensing from God?

Accurate/Active Spiritual Listening: Faith-Drenched Alertness—John 2:23-4:43

Having a model of suffering is vital, unless the model misses the person. Sustaining starts with understanding *universal* suffering—exegeting the Scripture to develop a biblical sufferology (theological listening). It continues with understanding *unique* individual suffering—exegeting the soul by listening with a poet's ear to the sufferer's heart (spiritual listening). Spiritual listening knows the theological nuances of universal suffering *and* the personal nuances of individual suffering because grievers do not all grieve the same.

Think of spiritual listening as *reflective paying attention*. It is passionate love that says, "I am not the center of my attention. God is. You are. I am third." As Deitrich Bonhoeffer teaches, "The first service we owe to others in fellowship is to listen to them. If we fail to listen, there are spiritual consequences. He who can no longer listen to his brother, will soon be no longer listening to God either."

**He who can no longer listen to his brother,
will soon be no longer listening to God either.**

Jesus listened spiritually to Nicodemus and the Samaritan woman. John places a "narrative marker" just before these two encounters. "He did not need man's testimony about man, for he knew what was in a man" (John 2:25). Jesus knew the scriptural, universal nature of human nature. He also tuned into the unique nature of individuals. As described in Chapter Six, Jesus could not have encountered two more unique individuals. His approach to them was idiosyncratic—uniquely fitting for each. Jesus listened to their souls and knew their individual stories. To follow his model, spiritual friends:

- Listen to Biblical Principles of Spiritual Listening: God's Word about Human Words
- Listen with Biblical Attentiveness: Theologically-Informed Listening
- Listen with Relational Competence: *LISTEN*

Listening to Biblical Principles of Spiritual Listening: God's Word about Human Words

Listening carefully to people's words is biblical, not secular. God's Word teaches that:

- Words Are Powerful
- Words Are Meaningful
- Words Convey Soul Messages
- Words Are Worthy of Soulful Attentiveness
- Words Reflect One of Two Life Interpretations

Words Are Powerful: Proverbs 18:21

"The tongue has the power of life and death" (Proverbs 18:21). That's power. The tongue, says James, is a small body part with power far beyond its size (James 3:1-5a). "Consider what a great forest is set on fire by a small spark. The tongue also is a fire, a world of evil among the parts of the body. It corrupts the whole person, sets the whole course of his life on fire" (James 3:5b-6). That's power. Listen carefully to the powerful, life and death words of your spiritual friends.

Words Are Meaningful: Proverbs 18:4; 20:5

"The words of a man's mouth are deep waters" (Proverbs 18:4). "The purposes of a man's heart are deep waters, but a man of understanding draws them out" (Proverbs 20:5). Words carry the soul's longings, beliefs, purposes, and feelings. Through careful, caring listening, you perceive the depth of the soul. Through active, accurate listening, you draw out the meaning of the soul—the hidden desires, convictions, goals, and emotions.

Words Convey Soul Messages: Psalm 39:1-3; Matthew 12:33-37

"Out of the overflow of the heart, the mouth speaks" (Matthew 12:34). Spoken words flow out of the depths of the heart revealing the content of the heart. The good heart bears nourishing fruit conveyed by wholesome words, while the evil heart bears poisonous fruit conveyed by unwholesome words. If you want to know your spiritual friends, then listen skillfully to their words.

Words Are Worthy of Soulful Attentiveness: Proverbs 18:13; James 1:19

"He who answers before listening—that is his folly, that is his shame" (Proverbs 18:13). "My dear brothers, take note of this: Everyone should be quick to listen, slow to speak, and slow to become angry" (James 1:19). The caring soul carefully listens to words spoken from the soul.

Words Reflect One of Two Life Interpretations: Job 42:7

"After the LORD had said these things to Job, he said to Eliphaz the Temanite, 'I am angry with you and your two friends, because you have not spoken of me what is right, as my servant Job has'" (Job 42:7). Job and his three friends witnessed one situation, but derived two vastly different interpretations. The set of information involved Job's life experience. The first interpretation consisted of the works, condemnation, cursing, and shame narrative of life inspired by Satan. The second consisted of the grace, faith, openness, and acceptance narrative inspired by God. According to God, Job got him right; Job's friends got God all wrong.

Whenever you listen, you listen for three sets of stories. Listen for your spiritual friends' life stories: listen attentively to what they're saying about what they're experiencing. Then listen to two possible interpretations of their stories. Listen attentively for signs of Satan's narrative creeping in. Additionally, listen attentively to God's narrative gaining dominance. These competing interpretive frameworks are at work in every life story.

Listening with Biblical Attentiveness: Theologically-Informed Listening

Everyone who knows anything about "counseling" knows the value of "listening." The more important question is, "What do you listen to?" Theory-guided, theologically-informed listening, listens to *soul* messages and *storied* messages.

Listen to Soul Messages

Since sustaining ministers to the suffering soul in the fallen world, you listen to soul messages spoken by suffering image bearers. You want to listen for things that are wrong, amiss, missing. God created your spiritual friends for Paradise, but they're living in a desert. They're created for joyful relationships and meaningful purposes and designed to live with passion, imagination, courage, and depth. When these are replaced with broken relationships and frustrated purposes, then you've entered the desert of suffering. When you hear distance, denial, disengagement, and deadness, then you know that you're hearing the hurting soul of the suffering image bearer. Since your spiritual friends are relational, rational, volitional, and emotional beings, you fine-tune your listening for soul messages in each of these *imago Dei* areas.

1. Listening to Relational Beings: Listen to the Romancer's Narrative—Sacrifice or Separation?

As a relational being, God designed Becky to love passionately. Passion relates not just to her intense feelings, but to her *selfless sacrifices*. When Becky is failing to give generously and sacrificially in relationships, then something is out of whack in her story.

Listen for separating narratives. How is Satan duping Becky? Where is she backing away from life, refusing to long, and quenching her thirsts apart from Christ? Listen also to how God's grace is enlivening Becky even in the midst of her soul's suffering. Where do you see signs of biblical groaning, awakened longings, and thirsts directed toward Jesus?

2. Listening to Rational Beings: Listen to the Dreamer's Narrative—Spiritual Eyes or Eyeballs Only?

As a rational being, God designed Alonzo to dream imaginatively. Imagination is not simply thinking in 3-D or thinking creatively, though it does include these capacities. Imagination is Alonzo's capacity to think about his own thoughts and to make sense of his world.

When Alonzo is failing to interpret his story through *grace eyes*, then something is amiss. Therefore, listen for works narratives where he's being duped by Satan to think small. Where is Alonzo handling life on his own, where is he thinking foolishly, and where are his mindsets rooted in the ruts of the flesh? Also listen for grace narratives where Christ is freeing Alonzo to think as big as God, for he is able to do abundantly above all that Alonzo could ever think, dream, or imagine. How is Alonzo perceiving his need for God, where are signs of wise interpretations, and where are his mindsets being led by the Spirit?

3. Listening to Volitional Beings: Listen to the Creator's Narrative—Courageous Risk or Compulsive Protection?

As a volitional being, God designed Becky to choose courageously, which is more than being "Wonder Woman." Courage includes her freedom to be responsible and her awareness of her ability to choose how to live an epic life in Christ.

When Becky is failing to see herself as an *active agent*, when she sees life controlling her, then something is wrong. So, listen for controlling narratives where Becky is being duped by Satan to surrender. Where do you hear Becky acting "choiceless," purposeless, and hopeless? What aimless purposes/pathways does she appear to be following? Listen also for freeing narratives where Becky is being led by the Spirit to persevere. Where do you hear Becky acting responsibly, purposefully, and hopefully? What focused and selfless purposes is she pursuing?

4. Listening to Emotional Beings: Listen to the Singer's Narrative—Poet or Stoic?

As an emotional being, God designed Alonzo to experience life deeply. Poetic living is not simply his ability to cry or sob, though it might include that, as well as his ability to laugh and jump for joy. Emotional depth is Alonzo's awareness, acknowledgement, and acceptance of his emotional state used to advance his relationships to God, others, and self. Alonzo can cry to keep you far from him by making you see him as too fragile to approach. This is not depth. On the other hand, he can cry as an offer for you to draw near to him. This is depth. It is an *aliveness that invites.*

When Alonzo is failing to feel alive, when he's in denial, when he's bland, then something is missing. So, listen for deadened, despairing emotions used by Satan to dupe Alonzo into drying up. When he comes alive, then he faces life fully, in living color. So, listen also for laments motivated by a groaning desire for deeper relationships. Listen for the mood state that predominates in Alonzo.

Listen to Storied Messages

While listening to soul messages, keep your ears tuned to "storied" messages. Remember that life is a story, a narrative. Job's miserable comforters told one story of his suffering, Job another. All the while, behind the curtain, Satan and God each had their stories to tell.

Becky's soul story requires soul listening. Start by *joining her journey* as a participant—incarnational listening. Connect, feel, and empathize.

As you journey, *listen for Becky's protagonist—God.* Where do you hear his grace, acceptance, forgiveness, faith, love, goodness, and new covenant story as she tells her story? Perhaps you hear it as you sense that Becky, though confused and much afraid, is still clinging.

She clings while in conflict. Therefore, *listen for Becky's antagonist.* Certainly her boss fits that bill. Perhaps her husband Jim does, too. However, her ultimate antagonist is none other than Satan. Do you hear his works, condemnation, rejection, old covenant, law, hate, fear, run and hide narrative when Becky talks about dreading the thought of approaching either HR or Jim?

Since Becky's husband and boss are lead actors in her story, *listen for the identity of these significant characters.* How does Becky see them, describe them, and relate to them?

Perhaps even more importantly, how does Becky see herself? *Listen for her self-identity.* Hear her suffering identities when you sense her desire to give up and when she begins to present herself as a helpless, fragile little child, rather than a wronged and harmed woman who is Father's adult daughter.

Then, too, *listen for your identity in Becky's story.* After all, you are a vital player now. How does Becky relate to you—as a rescuer, peer, friend, hero, distant helper, or perhaps another potential betrayer?

As with any good story, you need to *listen for the setting.* What are the details of her story? What is her background, her history? When is Becky worse, better?

Further, *listen for core story themes and threads.* Perhaps you hear in Becky's story the shame moral of: "Good girls are safe girls, so you must be a bad girl." Or, the grace theme of: "God is good even when life is bad—God can be trusted even while his people betray."

In *sustaining, listen for life's losses and crosses.* What death/separation events do you hear? What are the external losses (level one suffering) and what are the internal losses (level two suffering)?

Listening with Relational Competence: *LISTEN*

Use the following simple acrostic to remind yourself of basic components of competent spiritual listening.

- ♦ *L*   Loving Motivation: Proverbs 21:13
- ♦ *I*   Intimate Concern: Galatians 6:1-3; Colossians 4:6; James 3:17-18
- ♦ *S*   Slow to Speak: Proverbs 18:13; James 1:19
- ♦ *T*   Timing: Proverbs 15:23; 25:11
- ♦ *E*   Encouraging: Hebrews 3:7-19; 10:24-25
- ♦ *N*   Need-Focused Hearing: Ephesians 4:29

L   Loving Motivation: Proverbs 21:13

"If a man shuts his ears to the cry of the poor, he too will cry and not be answered" (Proverbs 21:13). Relationally competent spiritual friends are motivated, like God, to listen for, hear, care about, empathize with, and respond to the hurts of the wounded. Neither secular theory nor human curiosity drives careful listening. Care does. Concern does. Compassion does.

I   Intimate Concern: Galatians 6:1-3; Colossians 4:6; James 3:17-18

Paul (Galatians 6:1-3; Colossians 4:6) emphasizes the humble, spiritual, gentle, and gracious concern that ought to accompany spiritual listening. James (James 3:17-18), in a context sandwiched between the use of the tongue and the cause of quarrels, explains that true wisdom for living flows from a heart that loves people and peace, a heart that is considerate and submissive, impartial and sincere.

S   Slow to Speak: Proverbs 18:13; James 1:19

James is quite emphatic. "My dear brothers, take note of this: Everyone should be quick to listen, slow to speak, and slow to become angry" (James 1:19). Solomon explains why. "He who answers before listening—that is his folly and his shame" (Proverbs 18:13). Relationally competent spiritual friends hear their friend's story before they tell God's story to their friend.

T   Timing: Proverbs 15:23; 25:11

"A man finds joy in giving an apt reply—and how good is a timely word!" (Proverbs 15:23). "A word aptly spoken is like apples of gold in settings of silver" (Proverbs 25:11). "Apt" means fitting, timely, given in due season—words said at the right time, in the right way, for the right reason because of right listening.

E   Exploring: Hebrews 3:7-19; 10:24-25

Both Hebrews 3 and 10 speak of encouraging and clearly imply the necessity of exploratory listening before profitable encouraging. Before encouraging, spiritual friends tune into, see, listen, and hear what is going on in the heart of their spiritual friend.

N   Need-Focused Hearing: Ephesians 4:29

To benefit those who listen, spiritual friends listen for specific needs. "Do not let any unwholesome talk come out of your mouths, but only what is helpful for building others up according to their needs, that it may benefit those who listen" (Ephesians 4:29). Spiritual friends ask, as they listen, "What is it that my spiritual friend most needs? What are his hurts and wounds? What are her fears and scars? What wholesome words relate to her specific situation? Specifically, given his situation, what words will benefit him?"

Maturing Your Spiritual Friendship Competency
Accurate/Active Spiritual Listening

1. You're in the parking lot after church. You casually ask a friend, "How's work?" Your friend responds, "I'm makin' it."

   a. What are some possible meanings of your friend's response?

   b. How would you be able to discern the more accurate meaning?

   c. What type of reply might you make in order to draw out any possible additional meaning?

2. With a partner, role-play the "parking lot scenario." The counselor/spiritual friend should try to listen according to theory, by listening for relational, rational, volitional, and emotional messages. When you are finished listening, share the soul messages that you heard in each area. If you are working through this material alone, then write possible relational, rational, volitional, and emotional messages that your friend might share.

3. Respond to the following two sub-questions using the *LISTEN* acrostic:

   a. Rate yourself on each of the six aspects of listening.

   b. Describe ways that you could improve your spiritual listening skills, especially in those areas where you rated yourself lower.

Caring Spiritual Conversations: Sustaining Theological Trialogues—Ephesians 4:29

People in pain need whispers, not shouts. Don't holler curses; whisper grace because pain requires love and lovers whisper.

In caring spiritual conversations, you use biblical wisdom principles to engage your spiritual friends in discussions that help them to think through their external and internal situation. The core relational competency necessary for this soul care art is the ability to trialogue.

Earlier I contrasted monologues (you speak to me), dialogues (we speak to each other), and trialogues (together we listen to God). In trialogues, you want to make the presence of God the central dynamic in your conversation. You interact in Jesus' name helping people to face personal issues on a personal level. Your personal relationship with them helps them to deepen their personal relationship with Christ. Spiritual conversations invite your spiritual friends into an exchange so they can experience the passion of having been changed. They invite your spiritual friends into a vivid, robust experience of grace narratives through grace relationships.

Consider just a sampling of biblical passages that depict trialogues:

- "For where two or three come together in my name, there am I with them" (Matthew 18:20).
- "See to it, brothers, that none of you has a sinful, unbelieving heart that turns away from the living God. But encourage one another daily, as long as it is called 'Today,' so that none of you may be hardened by sin's deceitfulness" (Hebrews 3:12-13).
- "Let us draw near to God with a sincere heart in full assurance of faith . . . And let us consider how we may spur one another on toward love and good deeds. Let us not give up meeting together, as some are in the habit of doing, but let us encourage one another—and all the more as you see the Day approaching" (Hebrews 10:22, 24-25).

The Nature of Spiritual Conversations

The tongue has the capacity to offer life-giving resources that nourish the soul, or to be a power for life-draining energies that poison the soul. "Words satisfy the mind as much as fruit does the stomach; good talk is as gratifying as a good harvest. Words kill, words give life; they're either poison or fruit— you choose" (Eugene Peterson, *The Message*, p. 1130, Proverbs 18:20-21). Spiritual conversation is simply good talk about our good God in the midst of our bad life.

"Do not let any unwholesome talk come out of your mouths, but only what is helpful for building others up according to their needs, that it may benefit those who listen" (Ephesians 4:29). Spiritual conversations are grace conversations. Law conversations crush people and destroy relationships (compare Matthew 23). Grace conversations edify people and build relationships.

"Unwholesome" words are corrupt and rotten like decaying fruit. They're putrid, defiling, and injuring words. They're toxic speech—words that poison others, making their spirit sick. Paul's emphasis is clear in the original language: "All words of rottenness, do not let come out of your mouth." Spiritual friends restrain themselves, refusing to speak until they understand what words will be:

- *Helpful*: Good because they flow from moral character and promote beautiful living.
- *Strengthening/Building Up Others*: Edifying words that bring improvement and promote maturity.
- *According to Their Need*: Carefully chosen words that specifically fill up a need, meet a lack, minister to a want, or express care in a difficulty, where it is most necessary.

♦ *Beneficial/Ministering Grace*: Attractive speech that helps others to receive God's love poem and become God's love poetry. They are gift words—generously given, freely granted words that accept, that free, that empower, and that give hope.

To the Colossians, Paul writes, "Let your conversation be always full of grace, seasoned with salt, so that you may know how to answer everyone" (Colossians 4:6). Grace words are words of connection, giving, affirming, accepting, freeing, and justifying. They are seasoned with salt—they preserve relationships with God, others, and self.

James, after describing the fiery and poisonous nature of words (James 3:1-8), notes that, "with the tongue we praise our Lord and Father, and with it we curse (*katarometha*) men, who have been made in God's likeness" (James 3:9). In James 3:10-16, James teaches that Satan is the ultimate source of cursing words (*katarometha*)—harmful, hurtful, damaging words that wish a judgment upon someone. The most harmful words involve cursing conversations, law relationships, and condemning speech filled with wrath and scorn. Grace words, by contrast, are motivated by purity, pursue peace, and produce the fruit of righteousness (James 3:17-18).

The Careful Use of Spiritual Conversations

Throughout *Spiritual Friends*, you will read literally thousands of sample spiritual conversations. Because of the nature of the printed word, you will not be able to hear the inflection and tone of these sentences. You also will not be able to fully sense the spontaneity and individuality necessary in the skillful use of spiritual conversations. In other words, if you simply repeat to your spiritual friends these samples, then you will come across wooden, generic, academic, and out of touch. The samples are simply meant to stir your imagination, not to limit your creative, individual, personal interaction with your spiritual friends.

Additionally, be careful in the use of questions. I put many of the dialogues/trialogues in question form because they need to be so generic. However, think of spiritual conversations more as a quest to invite Jesus in, not as questions that push Jesus out and people away.

It is wise to question the use of questions, especially the poor use of questions. A few principles might help.

♦ As a spiritual friend, you're not an interrogator. You're not like Detective Joe Friday saying, "Just the facts, Ma'am. Just the facts." Spiritual friendship is a conversation, not a cross-examination.

♦ Be aware that questions can cause your spiritual friend to feel like an object to be diagnosed or a lab specimen to be dissected.

♦ Never use questions as an excuse to avoid intimacy.

♦ Don't use questions as filler because you're unsure what to say. Instead, simply say, "I'm not sure where to go from here."

When you do use questions, consider some suggestions for using them effectively:

♦ Always ask yourself, "Will this question further or inhibit the flow of our relationship, of our conversation?"

♦ Normally ask open-ended questions—ones that can't be answered with a "Yes" or "No."

♦ Use indirect questions that imply a desire for further exploration, without having a question mark at the end of your sentence. "That must have been hard when your wife left the room." "I bet a million thoughts were going through your mind when your boss said that."

The Practice of Spiritual Conversations

Your desire in spiritual conversations is to help your spiritual friends to live *coram Deo*. Your quest is to help your friends find God in the midst of their suffering. You want to send them on a God-quest where they bring God back into the center of their life journeys. Spiritual conversations in *sustaining* are a quest to encourage spiritual friends to invite God into their casket.

Spiritual Conversations and a Quest to Face God

I'm often asked, "Can you employ spiritual conversations with "unspiritual people," with unbelievers, with pre-Christians?" Yes. The following sample spiritual conversations are especially appropriate when working with an unsaved seeker because they probe and plant seeds. (For additional spiritual conversations with unsaved people, see the samples under *Trialogues and a Quest to Not Lose Faith/A Quest to Sustain Faith*, p. 140.)

- *I'm interested in how your spiritual values relate to this issue.*
- *I'm interested in how you are relating your spiritual values to this issue.*
- *Has your loss made any difference in your spiritual life?*
- *How are these problems influencing your view of God?*
- *How are these issues influencing your relationship to God?*
- *Has the issue you want to resolve made any difference in your feelings about God?*
- *What source of strength have you turned to in your distress?*

Spiritual Conversations and a Quest to Face What Was Lost: "Life is Bad!"

Sufferology teaches that before your spiritual friends can see how truly good God is, they have to first be brutally honest about how horribly bad life is. Therefore, you'll want to engage your spiritual friends in conversations that help them to face what was lost. You might call these "casket questions and integrity conversations." They help your spiritual friends to muster the integrity to explore honestly their disappointments and damages from a triune relational perspective—how it affects their relationships to God, others, and themselves.

- *I'm so sorry this has happened to you.*
- *I'm so sorry you're going through this.*
- *I can see and feel your grief and pain.*
- *What is this loss like for you?*
- *What are you feeling right now?*
- *What do you wish were happening instead of what you're going through?*
- *Have you ever faced a loss like this before?*
- *Has your hurt ever been this deep before?*
- *What has been robbed from your life due to this? What is missing?*
- *What are you grieving over the most? What hurts the most in this situation?*
- *What do you fear the most in this situation?*
  - *What if that happened?*
- *What's the worst-case scenario?*
  - *What if that happened?*

Spiritual Conversations and a Quest to Face God in Loss

First, trialogue about how bad life is. Next, trialogue about bringing God into the center of the loss.

- *What are you doing with God in your suffering?*
- *Where is God in all this?*
- *What might God be up to in all of this?*
- *Have you been able to share your heart with God?*
  - *What have you said?*
- *What are you sensing from God?*

Spiritual Conversations and a Quest to Wrestle with God

Biblical characters like Jacob, Job, David, and Paul, among many others, not only knew that life was bad. They not only knew that God was good. They also wrestled with the tension between a good God who allows evil and suffering. Spiritual friends encourage their friends to do the same.

- *What do you think the Bible says about feeling anger or disappointment toward God?*
- *What do you think about expressing your anger, disappointment, or complaint toward God?*
- *What Scriptures could we look at that illustrate how God's people have talked to God when they felt that he was not hearing their cry?*
- *If you were to write a Psalm 13 or a Psalm 88 to God (Psalms of Lament and Complaint), how would it sound? What would you write?*
- *How would you compare your response to your suffering to Jacob's response to God in his suffering?*
  - *To Job's response?*
  - *To David's response?*
  - *To Paul's response?*
- *If you painted a picture of how you sense God right now, what would you paint?*
- *In what ways, if any, do you sense that God has not heard the cry of your soul?*
- *What is it like for you when you sense that God has not heard the cry of your soul?*
- *What is it like for you when God seems deaf to your cry?*
- *When your soul shouts, "Where is God now? Where are his great and precious promises when I need them?" and the Scriptures teach that God is everywhere present and always faithful, which do you believe?*
  - *How do you go about choosing which to believe?*
- *If you weren't a believer, what do you think you would want, think, do, feel, and say?*
- *If you did not have the Scriptures to turn to, how would your perspective on this be different?*

Spiritual Conversations and a Quest to Cling to God

Wrestling with God is biblical (remember candor and complaint). As your spiritual friends wrestle, they must cling.

- *What is your suffering teaching you about God's power and your weakness?*
- *How could your agony cause you to cry out to God for help, love, strength, joy, peace, or deliverance?*

- *If you knew that God would say, "Yes," to your prayer about your situation, what would you be praying?*
- *If God were to immediately answer, "Yes," how would you respond?*
  - *How would things be different for you?*
  - *What would you do differently?*
- *What Scriptures could you turn to in order to understand God's perspective on your suffering?*
- *What Scriptures have you turned to in order to understand God's perspective on your suffering?*
- *What passages have you found helpful in gaining a new perspective on your suffering?*
  - *To find comfort as you go through your suffering?*
- *When else have you experienced suffering similar to this?*
  - *How did you respond?*
  - *What did you learn about God in that situation?*
  - *What would you repeat and what would you change about your response to that situation?*

Spiritual Conversations and a Quest to Not Lose Faith/A Quest to Sustain Faith

Historically, one of the main roles of sustaining has been to help believers to draw a line in the sand of retreat. To say, "My faith has been shaken, doubts have arisen, but I will not give up. I will not surrender to despair. My hope will remain. My faith is sustained."

The following trialogues, in addition to helping believers to explore and sustain their faith relationship with God, can be helpful when relating to the unsaved.

- *Has your loss made any difference in your feelings about God?*
- *It feels like your faith is slipping away from you and that's scary for you.*
- *You feel like your faith is fading. That frightens you, and you'd like to find your way to genuine faith.*
- *Tell me your perspective on the age-old question, "Why do bad things happen to good people?"*
- *What do you think? Is God good even when life is bad?*
- *When did you feel your faith beginning to slip?*
  - *What was happening in your life at that time?*
- *Your son's sudden death has left you terribly dejected; you feel this pervasive grief, and at the moment can find no consolation in your life or your religious faith.*
- *It's hard to feel anything but sadness because of your son's death, and this is made even worse by the feeling that it was terribly unjust, a betrayal by God.*
- *It's hard to feel anything but sadness because of your son's death, but some part of you would welcome genuine faith and consolation.*
- *How does your faith in Christ fit into your feeling and thinking about the loss of your son?*
- *What does your anger stir you to say to God about the loss of your son?*
- *One part of you wants some genuine relief from your deep sorrow, but you don't feel open to the peace and assurance that your faith might give.*
- *One part of you is terribly angry at God for taking your son from you, but you are reluctant to express that anger, to tell God how you feel and what you think.*

Exploring Your Spiritual Journey

1. Reflect on a casket experience in your life (distant past, recent past, or current). Select a few of the trialogues under *A Quest to Face God* to help you to explore your responses.

2. Reflect on a casket experience in your life (distant past, recent past, or current). Select a few of the trialogues under *A Quest to Face What Was Lost* to help you to explore your responses.

3. Reflect on a casket experience in your life (distant past, recent past, or current). Select a few of the trialogues under *A Quest to Face God in Loss* to help you to explore your responses.

4. Reflect on a casket experience in your life (distant past, recent past, or current). Select a few of the trialogues under *A Quest to Wrestle with God* to help you to explore your responses.

5. Reflect on a casket experience in your life (distant past, recent past, or current). Select a few of the trialogues under *A Quest to Cling to God* to help you to explore your responses.

6. Reflect on a casket experience in your life (distant past, recent past, or current). Select a few of the trialogues under *A Quest to Not Lose Faith/A Quest to Sustain Faith* to help you to explore your responses.

Empathetic Scriptural Explorations: Sustaining Biblical Trialogues—Isaiah 61:1-3

Spiritual conversations use broad theological concepts to prompt people to ponder more deeply their walk with God. *Scriptural explorations* use specific applicable biblical passages to help people to relate God's truth to their circumstances.

Isaiah 61:1-3 provides the purposes for soul care (sustaining and healing) scriptural explorations:

- Preach good news to the poor.
- Bind up the brokenhearted.
- Proclaim freedom for the captives and release from darkness for the prisoners.
- Proclaim the year of the LORD's favor and the day of vengeance of our God.
- Comfort all who mourn.
- Provide for those who grieve in Zion—bestowing on them:
  - A crown of beauty instead of ashes,
  - The oil of gladness instead of mourning, and
  - A garment of praise instead of a spirit of despair.
- Call and envision people as:
  - Oaks of righteousness and
  - A planting of the LORD.
- Display the LORD's splendor.

Notice the ultimate purpose of all soul care—helping your spiritual friends to display God's glory by trusting in his goodness in the midst of life's badness.

Specifically for sustaining, empathic scriptural explorations relate God's truth to your spiritual friend's life to encourage candor, complaint, cry, and comfort/communion. Imagine that you've connected with Alonzo. He senses that you're in his casket with him. You sense that you understand something of what he's going through both in level one and level two suffering. Having heard some of the depths of his soul through listening to his words, you're praying silently for opportunities for the two of you to listen together to God's Word.

In a natural, friend-to-friend manner, you long to help Alonzo to invite God back into the picture, into the casket with him. Your quest requires a loving understanding of Alonzo, biblical wisdom about the character and purposes of God, and biblical knowledge of Scripture. It also requires a wise, humble, and bold commitment to helping Alonzo to connect with God—his ultimate Spiritual Friend.

To get there, Alonzo needs to face life. He has to look in the mirror and acknowledge the ashes. Like the Jews of old, he must tear his garments and cover his head with ashes. He must mourn and grieve, singing the psalmists' laments. He has to face life so he can face God. In other words, he needs to practice biblical candor, complaint, cry, and comfort.

How do you help Alonzo to experience candor, complaint, cry, and comfort? You could tell him— "Cry now!" Not so wise. Or, you could teach him the four stages of biblical suffering. "Alonzo, for you to heal there are some biblical stages that we see evidenced in person after person throughout the Bible: candor, complaint, cry, and comfort. Let me share the passages and teachings that show us why we should do these, how we should do them, and the help they offer." Better—in a given situation, in a given way. However, still not best. The most helpful, effective way is the way of trialogues that use scriptural explorations to encourage personalized candor, complaint, cry, and comfort.

With Alonzo, Becky, and others, you can use the following trialogues as a basic pattern for exploring biblical narratives/stories, psalms, or passages together.

- *How do you react to this biblical story/psalm/passage?*
  - *How is it different from your situation? How is it similar?*
  - *How have you been responding differently? Similarly?*
  - *What in this story/psalm/passage would you like to add to your response? How could you do that?*
- *Imagine writing a story/psalm/passage somewhat like this one regarding your current suffering.*
  - *What would your relationship to God be like in your story/psalm/passage?*
  - *What role would you play in your story/psalm/passage?*
  - *Who else might be in your story/psalm/passage?*
  - *Are there any characters in this story/psalm/passage who remind you of any people in your life?*
  - *How would God give you strength in your story/psalm/passage?*
  - *What would the theme of your story/psalm/passage be?*
  - *How might your story/psalm/passage turn out?*
  - *How would God work out your story/psalm/passage for good?*

You can use this pattern of personal scriptural explorations with candor, complaint, cry, and comfort. All you need is biblical knowledge of appropriate passages and spiritual discernment to know what "stage" (candor, complaint, cry, or comfort) your friend is in.

Empathetic Scriptural Explorations and Candor

You sense that Alonzo is on the verge of embracing his loss, but he's fearful. Tentative. You'd love to see him "step on the mat with God so the wrestling match can commence." Perhaps you share:

- *Alonzo, you've shared a lot. There's obviously so much going on inside. Rightly so. Yet, so far we've not talked much about where God fits into your picture . . .*

You have all sorts of options concerning how you proceed. You could be quiet, sit back, and wait, which might be quite useful. Or, you could share:

- *I'm curious about where God is in your suffering.*
- *Alonzo, could you tell me what you're doing with God in your suffering?*
- *I'm wondering where God is in all this.*
- *What might God be up to in all of this?*

Perhaps your conversation might run like this.

> *"Alonzo, have you been able to share your heart with God?"*
> *"Well, yeah. Some. I guess."*
> *"Great. What have you said?"*
> *"Well, I've told him how confused I am. And shocked. And worried . . ."*
> *"Wow. That's a lot. You and God sure are on great speaking terms! What are you sensing from God as you share with him?"*

As you continue to talk, you sense Alonzo's openness to explore further his relationship to God. Now you have the opportunity, together, to explore a relevant biblical narrative or character. As you do, you can explore specific implications and applications.

♦ *Alonzo, David experienced something like this. Stalked by Saul, his life was on the line. He faced the valley of the shadow of death. Could we look at his situation and his response?*

If you're talking with Becky, it might sound more like this:

♦ *Becky, Tamar experienced something like this. Her half-brother betrayed her sexually. Could we look at her situation and her response?*

Empathetic Scriptural Explorations and Complaint

Below you'll find some examples of scriptural explorations and complaint. These are wooden because they're generic, one-size-fits-all. I've left space after each one. Use the scenario with Alonzo or Becky to make them more personal. Turn some of the questions into open-ended statements.

♦ *What does Psalm 88 suggest about expressing your anger, disappointment, or complaint toward God? How could you relate this to your response to God?*

♦ *God promises that all things work together for good for his children (Romans 8:28). What are your thoughts about that promise? What do you think about a passage like this? What good purposes has God already provided to you or in you through these events?*

♦ *If you were to write a Psalm 13 or a Psalm 88 to God (Psalms of Lament and Complaint), how would it sound? What would you write?*

Empathetic Scriptural Explorations and Cry

Below you'll find some examples of scriptural explorations and cry. Again, they are wooden, generic, one-size-fits-all. I've left space after each one. Use the scenario with Alonzo or Becky to make them more real. Turn some of the questions into open-ended statements.

♦ *What Scriptures could we look at that illustrate how God's people have talked to God when they felt that he was not hearing their cry?*

♦ *If you were to write a Psalm 72 or 73, how would it sound? What would you write?*

♦ *Based upon Psalm 13, how could your situation cause you to cry out to God for help, love, strength, joy, peace, and deliverance?*

Empathetic Scriptural Explorations and Comfort/Communion

Below you'll find some examples of scriptural explorations and comfort/communion. Once again, these are wooden, generic, and one-size-fits-all. I've left space after each one. Use the scenario with Alonzo or Becky to make them more personal. Turn some of the questions into open-ended statements.

♦ *Let's explore John 9, God's purposes in suffering, and how they may relate to your suffering.*

♦ *If you were to write a Psalm 42 and 43, where David moves from confusion to communion with God, how would it sound? What would you write?*

♦ *Based upon Deuteronomy 8, how do you think you can grow through your suffering?*

♦ *How could you relate Paul's perspective on his suffering in Romans 8:17-28 to your life? How could taking on his perspective alter your perspective?*

♦ *Let's explore how Paul found comfort in his despair in 2 Corinthians 1. What applications could you make from his life to yours?*

You can use scriptural explorations as powerful homework assignments. For instance, between now and the next time you meet, Becky could write her own psalm to God. Or, she could simply "journal her feelings to God." When you meet again, you trialogue about her writings.

Where We've Been and Where We're Headed

By God's grace, you've sustained your spiritual friend. Her faith has survived the onslaught of doubt. His retreat has been stopped, his hemorrhaging halted. Now what?

Now healing can and must begin. Climbing in the casket is a wonderful start. However, celebrating the resurrection is the necessary and magnificent culmination of soul care. Chapters Eight, Nine, and Ten (Section Three: Maturing the Art of Healing Spiritual Friendship) teach how to diagnose and treat spiritual friends through healing so that they can say, "it's possible to hope."

Maturing Your Spiritual Friendship Competency
Empathetic Scriptural Explorations

1. Reflect on a casket experience in your life (distant past, recent past, or current). Use the basic pattern for exploring biblical narratives, select a few of the trialogues under *Candor*, and use an appropriate passage of Scripture to help you to explore your responses.

2. Reflect on a casket experience in your life (distant past, recent past, or current). Use the basic pattern for exploring biblical narratives, select a few of the trialogues under *Complaint*, and use an appropriate passage of Scripture to help you to explore your responses.

3. Reflect on a casket experience in your life (distant past, recent past, or current). Use the basic pattern for exploring biblical narratives, select a few of the trialogues under *Cry*, and use an appropriate passage of Scripture to help you to explore your responses.

4. Reflect on a casket experience in your life (distant past, recent past, or current). Use the basic pattern for exploring biblical narratives, select a few of the trialogues under *Comfort/Communion*, and use an appropriate passage of Scripture to help you to explore your responses.

Chapter Eight

Healing Diagnosis
Compassionate Discernment in Healing

> *"Being a spiritual friend is being the physician of a wounded soul. And what does a physician do when someone comes with a bleeding wound? Three things: He or she cleanses the wound, aligns the sundered parts, and gives it rest. That's all. The physician does not heal. He or she provides an environment for the dominant natural process of healing to take its course. The physician really is midwife rather than healer"* (Tilden Edwards, *Spiritual Friend*, p. 125).

A Biblical Model of Healing

Sufferology Part I examines the connection between suffering and sustaining—what is it like to live in the desert of level one and level two suffering? Sufferology Part II explores the relationship between suffering and healing—what is the nature of the warfare between hope and despair in the thirsty soul?

Through sustaining, you've helped your spiritual friends to face their suffering. Now they recognize that life is bad. They're experiencing their thirsty soul. Now what? Now you want to ponder:

- *Relationally*: Where is my spiritual friend experiencing the greatest relational despair? Where is she enduring the greatest "groaning"? What are the unmet thirsts of her soul? In her thirsts, who is she turning to? In what ways is she drinking from her Spring of Living Water? What is her agony like? Where do I see glimpses of hope? Evidences of grace?
- *Rationally*: Where is my spiritual friend enduring the greatest mental battles? What is the battle like in his mind between Satan's lying narrative and Christ's grace narrative? What is it like to "be in his head"? How is he sorting out questions about God's goodness?
- *Volitionally*: What evidence do I see that my spiritual friend is re-engaging the battle? What would it look like for her to respond courageously even as she feels deeply? What does the "way of the fool" look like in her response? What does the "way of the godly" look like in her response? Is she worshipping and ministering?
- *Emotionally*: How well is my spiritual friend managing his moods? Is he self-aware? Is he gaining self-control? What would joy in the midst of sorrow be like for him? Is he crying out to God? Suffering *coram Deo*?

Exploring Your Spiritual Journey

1. When were you duped into believing Satan's lie that "God is your enemy"? How were you able to demolish his lie with Christ's truth?

2. Imagine that every second of your life your heart is captured by the truth that God is your pursuing Father, Christ is your forgiving Friend, the Holy Spirit is your inspiring Mentor, and you are a beloved son/daughter and a hero/heroine of epic proportions. How would your life be different?

3. Read 2 Corinthians 4:1-18.

    a. What is Satan's scheme as presented in this passage?

    b. In 2 Corinthians 4:7-12, Paul experiences life as bad but God as good.

        1.) How has your experience of life been similar to and different from Paul's?

        2.) How did Paul manage to be hard-pressed but not crushed, perplexed but not in despair?

        3.) How could 2 Corinthians 4:14-18 impact how you respond to suffering?

The Biblical Focus of Healing: "It's Possible to Hope"

Terry Waite, the British hostage released in 1991 after nearly five years of solitary confinement in Lebanon, was chained to the wall of his room for almost twenty-four hours a day. Reflecting on his circumstances, he noted:

I have been determined in captivity, and still am determined, to convert this experience into something that will be useful and good for other people. I think that's the way to approach suffering. It seems to me that Christianity doesn't in any way lessen suffering. What it does is enable you to take it, to face it, to work through it and eventually convert it (Waite, *Taken on Trust*, p. 11).

Call it *creative suffering*. God transforms suffering, composing good from evil, turning mourning into dancing, and creating beauty for ashes. British Christian psychiatrist, Frank Lake, pictures it powerfully. "There is no human experience which cannot be put on the anvil of a lively relationship with God and man, and battered into a meaningful shape" (Lake, *Clinical Theology*, p. 97).

> **There is no human experience which cannot be put on the anvil of a lively relationship with God and man, and battered into a meaningful shape.**

What role do soul care givers play in converting suffering? How do we cooperate with God to batter mangled caskets into meaningful shapes? In suffering, we compassionately identify with people in pain and redirect them to Christ and the body of Christ to *sustain* and *heal* their faith so they experience communion with Christ and conformity to Christ even in the midst of suffering in a fallen world.

Sufferology exists because sin, death, and separation exist. Created for life in Paradise, we now reside east of Eden. Designed for the refreshing, rejuvenating waters of relational connection, now we endure the arid desert of forsakenness, betrayal, and dis-integration. Desperately thirsty, we clamor for communion and long for resurrection. During Sufferology Part I, soul care givers *climb in the casket* of daily desert deaths—*sustaining* we call it. During Sufferology Part II, soul care givers *celebrate the resurrection* that promises a future day when all thirsts are quenched—*healing* we call it.

Sustaining helps faith *survive*. We fortify faith to resist retreat and to promote spiritual *stability*. Healing helps faith *thrive*. We deepen faith to move forward promoting spiritual *maturity*. In sustaining, we taste God's comfort; in healing, his goodness. In sustaining, we face the world's evil; in healing, God's goodness. In sustaining, we learn that we need something. In healing, we learn that we need Christ and Christians. In sustaining, we participate in the fellowship of Christ's suffering. In healing, we appropriate the power of Christ's resurrection. Together, sustaining and healing teach that even when life is bad, it's possible to hope because God is good. "It's normal to hurt and possible to hope."

The Biblical Theology of Healing: "I Believe in the Power of Christ's Resurrection"

In healing, we use thirsts (John 7), longings (Psalms 42-43; 63), and the groanings of life (Romans 8) as points of contact to share Christ. We share the mystery of grace in the midst of suffering. Our spiritual friend begins to understand that the "problem" is part of the larger story of what God is up to in his universe.

In healing, we become interpreters of God's eternal story. We dispense the spiritual medicine of a grace perspective so people can see the unseen grace and goodness of God.

Therefore, we do not lose heart. Though outwardly we are wasting away, yet inwardly we are being renewed day by day. For our light and momentary troubles are achieving for us an eternal glory that far outweighs them all. So we fix our eyes not on what is seen, but on what is unseen. For what is seen is temporary, but what is unseen is eternal (2 Corinthians 4:16-18).

In suffering, the Tempter tempts us to despair. Outwardly, life is bad. Nevertheless, inwardly, we perceive that God is good. We gain his larger perspective. "Wow! So that's what God's about. You mean that he takes the ugliness of my situation, and reshapes it, and me, into something glorious! He's making me spiritually beautiful. Oh, so all of this is his cosmic beauty treatment!"

Biblical Sufferology in Healing: Triumph of Faith

Consider where you last saw your suffering friend in sustaining: in a casket. Not alone, not dead, not separated. Nevertheless, in a casket. You're in the casket with her. She's invited Christ, also. Her soul gushes forth, spilling a lifetime of daily deaths. At this threshold of awareness of the fragility of her life and the frailty of human existence, a door of opportunity opens. Surprisingly, a door of hope.

More surprisingly, a door of eternal hope entered by way of the death of earthly hope. A rudimentary principle of spiritual existence teaches that until death crucifies our earthly hope, we refuse to surrender ourselves to resurrected heavenly hope.

We were under great pressure, far beyond our ability to endure, so that we despaired even of life. Indeed, in our hearts *we felt the sentence of death*. But this happened *that we might not rely on ourselves but on God, who raises the dead* (2 Corinthians 1:8a-9, emphasis added).

It's what happened to the woman at the well in John 4. "Water. Give me water!" She knew she was thirsty, but she was not yet at the end of her rope. She was consciously aware only of her physical thirst and all the self-effort it took to placate it. "I don't want to have to keep coming here to draw water." Hard work, but doable in human strength.

So Jesus shifted her sights from physical thirsts to relational ones. "Go get your hubby."

"Husband? I have no husband."

"That's right. The fact is, you have five husbands, and the man you now have is not even your husband."

What was Jesus up to? The same thing he's always up to in all our thirsty desert journeys—*inviting us to himself based on acknowledged relational thirsts*. "If anyone is thirsty, let him come to me and drink" (John 7:37).

No matter how hard the woman at the well worked, no matter how many times she pursued her relational strategy of "having a man," it was never enough. Thirsty, with only a broken cistern to draw from, she gave up all human hope. She surrendered to heavenly hope, placing her trust in the "Savior of the world" (John 4:42).

Soul thirsts are too deep to be fulfilled by works. Thank God! Hope prompted by thirsts (John 4 and 7), watered by longings (Psalms 42-43; 63), and seeded by the groanings of life (Romans 8) grow into a contact point to embrace and be embraced by Christ.

In sustaining, we face our loss. That's good. However, secular counseling can enter here offering solutions—secular healing. "Here, do this. Regroup. Start afresh. Grieve. Then move on. In your own strength. You can do it. Others have. You're okay. Life must go on. Don't quit."

Christian healing is soul *care* at its purest. It is not so much a cure, if by that we mean a definitive change in circumstances, or even a return to the previous state of being. Rather, it is *care*. We care about what is most important internally and eternally—a dependent, intimate grace relationship with Christ.

Spiritual friends say, "Stop trying to regroup on your own. Don't even think about climbing out of that casket alone. Cry out for resurrection help. Drink from the Spring of Living Water. Entrust yourself to Jesus and streams of living water will flow from within you." Or, put in Paul's terms, "He has *delivered* us from such *deadly* peril, and he will *deliver* us. On him we have set our *hope* that he will continue to *deliver* us (2 Corinthians 1:10, emphasis added).

Healing makes what cannot be removed, creatively bearable. It is the divinely creative use of pain and loss that cannot be cured. In our weakness, he is strong; in our parched condition, he is satisfying. His strength is made perfect in our weakness. Healing blossoms in the souls of thirsty image bearers who groan for what only God can supply.

Healing makes what cannot be removed, creatively bearable.

Spiritual emergencies allow for spiritual emergence. We heal spiritual disabilities by encouraging spiritual maturity through a greater awareness of God's good heart and his good purposes even in the middle of suffering. We plant seeds that help faith to thrive as people experience the benefits of faith to see the benefits of trials. Thirsty sufferers move forward with a new beginning through a new hope based upon a new perspective.

Biblically Diagnosing Suffering: Stages of Healing

Sufferology II opens with a theology of healing that teaches that God always uses parched thirsts to invite us to the Spring of Living Water. Sufferology through healing continues with a four-stage diagnostic process that helps you to discern how your spiritual friends are responding to suffering. You're trying to diagnose whether their responses to their thirsts are unhealthy (grieving without hope) or healthy (grieving with hope). Are they characterized by regrouping *or* waiting, deadening *or* wailing, despairing *or* weaving, digging cisterns *or* worshipping?

Stage	Unhealthy Thirst Responses	Healthy Thirst Responses
Stage One	Regrouping/Immediate Gratification	Waiting: Trusting with Faith
Stage Two	Deadening/Anesthetizing	Wailing: Groaning with Hope
Stage Three	Despairing/Doubting	Weaving: Perceiving with Grace
Stage Four	Digging Cisterns/False Lovers	Worshipping: Engaging with Love

What does hope look like? It looks like waiting, wailing, weaving, and worshipping. When I say that "it's possible to hope," I'm saying that it's possible to trust God with faith, groan to God with hope, perceive God's goodness with grace, and engage God and others with love. (Because sustaining and healing are so interrelated, I've repeated the full depiction of "Biblical Sufferology" in Box 8:1.)

Box 8:1
Biblical Sufferology

Levels of Suffering

Level One Suffering: External Suffering

♦ Circumstances: What Happens *to* Us—Separation
♦ Theological Reality: Our World Is Fallen and It Falls on Us

Level Two Suffering: Internal Suffering

♦ Condemnation: What Happens *in* Us—Spiritual Depression
♦ Experiential Reality: Our World Is a Mess and It Messes with Our Minds

Sustaining in Suffering
"It's Normal to Hurt and Necessary to Grieve."

♦ Stage One: Candor—Honest with Self
♦ Stage Two: Complaint—Honest to God
♦ Stage Three: Cry—Asking God for Help
♦ Stage Four: Comfort—Receiving God's Help

Healing in Suffering
"It's Possible to Hope in the Midst of Grief."

♦ Stage One: Waiting—Trusting with Faith
♦ Stage Two: Wailing—Groaning with Hope
♦ Stage Three: Weaving—Perceiving with Grace
♦ Stage Four: Worshipping—Engaging with Love

Stage One: Waiting—Trusting with Faith Rather Than Regrouping and Immediate Gratification

You're in a casket. Finally you've come face-to-face with death and with utter human hopelessness. Do you want to stay there? No! Frantic to escape? Yes! You cry out to God for help. What's he say? "Wait." Now you're at a faith-point. "I trust him; I trust him not. I'll wait; I'll not wait." Which will it be? Will you wait or regroup?

The woman at the well is in a husband-casket. One leaves the scene, "Encore! Encore!" she shouts, bringing the curtain down on another failed marriage. Frantically she searches time after time for a man she could have—a man she could desperately clutch who would meet her desperate needs by desperately desiring her above all else.

We don't know what came next for her after she surrendered her thirsts to Christ. Certainly, if she were to live out her new Christ-life, she would have to change her habitual pattern of regrouping through "having" a man. Suppose that she took her longing to God in prayer. Presuppose God told her to stop living with this man who was not her husband. Don't you think that on a human plane, she would experience excruciating emptiness, starving hunger? So she prays to God, "Father, I know that all I need is you and what you choose to provide. I'm cleaning up my life. Would you please send me a godly man." God says, "Wait. Delay your gratification. Don't get involved with a man." Everything inside her—her flesh-habituated past way of surviving, her cistern-digging style of relating—craves satisfaction *now*. If she regroups, she grasps another husband on the rebound. So, what would "hope" look like in her immediate context? Hope in God chooses delayed gratification over immediate gratification. Hope waits. Hope is the refusal to demand heaven now.

> **Hope waits.**
> **Hope is the refusal to demand heaven now.**

Tony Compolo preaches a message where he repeatedly says, "It's Friday, but Sunday's comin'." He's focusing his audience on Friday-truth—the crucifixion of Christ, and on Sunday-truth—the coming resurrection of Christ. I would change the metaphor a tad because we aren't living on Friday, we're living on Saturday. Symbolically, life lived on fallen planet Earth is Saturday living—the day between the crucifixion and the resurrection. The day of waiting. The day that tests our trust.

Waiting is rooted in the Old Testament. Prophets promised Israel that a better day was coming, *later*. The New Testament writers develop the waiting motif when they urge us toward patience and perseverance. Both teach that waiting is refusing to take over while refusing to give up. As we wait, we trust God's provision without working to provide for ourselves. That's the message of Romans 5, Hebrews 11, James 1, and 1 Peter 1-2. In waiting, we hold on to God's rope of hope, even when we can't feel it or see it.

Additionally, we refuse self-rescue. We neither numb our longings, pretending they don't exist, nor do we illegitimately fulfill our longings. The opposite of waiting is immediate gratification—meeting our "needs" *now*, taking matters into our own hands now and acting as if we're our only hope. Saturday living makes us thirsty. We can wait for the everlasting feast, or we can stuff our faces now.

Esau embodies immediate gratification. In fact, God says Esau embodies godlessness (Hebrews 12:16). For a single meal, a bowl of soup, he sells his birthright. He refuses to look ahead, to wait, to delay gratification. What is your bowl of soup? Mine? What am I convinced that I must have now that I believe is more pleasing to my deepest appetite than God and what he promises?

Moses exemplifies delayed gratification.

> By faith Moses, when he had grown up, refused to be known as the son of Pharaoh's daughter. He *chose to be mistreated* along with the people of *God rather than to enjoy the pleasures of sin for a short time*. He regarded disgrace for the sake of Christ as greater value than the treasures of Egypt *because he was looking ahead to his reward* (Hebrews 11:24-26, emphasis added).

No quick fix for him. No "Turkish Delight" from the White Witch of Narnia. No pleasures of sin for a season. Why? How could he? He chose eternal pleasure over temporal happiness. *He remembered the future.* Faith looks back to the past recalling God's mighty works saying, "He did it that time, he can do it now." Hope looks ahead remembering God's coming reward saying, "I consider that our present sufferings are not worth comparing with the glory (beauty) that will be revealed in us. The creation *waits* in eager expectation for the sons of God to be revealed" (Romans 8:18-19, emphasis and parenthesis added). Hope gives love time to take root.

Stage Two: Wailing—Groaning with Hope Rather Than Deadening and Anesthetizing

When I use the word "wailing," I don't mean weeping as in the complaint or cry of sustaining (though weeping is sure to be a part of wailing). I mean the utter agony of waiting that causes us to groan inwardly as we wait eagerly. Wailing is longing, hungering, thirsting, and wanting what is legitimate, what is promised, but what we do not have. It is grieving the "not yet."

> For the creation was subjected to *frustration*, not by its own choice, but by the will of the one who subjected it, *in hope* that the creation itself will be liberated from its bondage to decay and brought into the glorious freedom of the children of God. We know that the whole creation has been *groaning* as in the pains of *childbirth* right up to the present time. Not only so, but we ourselves, who have the firstfruits of the Spirit, *groan inwardly as we wait eagerly* for our adoption as sons, the redemption of our bodies (Romans 8:20-23, emphasis added).

Designed for paradise, we live in a desert. No wonder we're thirsty image bearers. No wonder we groan for heaven. We might picture the big picture like this:

- ◆ Paradise: "Now!"   Full
- ◆ Desert: "No!"   Empty
- ◆ Thirst: "Not Yet!"   Groaning

Everything was very good and completely satisfying in Paradise. Generous Father gifted less-than-grateful Eve and Adam with all they needed and so much more. They were full. Because they refused to rest in Father's fullness, they were barricaded from the Garden, sent roaming east of Eden into the desert. Instead of the happy cry of "Now! All my needs are met now!" they now cry, "No! We're empty. Thirsty. Hungry." Created for Paradise and living in a desert, they and their offspring become thirsty. The new cry is "Not yet!" We say, "I want what I want and I want it now." God says, "I promise you that I will quench all your legitimate thirsts, but not yet." So we groan.

What type of groans? Paul couples inward groaning with eager waiting (Romans 8:22-23), eager expectation (Romans 8:19), and frustration (Romans 8:20). "Eager waiting" pictures ferocious, desperate desire. "Frustration" suggests the ache that we feel due to the emptiness and void we experience living in a fallen world. It's the same Greek word used in the Septuagint to translate Solomon's word "vanity"—meaningless, soap bubbles, unsatisfying, pointless, absurd—all of this describes life south of heaven. When we wail, we declare how deeply out of the nest we are, how far from home we've wandered, how much we long for heaven.

Paul illustrates our desperate desire using the image of pregnancy. He describes a woman groaning as in child labor that lasts not hours, not nine-months, but a lifetime. Ouch. Ugh. Cringe. Imagine that. A pregnant woman in labor for seventy years! That's groaning. Groaning not only the pain of seemingly unending labor, but *groaning the pain of not having the joy of the baby*. That's our current condition. For our allotted years on this Blue Planet, we are pregnant with hope, groaning for Paradise, for Eden, for walking with God in the cool of the day, for being naked and unashamed, for shalom. When we groan, we admit to ourselves and express to God the pain of our unmet desires, the depth of our fervent longing for heaven's joy, and our total commitment to remain pregnant with hope.

We don't like to groan. Groaning exposes us for the needy people that we are. Groaning acknowledges our weakness, our brokenness—a brokenness that only God can fix. Paul knows the process. He candidly complained and cried out to God three times, pleading with the Lord to take away his suffering. But the Lord said to Paul, "My grace is sufficient for you, for my power is made perfect in weakness" (2 Corinthians 12:9). To which Paul replies, "When I am weak, then I am strong" (2 Corinthians 12:10). Wailing admits weakness and neediness that only grace can remedy.

Refusal to groan is disobedience and distrust of God. When we deaden our souls from groaning, we refuse to humble ourselves; we refuse to admit that we need God; we refuse to acknowledge that we are more than flesh and bone needing only meat. God uses hunger to teach us that we are souls who need him.

In 2 Kings 4, the barren Shunammite bears a son. He fulfills a lifetime of her hopes and dreams. Tragically, he dies. Rather than face her groaning, she repeats, "It's all right." Her heart is sick, her soul vexed, yet she keeps insisting, "It's all right. I'm all right." Life sent her two caskets, the first her inability to conceive, the second the death of the child she finally bore. She eventually screams at Elisha, "Did I not say to you, 'Don't deceive me! Don't get my hopes up.'"

Hope deferred makes the heart sick. Hope hoped for, received, then lost again, makes the heart deathly ill. Fragile. Needy. We hate being there. So we block it out.

How do we deaden our souls from groaning? By living as if this world is all there is. By making our bellies our God (Romans 16:18; Philippians 3:19). By eating meat. If we wait for the feast without snacking on junk food, then we'll hunger. Refusing to hunger for heaven, we spurn delaying our gratification, instead stuffing our faces with Twinkies until we lose all sensitivity (Ephesians 4:19). Eventually we give ourselves over to sensuality so as to indulge in every kind of impurity (any attempt to meet our needs apart from God, to self-sufficiently satisfy our appetites) with a continual lust for more (Ephesians 4:19). We preoccupy our minds with our bodies, thus shutting out the wail of our souls.

There is a costly loss of wailing in our anesthetizing world. False selves faking it with God. Docility, quietness, phoniness, deadness. The message of life is death, but we let the message of life slip. We drift, glide by, flow past, refusing to pay attention to sorrow's messengers. We don't turn our attention to sorrow; we fail to tune our radios toward suffering. Carelessly we waste suffering by refusing to wait and wail.

Instead, we must wait on God refusing to gratify our desires. Asaph models our message. "But as for me, it is good to be near God. I have made the Sovereign LORD my refuge; I will tell of all your deeds" (Psalm 73:28). Since his goodness is our refuge, we will wait on him.

> **We taste our thirsts for the promised feast
> even as we sense our stomachs growling with holy hunger pangs.**

We wail to God and ourselves. We experience and express the agony of hope deferred. We taste our thirsts for the promised feast even as we sense our stomachs growling with holy hunger pangs. With Asaph we wail, "Whom have I in heaven but you? And earth has nothing I desire besides you" (Psalm 73:25).

Stage Three: Weaving—Perceiving with Grace Rather Than Despairing and Doubting

In the world's model of the stages of grief, acceptance is as good as it gets. Acceptance acknowledges the loss, integrating it into the reality of life as we now experience it. Certainly, we want to do that, but in Christ we can do so much more. Candor and complaint correspond to the world's grief stage of acceptance. Weaving is our integrating stage where we integrate our smaller story loss into God's larger story picture.

It's in the soil of weaving that our concept of life as two competing love stories grows. Here we learn that God weaves beauty out of ashes. It is in weaving that we meet wounds healed.

Grace Narratives

Joseph mastered this message. Facing his fearful family, Joseph said to them, "Don't be afraid. Am I in the place of God? You intended to harm me, but God intended it for good to accomplish what is now being done, the saving of many lives" (Genesis 50:19-20). Joseph uses "intended" both for his brothers' plans and God's purposes. The word has a very tangible sense of weaving, plaiting, and interpenetrating as in the weaving together of fabric to fashion a robe, perhaps even a coat of many colors. It was also used in a negative, metaphorical sense to suggest a malicious plot, the devising of a cruel scheme. Additionally, the Jews used "intended" to symbolically picture the creation of some new and beautiful purpose or result through the weaving together of seemingly haphazard, miscellaneous, or malicious events.

"Life is bad," Joseph admitted. "You plotted against me for *evil*." That is, his brothers *intended* to spoil or ruin something wonderful. "God is good," Joseph preached, choosing a word that is the superlative of pleasant, beautiful. That is, God *intended* to create beauty from ashes.

Joseph discovers healing through God's grace narrative. Further, he offers his blundering brothers a taste of grace.

And now, do not be distressed and do not be angry with yourselves for selling me here, because it was to save lives that God sent me ahead of you. For two years now there has been a famine in the land, and for the next five years there will not be plowing and reaping. But God sent me ahead of you to preserve for you a remnant on earth and to save your lives by a great deliverance. So then, it was not you who sent me here, but God. He made me father to Pharaoh, lord of his entire household and ruler of all Egypt (Genesis 45:5-8).

Amazing! I hope you caught the words. "To save lives," "to preserve," "by a great deliverance." That's a grace narrative, a salvation narrative. Think about it. Had God not preserved a remnant of Abraham's descendents, then Jesus would never have been born. Joseph used his spiritual eyes to see God's great grace purposes in saving not only Israel and Egypt, but the entire world.

I hope you caught Joseph's repetition. "God sent me." "God sent me ahead of you." "It was not you who sent me here, but God." I'm sure you detect the smaller story and the larger. There was a smaller story of human scheming for ruin. However, God trumps that smaller scheme with his larger purpose by weaving beauty out of ugliness.

Life hurts. Wounds penetrate. Without grace narratives, bitterness flourishes. With a grace perspective, forgiveness flows.

Instead of our perspective shrinking, suffering is the exact time when we must listen most closely, when we must lean over to hear the whisper of God. True, God shouts to us in our pain, but his answers, as with Elijah, often come to us in whispered still, small voices amid the thunders of the world.

In weaving, our wounds are healed as we envision a future while all seems lost in the present. Through hope, we remember the future; we move from Good Friday to Easter Sunday while living on Saturday. Grace narratives point the way to God's larger way, assuring us that our Worthy Groom is worth our wait.

Grace Math

To heal wounds, we need grace narratives plus grace math. Grace math teaches us that *present suffering plus God's character equals future glory*. The equation we use is the Divine perspective.

From a Divine faith perspective on life, we erect a platform to respond to suffering. *Coram Deo* faith perceives the presence of God in the presence of suffering. Since God's heart is good beyond question, we don't have to live in denial. Like Paul, we can groan over how horrible this world is (Romans 8:17-27).

In our pain, God shouts to us. He has our attention. And we have his attention. He is listening, waiting for us to cry out to him. He longs for us to face our suffering face-to-face with him. "Trust in him at all times, O people; pour out your hearts to him, for God is our refuge" (Psalm 62:8).

How a person views life makes all the difference in life. Luther understood this. "The Holy Spirit knows that a thing only has such value and meaning to a man as he assigns it in his thoughts" (Luther, *Luther's Works*, Vol. 42, p. 124). Therefore, Luther sought to help people to reshape their perspective or interpretation of their life situation. He wanted his followers to contemplate suffering from a new, divine perspective. He nurtured alternative ways to view life.

Speaking of Luther's *Letter of Fourteen Consolations*, J. E. Strohl writes:

The whole treatise is concerned with what one sees. It presents fourteen images for contemplation, and their purpose is to renew our sight. The consolation offered by the Word is a new vision, the power of faith to see suffering and death from the perspective of the crucified and risen Lord. It turns our common human view of these matters upside down, lifting us as Luther puts it, above our evils and our blessings, making them *res indifferentes*. This does not eradicate the pain or the fear of our misery, but it robs it of its hopelessness (Strohl, *Luther as Spiritual Advisor*, 1989, p. 179).

Our earth-bound or non-faith human story of suffering must yield to God's narrative of life and suffering—to God's grace narrative and grace math.

If only a man could see his God in such a light of love . . . how happy, how calm, how safe he would be! He would then truly have a God from whom he would know with certainty that all his fortunes— whatever they might be—had come to him and were still coming to him under the guidance of God's most gracious will (Luther, *Luther's Works*, Vol. 42, p. 154).

That's the perspective that prompts healing.

For Luther, and for us, the Cross forever settles all questions about God's heart for us. Without faith in God's grace through Christ's death, we are deaf to God-reality.

He who does not believe that he is forgiven by the inexhaustible riches of Christ's righteousness is like a deaf man hearing a story. If we consider it properly and with an attentive heart, this one image—even if there were no other—would suffice to fill us with such comfort that we should not only not grieve over our evils, but should also glory in our tribulations, scarcely feeling them for the joy that we have in Christ (Luther, *Luther's Works*, Vol. 42, p. 165).

The Christ of the Cross is the only One who makes sense of life when suffering surfaces. Only the Cross of Christ can make sense out of the sufferings of life.

Stage Four: Worshipping—Engaging with Love Rather Than Digging Cisterns and False Lovers

As we progress through the stages of healing, we are transformed:

♦ From Regrouping to Waiting: Delayed Gratification—Trusting with Faith
♦ From Deadening to Wailing: Groaning—Groaning with Hope
♦ From Despair to Weaving: Grace-Healed Wounds—Perceiving with Grace
♦ From Digging Cisterns to Worshipping: Glorifying—Engaging with Love

Put yourself back in that casket. You've tried to claw your way out through immediate gratification. Your bowl of soup may be power, prestige, pleasure, pleasing people, or any multitude of pathways of relating. Since soup never satisfies the soul, only the stomach, you still ache. What to do with your ache? Well, if you face it, then you have to admit your insufficiency. That simply will not do. So, you deaden it. You block out and suppress the reality of your hungry heart. Keep busy. Fantasize. Climb the corporate ladder. These tricks of the godless trade work no better than immediate gratification. Somewhere, deep down inside, despair brews. "Is this all there is?"

Now what? If you follow the beaten path, then despair guides you to false lovers. Idols of the heart. Digging cisterns, broken cisterns that can hold no water. Something or someone who will rescue you from agony's clutches—or so you imagine.

If, on the other hand, you have been waiting in the casket, wailing out to God, weaving together in your imagination his good plans from his good heart, then your path is marked "Worship." Waiting, wailing, and weaving glorify God. We glorify God when we rest in him even in our casket.

> # We magnify him when we trust him so much
> # that we tell him so much.

We magnify him when we trust him so much that we tell him so much. When we wail, we say to the watching world, "Even in suffering I am known by God, belong to God, and loved by God." God's larger story of home groaning and home going is dramatized in Christ's death and resurrection, and in our daily deaths and our daily resurrections.

We exalt Christ when we help one another to weave together grace narratives. We defame him when we forget him. The children of Israel "did not remember the LORD their God, who had rescued them from the hands of all their enemies on every side" (Judges 8:34). We need to constantly stir one another's Christ-memory. Death and resurrection stories are stories of God's deliverance. If we grab for all the gusto now in an attempt to anesthetize our groaning hearts, then we can never testify to a watching world about Christ's resurrection power. But if we will rest in God, awaiting his rescue in his time, then we can shout, "Consider what great things he has done" (1 Samuel 12:24).

Rather than turning to false lovers who tame our souls, we turn to our untamed God who enraptures our souls. Then we give witness—testimony to God's glory, to his personal and universal beauty and majesty.

Exploring Your Spiritual Journey

♦ Think back to a time when God brought hope, joy, newness, and "resurrection" into your life after a casket time.

1. What did God use to bring about your spiritual victory?

2. How did you cooperate with God by waiting, wailing, weaving, and worshipping?

3. How did you depend upon God to defeat Satan's way of regrouping, deadening, despairing, and digging cisterns?

4. How did you begin to see God differently? How did you begin to experience more of his goodness? How were you able to love him more?

5. As you found his strength in your weakness, what was God able to accomplish through you? How was he able to use you as his hero/heroine in his grand adventure?

Assessing Your Spiritual Friends' Thirst Responses

Before you can assist your spiritual friends to handle their thirsts well, you must determine how well or poorly they're currently facing their emptiness. Specifically, you want to diagnose whether they're experiencing and practicing:

+ Regrouping *or* Waiting
+ Deadening *or* Wailing
+ Despairing *or* Weaving
+ Digging Cisterns *or* Worshipping

Based upon the preceding notes, you can conceptualize two basic responses to thirsts:

+ Thirsting without God: Facing Our Thirsts with Our Backs to God
+ Thirsting with God: Facing Our Thirsts Face-to-Face (*coram Deo*) with God

These two categories assist you in assessing your spiritual friends' responses to thirsts. You do this by "collating" biblical ideas about stages of suffering, image bearers (relational, rational, volitional, and emotional), and these two possible ways of trying to quench thirsts.

Are My Spiritual Friends Facing Thirsts without God?: Diagnostic Indicators

Relationally as Romancers, people who face thirsts without facing God will be distant from God, alienated. You'll note that their relationships with God will either be like Job's wife, "Curse God and die" (give up on God, on yourself, and on life), or like Job's "comforters,"—rigid, religious, ritualistic, and pharisaical.

When they do turn to God, it's the "Santa Claus god," or the "Genie-in-a-Bottle god," or the "Spoiling Grandfather god." Their image of God frames a God who must respond on demand to their demand. Their God is the butler upstairs who is at their beck and call, racing to fix them what they need the second they call on the intercom.

They respond to their thirsts with grasping, not groaning. "I want what I want and I want it now!" "I must fill my emptiness or I die."

When we refuse to live supernaturally, naturally we live selfishly. We kill and we covet (James 4:1-4). We manipulate others into feeding our hungry souls. When they fail us, we retaliate against them. "You left me hungry and hurting. Now it's your turn to hurt and go hungry!" We blame and shame (Genesis 3:7-16) trying to guilt others into coming through for us.

Alienated relationally from God and others, we end up tormented in our own souls. Father never designed us to clutch and grasp. Like Jacob, we live a fearful, small life of trying to eke out what we can. Like Gollum in *The Lord of the Rings*, we grow increasingly pathetic the more we allow ourselves to be consumed by quenching our thirsts. As Gollum pitifully cries, "My precious," to the Ring of Power, so we clamor for the secret sauce to satisfy our souls.

Rationally as Dreamers, people who face thirsts without facing God will do everything possible to deny the hole in their souls. They'll shrink life, trying to make it manageable. Like Job's counselors and modern-day "health and wealth gospel thinkers," they might say, "I must be hungry due to God being angry with me. If only I can get him on my good side or get on his good side, then he will bless my socks off." Or like Job's wife, ancient Stoics and Epicureans, and modern-day existentialists, they might conclude, "God? What God! Give up on God. Eat, drink, and be merry, for tomorrow we die."

They'll see life with eye-balls only, refusing to view life from God's eternal perspective. Their works approach to quenching their thirsts will leave them troubled. If they seem to be able to quench some of their thirsts apart from God, then they will incessantly worry about whether they can pull off the next heist on their own. If they recognize their failure to quench their thirsts apart from God, then they are left in the precarious position of needing God while refusing to turn to God.

Volitionally as Creators, people who face their thirsts with their backs to God inevitably turn to false lovers. They live to survive, not to thrive, and certainly not to help others to thrive. Their wills grow weaker and weaker, since God intended our wills to grow strong as we sacrificially give, not as we selfishly hoard. You'll detect selfishness, relational turmoil, and enslavement.

Emotionally as Singers, people who face their thirsts without God end up in despair. They're ever restlessly trying to deal with the God-shaped vacuum in their souls. As Ephesians 4:17-20 details, they then live more and more for the fleeting pleasures of the flesh. Addictive behaviors develop, directly traceable to foolish attempts to quench thirsts without Christ. Mismanaged emotions will abound.

Are My Spiritual Friends Facing Thirsts with God?: Diagnostic Indicators

What diagnostic indicators can you use to discern if your spiritual friends are facing thirsts face-to-face with God? You can answer this question by integrating waiting, wailing, weaving, and worshipping with your understanding of image bearers as relational, rational, volitional, and emotional beings.

Relationally as Romancers, when your spiritual friends face their thirsts face-to-face with God, you'll detect deep longings. Like David, they'll pant after God as the deer pants for streams in the desert. Further, they'll "use" their thirsts not as an excuse to demand, but as further reason to pursue connection with God and others.

Rationally as Dreamers, spiritual friends who face thirsts *coram Deo* are reflective. Their lives are the antithesis of shallow. They face the complexity and confusion of a good God who allows evil and suffering. Like Paul, they'll groan as in the pains of childbirth, pregnant with hope that some day they will see God face-to-face. Their perspective on life will be grace-governed, knowing that every good gift that does come their way comes by way of their good God.

Volitionally as Creators, you'll note how your spiritual friends are engaged with life, God, and others. The weeds of life hurt, but do not thwart. Whether feeling empty or full, they still courageously choose to give to others, strong in the strength of the Lord.

Emotionally as Singers, you'll detect how your *coram Deo* thirsting spiritual friends rest in Christ's promise that he has overcome their world of trouble. They are roused to live fully alive lives that face emptiness and fallenness boldly and honestly. They hurt deeply, even profoundly. Like Jesus, they are men and women of sorrow, acquainted with grief. Also like Jesus, they still choose to die to self and live for others. Like Paul, they find contentment no matter what thirst-state they find themselves in.

In summary, with thirsty *Romancers*, listen for *groaning or gratification*. If they're suffering and not groaning, then they're either denying or gratifying their flesh to shush their spirit. The great women and men of faith in Hebrews 11 delayed their present gratification and longed for a future home. At the beginning of the healing stage, you are face-to-face with a homeless person. How is he or she relating?

With thirsty *Dreamers*, listen for *reflection or anesthetizing*. If they're suffering and not reflecting, then they're either denying or anesthetizing their minds by focusing their brains on earthly pleasures. Fixing spiritual eyes on Jesus (Hebrews 12:1-4) involves considering him—pondering him, reflecting on him, thinking deeply about the choices he made, the relationships he maintained, and the way he thought. As you progress through the healing stage, you're face-to-face with a confused person. How is he or she thinking?

With thirsty *Creators*, listen for *strength or weakness*. If they're suffering and not tempted to give up and give in, then they're either denying, or they've already given up or given in! The author of Hebrews uses the example of Old Testament witnesses (Hebrews 11) along with the example of Christ (Hebrews 12:1-4) to challenge believers to "endure hardship" and to "strengthen feeble arms and weak knees" and to "make every effort to live in peace" (integrated relationships). As you continue in the healing stage, you're face-to-face with a de-energized person. How is he or she choosing?

With thirsty *Singers*, listen for *wailing or silence*. If they're suffering and not wailing, then they're either denying or already emotionally dead. Jesus conquered shame not by silencing it, but by facing it with songs of joy (Hebrews 12:1-4). He experienced both lamentation and celebration. As you move further into the healing stage, you're face-to-face with a hurting soul. How is he or she experiencing?

Box 8:2 summarizes these contrasting approaches to thirst-quenching. Consider it a visual reminder of some of the primary diagnostic indicators to search for and sense as you provide healing soul care to thirsty image bearers.

Box 8:2
Thirsty Image Bearers

Thirsting without God
Facing Our Thirsts with Our Backs to God

Romancer	Dreamer	Creator	Singer
Regrouping	Deadening	Digging Cisterns	Despairing
Alienated	Misinterpretation	Disengaged	Restless
Grasping	Simple	Weak	Incited
Shame Relationships	Works Narratives	Manipulating	Denying Loss
Loving Selfishly	Thinking Carnally	Choosing Meaninglessly	Feeling Fleshly
Tormented	Troubled	Tortured	Trite

Thirsting with God
Facing Our Thirsts Face-to-Face with God: *Coram Deo*

Romancer	Dreamer	Creator	Singer
Longing	Reflection	Engagement	Peace
Reintegration	Reinterpretation	Reengagement	Rest
Groaning	Complexity	Strong	Roused
Grace Relationships	Grace Narratives	Works of Ministry	Wailing Loss
Loving Passionately	Thinking Spiritually	Choosing Hopefully	Feeling Honestly
Hallelujah	Humbled	Holding On/Helped	Hurt

Maturing Your Spiritual Friendship Competency
Diagnosing the Thirsty Soul

1. In the space provided below, record comments that Alonzo might make that could indicate that he was facing his thirsts without facing God. List examples of relational, rational, volitional, and emotional comments and attitudes that could indicate Alonzo's failure to face his thirsts with God.

2. In the space provided below, record comments that Alonzo might make that could indicate that he was facing his thirsts face-to-face with God. List examples of relational, rational, volitional, and emotional comments and attitudes that could indicate Alonzo's success in facing his thirsts *coram Deo*.

3. As you talk with Alonzo, you assess that he's saying in his soul: "I'm thirsting without God." How would you attempt to move with him from:

   a. Regrouping to waiting?

   b. Deadening to wailing?

   c. Despairing to weaving?

   d. Digging cisterns to worshipping?

Healing Intervention

After compassionately discerning the stages of thirsts and the styles of handling unquenched thirsts, you're ready to provide healing treatment and intervention. In the next two chapters, you'll learn and practice many specific healing relational competencies. In the remainder of this chapter, you're learning how to answer the broader question, "What is necessary for my spiritual friends' faith to heal?" You stretch their faith to God's larger story, to Christ himself, through the following *imago Dei* interventions:

- ◆ Romancer: Relational Reintegration
- ◆ Dreamer: Rational Reinterpretation
- ◆ Creator: Volitional Re-engagement
- ◆ Singer: Emotional Refreshing

Relational Reintegration: Healing the Soul by Reintegrating Your Spiritual Friends to God, Themselves, and Others

In sustaining, your spiritual friends felt a distance, an alienation from God, others, and self. Now in relational healing, you stretch your spiritual friends to a higher level of spiritual awareness and experience through *coram Deo* relating. That is, you bring God not only back into the picture, but back into their souls—face-to-face.

Reintegrated Relationship with God: Cross-Based Reintegration

Imagine that you've continued to work with Becky and that you're now in the healing process. Like any honest person, she's asking "What sort of God works good out of evil?"

How do you answer Becky's question? What's involved in relational healing for Becky?

You want to help Becky to explore *an integrated view of God's character*. She needs to see God as a God of absolute grace and perfect holiness. So, you help Becky explore who God is. She'll need to personally grasp the depths of God's sovereign love (Ephesians 3:15-21). She'll need to trust what Luther called, "the inscrutable goodness of the Divine will" (G. Tappert, *Luther: Letters of Spiritual Counseling*, p. 69).

The heart of healing involves turning people back to the heart of God.

Becky also needs *an integrated view of God's relationship to his children*. She needs to see God as a loving Father and gracious Savior. The heart of healing involves turning people back to the heart of God. The heart of God is eternally, infinitely, and ultimately revealed in the Cross of Christ. Becky will need to know the Christ that Luther struggled to know. "I know nothing of any other Christ than he whom the Father gave and who died for me and for my sins, and I know that he is not angry with me, but is kind and gracious to me; for he would not otherwise have had the heart to die for me and for my benefit" (Luther, *Luther as Spiritual Advisor*, pp. 180-181). Becky needs to "fix her eyes on Jesus, the Author and Finisher of her faith" (Hebrews 12:2, author's paraphrase).

Additionally, Becky needs clear biblical images of herself in relationship to God. She is:

♦ The Father's Adult Daughter (Romans 8:14-17)
♦ The Son's Virgin Bride (Ephesians 5:21-33)
♦ The Spirit's Cleansed Disciple (2 Timothy 1:5-7)

Becky needs to see that even in trials, God is dealing with her as a daughter—out of a love relationship and with positive purposes (Hebrews 12:5-11). The next two chapters teach how to accomplish this through using healing trialogues, spiritual conversations, and scriptural explorations.

Reintegrated Relationship with Self: Compassionate Reintegration

Imagine now that you're working with Becky's husband, Jim. He not only needs to experience a reintegration with God, he also needs to encounter relational healing through personal integration. In talking with Jim, you've heard him question himself. "How could I have been so naïve? So stupid to trust Bill (Becky's boss)? Why was Becky so afraid to tell me? Am I such a monster?"

You can't talk Jim out of Satan's cursing narrative. Instead, you have to provide *compassionate reintegration*. Luther called it *viva vox evangeli*—personal encounter as the voice of the Gospel is carried by the human voice. I've called it, "Jesus with skin on him." Your relationship with Jim allows you to become a mirror for him so that he can see himself and God more clearly.

Luther used cure by charity, company, *societas*—human companionship. He practiced the art of ingenious persuasion through human contact, using personal encounter as a way of encountering another person on behalf of God—compassionate reintegration.

In summary, compassionate reintegration helps Jim to sense, "If God be for me, who can be against me? And if you are for me on behalf of God, I could never imagine how much God himself is for me! So I can face whatever is true about me. I can discard whatever is false." The next two chapters teach how to accomplish this through using healing trialogues, spiritual conversations, and scriptural explorations.

Relational Reintegration with Others: Reconciliation

Picture beginning to meet with Jim and Becky jointly. They need to find healing in their personal relationship and in their relationship with Bill. Because they overlap, I'll outline the biblical process of reconciliation, restitution, and forgiveness under the heading of "Volitional Reengagement" (see below). I'll also explore much more about the processes of confession, repentance, and restoration in three chapters on reconciling.

Rational Reinterpretation: Healing the Mind through Biblical Reinterpretation

If relational healing requires *presence* (grace relationships), then rational healing requires *perspective* (grace narratives). The medicine for Becky's mental healing is a grace/faith perspective. Like Joseph in Genesis 50:20, at some point Becky will need to be able to say, "Bill meant this for evil, but Christ can bring about good even in this." She can find comfort deeper than her pain and peace beyond her human understanding.

It won't be easy. Becky will need to have a "Cross focus" where she fixes her eyes on Jesus (Hebrews 12:2). You need to help her to engage all of life through grace-eyes, looking everywhere for evidence of Christ's care. For Christ's Cross is life's final arbiter, interpreter. That one image of Christ dying for her is enough. In the mystery of life, Becky can say, "It is enough for me that I have a gracious

God." The next two chapters teach how to accomplish these goals using healing trialogues, spiritual conversations, and scriptural explorations.

Volitional Reengagement: Healing the Will by Challenging Your Spiritual Friends to Reengage the World

Jim's faith will be tested by his ability to relate intimately to Becky. He'll need to have the courage to choose to say, "Becky, I've let you down. Somehow I haven't been a safe person for you. I want to change. I want our relationship to change." He'll also need to have the courage to face Bill, Becky's boss. This is not something she should have to face alone.

Responsible reengagement includes several biblical concepts. If Jim and Becky have areas where they have been sinned against, then they need to:

♦ Experience Healing from God: 1 Peter 2:19-25
♦ Forgive: Matthew 18:21-35; Romans 12:17-21; 2 Corinthians 2:3-11; Ephesians 4:32; Colossians 3:8-14
♦ Examine Any Logs in Their Eyes/Lives: Matthew 7:1-5
♦ Seek Restoration/Reconciliation: Matthew 18:15-20; 2 Corinthians 6:11-13

If Jim and Becky have become aware of areas of sin in their lives, then they would need:

♦ Repentance/Confession to God: Hosea 14:1-9; 1 John 1:8-10
♦ Acceptance of God's Forgiveness: 1 John 1:8-2:2
♦ To Seek Forgiveness from and Confess Sin to One Another: James 5:16
♦ Restitution: 2 Corinthians 7:10-12

Satan will tempt Becky and Jim to buy the lie that suffering cripples and does so permanently. Becky might falsely think, "I'll never be able to face life again. I'm ruined. A misfit. Unhealthy." God says, "No! I am the Healer. I mend your broken will so that you come out even stronger than before. I'm the God of creative suffering and miraculous healing."

God uses difficulties, discipline, pain, and unpleasantness to produce a harvest of righteousness and peace. Suffering is God's gymnasium of training intended to strengthen people to enter the world courageously. After connecting suffering and training (Hebrews 12:11), the author of Hebrews emphasizes strength and healing. "Therefore, strengthen your feeble arms and weak knees. Make level paths for your feet, so that the lame may not be disabled, but rather healed" (Hebrews 12:12-13).

It's also interesting to note a second connection made in Hebrews 12, this one between suffering and peace. "Make every effort to live in peace with all men and to be holy" (12:14). This, too, counters Satan's lie about suffering. "Your boss did what!? Never, ever forgive him. Never speak to him again! Persecute him. Shun him. Guilt him. Shame him. Avoid him." While God says, "You do everything in your volitional power to reconcile with bold love—love that confronts sin *and* forgives sin."

Emotional Refreshing: Healing Damaged Emotions—Biblical Mood Management

What does healing look like? It looks like renewed connections relationally, renewed thinking rationally, renewed commitments volitionally, and renewed, refreshed moods emotionally.

As the author of Hebrews continues to explore God's way with suffering, he highlights the need to not allow any bitter root to grow up and cause trouble (12:15). He then connects unchecked bitterness with ungoverned emotions and lusts (12:16).

If Becky fails to turn to Christ to quench her thirsts, especially thirsts exacerbated by suffering, she'll find herself in a downward spiral. Relationally she rejects God, rationally she dismisses his goodness, volitionally she refuses his power, and then emotionally she resists his peace, comfort, and rest. Would it be any surprise if her emotions became ungoverned and her evil desires uncontrolled?

Emotional self-awareness and emotional self-control are two hallmarks of the godly Christian. Throughout the next two chapters, you'll learn how relationally competent spiritual friendship promotes emotional maturity.

The rest of Hebrews 12 offers a hint, a glimpse you might not expect. Want to be at peace with God, at peace in your soul, at peace with others? Then fear God! When you fear God, you hold him in absolute awe as the most powerful Lover in the universe. Therefore, you know that your final home, the kingdom that you are receiving, cannot be shaken (12:28), for who can shake God? So you can rest. And rejoice. "You have come to thousands upon thousands of angels in joyful assembly, to the church of the firstborn, whose names are written in heaven" (12:22a-23).

Where We've Been and Where We're Headed

Having diagnosed the *stages* of healing, now it is time to explore the *process* of healing. Chapters Nine and Ten teach you how to help your spiritual friend's faith to heal through *RESTS* relational competencies:

- ◆ *R*   Relational Treatment Planning: John 2:23-25
- ◆ *E*   Encouraging Communication: Ephesians 4:29
- ◆ *S*   Story Reinterpreting: Philippians 3; 2 Corinthians 10
- ◆ *T*   Thirsts Spiritual Conversations: Hebrews 10:24-25
- ◆ *S*   Stretching Scriptural Explorations: Hebrews 8

Maturing Your Spiritual Friendship Competency
Stages of Healing

♦ If you are working through this material individually, then instead of role-playing, use the space after each scenario to write your responses to each situation.

♦ Scenario: You're meeting with Becky's husband, Jim. You've been through the sustaining process with him. You sense that he is battling hard in Christ's strength to handle his thirsty soul in a godly way (healing).

1. With a partner, role-play how you might use Hebrews 12 and other passages to help Jim to explore how to relationally reintegrate with God, self, and others.

2. With a partner, role-play how you might use Hebrews 12 and other passages to help Jim to explore how to rationally reinterpret what happened to Becky and God's view of it.

3. With a partner, role-play how you might use Hebrews 12 and other passages to help Jim to explore how to volitionally reengage his world.

4. With a partner, role-play how you might use Hebrews 12 and other passages to help Jim to explore how to emotionally rest in and be refreshed by God.

Chapter Nine

Healing Treatment and Intervention
RESTS Relational Competencies, Part I

"The Christian clergy have been a talkative lot. But for almost twenty centuries they have spent more time listening to people than preaching to them, and from the beginning they discovered that it was hard to listen, but even harder to respond appropriately to what they were hearing" (E. Brooks Holifield, *A History of Pastoral Care in America*, p. 15).

God Questions

Picture Alonzo. For weeks you've been walking beside him empathizing with his level one and level two suffering. Because of you, he's not walking through the valley of the shadow of death alone. God is enabling you to sustain him, forestalling retreat into despair.

Now Alonzo is asking hard questions. Honest questions. God questions. Casting aside doubt, he wants to know the nature of the hope that Christ offers him. Though the cancer infecting his body may be incurable, the doubt invading his soul can be healed. How do you encourage him to find God? What relational competencies will you need to artfully practice healing as you continue to journey with your brother?

GRACE summarizes sustaining relational competencies, which is fitting because Alonzo needs grace to help in his time of need. *RESTS* summarizes healing relational competencies, equally fitting because he needs to rest in the hope he has in Christ. Sustaining seeks to help suffering Alonzo to acknowledge, "It's normal to hurt." Healing seeks to assist him to believe, "It's possible to hope."

In healing, you address the question, "How can my spiritual friends and I engage in *RESTS* relationships and conversations that heal their faith by offering hope that rests in Christ?" *RESTS* stands for the following five healing relational competencies:

- ◆ *R*   Relational Treatment Planning: John 2:23-25
- ◆ *E*   Encouraging Communication: Ephesians 4:29
- ◆ *S*   Story Reinterpreting: Philippians 3; 2 Corinthians 10
- ◆ *T*   Thirsts Spiritual Conversations: Hebrews 10:24-25
- ◆ *S*   Stretching Scriptural Explorations: Hebrews 8

Exploring Your Spiritual Journey

1. Think about an issue you're facing. Though this situation screams, "Life is bad!" what evidences are you seeing that "God is good"?

2. How is the issue you're facing helping you to cling to Christ, depend on him, and hunger and thirst for him?

3. What would it be like to worship God in the middle of your situation?

4. Read Psalms 42 and 43 (Psalms of Thirst). Write your own Thirst Psalm based upon Psalms 42-43, relating it to the issue you're facing.

Relational Treatment Planning: Mutuality in Hope Building—John 2:23-25

Relational treatment planning is so much more than altering the symptoms of a disease, promoting a more balanced personality, or exposing unconscious causes underlying surface symptoms. Relational treatment cooperates with God in the process of sanctification. Biblical treatment empathizes with, encourages, exposes, and empowers spiritual friends so that they move toward communion with Christ and conformity to Christ. They come to love him more and reflect him better. Those are treatment plans and goals worth pursuing.

Given the nature of spiritual friendship, there are three types of treatment plans to learn and implement:

- Spiritual Friendship Treatment Planning (Chapter Nine)
- Soul Care Treatment Planning (Chapter Nine)
- Spiritual Direction Treatment Planning (Chapter Fifteen)

By *Spiritual Friendship* treatment planning, I mean the overall focus and goals of spiritual friendship encompassing sustaining, healing, reconciling, and guiding. *Soul Care* treatment planning describes specific sustaining and healing goals for "sufferology" (the evils people have suffered). *Spiritual Direction* treatment planning depicts specific reconciling and guiding goals for "sancticology" (the sins people have committed).

Spiritual Friendship Treatment Planning

Relational treatment planning builds upon compassionate discernment. Spiritual friends diagnose the state of the soul (relational, rational, volitional, emotional) in the world (desert/sustaining, thirst/healing, cistern/reconciling, and spring/guiding). Thus, spiritual friendship treatment plans are *imago Dei* treatment plans with two primary areas of focus and eight primary goals.

- *Focus One*: Discipling people so their inner lives are increasingly like the inner life of Christ:
  - Goal One: *Relational* Romancers who love God and others passionately while accepting their acceptance in Christ—purified affections.
    - Souls captivated by God, saying "I enjoy you, Father."
  - Goal Two: *Rational* Dreamers who think imaginatively while wisely perceiving life from Christ's perspective—wise mindsets.
    - Hearts enraptured by Christ's loving adventure narrative saying, "I trust you, Savior."
  - Goal Three: *Volitional* Creators who choose courageously by pursuing God's purposes with the Holy Spirit's power—other-centered purposes.
    - Wills captured by and surrendered to the Spirit saying, "Empower me, Holy Spirit."
  - Goal Four: *Emotional* Singers who experience deeply as they understand and manage their moods for God's glory—managed mood states.
    - Emotions fully opened to the Triune Lover of their souls saying, "I rest in you, God."
- *Focus Two*: Providing soul care and spiritual direction:
  - Goal One: *Sustaining* people so they know that "It's normal to hurt."
  - Goal Two: *Healing* people so they know that "It's possible to hope."
  - Goal Three: *Reconciling* people so they know that "It's horrible to sin, but wonderful to be forgiven."
  - Goal Four: *Guiding* people so they know that "It's supernatural to mature."

When you're sitting in front of Alonzo and the complexity and intensity overwhelms you, where do you focus? Simplify by focusing on the eight goals of *imago Dei* diagnosis. Often in a spiritual friendship meeting you're wondering, "What's a spiritual friend to do? Where are we in the process? Where should we go next?" Simplify by pursuing the eight goals of *imago Dei* diagnosis. They are the core goals, results, purposes, and desires that you pray for and work toward as you offer spiritual friendship.

Yes, spiritual friendship is an art. However, some make it so much art that they lose sight of the truth behind the art—the biblical truth about image bearers in a fallen world. Even the best artists follow a few aesthetic principles and obey a few basic rules of "design." In all creativity, people integrate form and function.

Spiritual friends follow a few aesthetic principles, a few basic biblical rules of God's design. Simplifying them even more, the following eight goals are signposts to follow:

- Relational Beings: Affections/Lovers
- Rational Beings: Mindsets
- Volitional Beings: Purposes/Pathways
- Emotional Beings: Mood States
- Sustaining: "It's normal to hurt."
- Healing: "It's possible to hope."
- Reconciling: "It's horrible to sin, but wonderful to be forgiven."
- Guiding: "It's supernatural to mature."

There are some basic ways to keep focused and to drill these goals into your mindset as a spiritual friend. They include:

- The Disclosure Statement (Welcome Form)
- The Spiritual Friendship Treatment Plan Sheet
- The Spiritual Friendship Tape Self-Evaluation
- The Spiritual Friendship Evaluation (Evaluations from "Clients")

Relational Treatment Planning and the Disclosure Statement (Welcome Form)

People often ask, "Do you tell your clients/parishioners/spiritual friends that these are your goals?" Absolutely. Spiritual friends work together, mutually. Ethical integrity demands a disclosure of treatment goals. One of the best ways to accomplish this is through a *Disclosure Statement* or *Welcome Form* distributed and discussed during the first meeting.

The two-page *Welcome Form* (see pages 174-175) provides a sample *Disclosure Statement* explaining your approach and obtaining your spiritual friend's commitment to work from that perspective. It is crucial to spend time explaining and discussing it at the start of your first meeting.

Relational Treatment Planning and the Spiritual Friendship Treatment Plan Sheet

Sometimes the problem in intervention is not ascertaining the person's agreement to work toward biblical treatment goals. Sometimes pastors/counselors/spiritual friends fail to follow their own stated goals. Other times they inconsistently follow them. The two-page *Spiritual Friendship Treatment Plan Sheet* (see pages 176-177) keeps pastors/counselors/spiritual friends on track toward biblical goals, toward relational treatment planning and intervention.

Before meeting with your spiritual friend, complete the top part of the front side of your *Spiritual Friendship Treatment Plan Sheet*. It contains basic "client identification information" as well as your summary regarding where you might focus during this meeting, based upon your reflections from your past meetings. Notice that it also has room to record your spiritual friend's goals—thus enhancing mutuality in treatment planning.

You can use the middle part of the front page either during or immediately after (or both) your meeting. Record here a synopsis of central points that arose and essential insights you gleaned during your meeting.

Use the bottom of the front page to remind yourself of directions you and your spiritual friend determined to take between now and the next meeting. You can also begin to work on treatment plans for the upcoming week. Additionally, you'll find a place to record your next meeting date and time.

The backside of the *Spiritual Friendship Treatment Plan Sheet* uses basic *Spiritual Friends* concepts as a format for you to diagnose how your spiritual friend is doing and to plan treatment as you work with your spiritual friend. Every meeting will not cover every area. You can highlight what was most pertinent, insightful, and moving. Over time, you can collate your records and plans, noting themes and movement on your spiritual friend's path to maturity.

Relational Treatment Planning and the Spiritual Friendship Tape Self-Evaluation

Wise spiritual friends often tape (audio or video) themselves (with their friend's permission). After taping, you can use the sample *Spiritual Friendship Tape Self-Evaluation Form* (see pages 178-179) to evaluate yourself using *imago Dei* goals.

The front side is more "quantitative." On it, you simply list the number of times you focused on a certain aspect of spiritual friendship. This is especially helpful for beginning spiritual friends/counselors to determine what their natural tendencies lean toward. Of course, some sessions will lend themselves more to sustaining, for instance. So, it is important to track your focus over time—over several meetings with your spiritual friend.

The backside of this two-sided form is more "qualitative." Here you evaluate not how many times, but how well you sense you are providing major aspects of spiritual friendship. You can also use this form to have other people, like co-workers, supervisors, professors, lab encouragement partners, and lab mentors, evaluate your spiritual friendship/counseling.

Relational Treatment Planning and the Spiritual Friendship Evaluation

On page 180, you'll find a one-page *Spiritual Friendship Evaluation Form* that you can give to your spiritual friend to evaluate you, especially at the commencement (termination) of your meetings together. Again, you'll note how this form uses the basic treatment thinking of spiritual friendship to assess your relational competencies.

All of these forms are aids meant to help you to follow a biblical treatment planning methodology in spiritual friendship. Your "goal" is to help your spiritual friends to mature relationally, rationally, volitionally, and emotionally as they live in a fallen world of desert (sustaining), thirst (healing), cistern (reconciling), and spring (guiding).

"Welcome!"

We welcome you to the *Spiritual Friendship Ministry* of Grace Fellowship Church. We desire to be used by God to "speak his truth in love." We know that the path to maturity is often steep and rough and at times filled with pain and confusion.

However, there really are answers. Our basic premise is that the Bible is *a sufficient guide to relational living*. There really is a route to life. Our Lord is that *way*. Christ is the *truth* who frees us to love. He is the *life* who satisfies the deepest thirsts of our soul.

Spiritual Friendship Ministries Offered

As a *ministry* of Grace Fellowship Church, our services are *free*. Because we are a discipleship ministry of a *local church*, and because our human resources are limited, our first priority is to those who are members and/or regular attendees of our church. We offer to you:

♦ Individual spiritual friendship regarding spiritual and personal issues.
♦ Pre-marital spiritual friendship.
♦ Marital spiritual friendship.
♦ Family (parental) spiritual friendship (with children under the age of thirteen we work primarily with the parents and/or with the parents and children).
♦ Adolescent spiritual friendship.
♦ Small group discipleship (see our brochure on various groups).
♦ A referral network.

Confidentiality

All communications between you and our *Spiritual Friendship Ministry* personnel will be held in strict confidence, unless you (or a parent in the case of a minor) give authorization to release this information. The exceptions to this would be that instance in which either you or someone else was felt to be in immediate danger secondary to your actions. In this instance, it would be our ethical and biblical responsibility to act to try to ensure the safety of these individuals. A second exception would be that instance in which you evidenced habitual unrepentant rebellion against the Word of God. In this instance, it would be our biblical duty to initiate our church's restoration procedure in order to encourage repentance and restoration (see our statement: *Restoring the Purity of Christ's Bride*).

Appointments

Our lay and pastoral spiritual friends work by scheduled appointments. Of course, in emergencies, exceptions are made. We need your prompt and consistent participation in your scheduled meetings. Please contact our office 24 hours in advance if you must cancel an appointment. This will allow us to schedule another individual during this time.

If you will arrive 30 minutes early for your first appointment, you will then be able to complete any necessary forms. During your initial meeting, you will determine the goals you would like to work toward. After approximately five sessions, you and your spiritual friend will evaluate your progress toward those goals and together determine what further action needs to be taken.

Our Commitments to You in Spiritual Friendship

You've read our term "spiritual friendship." We'd like to explain what we mean by it. In spiritual friendship we commit to the historic roles of *soul care* and *spiritual direction* through:

♦ *Sustaining*: Empathizing with your suffering, helping you to understand that *"It's normal to hurt."*
♦ *Healing*: Enlightening current ways of viewing life to encourage you to see life from a more biblical perspective, helping you to know that *"It's possible to hope."*
♦ *Reconciling*: Examining and exposing your current responses to life and suggesting new ways of handling problems, helping you to see that *"It's horrible to sin, but wonderful to be forgiven."*
♦ *Guiding*: Exploring how and empowering you to mature through Christ, helping you to grasp that *"It's supernatural to mature."*

Because we care about *you*, our desire is for you to be drawn closer to Christ and to become more like Christ, which we see as *your inner life increasingly reflecting the inner life of Christ*:

♦ *Relational Maturity*: Loving God wholeheartedly and loving others as yourself.
♦ *Rational Maturity*: Wisely living according to the truth of Christ's Gospel of grace.
♦ *Volitional Maturity*: Courageously choosing to pursue God's purposes in your life through the Spirit's power.
♦ *Emotional Maturity*: Deeply and honestly experiencing life with integrity, fully open to God while managing your moods for God's glory.

Your Commitments to Christ, to Yourself, and to Us in Spiritual Friendship

We ask that you commit to:

♦ Honestly and openly sharing your hurts and struggles.
♦ Evaluating your own emotions, actions, goals, beliefs, images, relationships, and longings.
♦ Actively participating in the development of renewed emotions, actions, convictions, and affections.
♦ Coming to each meeting prepared to review your progress throughout the last week (including the completion of personalized "homework" assignments) and prepared to share your goals for the present meeting.

Because the Scriptures teach that growth in Christ requires all the resources of the Body of Christ (not only spiritual friendship, but also discipleship, worship, stewardship, ambassadorship, and fellowship), we believe that it is essential that those seeking spiritual friendship at our church commit themselves to the following:

♦ Regular church attendance.
♦ Active participation in our ABFs (Adult Bible Fellowship/Sunday School).
♦ Participation in at least one of our small groups (we'll discuss the appropriate group for you).

We ask that you sign below to indicate your agreement with and commitment to our *Spiritual Friendship Ministry*.

Your Name	Parent if Minor	Date

Spiritual Friendship Treatment Plan Sheet

Spiritual Friend's Name: _____
Session Number: _____
Date: _____

Pre-Meeting Information

Spiritual Friend's Review/Update/Report:

Your Review/Summary:

Spiritual Friend's Goals:

Your Goals/Focus:

Spiritual Friendship Meeting Notes

Spiritual Friendship Post-Session Homework Assignment(s)

Next Meeting Date and Time: _____
Continue on the Backside with Post-Meeting Diagnosis and Treatment Plan

Spiritual Friendship Post-Meeting Diagnosis and Treatment Plan

- **Sustaining: "It's Normal to Hurt."**

  - Diagnosis: I discerned . . .

  - Treatment Plan: We need to work on . . .

- **Healing: "It's Possible to Hope."**

  - Diagnosis: I discerned . . .

  - Treatment Plan: We need to work on . . .

- **Reconciling: "It's Horrible to Sin, but Wonderful to Be Forgiven."**

  - Diagnosis: I discerned . . .

  - Treatment Plan: We need to work on . . .

- **Guiding: "It's Supernatural to Mature."**

  - Diagnosis: I discerned . . .

  - Treatment Plan: We need to work on . . .

- **Relationally: Romancers, Affections/Lovers, Spiritual, Social, Self-Aware**

  - Diagnosis: I discerned . . .

  - Treatment Plan: We need to work on . . .

- **Rationally: Dreamers, Mindsets, Images, Beliefs**

  - Diagnosis: I discerned . . .

  - Treatment Plan: We need to work on . . .

- **Volitionally: Creators, Purposes/Pathways, Goals, Actions**

  - Diagnosis: I discerned . . .

  - Treatment Plan: We need to work on . . .

- **Emotionally: Singers, Mood States, Awareness, Management**

  - Diagnosis: I discerned . . .

  - Treatment Plan: We need to work on . . .

Spiritual Friendship Tape Self-Evaluation

Spiritual Friendship Self-Evaluation, Part I: Interaction Log

1. Record the number of times your interactions focused upon:

    a. Sustaining: *"It's normal to hurt."*   _____

    b. Healing: *"It's possible to hope."*   _____

    c. Reconciling:

        1.) Part A: *"It's horrible to sin."*   _____

        2.) Part B: *"It's wonderful to be forgiven."*   _____

    d. Guiding: *"It's supernatural to mature."*   _____

2. Record the number of times your interactions focused upon:

    a. Creation: God's Design   _____

    b. Fall: Person's Depravity   _____

    c. Redemption: Renewed Dignity   _____

3. Record the number of times your interactions focused upon:

    a. Relational Longings (Affections/Lovers):

        1.) Spiritual   _____

        2.) Social   _____

        3.) Self-Aware   _____

    b. Rational Concepts (Mindsets):

        1.) Images   _____

        2.) Beliefs   _____

    c. Volitional Choices (Purposes/Pathways):

        1.) Goals   _____

        2.) Actions   _____

    d. Emotional Responses (Mood States):   _____

    e. Physical Issues (Habituated Tendencies):   _____

Spiritual Friendship Self-Evaluation, Part II: Personal Assessment

Using the scale below, evaluate yourself in the following spiritual friendship areas:

1. I disagree strongly
2. I disagree
3. I'm not sure
4. I agree
5. I agree strongly

_____ 1. Sustaining: I listened to and really sensed my spiritual friend's hurts.

_____ 2. Sustaining: I climbed in the casket with my spiritual friend, empathizing with and embracing my spiritual friend's pain.

_____ 3. Healing: I encouraged my spiritual friend to embrace God.

_____ 4. Healing: I trialogued (spiritual conversations and scriptural explorations) with my spiritual friend encouraging him/her to see God's perspective on his/her suffering.

_____ 5. Reconciling: I exposed the horrors of my spiritual friend's sin.

_____ 6. Reconciling: I dispensed grace, showing how wonderful it is to be forgiven.

_____ 7. Guiding: I enlightened my spiritual friend to God's supernatural work of maturity.

_____ 8. Guiding: I equipped and empowered my spiritual friend to mature.

_____ 9. Relational: I effectively used the concept of "affections/lovers" to assess and expose the relational motivations in my spiritual friend's soul.

_____ 10. Rational: I effectively used the concept of "mindsets" to assess and expose the rational direction (images and beliefs) in my spiritual friend's heart.

_____ 11. Volitional: I effectively used the concept of "purposes/pathways" to assess and expose the volitional interactions (styles of relating, goals, purposeful behaviors) in my spiritual friend's will.

_____ 12. Emotional: I effectively used the concept of "mood states" to assess and expose the emotional reactions in my spiritual friend's moods.

_____ 13. Truth/Discernment: I used theological insight to understand the spiritual dynamics and root causes related to my spiritual friend.

_____ 14. Love/Compassion: I compassionately identified with my spiritual friend—I was engaged, involved, and related from my soul.

_____ 15. Overall: I would go to myself for spiritual friendship.

Spiritual Friendship Evaluation

As spiritual friends, we desire to grow in our ability to speak the truth in love. Honest feedback from those we minister to is very helpful. Please evaluate your spiritual friend based upon the following scale:

1. I disagree strongly
2. I disagree
3. I'm not sure
4. I agree
5. I agree strongly

_____ 1. My spiritual friend listened to and sensed my hurts.

_____ 2. My spiritual friend empathized with and embraced my pain.

_____ 3. My spiritual friend encouraged me to embrace God in my pain.

_____ 4. My spiritual friend encouraged me to see God's perspective on my suffering.

_____ 5. My spiritual friend courageously, yet humbly, exposed areas of sin in my heart.

_____ 6. My spiritual friend helped me to see the wonders of God's grace so I could experience God's forgiveness.

_____ 7. My spiritual friend helped me to see that I can mature only through Christ's resurrection power.

_____ 8. My spiritual friend equipped and empowered me to love like Christ.

_____ 9. My spiritual friend helped me to assess the deepest longings of my soul exposing the false idols of my heart as well as my soul's deepest thirsts for Christ.

_____ 10. My spiritual friend helped me to assess my images and beliefs enlightening me to foolish beliefs and helping me to renew my mind according to Christ's wisdom.

_____ 11. My spiritual friend helped me to assess the goals and purposes behind my behaviors and relationships helping me to put off old, self-centered ways and to put on new, other-centered patterns.

_____ 12. My spiritual friend helped me to assess my moods assisting me to become more emotionally self-aware and better able to manage my moods.

_____ 13. My spiritual friend used biblical principles to understand the spiritual dynamics and root causes at work in my life.

_____ 14. My spiritual friend compassionately identified with me engaging me with deep personal involvement and relating to me with Christ-like love.

_____ 15. The goals that we set for spiritual friendship were successfully met.

_____ 16. Because of our spiritual friendship relationship, I love Christ more.

_____ 17. Because of our spiritual friendship relationship, I love other people more.

_____ 18. Because of our spiritual friendship relationship, I more readily accept my acceptance in Christ (more deeply knowing and enjoying who I am in Christ and who I am to Christ).

_____ 19. I would go to my spiritual friend again for spiritual friendship.

_____ 20. I would recommend my spiritual friend to others for spiritual friendship.

Please share any additional suggestions, thoughts, questions, or comments (feel free to use the back):

Your Name: _____ (Optional) Spiritual Friend's Name: _____

Maturing Your Spiritual Friendship Competency
Relational Spiritual Friendship Treatment Planning

1. If you are working through this material individually, then instead of role-playing, use the space below to write your responses. Otherwise, with a partner, role-play using the *Welcome Form* to begin a first meeting. Cover it in "user-friendly language." Clarify any questions your spiritual friend has and explain the focus, goals, and treatment plans that you will pursue. After doing so, respond to the following questions:

   a. What was easy? What would you keep the same on the *Welcome Form*?

   b. What was difficult? What would you change/reword on the *Welcome Form*?

2. Use the *Spiritual Friendship Tape Self-Evaluation Form*, both sides, to evaluate yourself. You can use it based upon your most recent spiritual friendship meeting (whether you have a tape or not, though a tape is most helpful). Or, you can use it based upon how you see your overall spiritual friendship competencies at this point.

3. With a client, parishioner, spiritual friend, protégé, mentor, supervisor, or encouragement partner, use the *Spiritual Friendship Evaluation Form* to gain feedback Again, you can use it based upon your most recent spiritual friendship meeting or based upon your overall spiritual friendship to this point.

Soul Care Treatment Planning

In soul care, treatment planning focuses on how your spiritual friends are handling the evils they are suffering. Through sustaining and healing, you empathize with and encourage them to face their suffering face-to-face with God and to turn to Christ for the quenching of their thirsts.

Treatment planning in soul care, as I've emphasized, has more to do with care than cure. Cure is the sovereign work of Christ. Care is the sympathetic calling of Christ's people.

Removal of symptoms, though wonderful when it occurs, is not the "solution" to target. Your treatment plans in soul care have other, deeper, *relational* aims, such as:

♦ Caring about the evils your spiritual friends have suffered.
♦ Helping your spiritual friends to experience the truth that "God is good even when life is bad."
♦ Compassionately identifying with your spiritual friends in their pain and redirecting them to Christ and the Body of Christ to sustain and heal their faith so they experience communion with Christ and conformity to Christ as they love God (exalt him by enjoying and entrusting themselves to him) and others.

What does soul care treatment planning look like? What is it that you want to "do," want to "accomplish," when your spiritual friends bring you the evils they have suffered? What are the "goals" of soul care for sufferology?

Chapter Four emphasized diagnosis using the concept of "compassionate discernment." It highlighted how to diagnose the state of the soul (relational, rational, volitional, and emotional) in the world (desert/sustaining, thirst/healing, cistern/reconciling, and spring/guiding).

Chapter Five presented diagnosis for sustaining, including how to diagnose level one and level two suffering. It focused upon diagnosing how your suffering spiritual friend was handling life in the desert as a relational, rational, volitional, and emotional being. It used candor, complaint, cry, and communion *versus* denial, anger, works, and alienation as the model for sustaining diagnosis.

Chapter Eight shared diagnosis for healing. It focused on how your thirsty spiritual friend was dealing with thirsts as a relational, rational, volitional, and emotional being. It used waiting, wailing, weaving, and worshipping *versus* immediate gratification, anesthetizing, despairing, and cistern digging as the pattern for diagnosis in healing.

Spiritual friendship unites these categories to develop a two-level, eight-stage soul care treatment plan: *Sufferology Soul Care Treatment Plan Sheet* (see pages 184-185). You can use this form to diagnose where your spiritual friends are and to plan how to move them to where God wants them to be. The vignette that follows illustrates its use.

Imagine that you're counseling Juan. Juan's been a committed believer for years. Lately he's been hammered by life—loss, after loss, after loss. Not quite Job-like losses, but daily casket experiences, nonetheless. Where do you start? What does your soul care treatment plan look like?

Start where Juan is—level one suffering. Using spiritual listening competencies, draw out Juan's external losses. He explains that his last child has left for college—all three children are now out-of-state; he was denied the promotion at work and it now looks like, at his age, he will never enter management; his parents have recently moved away, retiring to Florida; the church he attends just endured a split; and his best friends are moving to California.

Using your sustaining relational competencies, you connect with and embrace Juan. As you do, you start to tap into his level two suffering. How is he responding internally to his external losses? He's beginning to blame himself, wondering if he is driving people away. He's also shaming himself, telling himself that he is worthless since he will never enter management. He's wrestling with God. "Why would God move all my connections away at the same time and not give me any options?"

Continue with the four stages of sustaining so you can help Juan to grieve deeply, biblically. He's well on his way toward candor already. He's not in denial. He needs you to join him in his valley of the shadow of death. As you join him, help him to be fully honest with God—complaint. Trialogue with him concerning his questions about God's plan in his life.

Now that Juan's openly sharing his soul with his Savior, use spiritual conversations and scriptural explorations to encourage him to cry out to God. To cry, "Uncle." To admit his absolute dependence upon a God who will never leave him nor forsake him.

As your spiritual friendship merges from sustaining to healing, you'll move Juan to communion. Help him to embrace and be embraced by the God who comes when he cries.

This is the goal of sustaining—drawing the line in the sand of retreat. The world beats Juan down then tempts him to "Curse God and die." Sustaining entices him instead to "Commune with God and live." How do you know that sustaining has been or is being "successful"? When Juan is facing suffering face-to-face with God. No denial. No retreat. Raw honesty. Courageous integrity. Desperate dependency. Clinging communion.

Great start, but there's more "grace-work" to be done in Juan's heart. As you move to healing, Juan needs to learn the humbling experience of waiting on God. God comes when Juan cries, but he does not necessarily "cure" his ache. He will not necessarily give Juan the promotion, move his kids back home, or return his parents. Juan must resist the temptation to quench his own thirst through immediate gratification.

As he waits, Juan wails. He groans. He faces not only his losses, but also his thirsts. He admits that he's not home yet. That he longs for the day when there will be no more sorrow, no more separation. Now he is grieving and groaning deeply. Such wailing leads to weakness, brokenness, and dependency. When Juan is weak, then God is strong.

Throwing himself on God's mercy, Juan experiences grace relationships with Christ. He also needs grace narratives, weaving. Not answers or explanations, but spiritual eyes to believe by faith that God is good and has good purposes for Juan's losses. Not fully seeing God's plan, he trusts God's heart.

His faith now not only survives, it thrives. So he worships and works. He loves God and ministers to others. He allows his losses to entice him to deeper connection with others and communion with Christ.

> **This is the goal of healing—creative suffering—surrendering to God's sovereign plan to work good out of evil, to create beauty from ashes.**

This is the goal of healing—creative suffering—surrendering to God's sovereign plan to work good out of evil, to create beauty from ashes. You know that healing has been and is being "successful" when Juan faces suffering face-to-face with God *and* becomes more like Christ in the process.

You can use the *Sufferology Soul Care Treatment Plan Sheet* to record Juan's progress, or lack thereof, as you minister to him. Again, it keeps it simple by simply collating in one place the two levels of suffering and the eight stages of grieving. Though simple, it helps you to focus your diagnosis, treatment planning, and interventions.

Some may be wondering. "Wait a minute! I see idols in Juan's heart. Sin in his attitude. What ever happened to sin?" Sin issues must be explored. They will be in reconciling and guiding through *Sancticology Spiritual Direction Treatment Planning*. In a given meeting, you might explore sin in the same session where you explore suffering. However, for the sake of teaching in a logical sequence, the focus now is on suffering treatment planning. Spiritual friendship neither ignores sin, nor suffering.

Sufferology Soul Care Treatment Plan Sheet
Part I: Sustaining Treatment Planning

Sustaining in Suffering—"It's Normal to Hurt and Necessary to Grieve."

Stage	Unhealthy Desert Suffering	Healthy Desert Suffering
Stage One	Denial	Candor: Honest with Self
Stage Two	Anger	Complaint: Honest to God
Stage Three	Bargaining/Works	Cry: Asking God for Help
Stage Four	Depression/Alienation	Comfort: Receiving God's Help

Level One Suffering: External Suffering

♦ Circumstances: What's happening *to* my spiritual friend? Where is the fallen world falling on my spiritual friend?

Sufferology Diagnostic Indicators: Sustaining

♦ Sustaining Stage One: Is my spiritual friend practicing denial or candor?

♦ Sustaining Stage Two: Is my spiritual friend practicing anger or complaint?

♦ Sustaining Stage Three: Is my spiritual friend practicing bargaining/works or cry?

♦ Sustaining Stage Four: Is my spiritual friend practicing depression/alienation or comfort?

Sufferology Treatment Plan Evaluators: Sustaining

♦ Sustaining Stage One: How can I move with my spiritual friend from denial to candor? How well am I doing so?

♦ Sustaining Stage Two: How can I move with my spiritual friend from anger to complaint? How well am I doing so?

♦ Sustaining Stage Three: How can I move with my spiritual friend from works to bargaining/cry? How well am I doing so?

♦ Sustaining Stage Four: How can I move with my spiritual friend from depression/alienation to comfort? How well am I doing so?

Sufferology Soul Care Treatment Plan Sheet
Part II: Healing Treatment Planning

Healing in Suffering—"It's Possible to Hope in the Midst of Grief."

Stage	Unhealthy Thirst Responses	Healthy Thirst Responses
Stage One	Regrouping/Immediate Gratification	Waiting: Trusting with Faith
Stage Two	Deadening/Anesthetizing	Wailing: Groaning with Hope
Stage Three	Despairing/Doubting	Weaving: Perceiving with Grace
Stage Four	Digging Cisterns/False Lovers	Worshipping: Engaging with Love

Level Two Suffering: Internal Suffering

♦ Condemnation: What's happening *in* my spiritual friend? Where is the messy world messing with my spiritual friend's mind?

Sufferology Diagnostic Indicators: Healing

♦ Healing Stage One: Is my spiritual friend practicing regrouping or waiting?

♦ Healing Stage Two: Is my spiritual friend practicing deadening or wailing?

♦ Healing Stage Three: Is my spiritual friend practicing despairing or weaving?

♦ Healing Stage Four: Is my spiritual friend practicing digging cisterns or worshipping?

Sufferology Treatment Plan Evaluators: Healing

♦ Healing Stage One: How can I move with my spiritual friend from regrouping to waiting? How well am I doing so?

♦ Healing Stage Two: How can I move with my spiritual friend from deadening to wailing? How well am I doing so?

♦ Healing Stage Three: How can I move with my spiritual friend from despairing to weaving? How well am I doing so?

♦ Healing Stage Four: How can I move with my spiritual friend from digging cisterns to worshipping? How well am I doing so?

Maturing Your Spiritual Friendship Competency
Relational Soul Care Treatment Planning and Intervention

♦ Summarize a level one area of suffering (or a combination of several level one areas of suffering) that you are now, or have recently, endured. Write about your level two suffering and the eight stages that you have gone through or are going through in your own soul care process.

♦ Then, if you are working with a partner, take turns sharing and working through the ten areas of relational soul care treatment planning, helping each other to move through the soul care process.

1. Level One Suffering: I have been facing the following losses and crosses (separation experiences):

2. Level Two Suffering: Responding to these losses, my inner battle has been (spiritual depression):

3. Stage One Sustaining: How can I move from denial to candor?

4. Stage Two Sustaining: How can I move from anger to complaint?

5. Stage Three Sustaining: How can I move from bargaining/works to cry?

6. Stage Four Sustaining: How can I move from depression/alienation to comfort?

7. Stage One Healing: How can I move from regrouping/immediate gratification to waiting?

8. Stage Two Healing: How can I move from deadening/anesthetizing to wailing?

9. Stage Three Healing: How can I move from despairing/doubting to weaving?

10. Stage Four Healing: How can I move from digging cisterns/false lovers to worshipping?

Encouraging Communication: Hope-Based Interactions—Ephesians 4:29

Since people do come to us with *problem-saturated stories*, we need to *infuse hope*. How we define situations is critical. Do we so define problems that we make them unsolvable? Modern Christianity has lost hope, succumbing to a pessimistic, negative, and critical mood. This is so unlike New Testament Christianity:

- "My grace is sufficient for you, for my power is made perfect in weakness" (2 Corinthians 12:9).
- "Being confident of this, that he who began a good work in you will carry it on to completion until the day of Christ Jesus" (Philippians 1:6).
- "I can do everything through him who gives me strength" (Philippians 4:13).
- "And my God will meet all your needs according to his glorious riches in Christ Jesus" (Philippians 4:19).
- "You, dear children, are from God and have overcome them, because the one who is in you is greater than the one who is in the world" (1 John 4:4).
- "For everyone born of God overcomes the world. This is the victory that has overcome the world, even our faith" (1 John 5:4).

Lately I've pondered why we're blind to our resources in Christ.

- We're not praying for enlightenment to know the power and love of God (Ephesians 1:15-23; 3:14-21).
- Satan blinds us to God's good work in us (2 Corinthians 4:1-18). (It's vital to note the context here: "Do not lose hope! Hope in the glorious power of the Gospel of Christ!")
- We forget that Paul's relational principles (Ephesians 5:22-6:9) are sandwiched between the Spirit's filling and our spiritual armor (Ephesians 5:18-21 and Ephesians 6:10-18).
- We fail to stir up, provoke, encourage, and fan into flame the gift of God within each other (2 Timothy 1:6-7; Hebrews 3:12-19; 10:24-25).
- We look at life with eyeballs only rather than with spiritual eyes (2 Corinthians 10:3-7).

I've also reflected upon how God's meta-narrative ("I am generously good and gracious") relates to hope-based spiritual friendship.

- Since God is the great Rewarder (Hebrews 11:6), he will certainly reward, equip, and provide grace to help all those who diligently seek him in their time of need (Hebrews 4:16; 11:6).
- Where sin abounds, grace does much more abound, therefore, God provides us with all the resources we need to exalt and enjoy him (Romans 5:20-21; 2 Peter 1:3-4).
- Because life has the eternal purpose of glorifying him, God will stop at nothing to protect his reputation and display his glory through our lives (Ephesians 3:1-21; 5:21-33).

Hope-based spiritual friendship never denies suffering and sin. Just the opposite. Hope-based spiritual friends keep their eyes wide open to sin and suffering while looking with spiritual eyes to the God who sustains and heals people in their suffering and reconciles and guides them to overcome sin.

Though I encourage you to empathize with hurting people, I don't want you to join with them in their *shrunken perspective*. All too often people wait so long to seek help, and churches do so little to offer preventative discipleship, that by the time people enter formal spiritual friendship their eyes are closed shut. They present to you shrunken narratives:

◆ Concerning Self: "I don't have the resources to deal with these problems." "My mess is beyond cleaning up." "I don't have what it takes to make this work."
◆ Concerning Others: "They're all to blame." "No one cares about me." "Everyone is my enemy."
◆ Concerning God: "Where are your great and precious promises when I really need them?" "Where are you when I really need you?"

That's why one of your primary roles involves infusing hope. You need to *undeceive* people. They buy Satan's lie that their lives are *hopeless*. Then they begin to surrender to despair.

To infuse hope, you have to have hope. You must believe that God exists, and that he is a rewarder of those who diligently seek him. You also must have respect for your spiritual friends. You must believe that as image bearers they have a God-created design and desire to mature. Sometimes you can't see that desire. It seems deeply buried, even carefully hidden. However, based upon your theology, you can unconditionally respect their potential in Christ to avail themselves of God's resources to be sustained, healed, reconciled, and guided.

The Bible teaches that "hope deferred makes the heart sick" (depleted, weak, dying, dried up, hard) (Proverbs 13:12). It also teaches that hope is an essential ingredient in the diet of healthy Christians, especially during times of suffering (Romans 5:1-11, 8:14-39; Hebrews 10:19-39; 11:1-40; 12:1-29). So in the crisis of despair you:

◆ Help people to realize that their problems are not bigger than God and his resources. They realize that their problems are not as all-encompassing as they thought.
◆ Identify people's hopes, dreams, aspirations, and the relational routes for getting there.
◆ Focus on people's strengths, searching for any resources to build upon and nurture.
◆ Avoid the typical Freudian search for hidden trauma and subconscious depth issues. It seems paradoxical to ask people to focus on their failures in order to build skills. Instead, when you ask people about their strengths, they inevitably show up more capable and creative and have renewed energy to find solutions.

Hope-Based Initial Interactions

From your very first interaction with your spiritual friend, parishioner, or counselee, you can use encouraging interactions. In other words, you don't have to "wait until you get to healing to talk about hope." Suppose Becky and Jim call you to arrange a meeting to talk about their marriage relationship. You could say at the end of your phone contact:

◆ *Between our phone call and our first meeting, I'd like you to discuss something. What was different about the time in your marriage when there was magic, when you felt excitement about being together?*
◆ *Many couples report that the simple act of asking for help starts a positive chain reaction. I'd like you to do your marriage a favor this week. Notice what is happening that you want to continue to happen.*
◆ *Before our first meeting, I'd like you to look for any signs of improvement. Notice any positive experiences in your relationship.*
◆ *Though you express some deep concern, I'm convinced that all is not lost. Over the next week, consciously focus on any positive signs. When we meet next week I want you to recall for me what you have done differently over the past week that has worked for you, that has improved an area of your relationship.*
◆ *I want you to think about one question. What is different about those times when you get along?*

When Becky and Jim arrive, you can continue your hope-based interactions.

- *People often notice that things already seem different from the time they made an appointment for counseling to the first meeting.*
  - *What have you noticed about your situation?*
  - *Do these changes relate to the reasons you're coming for counseling?*
  - *Are these the kinds of changes that you would like to continue to have happen?*
- *So how will you know that coming here has been helpful to your marriage relationship?*

During your first meeting together, you can *combine empathy with encouragement*, sharing comments such as:

- *Both of you have experienced some deep hurts. I'm truly sorry for that. I'm also wondering how you have found the strength to maintain your commitment to each other.*
- *No doubt, these are some serious issues that we will need to face. Would you care to see how good you can make your marriage?*
- *You've discussed several things that you have tried, and I sense some exasperation in your voices. I do want you to realize that in coming here you have added a "third pair of eyes." You have added another voice, another perspective to the mix. So, already, you have taken a positive step that has changed the way you handle these issues.*
- *As you talk about some of your struggles, I'm wondering if we also could explore some of your successes. What is occurring in your relationship that you would like to nurture?*
- *How have you learned to overcome _____?*
- *Though these issues seem almost insurmountable to you, I want you to know that through Christ you can do all things. You can change no matter how entrenched the patterns seem.*
- *These are hard issues. They have grown over time. However, with your commitment and God's resources, we can see lasting changes. Would it be okay if I prayed for you right now asking God to fill you with his hope, love, faith, and power? "Dear Lord . . ."*
- *You've experienced some very difficult things. I want you to know that as long as I am your counselor one of my roles will be to police how you treat each other. While you are in here, I want you to be honest, but **lovingly** honest, speaking the truth in love. If I sense either of you speaking destructively, I will confront you on that. Do you agree to this?*

By the time your first meeting has concluded, your prayer is simple: "Lord, may you have used me to help them to glimpse a vision of a better life together."

Infusing Hope

Empathy, feeling with, connecting, and climbing in the casket—these all partially describe the focus of sustaining. In sustaining, your goal is to help your spiritual friend's faith to survive, remembering the truth that it's normal to hurt and experiencing the truth that shared sorrow is endurable sorrow.

Encouraging, empowering, challenging, and celebrating the resurrection—these all partially describe the focus of healing. In healing, your goal is to help your spiritual friend's faith to thrive, remembering the truth that it's possible to hope and experiencing the truth that there's a larger story out there—Christ's eternal story that towers over our earthly story.

With Juan, if you never leave sustaining empathy, then he will remain lodged in his casket, buried six feet under. Having empathized, having heard his earthly story of suffering, now it's time to help him to find God's way out of the pit or, more importantly, to find God in his pit.

Hope is especially vital when you realize that Juan likely comes to you problem-saturated, overwhelmed, and believing only the worst about his situation. Certainly, you want to climb in the casket and hear his painful perspective. However, along the way, you also want to help Juan to achieve a more hopeful perspective.

To infuse hope, don't simply tell Juan to hope. Instead, develop mutuality in building hope as you interact and trialogue. Specifically, help him to develop his own hope-based treatment plans through responsibility trialogues, "faith eyes" trialogues, and encouragement trialogues.

Responsibility Trialogues

Imagine that you've diagnosed Juan's core responses to suffering and thirsts. You've begun to explore his hope-based responses. Help Juan to responsibly pursue biblical treatment plans through:

- Progressing Trialogues:

  - *As you leave here today, and you're making progress, how will you be relating to God differently?*
  - *As you leave here today, and you're making progress, how will you be relating to others differently?*
  - *As you leave here today, and you're making progress, how will you be seeing yourself differently in Christ?*
  - *As you leave here today, and you're making progress, how will you be thinking differently?*
  - *As you leave here today, and you're making progress, what will you be doing differently? How will your goals and purposes be altered?*
  - *As you leave here today, and you're making progress, how will you be feeling differently? How will you be managing your moods differently?*

- Instead Trialogues:

  - *What will you be longing for instead?*
  - *What will you be thinking instead?*
  - *What will you be doing instead? Pursuing instead?*
  - *What will you be feeling instead?*

- Faith-Focused Trialogues:

  - *When the problem is solved, how will you be relating differently?*
  - *When you have victory, what different perspectives will you have?*
  - *When Christ rescues you, what will you be doing differently?*
  - *When you manage your moods, how will you be feeling differently?*

- Answered-Prayer Trialogues:

  - *Imagine that God answers your prayer exceedingly abundantly above all that you can ask or dream. How would you know your prayer had been answered?*

    - *What would be different?*
    - *What would you be doing differently?*

- *How would others know?*

◆ Specifying Trialogues:

- *Specifically, how will you be doing this?*
- *Describe for me specifically what these changes will look like.*
- *Who, specifically, will notice these changes?*

"Faith Eyes" Trialogues

To infuse hope that treatment plans are not pipe dreams, implement "faith eyes" trialogues. Faith eyes conversations help your spiritual friends to detect undetected times when God is already giving them the victory in their responses to suffering.

◆ *How is this happening some now?*

- *How are you already clinging to Christ?*
- *How are you now trusting your faithful Father?*
- *How are you putting on these new mindsets now?*
- *How are these new images already occurring?*
- *How are these new patterns of relating happening now?*
- *How are you managing your moods already?*

◆ *When isn't the problem happening?*

- *A little bit?*
- *When isn't Satan's lying narrative controlling your perspective?*
- *When aren't you doubting God's goodness?*
- *When isn't your struggle to manage your moods happening?*

◆ *When are you already doing some of what you want (relationally, rationally, volitionally, and emotionally)?*

- *What is different about these times?*
- *What are you wanting/thinking/doing/feeling differently?*
- *How will you keep this going?*
- *How are others perceiving you as longing/thinking/acting/feeling differently?*
- *If I were a fly on the wall, what would I see you longing/thinking/doing/feeling differently?*

Encouragement Trialogues

As you and your spiritual friends mutually develop hope-based treatment plans, they will work! They'll change. Mature! When they report good news of growth, respond with empowering trialogues and agency trialogues.

◆ Empowering Trialogues:

- *Wow! How awesome! That's really great!*

- *How did you manage to do that!*
- *How did you decide to do that?*
- *How do you explain that?*
- *Who was surprised by that?*
- *How have you managed to stay on top of all these things as much as you have?*

- Agency Trialogues:

  - *How have you been cooperating with God to _____?*
  - *How will you keep this change going?*

Other times, at the start of a meeting, you might open with growth trialogues:

- Growth Trialogues:

  - *So, tell me what is different or better.*
  - *How are you enjoying God more?*
  - *How are you offering yourself to others?*
  - *How are your mindsets improving?*
  - *How are your decisions becoming more courageous?*
  - *How are your actions becoming more other-centered?*
  - *How are you managing your moods more victoriously?*

Even the best treatment plans sometimes do not result in "success"—in mature responses. Several interaction options can help your spiritual friends to face their perceived or real failures:

- Normalizing Setbacks:

  - *It's not at all unusual . . .*
  - *Even David, a man after God's own heart, failed.*
  - *Even the Apostle Paul battled intensely, sometimes victoriously and sometimes not.*
  - *Even Paul and Barnabas fought so fiercely that they had to endure a ministry split.*

- Predicting Struggles:

  - *Are there times you can imagine it being tempting to go back to the old ways rather than continuing to grow?*

Communication Options

You've listened, questioned, and explored. Now how do you know what an *apt reply* is? The Bible repeatedly emphasizes the importance of appropriate responses: Proverbs 9:7-9; 10:31; 15:1, 23; 25:11; Ephesians 4:29; and Colossians 4:6. The Bible also illustrates a plethora of possible responses. Consider a few biblical communication options:

- Question: Genesis 3:9, 11, 13; 4:6-7, 9, 10
- Remain Silent: Job 2
- Nourish: Proverbs 10:21

Exploring Your Spiritual Journey

◆ Think about an area of suffering/thirsting that you've been struggling with. Work your way through that issue and your responses using the following trialogues about mutuality in building hope.

1. Progressing Trialogues:

   a. As you progress toward victory in this, how will you be relating to God differently?

   b. As you progress toward victory in this, how will you be relating to others differently?

   c. As you progress toward victory in this, how will you be seeing yourself differently?

   d. As you progress toward victory in this, how will you be thinking differently?

   e. As you progress toward victory in this, what will you be doing differently?

   f. As you progress toward victory in this, how will you be feeling differently? How will you be managing your moods differently?

2. Faith Eyes Trialogues:

   a. In this situation, how are you already clinging to Christ?

   b. In this situation, how are you now trusting your faithful Father?

   c. In this situation, how are you putting on new mindsets now?

   d. In this situation, what new biblical images are controlling your thinking?

   e. In this situation, what new patterns of courageous choices are you making?

   f. In this situation, how are you managing your moods?

- Refresh: Proverbs 11:25
- Heal: Proverbs 12:18
- Uplift: Proverbs 12:25
- Answer Gently: Proverbs 15:1
- Share Pleasant Words: Proverbs 16:21
- Guide: Proverbs 20:18
- Rebuke Openly: Proverbs 27:5
- Wound: Proverbs 27:6
- Admonish: Romans 15:14; Colossians 3:16
- Strengthen, Encourage, and Console: 1 Corinthians 14:3
- Comfort: 2 Corinthians 1:3-8
- Restore: Galatians 6:1
- Affirm: Ephesians 1:1-14
- Equip: Ephesians 4:11-12
- Communicate Lovingly: Ephesians 4:15
- Edify: Ephesians 4:29
- Forgive: Ephesians 4:32-5:2
- Pray: Ephesians 6:18
- Proclaim, Admonish, and Teach: Colossians 1:28
- Encourage: Colossians 2:2; Hebrews 3:12-19; 10:25
- Sing: Colossians 3:16
- Teach: Colossians 3:16
- Urge, Warn, Encourage, Help, and Support: 1 Thessalonians 5:14
- Fan into Flame: 2 Timothy 1:5-7
- Entrust: 2 Timothy 2:2
- Remind and Warn: 2 Timothy 2:14
- Instruct Gently: 2 Timothy 2:25
- Teach, Rebuke, Correct, and Train: 2 Timothy 3:16-17
- Provoke/Stir Up: Hebrews 10:24
- Confess: James 5:16

No one word or one model can account for all the creative, artistic, and unique biblical ways of responding to people. Biblical counseling involves all of these diverse responses. Throughout *Spiritual Friends,* various exercises will assist you in learning how to apply these responding options.

Edifying Responses

To edify is to build up. When your words edify, they build a foundation of strength into another person's soul, giving them greater confidence and resources to face life with passion, imagination, courage, and depth. Non-edification tears down. It speaks Satan's native language of murder, lies, condemnation, and cursing.

Larry Crabb and Dan Allender, in *Encouragement: The Key to Caring*, discuss edifying and non-edifying responses under the useful and picturesque headings of "door closers" and "door openers."

Non-Edifying Responses: Door Closers

Door closers are comments prompted by fear of intimacy that force communication to remain on a surface or external level. They are often statements. Door closers that slam the soul shut include:

- *Denying Feelings*: "Oh, you don't feel that bad." "Christians don't . . ."
- *Minimizing Circumstances*: "You'll survive." "Buck up, buddy!" "It's not that bad."
- *Correctiveness*: Quick confrontations without depth or insight. "You've obviously sinned."
- *Quick Advice*: "I think you should . . ." "Things would improve if you would . . ."
- *Judging and Condemning*: "Well, if you hadn't . . ." "The cause of your problem is clear."
- *Subject Switching*: Bouncing from one shallow issue to another.
- *Talking at Instead of Talking to*: Monologue, not dialogue and trialogue.

Edifying Responses: Door Openers

Door openers are comments prompted by love that encourage further sharing of whatever might be there and that communicate an acceptance of whatever is there. Often they are questions or open-ended comments that draw out more communication. All of the spiritual conversation and scriptural exploration trialogues are designed as door openers. Other sample door openers include:

- *Reflection*: Serving as a mirror, putting their words into your words. "So it really upsets you when Jim makes light of this."
- *Clarification*: This is reflection with a stated or implied question. You're asking if you're getting it right. "So you feel like if Jim would back off, then you could handle this better?"
- *Exploration*: Implied questions and open-ended questions. "Tell me what was going on." "How did you feel?" "What did you do?" "What were you thinking?" "What would you have wanted?"
- *Intimate Interaction*: Here you communicate the commitment and the courage to go further, to go deeper, if your spiritual friend is ready. "This sounds really important to you. If you would like to explore this more, I'm right here with you."
- *Silence*: Attentive, interested silence can be one of the best door openers imaginable.

Hope-Based Spiritual Friendship Narrative Letter

Sending a letter to your spiritual friend is another means of infusing hope. Notice how the sample letter on page 196 highlights the positive aspects in Becky and Jim's relationship.

Where We've Been and Where We're Headed

Thus far in the healing process, we've learned how to mutually develop hope-based treatment plans and saturate conversations with hope-based interactions. In Chapter Nine, we've explored the *R* and the *E* of *RESTS*:

- *R*   Relational Treatment Planning: John 2:23-25
- *E*   Encouraging Communication: Ephesians 4:29

None of this assumes or implies that Satan's lies have vanished or that his dark doubts have been vanquished. He's insidious. Therefore, healing soul care continues with three relational competencies designed to assault the gates of hell by enlightening spiritual friends to Christ's larger story of hope. Chapter Ten explores how to practice the fine arts of:

- *S*   Story Reinterpreting: Philippians 3
- *T*   Thirsts Spiritual Conversations: Hebrews 10:24-25
- *S*   Stretching Scriptural Explorations: Hebrews 8

Hope-Based Spiritual Friendship Narrative Letter (Sample)

Pastor Jonathan R. Smith, Ph.D., LCPC
Grace Fellowship Church
321 Hope Lane
Union Bridge, MD 21777
Phone: 410-555-7000
pastorjrs@gfc.net

Dear Becky and Jim,

Wow! Quite a first meeting for the three of us, huh? I know that it was a very emotional time for both of you. And I'm convinced that it was yet another faith-step along your path to a marriage that is becoming stronger and stronger each week.

Having previously spent little time with the two of you together, I was so amazed to notice how well you complement (complete) each other. Jim, you were right there for Becky with your words and your hugs when she needed you most during our meeting. And Becky, you hung on Jim's every word. You were truly able to sense what it has been like for him to go through this with you.

I'm wondering where the two of you learned to connect so well. Has your marriage always been like this? How have the events of the past three months further sharpened your connection?

I'm curious about something else. I never once heard a word of blame or shame. There was no finger pointing. No faultfinding. Just honest, open sharing. Is this typical of your relationship? How do you intend to keep this good sharing going?

God never ceases to surprise me. For the two of you, he is taking what has been so incredibly painful and making something beautiful/powerful out of it. Rather than allowing what Bill did to cause the two of you to drift apart, you are using it to pull yourselves closer together. What role is your faith playing in your healthy response to this? I'm wondering what might have happened between the two of you if you did not share such a strong faith . . . I'm wondering, too, about the prayers you have prayed through this ordeal, both separately and together . . .

By the time you receive this letter, you will have had a few days to "do your homework." How's that coming? Let's be sure to pick up on your homework, and on your thoughts about my letter, at the start of our meeting next Tuesday.

I'm praying for you. I really am.

In Christ's Grace,

Pastor Jon

Maturing Your Spiritual Friendship Competency
Hope-Based Communicating

1. Picture yourself talking to Juan on the phone during your initial contact with him. Put in your own words, specific to his situation, some hope-based initial interactions that you might share with Juan.

2. Think about someone you are ministering to. Begin to sketch the outline/first draft of a hope-based narrative letter that you might write her or him. Feel free to use a separate sheet.

3. Look again at the communication options.

   a. What five options seem to characterize many of your interactions? Why?

   b. What five options do you seem to seldom use? Why?

   c. What patterns do you sense? What do you make of your pattern?

4. Someone says to you, "Our church is killing me!"

   a. Respond with "door closers."

   b. Respond with "door openers."

Chapter Ten

Healing Treatment and Intervention
RESTS Relational Competencies, Part II

"Are you bruised? Be of good comfort, he calls you. Conceal not your wounds, open all before him and take not Satan's counsel. Let this support us when we feel ourselves bruised. Christ's way is first to wound, then to heal. If Christ be so merciful as not to break me, I will not break myself by despair, nor yield myself over to the roaring lion, Satan, to break me in pieces" (Richard Sibbes, *The Bruised Reed*, p. 9).

Faith Is the Victory That Overcomes the World

Puritan Pastor Richard Sibbes had it right when he wrote, "It was Satan's art from the beginning to discredit God with man, by calling God's love into question with our first father Adam. His success then makes him ready at the weapon still" (Sibbes, *The Bruised Reed*, p. 63). Satan parades the circumstances of your spiritual friends' life stories and shouts, "God does not care about you!" The Author of their stories says, "I love you!" Which do they believe?

In sustaining, you face doubt and despair with your spiritual friends. Now, what do you do with their spiritual depression? How does faith defeat despair? Healing provides the answer.

In healing, you address the question: "How can my spiritual friends and I engage in *RESTS* narratives that heal their faith by offering hope that rests in Christ?" In the current chapter, you'll examine the final three of the five *RESTS* relational competencies:

- ◆ *R*   Relational Treatment Planning: John 2:23-25
- ◆ *E*   Encouraging Communication: Ephesians 4:29
- ◆ *S*   Story Reinterpreting: Philippians 3; 2 Corinthians 10
- ◆ *T*   Thirsts Spiritual Conversations: Hebrews 10:24-25
- ◆ *S*   Stretching Scriptural Explorations: Hebrews 8

Story Reinterpreting: Co-Authoring Resurrection Narratives—Philippians 3; 2 Corinthians 10

Faith is primal trust in the full reliability of God's good heart in the middle of life's messes. It's courageous trust: confident reliance upon God through reason redeemed by grace through faith. By

Exploring Your Spiritual Journey

1. Think about a situation you're facing.

    a. What are some of the negative mindsets that you have about your situation?

    b. Where do you think you were recruited into these mindsets? Where did you learn your way of looking at your situation?

    c. What biblical principles could counter your current negative mindset?

2. Thinking about the same situation:

    a. When have you faced something like that in the past? How did God bring you through it victoriously?

    b. Think hard now. Where is God *already* giving you some victory in your current situation?

    c. What are you doing to cooperate with God to find victory?

    d. How can you and God magnify your victory—keep it going and enlarge it?

reason alone, God's benevolent presence remains obscured. It seems to the mind that God either does not exist, does not care, or is capricious. Yet Father assures us that we can know him (Romans 1), that we can seek and find him (John 4), that he is good (Matthew 5:43-48; John 3:16), that he works everything together for good (Romans 8:28), and that he is our Rewarder (Hebrews 11:6).

With the benefit of faith we can see the benefit of trials.

It is as we face despair and honestly address real-life questions that we can truly know God. With the benefit of faith we can see the benefit of trials. Spiritual friendship in healing reveals the deeper meaning behind events by reinterpreting life from God's grace perspective. It does so by:

- Exploring the Universal Picture of Why God Allows Suffering
- Co-Authoring a Unique Individual Story of Specific Ways God's Goodness Is Triumphing
- Sharing Your Unique Story of How God Made Good out of Evil in Your Suffering

Exploring God's Universal Picture of Suffering's Purposes: Communion, Conformity, Contingency, Conversion, and Communication

The author of Psalm 119 knew the Author of life. Additionally, he knew the critical role that the Word plays in how we respond to suffering. "If your law had not been my delight, I would have perished in my affliction" (119:92). Want to help your spiritual friends survive and thrive through suffering? Then help them to know and delight in God's Word. "Sustain me according to your promise, and I will live; do not let my hopes be dashed" (Psalm 119:116).

In particular, you help your spiritual friends by exploring with them what God's Word says about the purposes of suffering. Why does a good God allow evil? Though not exhaustive, the following five purposes for suffering can keep suffering from exhausting energy and draining faith.

- Communion: In suffering, God is drawing us nearer to himself.
- Conformity: In suffering, God is conforming us to the image of his Son.
- Contingency: In suffering, God is demonstrating just how needy we are for him.
- Conversion: In suffering, God is offering us the opportunity to testify about our hope in him.
- Communication: In suffering, God is declaring to the entire universe that he is trustworthy even when life is unfair.

First, God uses suffering to reveal himself (his beauty and majesty) to us so we can experience deeper communion with him. As we daily risk our lives to him, he reveals himself to us through our struggles and uncertainties. God drew the psalmist back to himself during times of suffering, revealing his character (unfailing love) and truth. "Before I was afflicted I went astray, but now I obey your word" (119:67). "May your unfailing love be my comfort" (119:76).

Second, God uses suffering to conform us to the image of his Son. "It was good for me to be afflicted so that I might learn your decrees" (119:71). Affliction softens our hearts.

In this you greatly rejoice, though now for a little while you may have had to suffer grief in all kinds of trials. These have come so that your faith—of greater worth than gold, which perishes even though refined by fire—may be proved genuine and may result in praise, glory and honor when Jesus Christ is revealed (1 Peter 1:6-7).

Third, God uses suffering to cause us to hunger and realize our need for him (Deuteronomy 8:1-20). The last thing we want to be is *humbled*. Think of the words that humility brings to mind: repentant, remorseful, apologetic, sorry, penitent, lowly, meek, submissive, small, plain, ignoble, modest, unassuming, needy, poor, destitute, impoverished, naked, exposed, bare, uncovered, barren, infertile, impotent, powerless, unable, helpless, defensive, dependent, contingent, and reliant.

Like it or not, admit it or not, we are contingent beings. We're not self-sufficient or self-reliant. Having been made for God, we need the Other. Suffering brings us back home to Father—back to dependence. Desperate dependence. "My comfort in my suffering is this: Your promise preserves my life" (Psalm 119:50). "Let your compassion come to me that I may live" (Psalm 119:77).

Fourth, suffering is often God's path to show others how good he is, converting them to trust in him. "Let me live that I may praise you" (Psalm 119:175). When we cling to him in turmoil, others ask us for a reason of the hope that is within us (1 Peter 3:15).

Fifth, Job, John 9, Ephesians 1, Ephesians 3, Hebrews 12, and many other passages show us that God uses suffering to communicate to the entire universe that he is good—that he is so good that he can even make good out of bad and grace out of evil. "You are good, and what you do is good; teach me your decrees" (Psalm 119:68).

The point is not necessarily to "teach" these concepts, as much as it is to have them in mind. The most powerful way to "use" these concepts in personal ministry is to trialogue about them with your spiritual friends.

- *What do you think God's purposes might include in allowing you to experience this?*
- *In what ways is God drawing you nearer to himself through your suffering?*
- *How is God making you more like his Son through your suffering?*
- *As hard as this is, what lessons is it teaching you about your desperate need for God?*
- *What testimony of hope might spring from your suffering?*
- *How are you seeing and sharing God's trustworthy character even in this?*

Co-Authoring a Unique Individual Story: How God's Goodness Is Triumphing

When people first respond to suffering, they typically look at their lives with *eyeballs only*. No one has to tell them that "Life is bad." Nor does anyone need to inform them that their relationships are causing them pain. Clearly, they are in the desert of suffering in a fallen world—ready to give up hope.

As they progress through the sustaining process, God breathes back life into them. Still confused and hurting, but now resuscitated.

In healing, your spiritual friends need to become aware of Christ's larger story of victory over suffering and sin. However, before putting on victory narratives, you can assist them to put off the old defeat narratives.

Challenging the Old Works Narrative: Satan's Dominating Defeat Story

As you sit with your spiritual friends, be asking *yourself*:

- *What is the dominant story of defeat torturing my friend?*
- *What hopeless narrative is driving my parishioner to despair?*
- *What satanic lie is my counselee believing?*

Once you latch onto the dominant defeat story they're believing, then help them to challenge that old narrative and replace it with a narrative of hope. I label this process "undeceiving." Your spiritual friends are deceived by Satan's lies about God, others, and themselves. Help them to undeceive themselves through:

♦ Assessing the Unique Lie
♦ Labeling the Dominant Lie
♦ Exposing the Root Source of the Defeat Story
♦ Specifying the Root Source of the Temptation: The World, the Flesh, and the Devil

Start the process by assessing the unique messages people are believing about their level one suffering. Ponder questions like, "What is the particular dominant problem story?" "What is the impoverishing story that this unique person is believing?"

As you sense a theme developing in your mind, give it a metaphor—one compressed picture with power. Put their problem-saturated plot in a nutshell—in one picture, label, or image that captures the essence of how they see themselves. The more you can label it according to their language, lingo, or realm of experience, the better. For example:

♦ **To a Teenage Male High School Wrestler**: *It seems to me that you see yourself pinned before you ever step on the mat. It's like Satan is the defending heavyweight state champ, and you're a first-year JV lightweight. Where do you suppose you came to see yourself like this?*
♦ **To a Female Newspaper Reporter**: *If your view of your life were a front-page headline, it would be screaming, "Extra! Extra! Read All About It. Woman Buried in Avalanche of Problems." Who do you think wrote this headline?*
♦ **To a Male Lawyer**: *May I share a picture of what I sense as I hear you discuss your situation? It's like you're on trial and someone has stacked the jury against you. Without warrant, they have made your decision a capital offense punishable by death. I'm wondering where you were recruited into this view of your situation.*

Reread the last sentence in each of the three vignettes above. They model how to *expose* Satan's lying narrative. Though each person has problems, who says that those problems must overwhelm them? Who says that a few problems are a death sentence against hope? Who says that problems must leave people helplessly buried under an avalanche? As the old skit on *Saturday Night Live* used to put it, "Could it be . . . SATAN!!!!!???"

Acts 26:17-18; 2 Corinthians 10:3-7; Ephesians 5:6-14; and Colossians 1:13 all model exposing the works of darkness. Christ calls spiritual friends to give light to those blinded by Satan's deceptive darkness. Paul commands believers in Ephesians 6:10-14 to stand guard, while Peter exhorts Christians to stand watch in 1 Peter 5:8-10. Your job is to name Satan's scheme. Label the counter-plot and expose its author.

♦ *Who do you suppose is behind your way of thinking about your life?*
♦ *Are there any passages we could explore that might expose the true source of this viewpoint?*
♦ *Where were you recruited into this way of seeing your situation?*
♦ *Who is the real enemy here?*
♦ *Who do you suppose is really behind your conflict?*
♦ *Who is energizing this?*

Satan loves to keep Christians from seeing who they are in Christ. He loves believers to think that they're all fleshly, all worldly, and all sinful. He wants Christians to think that temptation is bigger than God is. He does not want saints to know the truth that their "old man" is crucified with Christ and that they're now, in their core, not fleshly, but one spiritual "new person" in Christ—God's adult sons and daughters, kings and queens, and more than conquerors.

You can help your spiritual friends take responsibility for their actions while also sensing their ability to defeat temptations. Do exactly what Paul, John, and James did. They *specified* the root source of the temptation, labeling it either "the world, the flesh, or the Devil."

- *In what ways do you think **the world** is trying to creep into your thinking in this issue? Perhaps if we explored 1 John 4:1-6 . . .*
- *How do you think **the flesh** is trying to dominate you here as you rip into each other like this? Perhaps if we looked at Galatians 5:13-21 . . .*
- *How do you think **the Devil** is involved in the mindset that seems to be developing around your suffering? Could we look at Ephesians 2:1-3 and 6:10-18 to explore this?*
- *I'm wondering what it is like for you to face **the temptation** to see your life in this negative light. Could we look at James 1 to answer that?*

Help your spiritual friends separate from the oppressive stories they're believing so they can reflect on them, re-examine them, and gain a new perspective on them. Then they can recognize that their narratives (their interpretations) are not God's. When they see these imaginations and strongholds for what they are, then they can cast them down (2 Corinthians 10:3-7).

Re-Authoring/Co-Authoring a New Grace Narrative: The Daring Victory Story

Whenever you help your spiritual friends "put off the flesh" or "cast off Satanic schemes," also equip them to "put on the Spirit" and "internalize the truth." Assist people to re-author a new grace story. Co-author (them, you, and Christ) a new way of looking at their problems—a hope-filled, grace-oriented view. I call this the *daring victory story*. They're developed as you help your spiritual friends to:

- Gain Perspective
- Garner Gender Resources
- Surface Exceptional Victory Narratives
- Create New Victory Narratives
- Generate Ongoing Victory Narratives

Gaining perspective helps people to gain hope. People must see that they're not trying to solve their problems from a dead stop. So trialogue:

- *Tell me about some times when you're already defeating some of these problems.*
- *Who else is on your side and in your corner as you work to overcome these struggles?*
- *Have you ever struggled with anything like this before? How did you overcome it then? What could you take from that past victory and use now?*
- *How has Christ already been giving you some victory in this area?*

You don't simply counsel image bearers, you counsel male and female image bearers. Therefore, you can draw out and stir up the masculine soul resources inside your male spiritual friends and the feminine soul resources inside your female spiritual friends.

Many biblical concepts summarize what reflects maleness: initiating, planting, protecting, guarding, evoking beauty, guiding, courageously confronting confusion and chaos, sacrificial strength, sacrificial love, shepherd, care taker, road maker, and protective provider. Many biblical concepts summarize what reflects femaleness: responding, watering, receiving, nurturing, incubating, respecting, giving refuge, bringing forth life, openness, reverence, softness, unconditional respect, life sustainer, encourager, and collaborative celebrator.

Fashion your trialogues with these truths in mind. Consider two samples:

♦ *Don, I know your heart. You're a protector. Nobody messes with those you love. You love June. I want to see you protect her right now. Protect her from your own anger, from your flesh. What could you say or do right this second that would offer June your strong protection?*

♦ *June, I've seen you nurture so many people in our church. Many times you've been my biggest fan. I'd like you to nurture Don right now by being his biggest fan. He feels defeated. He seems to think that you've lost all respect for him. What could you do or say right this second that would offer Don your nurturing respect?*

Believers have more resources within and around them from God than Satan wants them to know about. Due to Satan's deceits, they focus only on their defeats. You enter a safari searching for *exceptional times* when they are already finding victory.

♦ *What's different about the times when you are getting along well with others?*
♦ *How do your unpleasant interactions with your boss end? What triggers the cease-fire?*
♦ *Under what circumstances is the problem less intense? Less frequent? Of shorter duration?*
♦ *What is different when something constructive results?*
♦ *What is different when the same thing occurs, but it troubles you less?*

Help your spiritual friends to ponder what their exceptional times of victory say about them, God, their future, and the dominant negative narratives they've been believing. Exceptions lead to enlightenment. Enlightenment leads to *new victory narratives*. To create these new victory narratives, explore with them.

♦ *What do these recent times of victory say about you and Christ?*
♦ *Wow! After all you've faced, you're still facing life with Christ. What does that say about who you really are in Christ?*

Describe what you see in vivid, user-friendly (in their language) metaphors.

♦ **To a Teenage Male High School Wrestler**: *Hmm . . . It seems to me that some of your wrestling against Satan is state-caliber, top-notch. Those times when you turn to Christ as your Coach, play by his rulebook, and remain connected to his strength, you come out on top. How do you suppose you can keep your MVP spiritual season going?*

♦ **To a Female Newspaper Reporter**: *Wow! If we take a new look at your situation, as if it were a front-page headline, it would be shouting something very different. "Extra! Extra! Read All About It. Wife Risks All to Save Husband." How have you been able to write this sort of headline?*

- **To a Male Lawyer**: *May I share a new picture with you? It's like you're on trial and Jesus is your Defense Attorney. He knows the truth; he **is** the Truth. He's speaking on your behalf with authority. How have you been able to so drastically reshape the way you see this?*

Of course, it's not enough to simply look to the past or even to focus on the present. Your spiritual friends have issues to face today, tomorrow, and the next day. Spreading hope is the essence of *generating ongoing victory narratives*. Use your spiritual friends' past and current victories to motivate and energize them to keep moving, keep trusting, and keep loving. You want them to see that their future hope is greater than their past suffering, God's healing is greater than their hurts, and Christ's redemption is greater than their sins.

You want them to be more *opportunity-minded* than *problem-focused*, and you long for them to have faith in God and the resources that he has given them. Some trialogues will help.

- *What do you think your victory this past week says about the issue you're facing?*
- *If you applied what you learned from the time at your in-laws, what would you do to work through this issue?*
- *In light of that time of joint victory, what will you do differently this week?*

You're wanting to provoke ongoing action. This means helping your friends continue to *do more of the same*. Imagine working with a father and his teenage son:

- *Over the next week, I'd like you each to write down what happens in your relationship that you want to continue happening.*
- *During the time between now and our next meeting, I'd like each of you to write down times when you connect like a coach and an MVP. Also, jot down what you are doing differently during those times that helps you to connect and empower each other so well.*
- *Imagine into the future. How do you see the two of you working together to defeat your relationship problem?*

When father and son return, *expect the best*:

- *So, tell me what is different or better.*
- *So, give me an update. How did things go with last week's assignment?*
- *So, what's your report today? Tell me how you were able to apply what you learned last week.*
- *What was happening this past week that the two of you want to continue doing?*
- *What did the two of you accomplish together in your relationship that you would like to continue to nurture?*

When they report successes, *keep the ball rolling*:

- *That's great!*
- *How did you do that?*
- *What does this say about your newly recovered connection?*
- *I'm struck by your teamwork.*

When they report *no change*, then respond with:

- *Hmm. How have you been able to continue to cope with this?*

- *I'm sorry to hear that it feels like the same old, same old. How have you managed to stay on top of things as a father and son through all of this?*
- *How did the two of you keep matters from getting worse?*
- *None? Not even a little? Was there one time when you were able to experience a bit more victory together than previously?*
- *Are there actions, attitudes, or words that you would do differently if you could do the week over?*
- *What do you think kept you from drawing on God's power to do this together?*

Sharing Your Story: Counselor Self-Disclosure

You can help your spiritual friends create new narratives by sharing your narrative. Consider some principles:

- Don't preach.
- You don't have to share an identical experience of suffering; you may not have one. However, you can share the common experience of having suffered and having seen God at work.
- Share your struggle to trust.
- Share how God brought you to trust.
- Share how you gained new insights into God, others, and yourself.
- Ask for feedback. "Does this connect for you?" "Is there anything in my situation that you could use in yours?"

Use self-disclosure with discretion. Don't dominate the conversation. Don't turn the tables so that you become the counselee or the counselee pities and sustains you. Share enough that you have your spiritual friends' rapt attention. Then, be sure to check in. "Does this fit for you? How is it different? Similar?"

Thirsts Spiritual Conversations: Healing Theological Trialogues—Hebrews 10:24-25

In sustaining, your spiritual conversations revolve around candor, complaint, cry, and communion—helping your spiritual friends to honestly face life by admitting, "Life is bad." "It's normal to hurt." In healing, your spiritual conversations revolve around waiting, wailing, weaving, and worshipping—helping your spiritual friends to honestly face thirsts, longings, desires, and groanings by acknowledging, "God is good." "It's possible to hope."

I'll provide numerous sample categories and conversations. Don't repeat them word for word. Make them your own. More than that, create your own from your understanding of the Word and of your spiritual friends. Match Scriptures and souls.

Spiritual Conversations That Encourage Tasting Thirsts

- *Where are you finding tastes of Christ as the Lover of your soul?*
- *Have you ever loved Christ more than you do today? What was that love like? Describe it to me in terms of a dating relationship/marriage relationship. What was different then from now? How close are you to that now?*

Maturing Your Spiritual Friendship Competency
Story Reinterpreting

♦ If you're working through this material individually, then instead of role-playing, use the space after each scenario to write your responses to each situation.

1. With a partner, role-play challenging the dominant defeat story. The "counselee" shares a scenario replete with defeatist attitudes. The "counselor" follows the four aspects of:

   a. Assessing the Unique Lie

   b. Labeling the Dominant Lie

   c. Exposing the Root Source of the Defeat Story

   d. Specifying the Root Source of the Temptation: The World, the Flesh, and the Devil

2. With a partner, role-play co-authoring a daring victory story. The "counselee" continues the story from question number one. The "counselor" applies the five aspects of:

   a. Gaining Perspective

   b. Garnering Gender Resources

   c. Surfacing Exceptional Victory Narratives

   d. Creating New Victory Narratives

   e. Generating Ongoing Victory Narratives

Spiritual Conversations That Encourage Communion/Worship/Quenching Thirsts in Christ

- *What would it be like to worship God in the middle of this?*
- *What would it feel like for you to turn to Christ in the middle of this?*
- *Let's look at Psalms 42 and 43—Psalms of Thirst. If you were to write a Thirst Psalm like this to God, how would you word it?*
- *What are you longing for from God right now?*
- *If Christ were to walk into the room right now, what would you want from him?*
- *Tell me about some times when you were closest to Christ.*
- *Tell me about your first love for Christ. When was it? What did it feel like?*
- *When are you closest to Christ now?*
- *How is all of this helping you to cling to Christ, to depend on him, to hunger and thirst for him?*
- *Let's look at Revelation 7. How do these wonderful pictures of heaven give you hope today?*
- *Tell me about how you've been clinging to the anchor of God's character. To God's promises.*
- *Tell me about how you have been drawing nearer to God through this.*
- *Tell me what you have come to learn about yourself in this.*
- *How have you been able to rest in this? Find such peace in this?*
- *Someone defined worship as, **"Thankfulness for the poetry of God's plan and praise for the beauty of God's soul."** Tell me about your thankfulness for God's poetic plan. Tell me about your praise for God's lovely soul.*
- *I've heard someone say, **"Wisdom is a God-oriented sense of reality."** What's God's hidden reality behind your situation?*
- *Someone once said, **"Worship is hosting the holy."** When do you host God? What's it like when God hangs out in your home?*
- *What would it look like for you to rest in God right now? For you to surrender to God? To trust instead of work, to wait instead of demand?*

Spiritual Conversations That Enlighten Spiritual Friends to Grasp God's Love

- *How is your Lover loving you in this? Respecting you?*
- *How does this expose God's love for you? Respect for you? Plan for you?*
- *As you have gone through this, what thoughts or feelings have you had about God?*
- *How has your situation influenced your relationship to God? Your feelings toward God? Your image of God?*
- *What's your understanding of what the Bible says about God's purposes in suffering?*

Spiritual Conversations That Expose That God Is Good Even When Life Is Bad

- *How would you know that God was tuned into your distress?*
- *If you had one word or image to describe God right now, what would it be?*
- *If Christ were in this chair, what do you think you would be talking about? What would you want to ask, say, or do? What do you imagine him saying or doing?*
- *If Christ came walking into the room right now, what would he look like? What would the expression on his face be? What would he say to you? What would you want him to say or do?*
- *What do you think about the goodness of God as you experience this?*
- *How do you reconcile God's goodness with what you're facing?*
- *God is all-powerful, holy, and in control of everything. What impact do these characteristics of God have on you as you face this?*

- *What passages have helped and strengthened you to deal with this?*
- *What passages have deepened your relationship with God?*
- *Tell me about how God has proven his goodness to you.*
- *Tell me how it impacts you to know that Christ is suffering with you right now.*
- *Tell me how it impacts you to know that Christ is praying for you right now.*
- *How is life different for you when you see God as your Father and Christ as your Friend?*
- *God is loving, fatherly, accepting, gracious, and good. What impact do these characteristics of God have on you as you face this?*
- *In the middle of this, how do you relate to the image of God as your loving Father?*
- *God promises to work all things together for good for his children. What are your thoughts about his promise? What do you think about that passage now?*
- *What good purposes has God already provided to you or in you through these events?*
- *Tell me about some ways that all this has deepened your closest relationships.*
- *I'd love to hear how this has positively impacted your relationships.*
- *How have you been able to worship God in the middle of this?*
- *What would it be like to worship God as you go through this?*

Spiritual Conversations That Promote Resilience

- *What spiritual support network could be helpful to you in this?*
- *Are you remaining under without giving in?*
- *Are you accepting Saturday living?*
- *What have you done to not wait? To wait?*
- *What would a comeback look like?*
- *What would it look like to not quit while this lingers?*
- *What would quitting mean? What would it look like?*

Spiritual Conversations That Expose Satan's Lying Strategy

- *Where were you recruited into the belief that God is your enemy?*
- *What/who do you think is causing you to see yourself and your relationship to God in such a negative light?*
- *You've said some pretty harsh things about yourself. If your heavenly Father were physically here right now, what would he be saying about you and to you?*
- *I've noticed a sense of hopelessness developing in you. Where do you think that's coming from?*
- *You seem to feel that God doesn't care about you and your suffering. Is that how you see God?*
- *Let's contrast how you're seeing God right now with how God describes himself in his Word.*
- *You seem intent on handling this on your own. How has that worked for you before?*

Spiritual Conversations That Enlighten Spiritual Friends to Christ's Grace Narrative

- *What passages have you found helpful in gaining a new perspective on your situation?*
- *What Scripture have you found helpful in gaining comfort and hope as you go through this?*
- *What might God be wanting to accomplish in your life through your circumstances?*
- *If you did not have the Scriptures, how would your perspective on this situation be different?*
- *As you've gone through this, what thoughts or feelings have you had about God?*
- *How is this impacting your image of God?*
- *What do you believe the Bible teaches about God's purposes in suffering?*

- *What are you learning in God's school of suffering about yourself, others, God, Christ, and life?*

Spiritual Conversations That Encourage Spiritual Friends to Turn to God in Their Suffering

- *Who have you turned to during this tough time?*
- *What are you doing with God in your suffering?*
- *How is all of this impacting your relationship with Christ?*

Spiritual Conversations That Promote Conformity/Maturity

- *What person has been most influential on your beliefs and values? Picture that person experiencing what you are going through. How do you imagine her/him handling this?*
- *How have you been able to cooperate with God's grace to show such patience during all of this? Such love? Grace? Endurance? Hope? Strength?*
- *Wow! That's amazing. I'm so impressed with your attitude. Tell me how you've learned to handle this. How are you able to display that fruit of the Spirit? Keep your mind on Christ?*
- *Who do you suppose is watching you and wondering, "How's she/he doing this?" What would you tell them?*
- *We've talked about Job's story. Suppose Satan sent someone to you to say, "Curse God and die." How would you respond?*
- *We've talked about how the "whole world is watching" when God's child suffers. They're watching to see if God's heart is trustworthy. What message do you want to send?*

Spiritual Conversations That Promote Ministry

Describe their situation as a heroic adventure. Match your description to their situation, sharing your images with passion and power. Then co-author a heroic narrative.

- *Who sent you on this journey?*
- *Why were you chosen?*
- *What unique gifts do you bring?*
- *Who is the enemy here?*
- *Who are your comrades in arms? Fellow pilgrims? How could you work together? How have you been working together?*
- *Doubt says, "Things will never change." What might hope say?*
- *Tell me how you fight to maintain the faith perspective that God is faithful.*
- *Tell me about the future you hope for.*
- *What dead "things" do you anticipate Christ resurrecting? Your career? Marriage?*
- *What will your life look like when God resurrects it?*
- *Tell me about the eternal future you hope for.*
- *How have you worked through similar experiences of emptiness (fear, suffering) before and come to a point of healing? Maturity? Growth?*
- *What person has been most influential on your beliefs and values? Picture that person experiencing what you're going through. How do you imagine her/him handling this?*
- *When else have you experienced suffering similar to this? How did you respond? What did you learn about your spirituality in that situation? What did you learn about God in that situation? What would you repeat and what would you change about your response to that situation?*

Maturing Your Spiritual Friendship Competency
Thirsts Spiritual Conversations

♦ Reword each of the spiritual conversations listed below to fit something from your story and your soul regarding Satan's warfare against you. Then write your response to your reworded spiritual conversation:

1. Where were you recruited into the belief that God is your enemy?

2. What/who do you think is causing you to see yourself and your relationship to God in such a negative light?

3. You've said some pretty harsh things about yourself. If your heavenly Father were physically present right now, what would he be saying about you and to you?

4. I've noticed a sense of hopelessness developing in you. Where do you think that's coming from?

5. You seem to feel that God doesn't care about you and your suffering. Is that how you see God?

6. Let's contrast how you're seeing God right now with how God describes himself in his Word.

Stretching Scriptural Explorations: Healing Biblical Trialogues—Hebrews 8

If Scripture use in sustaining requires *courageous integrity*, then in healing it requires *hopeful imagination* and *grace perspective*. These abilities see what God is doing *behind* the scenes and what God might want to be doing *in* your friends.

The *process* is the same as with sustaining, however the *focus* differs. Now you explore Scriptures (and they are vast) that produce a *trialogue* that confirms that it's possible to hope.

Remember the model from sustaining: explore together a relevant biblical narrative or character. Then explore the implications and applications:

- *How do you react to this biblical story?*
- *How is it different from your situation? How is it similar?*
- *How have you been responding differently? Similarly?*
- *What in this story would you like to add to your story? How do you think you could do that?*
- *Are there any characters in this story who remind you of any people in your life?*
- *If you were to write your own story, somewhat like this biblical story, what would the theme of your story be?*
- *How might your story turn out?*
- *What role would you play in your story?*
- *What role would God play in your story?*
- *Who else might be in your story?*
- *What would your relationship to God be like?*
- *How would God work your story out for good?*
- *How would God give you strength in your story?*

I'll provide some sample hope-based Scripture trialogues. Don't "copy these" or say them with rote dispassion. Use them as guides for developing your own trialogues that fit your personality and your spiritual friends' lives.

Scriptural Explorations of Ephesians 3:15-21—Dreaming Big Narratives

- *Since Ephesians 3:20 says that you can never out dream God, what lofty dreams do you dream regarding the outcome of all of this?*
- *What's the best possible scenario you can imagine coming from your situation? Now, imagine even bigger. God does. Tell me what you imagine.*

Scriptural Explorations of Hebrews 8—Jesus, God's Perfect Provision for Peace

- *How are you trusting Jesus for peace?*
- *When you are at peace, what are you doing?*
  - *How are you relating to God? Others?*
  - *What are you thinking about yourself? Life? Future? Past? Present?*
- *When you are anxious, what are you doing?*
  - *How are you relating to God? Others?*
- *When you are worrying, how are you thinking about yourself? Life? Future? Past? Present?*
- *What condemning lies are you believing/clinging to? Works-related? Fear-based? Distancing?*

Scriptural Explorations of Hebrews 12:1-15—Heroic Narrative

- *How are you demonstrating to the audience (Hebrews 12:1-2) that God really is trustworthy?*
- *How are you showing that you really do trust God with childlike faith? That you're pursuing him with adult passion?*
- *What would it look like to persevere in the race God has set before you?*
- *How can you fix your eyes on Jesus?*
- *How could you imitate Christ's endurance?*
- *Tell me how God is training you through this.*

Some Sample Passages for Reengagement When Your Spiritual Friends Have Been Sinned Against

Chapter Eight (*Volitional Reengagement*, page 166) listed the following themes and passages, which you can use to develop scriptural explorations.

- To Experience Healing from God: 1 Peter 2:19-25
- To Forgive: Matthew 18:21-35; Romans 12:17-21; 2 Corinthians 2:3-11; Ephesians 4:32; Colossians 3:8-17
- To Examine Any Logs in Their Own Eyes/Lives: Matthew 7:1-5
- To Seek Restoration/Reconciliation: Matthew 18:15-20; 2 Corinthians 6:11-13

Some Sample Passages for Reengagement When Your Spiritual Friends Have Sinned in Response to Suffering

Chapter Eight (*Volitional Reengagement*, page 166) listed the following themes and passages, which you can use to develop scriptural explorations.

- Repentance/Confession to God: Hosea 14:1-9; 1 John 1:8-10
- Acceptance of God's Forgiveness: 1 John 1:8-2:2
- Seeking Forgiveness from/Confessing Sin to One Another: James 5:16
- Restitution and Renewal: 2 Corinthians 7:10-12

Where We've Been and Where We're Headed

Spiritual friendship consists of soul care for suffering *and* spiritual direction for sinning. Chapters Five through Ten have equipped us to diagnose and treat our *suffering* spiritual friends. Chapters Eleven through Sixteen will equip us to diagnose and treat our *sinning* spiritual friends.

That process begins in Section Four (Maturing the Art of Reconciling Spiritual Friendship). Chapter Eleven explains reconciling diagnosis, while Chapters Twelve and Thirteen teach reconciling treatment and intervention.

Maturing Your Spiritual Friendship Competency
Stretching Scriptural Explorations

♦ For each passage/section below, write a trialogue that you could use based upon that Scripture and situation.

1. When Your Spiritual Friends Have Been Sinned Against:

   a. To Experience Healing from God: 1 Peter 2:19-25

   b. To Forgive: Matthew 18:21-35; Romans 12:17-21; 2 Corinthians 2:3-11; Ephesians 4:32; Colossians 3:8-17

   c. To Examine Any Logs in Their Own Eyes/Lives: Matthew 7:1-5

   d. To Seek Restoration/Reconciliation: Matthew 18:15-20; 2 Corinthians 6:11-13

2. When Your Spiritual Friends Have Sinned in Response to Suffering:

   a. Repentance/Confession to God: Hosea 14:1-9; 1 John 1:8-10

   b. Acceptance of God's Forgiveness: 1 John 1:8-2:2

   c. Seeking Forgiveness from/Confessing to One Another: James 5:16

   d. Making Restitution and Experiencing Renewal: 2 Corinthians 7:10-12

Chapter Eleven

Reconciling Diagnosis
Compassionate Discernment in Reconciling

> *"We will take all things well from one that we know entirely loves us. We will put up with a blow that is given us in love sooner than with a foul word that is spoken to us in malice or in anger. If you be their best friends, help them against their worst enemies. And think not all sharpness inconsistent with love: parents correct their children, and God himself 'chastens every son whom he receives' (Hebrews 12:6)"* (Thomas Aquinas, *Commentary on Sentences,* I, Distinction 27, Q. 1, a. 1-4, AR, pp. 261-262).

Sharing God's Treasure

As I've viewed the landscape of ancient, modern, and post-modern ministry, I've detected a tendency toward extremes. Personal ministry has gravitated toward extremes of dealing only with suffering *or* only with sinning. When I "sovereignly stumbled" upon the four tasks of sustaining, healing, reconciling, and guiding, along with the twin concepts of soul care and spiritual direction, I felt like an archaeologist on the find of a lifetime.

Since that time, I've made it my lifelong calling to share the discovery. Surprisingly, I've heard a familiar refrain. "Oh yeah. I know about sustaining, healing, reconciling, and guiding." Then off people go to *either* sustain and heal for suffering *or* to reconcile and guide for sinning.

Finally, it dawned on me. No one has developed a comprehensive and comprehendible model of personal ministry through soul care (sustaining and healing) and spiritual direction (reconciling and guiding). No one has united all four of these "ancient arts" into a biblically based, culturally relevant, and practically useful method of diagnosis and treatment planning.

Now my lifelong calling has found its mission. My mission is to equip spiritual friends who practice soul care and spiritual direction by:

- Sustaining people so they experience the truth that it's normal to hurt.
- Healing people so they experience the truth that it's possible to hope.
- Reconciling people so they experience the twin truths that it's horrible to sin, but wonderful to be forgiven.
- Guiding people so they experience the truth that it's supernatural to mature.

Exploring Your Spiritual Journey

♦ We're moving into a difficult but vital aspect of spiritual friendship—talking about personal sin.

1. Why is it so much easier to talk about suffering (about how others have sinned against us) than it is to talk about our own sin?

2. Think back to a time when someone confronted you about sin in an unhelpful way that turned you off and pushed you away from God. What was it about how the person related and talked to you that was unhelpful?

3. Recall a time when someone talked to you about sin in your life in a helpful way that encouraged you to confess your sin and find God's forgiveness. What was it about how the person related and talked with you that was helpful?

4. What is your tendency when you become aware of sin in your life? Do you ignore it, do you become overwhelmed by guilt and despair, or do you confess it and find newness of life in Christ's gracious forgiveness?

My prayer for the first half of *Spiritual Friends* is that you become a soul care giver who compassionately identifies with people in pain, redirecting them to Christ and the Body of Christ to sustain and heal their faith. My prayer for the second half of *Spiritual Friends* is that you become a spiritual director who understands spiritual dynamics, discerns root causes of spiritual conflicts, and provides loving wisdom to reconcile and guide faith.

Moving now into that second half will likely motivate some to say, "Finally, we talk about sin!" Others will possibly think, "If we must." For a myriad of personal reasons including background, training, personality, and life experiences, we all have a propensity toward dealing with suffering *or* with sinning. I invite you to join me in both as we embark on spiritual direction: reconciling and guiding your spiritual friends struggling to find victory over sins through growth in grace.

Spiritual direction involves the twin processes of reconciling and guiding. In reconciling, you enlighten your spiritual friends to their sins and to God's grace. Repenting of their sins relationally, rationally, volitionally, and emotionally; they receive God's grace that super-abounds beyond their sins.

In guiding, your spiritual friends are forgiven prodigals returned home. How do they live in Father's house? How do they live with their siblings? Their neighbors? How do they live out their redemption? They do it supernaturally through Christ's resurrection power.

The Biblical Focus of Reconciling: "It's Horrible to Sin, but Wonderful to Be Forgiven"

Martin Luther summarized the whole life of the believer with one word: *repentance*. Hosea 14 and Luke 15 both describe repentance as *relational return*—turning from a position with backs to God, to a position facing God. Repentance is *coram Deo* living in the presence of our holy and loving Father. Sanctification begins with the personal awareness and acceptance of Father's holy love.

Reconciling seeks to *reestablish broken relationships* with God, others, and self. You reconcile your spiritual friends' *spiritual disharmonies* by empowering them to understand and live according to their *spiritual identities*. Sin is always separation, awayness, the break of connection, and the refusal to love. Sin obliterates communion, disintegrates fellowship, and shatters shalom.

That's why sin is horrible. Not simply bad or wrong, but horrible, horrendous. Sin runs away from home, slaps Father in the face, holds Christ in contempt, and grieves the Holy Spirit.

That's why forgiveness is so wonderful. We don't deserve it, can't earn it, and never merit it. Grace is God's prescription for our disgrace. Reconciling refuses to talk about cheap grace. Grace is costly. Sin is horrendous. Forgiveness is amazing.

The Biblical Theology of Reconciling: "I Believe in the Forgiveness of Sin"

Reflecting on the sanctification process, Luther urged his parishioners to recall and apply a core statement in the catechism of the faith: "I believe in the forgiveness of sin." Think about that. Do you? Do I? Do we believe in forgiveness? Do we grant it to others? Do we receive it from Christ? Do we accept our acceptance in Christ?

In our attempts to be biblical counselors, sometimes I fear that we've highlighted sin above grace. Paul did not. "But where sin increased, grace increased all the more" (Romans 5:20, NIV). "But where sin abounded, grace did much more abound" (Romans 5:20, KJV).

Biblical Sanctification in Reconciling: The Triumph of Grace

Reconciliation is the first aspect of the sanctification process. It begins when we put off our old affections/lovers, mindsets, purposes/pathways, and mood states through relational repentance.

Sin is relational betrayal. We betray our Creator. More, we betray Father and our Worthy Groom. In diagnosing sin, we ask the relational question, "Who captivates and captures your soul?"

As spiritual beings, a breakdown in our biblical image of God explains the core cause of our spiritual disharmony with God. We no longer treasure God's splendor (Romans 1:18-28). The author of Hebrews spells out how sin works. "See to it, brothers, that none of you has a sinful, *unbelieving heart*, that *turns away from the living God*" (Hebrews 3:12, emphasis added). Sin starts with unbelief—lack of faith in the goodness of God, and results in fleeing from the Father—turning away from the living God.

It's horrible to sin because of the horrible consequence of sin: *estrangement*. Sin results in alienation from God, separation from one another, and personal dis-integration.

Our chosen independence results in loneliness that leads to enslavement to addictive behaviors (Ephesians 4:17-19). Demanding that we be non-contingent, we become contingent. Demanding that we be independent results in dependencies of all sorts. Now we experience a life of shame instead of shalom, a life of separation instead of connection, a life of manipulation instead of ministry, a life of hoarding instead of giving, and a life of competing instead of cooperating.

Luther concluded that in this state, *the central motivating concern in the human personality is the longing for peace* (shalom, harmony, oneness, communion, and connection). As spiritual directors, we encounter this situation and raise the vital question: "In this condition, how do we help people find peace with God?"

Turning to Scripture, we discover God's answer: *we find peace with God through faith in Christ's grace*. Grace is the only power capable of attracting our souls back to Father, empowering our spirits to live lives of faith active in love toward our brothers and sisters, and enabling our minds to replace shame with shalom. What changes people? Grace relationships based upon grace perspectives. Reconciling is peacemaking where we help one another find peace with God through Christ's grace.

Biblical Diagnosis of Sin

Reconciling depends upon biblical discernment to address the questions: "Who is my spiritual friend?" "How do I diagnose the nature of my spiritual friend's sinful, separating soul?"

Throughout Church history, spiritual directors have produced spiritual nosologies: classifications of problems, issues, sins, and ills by developing culturally relevant spiritual diagnostic systems for use in identifying and overcoming besetting sins that separate people from God and others. Consider one example of historic nosology. "Awaiting the favorable opportunity, he corrects evil, diagnoses the causes of inordinate passion, extracts the roots of unreasonable lusts, advises what we should avoid, and applies all the remedies of salvation to those who are sick" (Clement of Alexandria, *Christ the Educator*, Bk. I, Ch. 12, FC 23, p. 99).

In *Spiritual Friends*, I present two categories of spiritual nosology:

- Diagnosing the State of the Sinning Soul:

  - Relational Adulterers: Impure Affections/False Lovers/Idols of the Heart
  - Rational Fools: Foolish Mindsets
  - Volitional Destroyers: Self-Centered Purposes/Pathways
  - Emotional Addicts: Ungoverned Mood States

- Diagnosing the Stages of Relational Return:

  - From Blindness to Awareness: Guilt—Ephesians 4:17-19
  - From Stubbornness to Acknowledgement: Grief/Repentance—Ephesians 4:18-24

- From Works to Acceptance: Grace—Ephesians 2:1-10
- From Stagnation to Advancement: Growth—Ephesians 2:10-22; 4:20-32

Diagnosing the State of the Sinning Soul: Impure Affections, Foolish Mindsets, Self-Centered Purposes, and Ungoverned Mood States

Boxes 11:1, 11:2, and 11:3 (along with *Soul Physicians: A Theology of Soul Care and Spiritual Direction*) portray the sinning soul. Chapters Twelve and Thirteen teach the relational competencies necessary to use these diagnostic categories to probe theologically into the state of your spiritual friend's soul.

I introduced the basic process in Chapter Four, sharing sample theory-guided questions to ask when dealing with sin, reconciling, and cistern digging.

- *Relationally*: Where is my spiritual friend experiencing the greatest separation in her relationships? What idols of the heart is she pursuing? In what ways is she alienated from God? In what ways is she separated from others? In what ways is she dis-integrated in her own soul? What would relational repentance and return look like for her? What are the horrors of her sinful response to her suffering? How can God's grace influence her soul? What will soulful godliness look like in her relationships? What old impure affections should she put off? What new purified affections should she put on?

- *Rationally*: Where is my spiritual friend losing the battle for his mind? What evidence do I detect of his buying Satan's lie? What fleshly mindsets prevail in his heart? What would repentance as a change of mind look like in his heart? What would mind renewal look like in his situation? What new images of Christ, himself, and his situation could he put on? What old mindsets should he discard?

- *Volitionally*: What evidence do I see of my spiritual friend following purposes/pathways of the world, the flesh, and the Devil? What sinful patterns might she need to put off? What would the putting off process entail in her life? What evidence do I see of her following pathways of the Word, the Spirit, and Christ? What godly patterns might she need to put on? What would the putting on process look like in her life? How could God's grace empower her to respond courageously?

- *Emotionally*: How poorly is my spiritual friend managing his moods? Is he failing to be self-aware? Is he lacking self-control? What would repentance look like in this area? How could he soothe his soul in his Savior?

- *Physically*: How are my spiritual friend's distancing life responses influencing her physically? How can I use her "physical energy meter" as a diagnostic tool to assess whether she is living wisely or foolishly? What spiritual disciplines would assist her to put off old ways and put on new ways?

Chapters Fourteen through Sixteen teach how to use "cistern questions," "spring questions," stages of reconciling and guiding, and the putting off and putting on process to develop spiritual direction treatment plans. Biblical theology is relevant. Our understanding of the state of the soul in the world provides the categories that we need to diagnose problems and propose biblical solutions.

Box 11:1
Image Bearers and Universal Life Themes

Creation: Designed by God

Image Bearing Capacities and Characteristic Approaches to Life

- Relational Romancers: Affections   Passion/Lovers
- Rational Dreamers: Mindsets   Cognition/Images
- Volitional Creators: Purposes   Volition/Pathways
- Emotional Singers: Mood States   Emotion/Moods

Original Personality/Motivational Structure and Characteristic Approaches to Life

- What I believe (mindsets) about my desires (affections) leads to my actions (purposes) and results in my emotions (mood states).
- I pursue (volitional) what I perceive (rational) to be pleasing (relational) which prompts internal reactions (emotional).
- I freely pursue (created volitionality) God as the Chief Affection of my soul (created relationality) because I perceive God to be my Spring of Living Water (created rationality) so I experience love, joy, and peace (created emotionality).

Fall: Depraved by Sin

Fallen Image Bearing Capacities and Characteristic Approaches to Life

- Fallen Romancers: Impure Affections   False Lovers/Idols of the Heart
- Fallen Dreamers: Foolish Mindsets   Fleshly Imaginations
- Fallen Creators: Self-Centered Purposes   Broken Cisterns
- Fallen Singers: Ungoverned Mood States   Survival Modes

Fallen Personality/Motivational Structure and Characteristic Approaches to Life

- I slavishly pursue broken cisterns (fallen volitionality) because I foolishly suppress perceptions of God's holy love (fallen rationality) so I sinfully worship false lovers of the soul experiencing God as less than pleasing, not my Supreme Good (fallen relationality), which prompts internal responses in which I selfishly react with ungoverned mood states (fallen emotionality).

Box 11:2
Sin's Developmental Stages

Sin Relationally: From Romancers to Adulterers
Impure Affections/False Lovers

Rejecting God's awesomeness, refusing to experience God as sufficient, I reject God by:

1. Relying on myself, not God.
2. Trusting in myself, not God.
3. Making myself god.
4. Worshipping false gods and loving false lovers.

Sin Rationally: From Dreamers to Fools
Foolish Mindsets

Without God in my life, my belly becomes my god. Without the Spirit, I believe counterfeit stories about where life is found. Without Christ, I worship what makes my life work to:

1. Quench my perceived thirsts—gain pleasure by self-fulfillment.
2. Deny my unmet longings/groanings—avoid pain by self-protection.

Sin Volitionally: From Creators to Destroyers
Self-Centered Purposes/Pathways

Not being God, but being finite, I can't pull off my goals on my own. So I:

1. Manipulate you (use you) to meet my perceived needs and false goals (gain pleasure/avoid pain).
2. Retaliate against you (abuse you) for not meeting my perceived needs and false goals.

Sin Emotionally: From Singers to Addicts
Ungoverned Mood States

Not being God, you fail to fill me. Now I dread feeling anything deeply. I become emotionally addicted to:

1. Experiencing shallow pleasure.
2. Avoiding personal pain.

Box 11:3
Fallen Image Bearers

Romancers turning themselves into spiritual Adulterers,
Dreamers turning themselves into arrogant Fools,
Creators turning themselves into mastered Destroyers,
Singers turning themselves into moody Addicts, and
Actors turning themselves into materialistic Traitors, living in a
cosmos diabolicus attractively organized to attack God and attach to the flesh,
enchanted by False Seducer's lies masquerading as truth.

Fallen Relational Beings: Adulterers

Sinners are passionate Romancers turning themselves into spiritual Adulterers
passionately pursuing anyone but the Worthy Groom.

Fallen Rational Beings: Fools

Sinners are imaginative Dreamers turning themselves into arrogant Fools
fooled into thinking that the Worthy Groom is unworthy and unloving.

Fallen Volitional Beings: Destroyers

Sinners are empowered Creators turning themselves into mastered Destroyers
unable to have dominion over their own passions, much less God's planet.

Fallen Emotional Beings: Addicts

Sinners are soulful Singers turning themselves into moody Addicts
existing to satisfy their deified bellies.

Fallen Physical Beings: Traitors

Sinners are contingent Actors turning themselves into materialistic Traitors
living like animals in heat.

Fallen World System: *Cosmos Diabolicus*

Cosmos diabolicus attractively organized to attack God and attach itself to the flesh.

False Seducer: Angel of Darkness

The Angel of Darkness masquerading as an Angel of Light
portraying God as evil, Christ as unworthy, and Messenger as a liar.

Diagnosing the Stages of Relational Return

Before effectively using hamartiology (a biblical theology of sinful image bearers), you need to understand the typical stages in the process of facing sin. As with suffering, people may experience unhealthy (ungodly) or healthy (godly) responses to sin in their lives.

Stage	Unhealthy Responses to Sin	Healthy Responses to Sin
Stage One	Blindness	Awareness: Guilt
Stage Two	Stubbornness	Acknowledgement: Grief/Repentance
Stage Three	Works	Acceptance: Grace
Stage Four	Stagnation	Advancement: Growth

Stage One: Awareness—Guilt Rather Than Blindness

As you interact with your spiritual friends in reconciling, you're trying to discern whether they are honestly facing their guilt with personal, biblical awareness *or* remaining blind to it. Obviously, your interactions will vary significantly dependent upon their mindsets.

Let's use the situation with Becky and Bill (her boss who "made a pass" at her at work) as an illustrative scenario. Imagine that you know Bill casually from church. He agrees to meet with you for coffee at a local restaurant. After some small talk and ordering, you move the conversation to the "incident" with Becky.

"Bill, as I mentioned on the phone, I want to talk to you about what happened with Becky. As you know, she claims that you made two clear passes at her . . ." You briefly paraphrase Becky's account.

Before you can really finish, Bill responds with indignation. He totally denies either of the events.

You respond. "Bill, I do know that false accusations occur. I know that misunderstandings can happen. That's why I wanted us to meet. It's also why I wanted to share another piece of information that has come to my attention." You inform Bill that two co-workers (one male, one female) have verified Becky's statements.

Bill is quiet at first, but calm. "You know, people take things out of context. They don't understand the long history that Becky and I have. I was being silly. Innocent flirting. They should know me, and Becky should know me well enough to know that nothing serious was meant. I'd be glad to clarify this with Becky, Vanita, and Steve" (the two co-workers).

Here we see "evidence" indicating that more is going on than Bill is able to see and that there is more going on *inside* Bill than he is able to admit. The Bible calls it blindness and relates it to "sin's deceitfulness."

"But encourage one another today, as long as it is called Today, so that none of you may be hardened by sin's *deceitfulness*" (Hebrews 3:13, emphasis added). As Ephesians 4:18 says, "Having the understanding *darkened*, being *alienated* from the life of God through the *ignorance* that is in them, because of the *blindness* of their heart" (KJV, emphasis added). "If we claim to be without sin, we *deceive ourselves* and the truth is not in us. If we claim we have not sinned, we make him (God) out to be a *liar* and his word has no place in our lives" (1 John 1:8, 10, emphasis and parenthesis added).

Bill's self-deception is a great enticement because through it he can enjoy the pleasant illusion that he's "together." Fearing and fleeing God, he's lost in a web of self-deceit. Therefore, he needs another listening heart that can help him to move from blindness to awareness. *Bill needs guilt.* He is guilty of sinning against (sin is always *against*) God, Becky, Jim, and his wife (Susan). He needs the blind eyes of his heart enlightened to the awareness of his guilt.

Stage Two: Acknowledgement—Grief/Repentance Rather Than Stubbornness

As you continue the diagnostic process, you're now looking for indications of acknowledgement *or* stubbornness. It's instructive to realize that both Hebrews 3:12-13 and Ephesians 4:18 link blindness and hardness. When Bill is blind, he closes his eyes lest he see any evidence. He keeps them closed to the truth by keeping his focus elsewhere, anywhere. Bill might keep his focus on his otherwise "spotless" record at work. He might keep his focus on his seemingly healthy marriage. Or, he might simply keep himself so busy at church that he never takes the time to pray, "Lord, search me and know me. Show me my secret sins. See if there be any wicked way in me."

In the pathology of relational *blindness*, Bill keeps his eyes wide shut to any unpleasant self-awareness. In the pathology of relational *hardness*, his eyes see the evidence, but he chooses to ignore and refuses to acknowledge it. Bill is *blind* when he denies the incidents, and he's *hard* when he counters the evidence that verifies them. Bill needs *awareness:* "I did that. I'm guilty." He also needs *acknowledgement:* "I'm responsible for what I did. I have no excuse. I am sorry. I sinned against you. Please forgive me."

Stage Three: Acceptance—Grace Rather Than Works

Reconciling diagnosis now discerns between works *or* grace. That is, confronted with sin, face-to-face with guilt, will Bill turn to Christ's grace for forgiveness *or* try self-sufficient, works-oriented means to reconcile relationships, cleanse his soul, and salve his conscience?

Bill could come to the point of awareness and acknowledgement but "sorrow like the world" (2 Corinthians 7:8-10). Worldly sorrow works. Godly sorrow entrusts. Worldly sorrow condemns. Godly sorrow frees. Worldly sorrow separates. Godly sorrow reconciles (2 Corinthians 7:10-12).

Some people, caught as Bill is caught, choose spiritual suicide. They simply can't surrender to redemption. They can't accept their acceptance as a sinner saved by grace. The result is spiritual "purgatory." They condemn themselves, curse themselves, and assign themselves to a mental hell of their own making. They serve the offended party like a slave, never again feeling worthy to be called a son, daughter, husband, wife, or friend.

Having repented and pursued restitution, restoration, and reconciliation, Bill needs to accept his acceptance by grace and rest from his works. He needs to hear two of the smallest, but greatest words in Scripture: "*. . . but God . . .*" (Ephesians 2:4). He needs to experience the importance of *confession*; and he needs to know the *character* of God. "If *we confess* our sins, *he is faithful* and *just* and will *forgive* us our sins and *purify* us from all unrighteousness" (1 John 1:9, emphasis added). If Bill does not accept Christ's gracious forgiveness and if he does not receive forgiveness from others, then he will become overwhelmed by excessive sorrow (2 Corinthians 2:5-8) and outwitted by Satan's scheme (2 Corinthians 2:9-11).

Stage Four: Advancement—Growth Rather Than Stagnation

In reconciling's final diagnostic stage, you seek to discern whether Bill is moved by grace to glorify God *or* simply misusing grace to cover sin but not change. In Hebrews 4, the author envisions his audience as "spinning their wheels." The faster they run, the "behinder" they get. The harder they work, the less productive they become. It is always true spiritually that *the more we work for forgiveness, the less we experience forgiveness*.

On the other hand, it is always true spiritually that the more we work *because* we are forgiven, the more we experience our forgiveness. Hebrews 4:11 paradoxically exhorts people to work hard at resting. Ephesians 2:10 teaches that we can't work for our salvation, but that we are God's workmanship (God's poem) created to do good works. Romans 6:1-23 clearly teaches that upon receiving grace, we will spiritually discipline ourselves to avoid sin and to lovingly serve God and others.

When Bill gives into carnality, he blindly, stubbornly works like a mad man but gets nowhere. When he lives from the new spirit within him by God's Spirit dwelling in him, then he is open, soft, restful, and fruitful.

Bill does need to deeply repent before God. He does need to sincerely confess his sin to and ask forgiveness from Becky, Jim, Susan, Vanita, and Steve. He does need to demonstrate a changed life. However, he must not surrender to worldly sorrow and satanic shame. These lead only to works of the flesh. Instead, he can experience godly sorrow that leads to grace-empowered newness of life (2 Corinthians 7:8-12).

Reconciling Intervention

Before exploring reconciling relational competencies in the next two chapters, the task at hand is to ask, "What is necessary for my spiritual friends' faith to be reconciled? What interventions are involved in the process of helping people to know that it's horrible to sin, but wonderful to be forgiven?" Reconciling shoulders the intervention tasks of:

- ♦ Exploring: James 4:1-8
- ♦ Exposing: Hebrews 3:7-19
- ♦ Enlightening: 1 John 1:8-2:2
- ♦ Empowering: Romans 8:1-39

Struggling spiritual friends need the truth dispensed in love. They need Jesus with skin on him. Jesus came full of grace and truth (John 1:14); we need to come to our spiritual friends full of grace and truth.

There are two sections, back to back, in Hebrews 4 that are often quoted separately. They're often explored theologically, but rarely together. How sad. Taken together they teach how Christ blends the message of sin with the glories of grace.

> For the word of God is living and active. Sharper than any double-edged sword, it penetrates even to dividing soul and spirit, joints and marrow; it judges the thoughts and attitudes of the heart. Nothing in all creation is hidden from God's sight. Everything is uncovered and laid bare before the eyes of him to whom we must give account. *Therefore*, since we have a great high priest who has gone through the heavens, Jesus the Son of God, let us hold firmly to the faith we profess. For we do not have a high priest who is unable to sympathize with our weaknesses, but we have one who has been tempted in every way, just as we are—yet was without sin. Let us then approach the throne of grace with confidence, so that we may receive mercy and find grace to help us in our time of need (Hebrews 4:12-16, emphasis added).

"Therefore" forms the bridge between loading the conscience with guilt and lightening the conscience with grace. Spiritual friends use the Word to explore and expose sin. Then they point their repentant friends to Christ's throne of grace enlightening them to forgiveness and empowering them to ministry.

Those who wield the piercing sword must dispense the healing medicine. Sinning spiritual friends need the cutting exposure of their sin (Hebrews 4:12-13) *and* the amazing grace of Christ's forgiveness (Hebrews 4:14-16).

Exploring Your Spiritual Journey

1. Using the concepts listed below, ask God to search your heart to show you areas of sin to confess and areas of maturity to continue.

   a. Relationally: As the pattern of my life, am I turning to impure affections/false lovers and independence from God, *or* am I loving God and others passionately, turning to pure affections/grace lovers and grace relationships?

   b. Rationally: As the pattern of my life, am I suppressing the truth with foolish mindsets and blindness, *or* am I thinking imaginatively with wise mindsets and grace narratives?

   c. Volitionally: As the pattern of my life, am I living for self, based upon self-centered purposes and pathways where I manipulate and retaliate against others, *or* am I living for others, choosing courageously based upon other-centered purposes and pathways, and ministering (death to self)?

   d. Emotionally: As the pattern of my life, am I ungoverned in my mood states resulting in anxiety and rage, *or* am I governing my moods resulting in peace and love?

2. Using the concepts below, evaluate how you typically respond to sin in your life.

   a. Do I tend to remain blind to my sin, *or* do I tend to ask God to make me aware of my sin and guilt?

   b. Do I tend to stubbornly refuse to face my sin, *or* do I tend to acknowledge my sin and grieve over it?

   c. Do I tend to deal with my sin through works-righteousness *or* through clinging to God's grace?

   d. Do I tend to respond to grace by simply being glad I'm forgiven *or* by being motivated by God's grace to live a more godly life?

Exploring: James 4:1-8

In reconciling, you explore *distancing relationships*. With Bill, you want to tap into his loss of shalom (relational wholeness) because sin is always awayness, separation, and failure to love.

Imagine again your conversation with Bill in the restaurant. You could confront him overtly. Likely he will withdraw more, harden more, and become even more self-deceived. Alternatively, you could explore his distancing relationships.

"Okay, Bill. Let me look at this from your perspective. You know Becky well, right? Steve and Vanita, you've worked with them for what, 6-10 years? I'm curious then. How is it that your read on this is so different from theirs?"

Bill responds. "That's what gets me. How could they misread me by so much?"

"Bill, I'd like to turn that question around a tad. How could you misread them by so much?"

"Well, er. I'm not sure I get what you mean."

"Let's focus just on Becky and you. She's floored by this. Devastated. Have you noticed that she has been keeping her distance from you lately?"

"No. I just thought she was busy."

"So you did notice some changes, even if only in the short term."

"Yeah. Yeah. I suppose I did."

"What did Becky say when you approached her and asked, 'Becky, I've noticed you seem busier than usual lately and that we haven't connected much lately. Is there anything wrong? Anything I could do to help? Anything I've done or said?'"

"Oh. I never said anything like that to Becky. I don't think I could or would."

"That's my point, Bill . . ."

Since relational godliness involves passionate, risk-taking, sacrificial, giving love, look for the opposite. Probe instances where Bill is distant from God—backing away, not worshipping, not enjoying God, and in a rigid, pharisaical relationship with God. Explore patterns where Bill is distant from others—manipulative, aloof, insensitive, dispassionate, building walls, putting on coverings (fig leaves), and hiding behind layers. Examine times when Bill is dis-integrated from self—unaware, self-contemptuous, arrogant, anxious, and lacking shalom. These become your diagnostic indicators—the exploratory probes that you send to discover the way Bill is separating from God, others, and self.

At this point you might be thinking, "Distancing relationships?! Bill needs to be 'hit over the head' with his sinful sexual harassment of Becky." Or, you might be thinking, "This guy needs a crash course on political correctness and sexual harassment." Both of these might be true; however, Bill needs to see the *heart sin* behind his *behavioral sin*.

Counseling is *discipleship*. Discipleship is concerned with what Jesus called "the more important matters" of social relationship, spiritual trust, and personal integrity (Matthew 23:23). In working with Bill, his whole pattern of life is of greatest importance to you. You're wanting to help him to become more like Christ. You want his inner life to more maturely reflect the inner life of Christ. Would Jesus mistreat a woman? Of course not! Why not? It's not enough to say, "Because Jesus wasn't a sinner." That's eternally true. However, it's spiritually true that Jesus would never mistreat a woman because of his submission to God the Father, his deep heart of love for people, and his absolute moral integrity. *Jesus always experienced shalom relationships*—communion with God, connection with others, and a clear conscience within himself. Therefore, not only would Jesus never make a pass at a woman, he would never treat a woman with aloofness.

Where was Bill's heart of love for Becky before, during, *and* after the incident? For his wife, Susan? For his good friend, Jim? Bill's "pass," his "sexual harassment," exposes something terribly wrong deep inside. It exposes a *pattern of relational sin*.

Freud incorrectly taught that the royal route to the soul was the unconscious, especially unconscious sexual desires revealed through dreams. Theologically, since all of reality is relational, then *the royal route to the soul is revealed through patterns of relating*. James 4:1-4 traces relational problems back to sinful responses to unmet relational desires. Bill's central false love will reflect itself in every relationship. How is he moving away from God and others and depending upon himself in response to his unmet relational desires? Bill demonstrates a pattern of relational distance. A "relational denseness." James 4 plots the trail of the relational distancing events to explore.

♦ Explore *Unmet* Relational Desires: James 4:1
♦ Explore *Social* Relational Distancing Events: James 4:2-3
♦ Explore *Spiritual* Relational Distancing Events: James 4:3-5
♦ Explore *Self-Aware* Relational Distancing Events: James 4:6

Explore Unmet Relational Desires: James 4:1

"What causes fights and quarrels among you? Don't they come from your desires that battle within you?" (James 4:1). Bill, like all image bearers, has relational longings. He can meet them in God-provided ways or in God-prohibited ways. What does Bill want? What does he long for? What sense of relational acceptance or relational respect is Bill sinfully attempting to fill through his advances toward Becky? What sense of self in the grand adventure and the great love affair of life is Bill pursuing through Satan's meta-narrative of self-sufficiency?

Explore Social Relational Distancing Events: James 4:2-3

"You want something but you don't get it. You kill and covet, but you cannot have what you want. You quarrel and fight . . . You ask with wrong motives, that you might spend what you get on your own pleasures" (James 4:2-3). Bill, like all fallen image bearers, has relational cisterns. He can worship God or worship his own satisfaction. Where is Bill manipulative (coveting)? Where is he living to get Becky to meet his needs? Where is he retaliating (killing)? Where is he striking out against Becky, Susan, Jim, and God? Where are his motives no longer hardwired to God (you ask with wrong motives)? Where is he living a "consumer" lifestyle (spending what he gets on his own pleasures)?

Explore Spiritual Relational Distancing Events: James 4:3-5

James 4 teaches that all social relationship problems are rooted in spiritual relationship problems. "You do not have, because you do not ask God. When you ask, you do not receive because you ask with wrong motives that you may spend what you get on your own pleasures. You adulterous people, don't you know that friendship with the world is hatred toward God? Anyone who chooses to be a friend of the world becomes an enemy of God. Or do you think Scripture says without reason that the spirit he caused to live in us envies intensely?" (James 4:3-5). As you relate to Bill, where do you detect false lovers and idols of the heart? How is Bill demonstrating a works philosophy of life, a self-sufficient approach to life, or a worldly approach to life that rejects God as the Spring of Living Water in favor of the world as a broken cistern that can hold no water?

Explore Self-Aware Relational Distancing Events: James 4:6

"That is why Scripture says: 'God opposes the proud but gives grace to the humble'" (James 4:6). Bill is distant from his own soul. The integrated soul humbly grasps that everything comes as a grace-gift from God. The dis-integrated soul arrogantly and stubbornly believes that God is not generously good. So Bill thinks he must hoard, cling, and grasp. When he does "get," he proudly interprets it as being due to his own efforts. Where is Bill proud, arrogant, self-sufficient, and self-deceived?

Exposing: Hebrews 3:7-19

To help Bill to experience the horrors of sin, you first explore his pattern of relating. This helps you to "gain a handle" on his heart condition. Then you need to communicate your sense of Bill's relational distancing in a way that makes sense to him. I'll explain the *how to* of exposing under the relational competencies of confronting, softening stubbornness, connecting intimately, scriptural explorations, and spiritual conversations. Now my purpose is to explain *why* this is important theologically.

All sin begins with distancing ourselves from God and ends with distancing ourselves from one another. Adam and Eve distanced themselves from God by not calling upon him when the serpent challenged God. How very soon they then distanced themselves from each other with their sad "finger pointing."

The author of Hebrews clearly explains *God-distancing* as the root of all sin. "See to it, brothers, that none of you has a sinful, unbelieving heart that *turns away from the living God*" (Hebrews 3:12, emphasis added). To "turn away" literally means to turn one's back upon as a show of disregard, disrespect, and disgrace.

Two Old Testament narratives, separated by forty years, capture our attention in Hebrews 3. The testing of the Lord in Exodus 17 is highlighted by the author's quotation from Psalm 95:7-11. Significantly, the word for the Israelite rebellion (chide, test, tempt, provoke, strive against, contend with, fight against, be angry and displeased with) is *meribah* (Psalm 95:8). The Old Testament uses it only one other time: Numbers 20:13. The mention of rebellious testing of God at the beginning and ending of the wilderness sojourn is meant to communicate that the conduct was repeated many times during the whole period of the wandering.

The apex of this heart-hardening comes in Numbers 13-14. Ten of the twelve spies claim that "we seemed like grasshoppers in our own eyes" (*self-aware contempt*) (13:33). That night, unbelief and division runs rampant in Israel. All the people weep. Speaker after speaker calls for deposing their leaders (14:1-4) and everyone talks about stoning Joshua and Caleb (14:10) (*social contempt*). Then God responds. "Then the glory of the LORD appeared at the Tent of Meeting to all the Israelites. The LORD said to Moses, 'How long will these people treat me with *contempt*? How long will they refuse to believe in me?'" (14:10-11, emphasis added) (*spiritual contempt* for God).

Their spiritual contempt and scorn for God spawns an ugly family of sinful step-children. They birth self-contempt: the "grasshopper complex." They generate social contempt: quarrelling, rebellion, social chaos, every man for himself, anger, and retaliation.

What can we deduce from these wilderness accounts? Heart hardening is always rooted in unbelief that expresses itself in contempt for God's goodness (beauty) and greatness (power) and results in distancing contempt first from God, then from one another, and then even from oneself.

It is into this context that the author of Hebrews sends the words, "But encourage one another daily" (Hebrews 3:13). Think how different things might have been for Israel if they had encouraged one another daily instead of falling into contempt. Isolation from the mutual encouragement of the Body is dangerous; it is spiritually life-threatening. When alone and unaccountable, it's tempting to take the easy course instead of the right one. It's tempting to follow the arrogant path instead of the humble one.

That's why God-distancing Bill needs to hear the words, "Today, brother, listen to God's voice, so that you may not be hardened by sin's deceitfulness. Sin has duped you into contempt for God. Your sin against Becky is just the tip of the iceberg. Your soul has drifted far from God. Your mind has believed lies about God. Your will has stubbornly chosen to rebel against God. Your emotions have become enslaved to self-satisfaction. Bill, your 'pass at Becky' was so much more than innocent flirting and your way of relating to Becky since then reveals a spiritually hard heart."

What "results" are you praying for as you expose Bill's sin? *Repentance and restitution leading to reconciliation.* "Submit yourselves, then, to God. Resist the devil, and he will flee from you. Come near to God and he will come near to you" (James 4:7-8). Repentance is relational return. Return to the "creaturely" posture of submission to God—dependence, connection, openness, and hands raised to God in praise and contingency.

Instead of fleeing from God, Bill needs to resist the Devil who will then flee from Bill. Bill needs to tell his false lover, the False Seducer, "It's over! Our relationship ends today. I don't need you. I don't want you. You're a liar and a murderer. Everything about my relationship to you has been only evil continually. Be gone!"

Bill then needs to say to God, "Father, I have sinned against you. Though I don't deserve to be called your child, I freely accept your free acceptance. I agree with you that I am guilty of spiritual adultery. I claim your forgiveness. I rest in you. I love you."

Bill's return to God is to be humble and heartfelt. "Wash your hands, you sinners, and purify your hearts, you double-minded. Grieve, mourn, and wail. Change your laughter to mourning and your joy to gloom. Humble yourselves before the Lord, and he will lift you up" (James 4:8-10).

He comes to his Worthy Groom and confesses that he has been "playing both sides of the fence." He's been "hedging his bets." In his double-minded state, he has doubted God's generous goodness (James 1:2-8, 16-18). Consequently, he took what he could from God, took what he could from Satan, and stole what he could from others.

Now Bill needs to approach Christ acknowledging his shame, while realizing that Christ died to take his shame upon himself. He became sin and shame for Bill that Bill might become the righteousness and acceptance of God in Christ.

Having experienced reconciliation with God, Bill pursues *restitution* in order to experience reconciliation with others. James 4:11-5:20 records Bill's need to move from his consumer mentality to God's cooperative mindset. From his manipulative, taking, and grasping actions, he turns to God's ministry, giving, and sharing lifestyle. Godly sorrow produces restitution that rights the wrongs done. Bill doesn't provide restitution as penance, but as a grace-gift to the ones he has harmed. "See what this godly sorrow has produced in you: what earnestness, what eagerness to clear yourselves, what indignation, what alarm, what longing, what concern, *what readiness to see justice done* (2 Corinthians 7:11, emphasis added). "Anyone, then, who knows the good he ought to do and doesn't do it, sins" (James 4:17). Help Bill pursue restitution and renewed relationships through trialogues like these:

- *What words of repentance do you need to and want to take to God?*
- *What words of confession do you need to and want to take to others?*
- *Who do you need to ask to forgive you?*
- *Specifically, what would restoration look like in your situation?*
- *Specifically, what would restitution look like, given what you're guilty of and forgiven for?*
- *Specifically, what would reconciliation involve for you and _____?*
- *Specifically, what would justice look like in your situation?*
- *Specifically, how could you demonstrate your earnestness to make things right?*
- *Specifically, how could you demonstrate your earnestness to be a different kind of person?*

Enlightening: 1 John 1:8-2:2

You want to help Bill to know, "It's horrible to sin." You also long for him to experience, "It's wonderful to be forgiven." Imagine that over the process of time, and through the process of spiritual friendship, Bill comes to see the horrors of his sin. He sees what he has done to his wife, to Becky, to her husband, to his co-workers, to his employer, to his own reputation, and to God. Now what?

Reconciling focuses on *calling back together the estranged*. It mends ruptured relationships by addressing the question: "How are alienated people helped to establish proper and fruitful relationships with God and others?" It endeavors to remove the burden of guilt by reuniting Bill with his loving and holy God. Further, it seeks to empower Bill's spirit to become the ruling captain over his flesh. Reconciling is the "how to" of taking care of Bill's relationship with God and others by applying the living voice of the Gospel to his life.

You want to enlighten Bill to understand his identity in Christ as a reconciled son of God and as a forgiven friend of Christ. He needs this because Satan is sure to tempt him to doubt God's grace. He's sure to tempt Bill to doubt his identity in Christ. In his struggle to sense God's forgiveness, you need to communicate to Bill, "Because Christ paid your penalty, God is at ease with you! Because Jesus suffered God's wrath, God is not incensed with you. He is not angry with you. Understand the true meaning of your forgiveness. Relax. Be at ease. Reach out to unburden others." From this supernatural stance, Bill's soul is filled with God's love overflowing to others.

You want to *bring peace (shalom) to Bill's conscience*. The most basic knowledge the soul must have to survive and thrive is that Christ is the friendly Friend of sinners. Bill needs to rest in his core grace identities: reconciled son and forgiven friend. These grace identities compete against Satan's cursing identity. The law identity is of Satan. It says, "God doesn't want to forgive you." The grace identity says, "I am incorporated into Christ. I am evil, but Christ is good and I am righteous in him."

You can help Bill to explore which meta-narrative he believes. Does he buy Satan's lie: the law condemning identity? Or does he take root in the truth: Christ's grace justifying identity? Grace is the Son's magnet attracting the soul back to the Father's waiting heart. You want to help Bill to live Galatians 5 (freedom from the law) and Romans 8 ("God is for me!"). *Magnify the magnet.* Magnify the liberty Bill has in Christ. Help Bill with trialogues like:

♦ *In 1 John 1:9, John teaches that when you confess your sin, God is faithful and just to forgive your sin against him, Becky, and your wife. What do you think about his promise?*
♦ *During times of doubt about God's grace, how might it help if you perceived Christ saying, "Father, forgive Bill"?*
♦ *How might it help if you picture God as the Pursuing Father of Luke 15, running to you, throwing his arms around you, kissing you, and throwing a wild party in your honor?*
♦ *Martin Luther used to say that when we feel like God is angry with us, we should shout at the Devil, laugh in his face, and remind him that Christ died for our sins and that God can never again be angry at his children. What do you think about Luther's advice? How would you say it differently? What might you add or subtract?*
♦ *Romans 8:1 teaches that there is now no condemnation to those who are in Christ Jesus. Since you are in Christ, what does that verse mean to you, say about you?*
♦ *Romans 8:31-34 teaches that there's a battle brewing in your mind at the point of repentance. Satan chants dirges of condemnation while Christ sings songs of justification. Which are you listening to? Are you dwelling on condemning lies or are you whistling hymns of justifying truth? How can you focus on the truth of your justification and forgiveness in Christ?*
♦ *Instead of seeing God as your angry Judge, how will you be seeing him now?*
♦ *Let's say that you begin to feel overwhelmed with guilt and thoughts that God no longer loves or forgives you. What will you do to fight these lies?*
♦ *I'm curious how God gave you the victory over Satan's condemning lies in the past.*
♦ *I'm curious how it would help if you saw Christ as your merciful best Friend with his arms around you, saying, "I love ya' man!"*

- *Ephesians 3:18-19 teaches that it is **together with all the saints** that we truly grasp how long and wide and high and deep is the love of Christ. Who can you connect with to better grasp God's love to you as he forgives you for these sins?*
- *In 2 Corinthians 2:5-11, Paul explains Satan's schemes **after** we repent. He wants to overwhelm us with excessive sorrow. Paul also teaches that we need to be comforted by others who will relate to us with forgiveness. Who is giving you tastes of Christ's grace, of Father's forgiveness?*
- *In 2 Corinthians 7:8-10, Paul warns against worldly sorrow that leads to death and separation—overwhelming feelings of condemnation. How can 1 John 1:9; Romans 8:1; Romans 8:31-34; Luke 15; and Ephesians 3:18-19 help you to experience godly sorrow that leads to life and reconciliation?*

Empowering: Romans 8:1-39

In enlightening, you help Bill grasp grace—to begin to understand and picture amazing grace. In empowering, you help Bill apply grace—to begin to live powerfully based upon God's grace. In guiding, you'll assist Bill to experience his victory in Christ over sin. However, even now in the reconciling process, you can empower Bill to live according to his new grace identity. The following trialogues begin that vital process.

- *Romans 8:31 says, "God is for you!" What pictures does that bring to mind for you, Bill? How can these images help you to defeat the condemning lies of Satan?*
- *If you truly received God's forgiveness, grace, peace, and "forness," how would you be feeling differently, Bill? Acting differently? Thinking differently? Relating differently?*
- *When the prodigal returned in Luke 15, the Father (God) ran to him, threw his arms around him, kissed him impetuously and continuously, dressed him in robes of dignity, and threw him a party! How does that compare to how you sense your heavenly Father right now? What would it take for you to live according to those biblical images? Do you have the faith to believe that God is treating you like that today? If so, how will you feel, act, think, and relate differently?*
- *When by faith you truly see yourself as the Father's forgiven son, what impact does this have on your Christian life?*
- *When you are relating to Christ as your merciful best Friend, what impact does this have on your other relationships?*

Where We've Been and Where We're Headed

Chapter Eleven presented a biblical model of reconciling, a biblical diagnosis of sin (the state of the sinning soul and the stages of relational return), and biblical reconciling interventions (exploring, exposing, enlightening, and empowering). Chapters Twelve and Thirteen explain the acrostic *PEACEE*—the six relational competencies needed to reconcile spiritual friends.

- *P*   Probing Theologically: Ephesians 4:17-19
- *E*   Exposing through Confronting Wisely: 2 Timothy 2:22-26
- *A*   Active Softening of Stubbornness: Hebrews 3:7-4:16; James 4:1-13
- *C*   Connecting Intimately: 2 Corinthians 6:11-13; James 5:13-16
- *E*   Enlightening Spiritual Conversations: Hebrews 3:12-19
- *E*   Empowering Scriptural Explorations: Hebrews 4:12-16

Exploring Your Spiritual Journey

♦ You want to help your spiritual friend to experience how wonderful it is to be forgiven. How about *you*? How are you accepting your acceptance? How well do you receive God's forgiveness—experience his grace? Read Psalms 32 and 51 (Eugene Peterson, *The Message*, pp. 948-949 and 975-976). Then respond to the questions on the next page, applying God's forgiveness to your life.

Psalm 32

Count yourself lucky, how happy you must be—you get a fresh start, your slate's wiped clean.
Count yourself lucky—Yahweh holds nothing against you and you're holding nothing back from him.
When I kept it all inside, my bones turned to powder, my words became daylong groans.
The pressure never let up; all the juices of my life dried up.
Then I let it all out; I said, "I'll make a clean breast of my failures to Yahweh."
Suddenly the pressure was gone—my guilt dissolved, my sin disappeared.
These things add up. Every one of us needs to pray; when all hell breaks loose and the dam bursts we'll be on high ground, untouched.
God's my island hideaway, keeps danger far from the shore, throws garlands of hosannas around my neck.
Let me give you some good advice; I'm looking you in the eye and giving it to you straight: "Don't be ornery like a horse or mule that needs bit and bridle to stay on track."
God-defiers are always in trouble; God-affirmers find themselves loved every time they turn around.
Celebrate God. Sing together—everyone! All you honest hearts, raise the roof!

Psalm 51

Generous in love—God, give grace! Huge in mercy—wipe out my bad record.
Scrub away my guilt, soak out my sins in your laundry.
I know how bad I've been; my sins are staring me down.
You're the One I've violated, and you've seen it all, seen the full extent of my evil.
You have all the facts before you; whatever you decide about me is fair.
I've been out of step with you for a long time, in the wrong since before I was born.
What you're after is truth from the inside out. Enter me, then; conceive a new, true life.
Soak me in your laundry and I'll come out clean, scrub me and I'll have a snow-white life.
Tune me in to foot-tapping songs, set these once-broken bones to dancing.
Don't look too close for blemishes, give me a clean bill of health.
God, make a fresh start in me, shape a Genesis week from the chaos of my life.
Don't throw me out with the trash, or fail to breathe holiness in me.
Bring me back from gray exile, put a fresh wind in my sails!
Give me a job teaching rebels your ways so the lost can find their way home.
Commute my death sentence, God, my salvation God, and I'll sing anthems to your life-giving ways.
Unbutton my lips, dear God; I'll let loose with your praise.
Going through the motions doesn't please you, a flawless performance is nothing to you.
I learned God-worship when my pride was shattered.
Heart-shattered lives ready for love don't for a moment escape God's notice.
Make Zion the place you delight in, repair Jerusalem's broken-down walls.
Then you'll get real worship from us, acts of worship small and large, including all the bulls they can heave onto your altar!

1. What are some of the phrases from Peterson's translation that stand out to you? Why?

2. What do you feel like when you confess your sin and you realize that God has wiped the slate clean?

3. Write about a time when God gave you a fresh start, when he made a Genesis week out of the chaos of your life.

4. When is the last time you penned a Psalm of Confession and Restoration? What was it like?

5. Spend some time praising God for his generous love and amazing grace.

Maturing Your Spiritual Friendship Competency
Stages of Reconciling

1. Exploring: Write whatever "pattern of distancing relationships" you sense in Bill. Jot down some thoughts about what you "make of this." What heart issues are at work in Bill's life? Refer to Boxes 11:1, 11:2, and 11:3 for some conceptual help. Don't worry about "getting it perfect." Relax. Think biblically. Think theologically. Think imaginatively.

2. Exposing: Imagine that you and Bill have finished lunch. You're now in your office. Together you read Hebrews 3:7-15 and Hebrews 4:12-13. Write the feedback that you might give Bill at this point concerning his distancing relationships.

3. Enlightening: Create your own trialogues that might help Bill to accept his acceptance, to perceive and receive forgiveness.

4. Empowering: Create your own trialogues that might help Bill to actively apply his acceptance in Christ.

Chapter Twelve

Reconciling Treatment and Intervention
PEACEE Relational Competencies, Part I

> *"We are all prodigal sons, and not disinherited; we have received our portion, and misspent it, not been denied it. We are God's tenants here, and yet here, he, our landlord, pays us rents; not yearly, nor quarterly, but hourly; every minute he renews his mercy"* (John Donne, *Devotions upon Emergent Occasions*, p. 10).

Ambassadors of Reconciliation

"Shame." We hear the word and think we've been transported back in time to our childhood. "You should be so ashamed of yourself!"

The troubling childhood indictment contains even more meaning than we might think. Biblical shame means: "Be at war. Be shattered. Be sick. Be troubled." Be at war relationally—alienated from God, separated from others, dis-integrated from self. Be shattered rationally—foolishly and insanely unglued mentally, confused and blinded by the chaos of life. Be sick volitionally—ill, weak, and powerless, fearfully living to hide from God and feed off others. Be troubled emotionally—overwhelmed by life and responding either by stoic resolve that refuses to face reality, or by fleshly indulgence that seeks to anesthetize reality.

"Shalom." We hear the word and think we've been transported to the Jewish section of Brooklyn. "Peace."

The cordial greeting means so much more than we might imagine. Biblical shalom means: "Be at peace. Be whole. Be well. Be calm." Be at peace relationally—communing with God, connected to others, and enjoying a clear conscience with self. Be whole rationally—single-minded not double-minded, integrity not duplicity. Be well volitionally—free to choose courageously for the glory of God and the good of others. Be calm emotionally—not unmoved by the storms of life, but at rest in the eye of the storm, governing what you feel inwardly even if unable to govern what happens to you externally.

Reconciling enters a world of shame speaking shalom. Ambassadors of reconciliation enter souls where shame shatters shalom to share Savior's stillness. Reconciliation seeks harmony—the binding together again of how God meant people and things. Reconciling asks the question, "How can my spiritual friends and I engage in grace relationships that produce peace (shalom) as their faith is reconciled?" Chapters Twelve and Thirteen answer the question with six reconciling relational competencies summarized by the acrostic *PEACEE*:

Exploring Your Spiritual Journey

1. When have you experienced Christ's conviction of sin leading to repentance and newness of life?

2. When have you been able to experience Christ's forgiveness? What has it been like? How did it happen?

3. The Bible talks so much about God's grace, forgiveness, and acceptance based on Christ's death for us. When are you most aware of and impacted by God's grace? What does God seem to do to bring you to a strong awareness of his forgiveness? How do you tend to be cooperating with God as he brings you to these points of awareness?

4. How are you allowing other Christians to help you to enjoy, magnify, and appreciate Christ's grace?

5. In what ways are you using the spiritual disciplines to help you to appreciate God's grace?

- ♦ *P*   Probing Theologically: Ephesians 4:17-19
- ♦ *E*   Exposing through Confronting Wisely: 2 Timothy 2:22-26
- ♦ *A*   Active Softening of Stubbornness: Hebrews 3:7-4:16; James 4:1-13
- ♦ *C*   Connecting Intimately: 2 Corinthians 6:11-13; James 5:13-16
- ♦ *E*   Enlightening Spiritual Conversations: Hebrews 3:12-19
- ♦ *E*   Empowering Scriptural Explorations: Hebrews 4:12-16

Probing Theologically: Theory-Guided Awareness—Ephesians 4:17-19

Before you can expose sin, you have to be aware of sin. Before you can become aware of sin, you have to embed in your mind biblical diagnostic categories of sin.

In Chapter Eleven, under the heading of reconciling diagnosis, you read several pages and viewed three boxes that overviewed theory-guided diagnosis of sin. Here in Chapter Twelve, you learn how to use these categories as you interact with parishioners, clients, and spiritual friends.

Theologically-Guided Probes

Imagine a spiritual friend named Larry asking for help with "my anger problem." Where do you start? How do you probe? Use your understanding of image bearers in a fallen world to guide your exegesis of Larry's situation and soul:

- ♦ Situational: Theologically-Guided Probes and Presenting Problems—Circumstances
- ♦ Emotional: Theologically-Guided Probes and Emotions—Mood States
- ♦ Volitional 1:   Theologically-Guided Probes and Actions—Purposes/Pathways
- ♦ Volitional 2:   Theologically-Guided Probes and Goals—Purposes/Pathways
- ♦ Rational 1:   Theologically-Guided Probes and Beliefs—Mindsets
- ♦ Rational 2:   Theologically-Guided Probes and Images—Mindsets
- ♦ Relational 1:   Theologically-Guided Probes and Self-Awareness—Affections
- ♦ Relational 2:   Theologically-Guided Probes and Social Relationships—Affections
- ♦ Relational 3:   Theologically-Guided Probes and Spiritual Relationships—Affections

Notice that you start with what is on "the outside of the cup"—external matters, situations, and presenting problems. Notice also how you move toward deeper and deeper areas "inside the cup," inside the soul. Emotions tend to point toward actions and goals which tend to point toward beliefs and images which tend to expose affections related to self, others, and God.

As you read the illustrative trialogues probing each area, assume that you've already worked through sustaining and healing issues, or that you and Larry decided to focus on spiritual direction issues of sin and sanctification. As you probe, your purpose is to raise to the surface specific responses in such a way that both you and Larry are clear about what is happening, when, and why.

Situational: Theologically-Guided Probes and Presenting Problems—Circumstances

- ♦ *When did your struggle with anger begin?*
- ♦ *When is your response worse? Better?*
- ♦ *With whom is your anger worse? Better?*
- ♦ *Who is your anger affecting the most?*
- ♦ *How often does this mood come over you?*
- ♦ *Describe a couple of specific times when your anger was out of control.*

- *How are others responding to your anger?*
- *How would things be different if your anger were under control?*

Emotional: Theologically-Guided Probes and Emotions—Mood States

- *Describe your anger for me.*
- *What all are you feeling inside at these times?*
- *How are you feeling now as you discuss your anger?*
- *What does it feel like to lose control?*
- *You sound frustrated, upset, impatient.*
- *How aware are you of your anger as it starts to build?*
- *How much of a sense of self-control do you feel over your anger?*
- *To what extent is this mood a pattern for you, a common, maybe even habitual response?*
- *Where do you think you learned and developed this emotional pattern of responding?*

Volitional 1: Theologically-Guided Probes and Actions—Purposes/Pathways

- *What do you normally do when you start feeling like this?*
- *If you had done exactly what you felt like doing, what would you have done?*
- *How do you respond differently with different people?*
- *What did you do after you blew up?*
- *How typical is this pattern of reacting?*

Volitional 2: Theologically-Guided Probes and Goals—Purposes/Pathways

- *What were you hoping would happen when you did that?*
- *What response do you typically receive when you do that?*
- *What would you have liked to have happened when you did that?*
- *What does that do for you?*
- *Where do you think you learned this way of relating to others?*
- *What happens instead when you don't get angry?*
- *Any guess as to what's motivating your actions?*

Rational 1: Theologically-Guided Probes and Beliefs—Mindsets

- *What were you thinking at the time?*
- *What was going on inside your mind?*
- *If I had a tape recorder recording your brain, what would I have heard?*
- *What sentences were flowing through your mind at that moment?*
- *What were your thoughts about the other person?*
- *What were your thoughts about God?*
- *Any thoughts about why you're thinking this way about life?*

Rational 2: Theologically-Guided Probes and Images—Mindsets

- *How would you picture yourself at that moment?*
- *If I had a VCR playing at that moment, what pictures would I have viewed in your mind?*
- *How do you see yourself in these situations?*

- *How do you see others in these situations?*
- *How do you see God in these situations?*
- *Any ideas why you view life like this?*

Relational 1: Theologically-Guided Probes and Self-Awareness—Affections

- *More than anything else, what did you want at that moment?*
- *What would peace, contentment, shalom, and wholeness be like for you?*
- *When have you felt most at peace with yourself? Least?*
- *How do you feel about yourself at these moments?*
  - *Before you explode?*
  - *As you explode?*
  - *After you explode?*
- *What are your thoughts about yourself at these times?*
  - *When have you felt that way before?*
- *Any sense of why you see yourself like this?*

Relational 2: Theologically-Guided Probes and Social Relationships—Affections

- *More than anything, what did you want from others at that moment?*
- *What were you longing for from the other person?*
- *What did you fear from the other person?*
- *What are your thoughts about others at these moments?*
- *What concerns do you have for others when you vent your anger?*
- *How are you viewing the other person at these times?*
  - *Any sense of why you view him/her this way?*
- *How do you think the other person feels at these times?*

Relational 3: Theologically-Guided Probes and Spiritual Relationships—Affections

- *More than anything else, what are you wanting from God at these moments?*
- *What are you longing for from God?*
- *How are you viewing God at these moments?*
- *Where is God in the picture when you blow up?*
- *Where do you suppose you were recruited into this attitude about God?*
- *What do you think God is thinking at these times?*
- *How might you respond if he showed up?*

Practical Procedures for Probing

Theologically-guided probes help you know what to probe. Some practical procedures help you to know how to probe those areas.

Situational: Theologically-Guided Probes and Presenting Problems—Circumstances

Specificity and categories are the most important principles when probing situations surrounding sin issues. To gain specifics, pinpoint who, what, where, when, how, and why. Discern when the response is better or worse. Diagnose when the problem began and what was happening at that time.

Categories help you gain a sense of the breadth of the problem—how extensive a pattern it is. They also help you gain a sense of the nature of the problem—where it exists and why. Because reality is relational, all categories will have a relational focus. However, you can still distinguish between typical areas where you might want to launch your probes. These include the following relationships and situations:

- Spiritual Relationship with God
- Marital Relationship
- Sexual Relationship
- Family Relationship
- Social/Friendship Relationships
- Church Relationships
- Work Relationships
- Finances
- Recreation/Leisure/Free Time
- Routine Responsibilities
- Health

Emotional: Theologically-Guided Probes and Emotions—Mood States

With emotions, you're working toward identification and acknowledgment. "This is what I feel and this is why I'm feeling it." "This is what I feel. I have control over how I respond to this feeling."

When direct questioning does not yield a clear appraisal of specific emotions, the following skills can be helpful:

- Direct Suggestion: *It sounds like you felt _____. It seems like you feel _____.*
- Feedback of Non-Verbal Clues: *Even as you discuss it, your body language seems to suggest _____.*
- Identification of How You Might Have Felt: *Given these circumstances, I think I might have felt _____.*
- Re-Enactment: *Picture yourself in the situation again. Describe it in detail. Now picture what you were feeling inside.*
- Role-Play: *Let's role-play the situation. I'll be your boss. Now, what are you feeling?*

Volitional 1: Theologically-Guided Probes and Actions—Purposes/Pathways

Volitionally, you pursue description and awareness. "This is what I did and I did it because this is what I wanted." The following practices can be useful when probing actions:

- Analyze Behavior: Create a specific description of the actions before, during, and after the incident. *What did you do? What was happening right before that? What resulted from your actions?*
- Push for Specifics: Stay with one event, one issue, one situation long enough to sense that you were there as an eyewitness.
- Question Directly: Generate a detailed report of what your spiritual friend actually did and why.
- Role-Play: *Let's role-play the situation. I'll be your boss. Now, what are you doing?*

Volitional 2: Theologically-Guided Probes and Goals—Purposes/Pathways

At this point theological probing becomes crucial. You're attempting to discern and expose sinful motivations. You're trying to help Larry to honestly appraise and answer questions such as: "What were you hoping would happen when you did that? What was your goal? What motivated your action/reaction? What were you hoping for? What were you pursuing?"

> **All of our actions are movements toward goals—**
> **either other-centered goals or self-centered goals.**

All of our actions are movements toward goals—either other-centered goals or self-centered goals. You want to establish a pattern of goal-oriented behavior (purposes/pathways). Some basic methods for aligning behaviors and goals include:

- Reaction Probes: Ask, *How did others react to what you did?* This begins to identify what others felt Larry wanted.
- Result Probes: Ask, *What typically results when you do this?* This begins to identify what Larry is hoping for from his behavior.
- Approach/Avoidance Survey: Explore what Larry avoids. *What sort of situations and reactions do you tend to shy away from?* Also explore what Larry seeks: *What sort of situations and reactions do you tend to frequently involve yourself in?*
- Pattern Interpretation: Through careful listening and behavioral analysis, you will begin to detect patterns—links between actions and reactions. Note the theme or primary direction of various actions. Begin to establish in your mind what motivates Larry's actions.
- Provision of Loving Feedback about Goals: Share what you sense. *I'm beginning to wonder whether you get angry in order to push others away so that you don't have to face the truth about yourself.*

Rational 1: Theologically-Guided Probes and Beliefs—Mindsets

Recall the basic principle of *imago Dei motivation*: we pursue (volitional) what we perceive (rational) to be pleasing (relational). Therefore, exposing goals is the first link in exposing beliefs. What sinful mindsets does Larry hold about God, others, self, and life? What sinful beliefs does Larry cling to about what makes life work?

You want to make connections between actions, goals, and beliefs. "Larry, you get angry and express your anger because you believe that life for you is never being shown to be wrong." You want Larry to be able to fill in the blanks: "I pursue _____ because I believe that life for me is _____." Some practical methods for probing beliefs include:

- Theory-Guided Questions: Ask Larry to ponder how he would complete the following sentences. *Life for me is _____. I can make it if _____. I am a somebody if _____. For me, happiness is _____.*
- General Suggestions: After you begin to discern a pattern of beliefs (mindsets), simply share: *It seems to me that you are saying _____.*

- Tape Recorder Method: Ask Larry, *If you had a tape recording of what you were thinking at that moment, of what you were hoping for, what would we hear after we pressed rewind?*
- Worst Case Scenario: Ask Larry, *In that situation, what would the worst case scenario have been? What might you have feared the most? What might have been most hard for you to handle?*

Rational 2: Theologically-Guided Probes and Images—Mindsets

We not only think in words, but also in pictures. God designed us with the power of imagination, the ability to summarize our thoughts with thematic pictures of reality. Some helpful methods for probing images include:

- Theory-Guided Questions: *What image of God stands out in your mind in this situation? Since you see God like that, what does that suggest about how you were seeing yourself?*
- Direct Suggestion: As you listen to patterns of actions, goals, and beliefs, ask God to give you the "imagination" to sense how Larry is seeing himself, others, and God. *Larry, it seems to me that you're seeing God as a Genie in a bottle. I wonder if your view of yourself at that point was like the older brother in the parable of the prodigal son.*
- VCR Method: Ask Larry, *At that moment, if I had a VCR recording of how you saw yourself and God, what pictures would we view?*
- Image History: You can trace the history of core images by asking questions about earliest recollections, deepest hurts, most painful memories, most enjoyable memories, and most significant life events. Then, with Larry, attempt to focus the core image or images of self, God, and others that he has chosen to develop.

Relational 1: Theologically-Guided Probes and Self-Awareness—Affections

Now explore longings, thirsts, hopes, and dreams for *self.* How is Larry attempting to find wholeness, peace, integration, and contentment apart from God? Some practical skills for probing self-aware affections include:

- Taste and Share: As you interact, tune into Larry. Taste what he longs for, how he sees himself, what his personal desires and dreams are. Then share what you sense.
- Probe Wounds and Fears: Larry's sense of self, in a fallen world, might flow from sinful beliefs about and responses to past wounds. Explore what impact past (and present) suffering is having on how Larry senses himself.
- Probe Joy and Happiness: What does Larry most enjoy? When does he feel safest?
- Probe Past History: Explore times when Larry experienced the greatest relational acceptance and the least. Examine times when he experienced the greatest relational respect and the least. What did he learn about life from these events? What longings did he experience? What commitments did he make?

Relational 2: Theologically-Guided Probes and Social Relationships—Affections

Next, explore longings, thirsts, hopes, and dreams in relationship to *others.* How is Larry attempting to use others to dig and fill his own cisterns? How is he manipulating others? In what ways is he retaliating against others for not meeting his needs? Where is he turning desires into demands? Some of the methods helpful in probing these issues include:

- Push for Specifics: Stay with one event, one issue, one situation long enough to sense that you were there as an eyewitness.
- Assess the Relationship: In significant relationships the true "me" comes out. Larry will eventually relate to you in similar ways to how he relates to others. Tune into how you feel as you interact, and share this as a sample biopsy of his relational style.
- Give Feedback Assignments: Assign Larry the task of seeking feedback from others about how he "comes across," about how he relates.
- Ask Theory-Guided Questions: Use the theory-guided questions suggested earlier for this category to explore what Larry really wants, longs for, and desires as he relates to others.
- Contrast and Compare: Contrast and compare how Larry is relating to how Jesus relates to people.

Relational 3: Theologically-Guided Probes and Spiritual Relationships—Affections

Finally, probe how Larry is turning to false lovers in relationship to *God*. Probe how he's forsaking God, his Spring of Living Water, and digging cisterns, broken cisterns that can hold no water. Some of the helpful skills to probe this area include:

- Theory-Guided Questions: To explore idols of the heart, use theory-guided questions to examine how Larry self-sufficiently attempts to quench his thirsts apart from God.
- Compare and Contrast: Compare and contrast Larry's relationship to God to the great commandment to love God with all his heart, soul, spirit, and strength.
- Connect the Dots: Share what you've seen as you've explored Larry's situational, emotional, volitional, rational, and relational patterns.

To connect the dots for Larry, you might share:

> *Larry, from everything you've said, I'm wondering if we're not hearing something like this. When others don't respect you like you believe you must be respected, you blow up. Blowing up has had the effect either of pushing people away so you can pretend that you don't care about their view of you or of getting them to apologize and tell you how right and wonderful you are. You're convinced that others must respect you, for you to have any sense of self.*
>
> *However, in doing this, you're all about **you**, all about **works**, and little about **God** and **others**. The image you portray to people is a bully. Yet that image covers another image you have of yourself—a loser. You cover up your contemptuous self-image with rags of works, specifically the rag of bullying. Rather than go to God to glorify his worth and to find your worth in Christ, you turn to yourself. Your deepest affection is your worth, not God's.*

Where you head from here will depend upon Larry's response. If he does not respond with humble repentance, then you might continue with other reconciling relational competencies such as confronting wisely, softening stubbornness, and connecting intimately. If he does respond humbly, you might continue with the reconciling relational competencies of enlightening spiritual conversations and empowering scriptural explorations.

Maturing Your Spiritual Friendship Competency
Probing Theologically

♦ Imaging that you're working with a spiritual friend who is struggling with the sin of envy toward other people in ministry who receive more attention and praise. Using the outline below, write a dialogue/trialogue between you and your spiritual friend. Use a few probes, questions, categories, or skills in each area, continuing to probe this one issue with each category.

1. Situational: Theologically-Guided Probes and Presenting Problems—Circumstances

2. Emotional: Theologically-Guided Probes and Emotions—Mood States

3. Volitional 1:   Theologically-Guided Probes and Actions—Purposes/Pathways

4. Volitional 2:   Theologically-Guided Probes and Goals—Purposes/Pathways

5. Rational 1:   Theologically-Guided Probes and Beliefs—Mindsets

6. Rational 2:   Theologically-Guided Probes and Images—Mindsets

7. Relational 1:   Theologically-Guided Probes and Self-Awareness—Affections

8. Relational 2:   Theologically-Guided Probes and Social Relationships—Affections

9. Relational 3:   Theologically-Guided Probes and Spiritual Relationships—Affections

Exploring Your Spiritual Journey

1. List some of the first words, thoughts, pictures, and concepts that come to mind when you hear the word "confrontation."

2. Summarize a "bad experience" you had when someone "confronted" you.

3. Summarize a "bad experience" you had when you "confronted" someone.

4. Write your definition of "confrontation."

Exposing through Confronting Wisely: Disclosing Discrepancies—2 Timothy 2:22-26

Confrontation has earned an undeserved "bad rap." To correct that, consider the following biblical definitions.

- Confrontation exposes discrepant worldviews.
- Confrontation exposes spiritual inconsistencies.
- Confrontation shows people how they are living inconsistently.
- Confrontation shows people how they are intoxicated by the lies of the world, the flesh, and the Devil.

In 2 Timothy 2:25, Paul commands Timothy to "gently instruct (confront, correct) those who oppose themselves" (author's translation). The phrase "oppose themselves" develops from the Greek word for antithesis, a contrary position. *Anti* means "against" and *tithemi* "to place." *Antitasso* means to set oneself against the natural order. Here in 2 Timothy the word is *antidiatithemenous*: *anti*—"against," *dia*—"through," and *tithemenous*—"to place." In the middle tense as it is here, it means *to stand opposed to oneself, to place oneself in opposition to oneself* (Ralph Earle, *Word Meanings in the New Testament*, p. 406).

Confrontation shows Larry how he is standing opposed to himself. It exposes how he is living inconsistently with his new heart. It demonstrates how his life is inconsistent with his stated beliefs. It reveals how he is buying the lie of the works narrative rather than being rooted in the truth of Christ's grace narrative. Confrontation points out discrepancies.

In 2 Timothy 2:22-26, Paul explains the character of the confronter, the process of confrontation, the goals of confronting, and the true enemy in confrontation.

Flee the evil desires of youth, and pursue righteousness, faith, love, and peace along with those who call on the Lord out of a pure heart. Don't have anything to do with foolish and stupid arguments, because you know they produce quarrels. And the Lord's servant must not quarrel; instead, he must be kind to everyone, able to teach, not resentful. Those who oppose him (oppose themselves) he must gently instruct (confront, correct), in the hope that God will grant them repentance leading them to a knowledge of the truth, and that they will come to their senses and escape from the trap of the devil, who has taken them captive to do his will (2 Timothy 2:22-26, parenthesis added).

Confrontation requires integrity. To confront another, Timothy first has to confront himself. He has to flee (put off) evil desires and pursue (put on) godly affections. He removes the log from his eye by living out of a pure heart, before he confronts the heart of another.

Confrontation also requires humility. Timothy shuns fights, quarrels, and stupid arguments. Instead, he is to be kind and patient toward others, especially with those who are refractory. He sees himself as the Lord's servant—his slave, voluntarily under Christ's authority.

Confrontation further requires spirituality. Biblical confrontation is not bold and bullying. It is gentle and patient. In confronting, Timothy practices patience (2:24). That is, he bears up under wrong. When confronting others, they frequently become displeased with him. To bear up without resentment, Timothy needs forbearance.

Timothy is also to confront in meekness (2 Timothy 2:25). Meekness includes a temper of spirit and managed strength released with gentleness, humility, and concern. The meek person neither fights against God nor enters power struggles with others. The meek spiritual friend displays the opposite of self-assertion and self-interest.

Confrontation also requires capability. Timothy has to be "able to teach" (2:24). He needs to skillfully relate doctrine to conduct. He has to relate truth to human relationships.

Paul uses the word *paideuonta* ("gently instruct") to describe the process of confrontation. The word relates to schooling and in this context emphasizes corrective instruction (A. T. Robertson, *Word Pictures in the New Testament*, p. 541).

Its root form *paideuo* literally means to train children. Such child training requires practicality. It also necessitates explanation, as opposed to simply handing down rules by fiat. Much more than mere exhortation to stop a behavior, it involves instruction in the process of heart change leading to behavioral change.

Finally, confrontation requires savvy. "Those who oppose themselves he must gently confront *in the hope that God will grant them repentance*" (2:25, author's translation, emphasis added). Timothy avoids power struggles and a quarrelsome spirit by realizing that it is not his role, but God's, to bring about repentance. His role is simply to gently instruct by demonstrating discrepancies.

The goal of instructive correction (confrontation) is maturity: love out of a pure heart, a good conscience, and a sincere faith (1 Timothy 1:5). Thus the goal is virtue (2 Peter 1:3-11): character, not simply content. Biblical instruction/confrontation includes a presentation of a clear worldview (grace narrative) and the implications derived from it (grace relationships). Confrontation promotes spiritual development through personal influence; it is the relational presentation of God's worldview. It skillfully explores any discrepancies between grace narratives and works narratives and grace relationships and works relationships.

Paul further develops the goal of gentle biblical confrontation when he writes, "that they may recover themselves" (2 Timothy 2:26, author's translation). Thus the goal is sobriety and sanity. To "recover" means to return to soberness as from a state of delirium where one is under the control of an outside element—the controlling passions of the flesh, intoxicated with false worldviews, and snared by the Devil (Earle, *Word Meanings in the New Testament*, p. 406). Confrontation helps a person like Larry to return to a sound mind—a whole, healthy mind that thinks and lives with integrity.

> **Confrontation helps a person like Larry to return to a sound mind—
> a whole, healthy mind that thinks and lives with integrity.**

An additional goal of confrontation is safety—escape from the snare of the Devil who has taken them captive to do his will. "Snare" (2 Timothy 2:26) is a trap that fastens or holds fast, a net, a noose. Various authors used the word for seductive women and for the Trojan Horse. A snare is anything that entices with something desirable. It promises pleasure, but gives pain. When snared, Larry is caught in the net of self-deception and captured by the Devil's delusion.

Notice, too, who the true enemy is here. Larry is not the ultimate enemy, Satan is. He has taken Larry captive. You attack Satan with God's armor rather than attacking Larry.

Let's consider some of the relational competencies necessary for biblical confrontation as you work with Larry and other spiritual friends.

Sense Discrepancies by Carefully Hearing the Human Story and God's Story

Since Larry's life is not lining up with God's will, you want to sense discrepancies.

Listen for Discrepancies between the Human Story and God's Story

Ask yourself as you interact:

- *How is Larry failing to live out God's grace narrative?*
- *How is Larry failing to see God's grace narrative?*
- *How is Larry failing to live out God's grace relationships?*
- *How is Larry failing to live like Christ's redeemed image bearer?*

Listen for Discrepancies within the Human Story

Ponder as you interact:

- *Where is Larry seeking false idols instead of worshipping Christ?*
- *Where is Larry following foolish mindsets rather than wise mindsets?*
- *Where is Larry pursuing self-centered pathways rather than other-centered ones?*
- *Where is Larry living according to ungoverned mood states instead of managed moods?*
- *How is Larry presenting one goal but pursuing another?*
- *How is Larry living one lifestyle but claiming another?*
- *How is Larry living a double-minded life filled with trust and doubt?*

Listen for Discrepancies between the Spirit and the Flesh

Seek to perceive:

- Inconsistencies: Mixed messages, goals, thoughts, explanations, and feelings.
- Incongruity: Disparity between two statements, between actions and words, as well as between words and non-verbals.

In all of your listening, push for specifics: Stay with one event, one issue, or one situation long enough to sense that you were there as an eye witness.

Provide Feedback Concerning the Discrepancies You Hear

What do you do once you've sensed Larry's spiritual discrepancies? Present statements that raise the issue of: "On the one hand . . . on the other hand . . ."

- *On the one hand, I hear you saying that you have a healthy relationship with your co-workers. Yet on the other hand, I sense that you're unable to sense the impact of your anger on them.*

Then allow Larry to confront his own discrepancies:

- *On the one hand, I hear you saying that you have a healthy relationship with your co-workers. Yet on the other hand, I sense that you're unable to sense the impact of your anger on them.*
  - *How does this appear to you?*
  - *What do you make of this?*
  - *How do you put these two together?*

The art of confronting discrepancies is essential in all areas of relationship, not only in exposing "sin issues." In Chapter Seven, you read spiritual conversations that explored discrepant feelings, thoughts, and experiences (see below). Though not noted as such at the time, these interactions confront discrepancies in "suffering issues."

- *Your son's sudden death has left you terribly dejected; you feel this pervasive grief, and at the moment you can find no consolation in your life or your religious faith.*
- *It's hard to feel anything but sadness because of your son's death, and this is made even worse by the feeling that it was terribly unjust, a betrayal by God.*
- *It's hard to feel anything but sadness because of your son's death, but some part of you would welcome genuine faith and consolation.*
- *One part of you wants some genuine relief from your deep sorrow, but you don't feel open to the peace and assurance that your faith might give.*
- *One part of you is terribly angry with God for taking your son from you, but you are reluctant to express that anger, to tell God how you feel and what you think.*

All of these conversations display humility and meekness. God never calls you to cause others to lose face or to sense that you think that you're superior to them. Satan is the enemy. Your spiritual friends are not.

Larry may respond to your biblical, gentle confrontation in any number of ways. He may meet your confrontation with denial. *"Nope. Not me. Don't see it like that at all."*

He may respond with partial acceptance. This may look like quick agreement and may feel like insincere agreement, or it might take the form of shifting blame or making excuses.

Additionally, he may respond with acceptance and acknowledgement that results in repentance (new attitudes), restitution (new actions), and reconciliation (renewed relationships). If this is his response, rejoice. If not, move on to softening stubbornness.

Active Softening of Stubbornness: Loosening Resistance to Repentance
Hebrews 3:7-4:16; James 4:1-13

Confrontation attempts to help Larry to see what he is *unaware of.* Softening stubbornness attempts to help him to face things he is aware of, but *refusing to change.*

> **Stubbornness is the inclination to continue in self-sufficient attitudes (rational) that lead to selfish relationships (relational) maintained by chosen suppression (volitional).**

Stubbornness is the inclination to continue in self-sufficient attitudes (rational) that lead to selfish relationships (relational) maintained by chosen suppression (volitional) (Romans 1:18-32). The beach ball of guilt pops to the surface, but we force it down. Our flesh would rather choose the same old stupid (foolish) ways than be God-dependent. Since we are not yet glorified, at times we resist the work of the Spirit. We resist change, growth, grace, faith, hope, love, and peace.

Maturing Your Spiritual Friendship Competency
Confronting Discrepancies Wisely

1. From the presentation of 2 Timothy 2:22-26 and Paul's teaching on biblical confrontation:

   a. What stands out to you as new and important concepts?

   b. What applications do you want to make to your life and ministry?

2. Write a dialogue (trialogue) with Larry that explores discrepancies in his life emotionally, volitionally, rationally, and relationally.

3. Remember that confrontation is useful in sustaining and healing as well as in reconciling and guiding. Write a dialogue (trialogue) with Alonzo that explores discrepancies in his feelings, goals, thoughts, and longings as he faces his battle with cancer.

Stubbornness is *our creative refusal to entrust ourselves to God and others. Spiritual* stubbornness involves our refusal to love God by clinging to his grace, submitting to his holiness, and enjoying his goodness (Romans 1:18-28). *Social* stubbornness involves our choice to manipulate and retaliate against our brothers and sisters because we doubt God's generous goodness (James 4:1-13).

In spiritual friendship, stubbornness is the current evidence of self-centered relationships. Stubborn resistance to growth exposes the difference between your agenda and Larry's.

You're saying, "Trust God, please God, obey God. Minister to others, love others."

Larry's saying, "Change my circumstances and improve my feelings. Agree with me. Side with me in my independence from God. Side with me as I refuse to abandon myself to God and reject risky relationships with others."

Talk about discrepancies! What clear discrepancies between your goals as a Christian counselor and Larry's goal for Christian counseling.

Stubborn resistance arises when Christianity is simply a plate that fits into our cupboard of denial. We like the status quo. "Don't unsettle me. I want to maintain control. Facing my dependency upon God is frightening because he will not put himself under my control." Stubbornness allows us to disengage our souls from life. "I will not be disturbed. All truth must reinforce what I already know!"

How do you handle stubborn resistance in biblical counseling? What can you do to soften Larry's stubborn heart?

Becoming Aware of Stubbornness

To soften stubbornness, you must be aware of it. You become aware of stubbornness by exploring distancing relational events. Ask yourself as you relate to Larry, "How is Larry relating to God? To others? To me? How is he relating as an image bearer?"

To become aware of Larry's stubbornness in his relationship to God, ponder:

- *How is he trusting in himself instead of in God?*
- *How is he meeting his own needs apart from Christ?*
- *What false cisterns is he drinking from to satisfy his thirsts?*
- *How is he living as if he can make life work apart from God?*
- *In what ways is he living for this life?*
- *In what ways is he refusing to depend upon, trust, enjoy, submit to, and glorify God?*
- *What wrong motives seem to be driving him?*
- *What faulty views of God does he seem to have?*
- *How is he choosing worldly satisfaction over loving God?*
- *How is he forsaking God as his Spring of Living Water?*
- *How is he cooperating with God to love others?*
- *How is he drawing near to God?*
- *How is he mourning the damage his sin has caused?*
- *How is he resisting Satan?*
- *In what ways is he evidencing dependence upon God? Ministry? Sacrifice? Passion? Courage? Depth?*

To discern how Larry is distancing himself from others, ponder:

- *How is he failing to love?*
- *What would it be like to be in a relationship with him as his spouse, co-worker, child, parent, or friend?*

- *How is he retreating from involvement?*
- *How is he failing to connect?*
- *What is he doing to protect himself?*
- *How is he living out the phrase, "I want what I want and I want it now!"*
- *How is he ministering to others?*
- *How is he open and vulnerable with others?*
- *How is he looking out for the interests of others?*
- *What evidence do I see of the fruit of the Spirit in his life?*

To discern how Larry is relating to you, consider some thoughts to probe as you provide spiritual direction (the next relational competency—connecting intimately—explores this area in more detail).

- *How do I feel as I relate to him? Invited in? Pushed away? Respected? Cared about? Discounted? Mistrusted? Discouraged? Intimidated? Loved?*
- *As I relate to him, do I sense: Sarcasm? Emotional withdrawal? A critical spirit? The cold shoulder? Aloofness? Faultfinding? Arrogance? A judgmental spirit? Harshness? Warmth? Trust? Mutuality? Teamwork? Intimacy?*

To probe how Larry is relating as an image bearer, return to categories previously used under reconciling diagnosis. They're helpful now in diagnosing patterns of possible stubborn sin relationally, rationally, volitionally, and emotionally.

- *Relationally*: What old false lovers should he put off? What impure affections motivate him? What idols of the heart control him? Where is his greatest separation in his relationships? In what ways is he alienated from God? In what ways is he separated from others? In what ways is he dis-integrated in his own soul? What are the horrors of his sinful response to his suffering? What would relational repentance and return look like for him? How can God's grace impact his soul? What will soulful godliness look like in his relationships? What new grace affections should he put on?
- *Rationally*: What fleshly mindsets prevail in his heart? What old mindsets should he discard? Where is he losing the battle for his mind? What evidence do I detect of him buying Satan's lie? What would repentance as a change of mind look like in his heart? What would mind renewal look like in his situation? What new images of Christ, himself, and his situation could he put on?
- *Volitionally*: What evidence do I see of him following purposes/pathways of the world, the flesh, and the Devil? What sinful patterns might he need to put off? What would the putting off process entail in his life? What evidence do I see of him following purposes/pathways of the Word, the Spirit, and Christ? What godly patterns might he need to put on? What would the putting on process look like in his life? How could God's grace empower him to respond courageously?
- *Emotionally*: How poorly is he managing his moods? Is he failing to be self-aware? Is he lacking self-control? What would repentance look like in this area? How could he soothe his soul in his Savior?

These questions are designed to tap into relational longings and the stubborn refusal to drink from God the Spring of Living Water. They help you to detect, and then to expose, stubbornness relationally, rationally, volitionally, and emotionally.

Dealing with Confusion

You must be careful not to label every disagreement "stubbornness." That would be arrogant. At times, Larry is open to considering the biblical perspective, but genuinely can't see or understand it. Perhaps you have explained things poorly or communicated ineffectively. Or, perhaps you are simply wrong in your assessment. When Larry is genuinely confused, respond with:

- A gentle answer (Proverbs 15:1).
- Gentle instruction (2 Timothy 2:22-26).
- Listening.
- Dialogue and trialogue.
- Patience.
- Prayer.
- Images: Creatively picture with words, illustrations, and narratives what you are attempting to communicate.
- Deep relationship.

The Art of Seeing Stubbornness

At other times, Larry will simply be stubbornly resisting the work of the Holy Spirit through you. He is willfully refusing to seriously consider and apply biblical truth to his life.

Not all such stubbornness is obvious. Depending on Larry's personality and relational "sophistication," he might express his stubbornness in any number of ways. For example:

- Helplessness.
- Sullenness.
- Excessive emotion whenever change is discussed.
- Insincere agreement.
- Surface changes.
- Excuse making.
- Formula Christianity: Living by rules, regulations, and external behavior.
- Hostility.
- Blaming.
- Guilting: Trying to cause you to feel guilty for his feelings of guilt.
- Intimidating.
- Rabbit trails.
- Objection hopping.
- Distance and aloofness.

Consider two broad styles of spiritual stubbornness. One cries, "I'm helpless." The other shouts, "I don't need any help!"

Larry might play the subtle role of the *despairing, needy, helpless* stubborn person. Acting helpless, he communicates, "Fix me. Save me. Magically change all that displeases me with no participation on my part." Rather than practicing spiritual discipline, he wishes for a magic wand, a magic word, or an ultimate prescription that makes life and growth easy. Like the Israelites of Jeremiah's day, he loves hearing prophets say, "Peace, peace," even when there is no peace (Jeremiah 6). Like the flesh-oriented Christians in Timothy's life, he gathers around himself teachers to say what his itching ears want to hear

(2 Timothy 4:3). He turns his ears away from the truth to myths (Satan's lying narrative) (2 Timothy 4:3-5). When you expose his stubborn helplessness, he wants you to rescue him, fix him.

Or, Larry might play the less subtle role of the *raging, autonomous, hostile* stubborn person. Acting as if he needs no help, he communicates, "Back off. Don't you dare confront me. I'll make you pay dearly. I am never wrong!" Rather than practicing spiritual humility, he's extremely self-sufficient, arrogant, and overtly or covertly hostile. He knows no alliances of equals and no comradeship, only competition. Like the rebellious in Timothy's day, his conscience has been seared as with a hot iron (1 Timothy 4:12). He will not easily respond to your attempts to expose his stubbornness.

Softening Stubbornness with God's Word

Hebrews 4:12-13 portrays the incredible power of biblical insight. God's Word lays bare the human soul. When a particular attitude or action is overtly and clearly unbiblical and this is demonstrable by reference to a specific passage or passages, then share that passage prayerfully with courageous meekness.

When the attitude or action is less overt, or stubbornly suppressed, then trialogue with Larry.

- *What Scriptures could we look at that might clarify God's position on your relationships? Thinking? Motivation? Actions? Feelings?*
- *What have you sensed God's Spirit saying to you?*
- *What does God's Word say concerning your current way of relating?*
- *What passages have you found helpful in gaining God's perspective on this?*

Softening Stubbornness with Your Words

You have several options at your disposal to soften stubbornness through sharing your words enveloped in biblical principles. Consider again the scenario with Bill and Becky. With Bill, you could ask about what a *perfect way of relating* to Becky might have been. This can help him to see the contrast between how he related and how he could have related.

Ask Bill *how he would have felt* if "the shoe had been on the other foot." Empathy for the victimized person is one means of softening hard-hearted stubbornness.

Explore with Bill *other possible relationships* where others have felt like Becky felt—threatened, intimidated, boundaries overstepped. You're hoping to identify *patterns* so that Bill can't flippantly say, "Oh, even if that were true, it's just an isolated incident."

With *loving firmness explain what you sense.* Provide specific feedback concerning the pattern of relating that you're sensing.

Share your own battles, scars, defeats, and victories. "Bill, I know that for me it's hard to admit when I'm intimidating. It's hard to admit when my desires have 'gotten the best of me.' But they have at times . . ."

Predict. "Bill, I'm no prophet, but I will make a prediction about what's likely to happen if you don't take a serious look at the patterns exposed by your actions . . ." The greatest power may come far down the line. When your prediction comes true, Bill may be at your door again seeking your wisdom.

Draw the line. There are times when you need to draw the line. Depending on the circumstances, this can take many shapes. It might involve an "intervention" where Becky, Susan, Jim, Vanita, Steve, and you provide group input to Bill. In a church situation, it may mean beginning the Matthew 18 process of church discipline/restoration by bringing in a third party. It may mean saying, "Bill, after a lot of prayer, effort, time, and consideration, I've decided that we can't continue to meet until you face up to your behavior . . ."

Pray. From first to last, prayer is essential. Remember 2 Timothy 2:22-26. You gently instruct in the hope that God will grant Bill repentance leading to the knowledge of the truth.

Where We've Been and Where We're Headed

Sin is insidious. As the saying goes, "Oh what tangled webs we weave, when at first we practice to deceive." Because that is true, probing theologically, exposing through confronting wisely, and active softening of stubbornness may still meet with resistance. What now? What next?

Or, perhaps Larry or Bill respond to your probes, exposure, and softening, but they are overwhelmed with sorrow and wracked with debilitating guilt. What now? What next?

Chapter Thirteen suggests three additional reconciling relational competencies that address both of these possible scenarios (refusal to repent and overwhelming sorrow). They are the final three competencies in the *PEACEE* acrostic:

- ♦ *C*   Connecting Intimately: 2 Corinthians 6:11-13; James 5:13-16
- ♦ *E*   Enlightening Spiritual Conversations: Hebrews 3:12-19
- ♦ *E*   Empowering Scriptural Explorations: Hebrews 4:12-16

Maturing Your Spiritual Friendship Competency
Softening Stubbornness

♦ Respond to the questions below based upon the following scenario. You've worked with your spiritual friend who is envious of others in ministry. You've probed and confronted, however, you sense resistance—stubbornness.

1. You think his/her resistance may be due to confusion. Write how you would use two or three of the following principles to deal with the confusion: a gentle answer, gentle instruction, listening, dialogue and trialogue, patience, prayer, images, and relating deeply.

2. Your spiritual friend's stubborn resistance is very subtle. Choose two or three of the following examples of subtle resistance and write sample statements he/she might make: helplessness, sullenness, excessive emotion, insincere agreement, surface changes, excuse making, formula Christianity, hostility, blaming, guilting, intimidating, rabbit trails, objection hopping, and aloofness.

3. Choose two or three of the following ways to soften stubbornness, then write descriptions of what you would say/do: ask about a perfect way of relating, ask your spiritual friend how he/she would feel, ask about other possible relationships where similar feelings arise, with loving firmness explain what you sense, share your own battle scars, predict, and draw the line.

Chapter Thirteen

Reconciling Treatment and Intervention
PEACEE Relational Competencies, Part II

> *"By the bruised here is not meant those that are brought low only by crosses, but such as, by them, are brought to see their sin, which bruises most of all. When conscience is under the guilt of sin, then every judgment brings a report of God's anger to the soul, and all lesser troubles run into this great trouble of conscience"* (Richard Sibbes, *The Bruised Reed*, pp. 10-11).

Spiritual Warfare

Recall Larry and his "anger issues" from Chapter Twelve. After probing theologically, exposing through confronting wisely, and actively softening stubbornness, you summarized Larry's heart issues.

> *Larry, from everything you've said, I'm wondering if we're not hearing something like this. When others don't respect you like you believe you must be respected, you blow up. Blowing up has had the effect either of pushing people away so you can pretend that you don't care about their view of you, or of getting them to apologize and tell you how right and wonderful you are. You're convinced that others must respect you, for you to have any sense of self.*
>
> *However, in doing this, you're all about **you**, all about **works**, and little about **God** and **others**. The image you portray to people is a bully. Yet that image covers another image you have of yourself—a loser. You cover up your contemptuous self-image with rags of works, specifically the rag of bullying. Rather than go to God to glorify his worth and to find your worth in Christ, you turn to yourself. Your deepest affection is your worth, not God's.*

Sitting back in your chair, you await Larry's "aha experience." It doesn't come.

> *I don't see it, Bob. Yeah, I get angry occasionally. We all do. But all this psychobabble makes me seem like a raving mad man. That's just not me. Ask anybody.*

Now what? Perhaps you enter a classic power struggle where you attempt to persuade Larry to accept your analysis. Maybe now's the time to draw the line in the sand and refuse to meet again until Larry "sees the light." Fortunately, the final three reconciling relational competencies provide better

Exploring Your Spiritual Journey

1. Read Hebrews 3:12-14. What impact could it make on your life if you had a spiritual friend or two who related to you according to Hebrews 3:12-14?

2. Read Hebrews 4:12-13. What impact could it make on your spiritual life if you and a spiritual friend used God's Word in each other's life the way Hebrews 4:12-13 suggests?

3. Read Hebrews 10:24-25. What impact could it have on your life if you were connected to a group of spiritual friends who consistently related to one another the way Hebrews 10:24-25 suggests?

4. Based upon the three preceding passages/questions, what longings are stirring in your soul? What are you motivated to do?

options. Taken together, the six reconciling competencies summarized by the acrostic *PEACEE* equip you to provide biblical spiritual direction to folks like Larry.

- ◆ *P*   Probing Theologically: Ephesians 4:17-19
- ◆ *E*   Exposing through Confronting Wisely: 2 Timothy 2:22-26
- ◆ *A*   Active Softening of Stubbornness: Hebrews 3:7-4:16; James 4:1-13
- ◆ *C*   Connecting Intimately: 2 Corinthians 6:11-13; James 5:13-16
- ◆ *E*   Enlightening Spiritual Conversations: Hebrews 3:12-19
- ◆ *E*   Empowering Scriptural Explorations: Hebrews 4:12-16

Connecting Intimately: Relating in the Moment—2 Corinthians 6:11-13; James 5:13-16

Because connecting intimately is so rare, I'll begin with some definitions and descriptions.

- ◆ *Coram Anthropos Intimacy*: Face-to-face relating with your friend about *your* friendship.
- ◆ *Dynamic Immediacy*: Dealing with what is taking place in *your relationship* at the *present* moment.
- ◆ *Relational Patterning*: Discussing the here-and-now with a view toward the *implications* for *other* relationships.

Throughout 1 and 2 Corinthians, Paul models intimate connecting as *he uses his relationship to the Corinthians as a catalyst to expose their relational immaturity.* Witness a beautiful and powerful example from 2 Corinthians 6:11-13.

We have spoken freely to you, Corinthians, and opened wide our hearts to you. We are not withholding our affection from you, but you are withholding yours from us. As a fair exchange—I speak as to my children—open wide your hearts also (2 Corinthians 6:11-13).

Paul follows a foundational principle: how people relate intimately to you mirrors how they relate intimately to others. We can only hide ourselves so long. Eventually, in significant relationships, our words either reveal or betray us, for out of the abundance of the heart, the mouth speaks. We relate in similar ways in all our meaningful relationships. Whatever is central to our style of relating will reflect itself in all our intimate relationships.

> **How people relate intimately to you mirrors how they relate intimately to others.**

The principle holds true only if your relationship is truly and purely intimate. Passionate love, imaginative thinking, courageous choosing, and experiential depth mark intimate relationships. If your pastoral ministry, professional counseling, and spiritual friendships are shallow and merely academic, then don't expect to detect significant relational patterns. Paul understood that insight alone never delivered anyone (1 Thessalonians 2:8; Philippians 1:9-11). He believed in and practiced the relational competency of being fully alive and present in his relationships.

Connecting intimately is vital because reality is relational. When you connect intimately with Larry, you become a main character in his life drama, instead of remaining simply a reader of his life story.

Connecting intimately is powerful because it's rare, even though it's exactly how God designed people to relate (Genesis 2:23-25).

The immediacy of your relationship with Larry provides here-and-now tastes of his pain, thirst, sin, and growth. It removes the wall between the two of you and the veil over his eyes, allowing you to catch Larry in the act of spiritual maturity or in the act of fleshly immaturity.

Connecting intimately requires much of you:

- *Relationally*: You need passionate love to touch soul-to-soul, not as an expert to a client, but as a friend to a friend.
- *Rationally*: You need the self-awareness and self-confidence to trust your intuition, your gut response, your instincts, your interpretive gifts, and your creative imagination.
- *Volitionally*: You need the vulnerability to deepen your friendship by sharing your friend's personal impact on you. You need the courage to risk the friendship by sharing that impact. You need to be so other-centered that you avoid the all-consuming question, "How am I coming across?" Connecting intimately requires a sense of "forness." "I'm for you. I'm on your side, on your team. I'm here to encourage and empower you."
- *Emotionally*: You need the openness to experience the impact of your friend right now.

Becoming Alive to Your Spiritual Friend's Impact on You

In order to connect intimately with Larry, you must become alive to his impact on you. This requires all the relational competencies explored thus far. Remember that these competencies are developmental; they build upon each other. You can't "practice" them in one stage, then toss them out. Intimate connecting requires listening, empathy, etc.

It requires an additional kind of listening: *listening to your own soul*. You need to trust your gut instinct as you relate to Larry. You're asking yourself, "Why does he intimidate me like this? What's going on that I always feel like we're in a competition? Why do I feel drawn to lecturing when I'm with him? How come I feel so distant and distracted when we talk?" You're asking yourself the question: "What do I feel drawn to feel, do, think, and want as we relate?" You're trying to assess the subjective sense of what you're experiencing while you're relating.

Sharing Your Spiritual Friend's Impact on You

Look for and put into words how Larry is relating to you at this moment. Share how you feel, how you experience him right now. "I sense that . . ." "It seems like . . ." Your sharing is done as a possible reflection of his general pattern of relating. How you relate and how you sense your relationship becomes a mirror of how Larry relates to others. You want to discuss the possible similar pattern in other relationships, examining how or if your present relationship is an example of his normal style of relating. Help Larry *to see by illustration* how he's relating to God and others. You explore themes, patterns, and styles of relating that either violate or illustrate love. Such intimate connecting has the potential to "catch him in the act" of distancing relational events, making suppression more difficult.

Experiencing Together Your Impact on One Another

In intimate connecting, you also invite Larry to focus on the here-and-now, not simply for comparison to his other relationships, but to experience yours deeply. This can lead to a level of intense interaction and open feedback.

Invitations to relate intimately can come in many forms.

- *Could we discuss what's happening between us now as we relate?*
- *How are you experiencing our relationship right now?*
- *What's going on inside you as we talk?*
- *How did you feel when _____?*
- *You seem _____ right now.*
- *May I share what I'm experiencing right now as we talk?*
  - *I wonder what we should make of this.*
  - *Is this how you really want to relate to me?*

The Process of Connecting Intimately

I fear turning something so personal into a "process." More than anything, connecting intimately involves your commitment to relate deeply. You refuse to maintain some aloof professional image or a distant pastoral stiffness. Instead, you:

- Taste the Horrors of Sin
- Catch Your Friend Red-Handed
- Paint Your Friend a Picture
- Provide Clarifying Feedback
- Explore God's Story of Sin

In *tasting the horrors of sin*, you enter Larry's soul, allowing him to impact you. You sense when he is conning you, manipulating you, or intimidating you. With Larry, you might be thinking, "Hmm, I'm not usually too easily intimidated. But I sure feel defensive now, put on the spot, jumped on. I wonder what's going on between us? Within him?" Of course, this takes the self-awareness to know how you normally respond and to distinguish your own sin from Larry's sin against you.

Catching the person red-handed requires that you keep your relationship within the room. Instead of only confronting Larry about his anger at work, you also confront him concerning his subtle intimidation of you now. "Larry, I've counseled for over two decades. I don't usually feel too defensive, but with you I feel put down and stepped on. I wonder what we should make of this?"

Painting the person a picture requires you to use imagery that fits the person and your current relationship. You might say, "Larry, you seem to need to use your foreman hat in order to not face relationships on an equal plane." Or, you might note, "I feel as if I've been put on review, or probation, and one more slip up and I'm out of here. Is that how you want to relate to me?"

In *providing clarifying feedback*, you wonder aloud about possible patterns. "Larry, is this how you relate to others?" Or, "Has anyone else ever given you feedback like this?" Or, "If I'm intimidated, and I'm your counselor, how do you think your children feel?"

Exploring God's story of sin allows Larry to face God's perspective on his way of relating.

- *What does God's Word say concerning your current way of relating?*
- *How would you compare and contrast your way of relating and Christ's way of relating?*
- *How would you compare your way of relating with the love chapter in 1 Corinthians 13?*
- *What passages might we find helpful in gaining God's perspective on your style of relating?*
- *What Scriptures could we look at that might clarify God's position on your pattern?*
- *What have you sensed God's Spirit saying to you about how you treat others?*

Maturing Your Spiritual Friendship Competency
Connecting Intimately

♦ Use the following scenario and the outline below to complete this exercise in connecting intimately. Larry's struggling with uncontrolled anger. You've probed, confronted, and softened stubbornness. But he's still non-responsive. Write dialogues and trialogues that you might use for each of the following skills of connecting intimately.

1. Taste the Horrors of Sin.

2. Catch Your Friend Red-Handed.

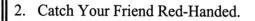

3. Paint Your Friend a Picture.

4. Provide Clarifying Feedback.

5. Explore God's Story of Sin.

Enlightening Spiritual Conversations: Reconciling Theological Trialogues—Hebrews 3:12-19

Through enlightening spiritual conversations, you illuminate Larry to his sin and to his Father's forgiveness. To accomplish this twin task, you need to trialogue with Larry about:

- The Nature of Repentance
- The Nature of Grace

Spiritual Conversations and the Nature of Repentance: "It's Horrible to Sin"

Through probing theologically, exposing through confronting wisely, softening stubbornness, and connecting intimately, you've exposed Larry's sinfulness relationally, rationally, volitionally, and emotionally. Now, in line with 2 Timothy 2:25-26, you want to:

Gently instruct in the hope that God will grant them repentance leading them to a knowledge of the truth, and that they will come to their senses and escape from the trap of the devil, who has taken them captive to do his will.

Gentle biblical instruction requires trialoguing about the process of mortification (death to self), or putting off the old, fleshly ways of relating. *Soul Physicians* teaches a six-step "process" of mortification based upon human beings as relational, rational, volitional, and emotional beings.

In designing the order of the process, *Soul Physicians* highlights biblical motivational structure. Why do we do what we do? We pursue (volitional) what we perceive (rational) to be pleasing (relational) which prompts reaction (emotional). Rational direction determines relational motivation, which decides volitional interaction, which results in emotional reaction. If we conclude (rational direction) that God is not our Supreme Good (relational motivation), then we will follow a self-centered lifestyle (volitional interaction) and end up emotionally out of control (emotional reaction). Therefore, one "order" of the putting off process includes:

- Rational: Putting Off Foolish Mindsets
- Relational: Putting Off Disordered Affections (Related to God, Others, and Self)
- Volitional: Putting Off Self-Centered Purposes
- Emotional: Putting Off Ungoverned Mood States

Regarding the three relational components (spiritual, social, and self-aware), *Soul Physicians* supports the order of God, then self, and then others. Until we open to God, we cannot open to others or self. Until openness to God changes who we are and how we see ourselves, we cannot open our hands to others.

Box 13:1 recapitulates the outline from *Soul Physicians*. The rest of this section follows that procedure. Chapter Sixteen follows the six steps of the vivification (putting on) process. There you learn how to guide a person like Larry to live according to his new nature and new nurture in Christ.

Spiritual Conversations Putting Off Old Foolish Mindsets: Rational Mortification

When Larry puts off his old mindset, he repents of the insane idols of his heart. He puts off his old contemptuous images of God and refuses to think like the old arrogant fool that he used to be.

Box 13:1
The Six Steps of Mortification
Putting Off the Old Fleshly Lifestyle

1. Step One: Rational Mortification—Putting Off Old Foolish Mindsets

   "I repent of the insane idols of my heart."
   "I break the stranglehold of strongholds."

2. Step Two: Relational Mortification—Putting Off Old Spiritual Disordered/Impure Affections

   "I divorce the adulterous false lovers of my soul."
   "I annul my attachment to alluring lovers."

3. Step Three: Relational Mortification—Putting Off Old Self-Aware Disordered/Impure Affections

   "I reject the ugliness of my self-beautification."
   "I shed my self-sufficient, defensive thematic identities."

4. Step Four: Relational Mortification—Putting Off Old Social Disordered/Impure Affections

   "I uproot my jealous hatred of others."
   "I dislodge my narcissistic, demanding relationships toward others."

5. Step Five: Volitional Mortification—Putting Off Old Self-Centered Purposes/Pathways

   "I put to death my enslaved acts of the flesh."
   "I discard my chosen style of destructive self-gratification."

6. Step Six: Emotional Mortification—Putting Off Old Ungoverned Mood States

   "I crucify my addictive passions that seek to make my belly god."
   "I jettison my emotional duplicity, deadening, and denial."

To mortify these idolatrous images, Larry must identify and repent of his unique mental strongholds. Mental stronghold sin takes a unique shape because Larry (like all of us) manufactures or carves his idol in his image—according to his non-God story of his life, according to his idiosyncratically chosen perception of reality. Each particular act of sin is a branch off the tree from which he carves his idol. The root of the tree is his imagination (his non-God image of God).

Personal sanctification and spiritual friendship require the identification and exposure of *person-specific* strongholds through trialogues like:

♦ *What is your image of God?*
♦ *What is your pattern of dethroning God?*
♦ *How do you typically try to make life work apart from God?*
♦ *What does your style of relating say about your underlying beliefs about life?*
♦ *Where were you recruited into this false belief about God?*
♦ *When did you begin to acquiesce to this lie?*
♦ *What sinful pleasure have you taken in this lie?*

Identification of unique mental strongholds begins the process of dehabituation. Repentance continues the work. Repentance is the daily putting off and breaking up of the whole complex of conformity to the world, the flesh, and the Devil. In mortification through repentance, you involve Larry in the life-long process of detecting his characteristic fleshly mindsets and turning from them.

To repent of a sinful mindset, Larry must recognize its insanity, see its vileness, and sense its ugliness. John Owen, in his classic work *The Mortification of Sin*, describes the process of loading the conscience with guilt: "Get a clear and abiding sense upon thy mind and conscience, first, of the guilt, secondly, of the danger, thirdly, of the evil, of that sin wherewith thou art perplexed" (Owen, *The Mortification of Sin*, p. 107).

Owen pictures a Christian struggling to defeat a besetting sin. Victory is stalled. The believer is perplexed, feels trapped, and senses defeat. How can this Christian uproot sin? What will motivate this believer to hate sin with a holy hatred? Owen suggests the following principles or steps of loading the conscience with guilt, which I "translate" into spiritual conversations.

♦ *Have you considered the danger of this particular mindset? Do you see the danger of being hardened by its deceitfulness (Hebrews 3:12-13)? Do you see the danger of God's discipline? The danger of loss of peace and strength?*
♦ *Have you considered the evil of this mindset? How it grieves the Holy Spirit? How the Lord Jesus is wounded afresh by it? How it will take away your usefulness in this generation?*
♦ *Have you considered the spirituality, severity, inwardness, and absoluteness of God's holiness?*
♦ *Have you brought your sin to the gospel not for relief but for further conviction? Have you looked on him whom you have pierced and in bitterness said to your soul: "What have I done? What love, mercy, blood, and grace have I despised and trampled on? Is this the return I make to the Father for his love, to the Son for his blood, and to the Holy Spirit for his grace? Have I defiled the heart that Christ died to wash, in which the Spirit has chosen to dwell? What can I say to my dear Lord Jesus? How shall I hold my head with any boldness before him? Do I account communion with him of so little value, that for this vile lust's sake I have scarce left him any room in my heart?"*
♦ *Have you considered the infinite patience and forbearance of God toward you? Have you reminded yourself of his gracious withholding of judgment?*
♦ *Have you prayed for and pursued a constant longing for deliverance from this mindset?*

- *Have you pondered what occasions led to your surrendering to this mindset? Have you guarded against those occasions?*
- *Have you reflected on the excellencies and majesty of God and how far short you are of him in holiness?*
- *Have you placed faith in Christ for the mortification of this sinful mindset?*

These practices seem foreign to us today because we've lost the spiritual awareness that Owen had. He knew that the defiled imagination glazed, adorned, and dressed the objects of the flesh—making them look beautiful, causing them to seem preferable to God and God's way. He understood that the fleshly imagination darkened the soul like a thick cloud intercepting the beams of God's love and favor (Owen, *The Mortification of Sin*, p. 53). Since Satan prettifies sin, you must putrefy sin; you must expose sin's horrible ugliness.

When you uncloak sin's sinfulness, then spiritual friends like Larry may be prepared to pray a prayer of rational repentance that might sound something like this.

Father, I've finally come to my senses. I confess as sin my foolish belief that I can make life work apart from you. I've arrogantly suppressed the truth of how perfectly well you care for me. I've denied your fatherly love for me. I've sinned against you by believing Satan's smaller story, fleshly mindset that you are not my Supreme Good. I've allowed my view of reality to become filled with contemptuous images of you. I've allowed my mind to be squeezed into the mold of this temporal world, living according to the dominant plot/theme of the earthly story. I've been like a deaf man straining to hear the Gospel story. I've denied the Cross. I return to you now repenting of these idols of my heart. Though I am not worthy in myself to be called your child, by faith I claim my adoption in Christ. Thank you for forgiving me.

Spiritual Conversations Putting Off Old Spiritual Disordered Affections: Relational, Spiritual Mortification

By "spiritual," I mean affections in relationship to God. Satan belittles Christ, then exalts himself, all in the sick hope of causing Larry to be unfaithful to Christ. He attempts to tempt him with foolish mindsets about God so he can allure him toward false lovers of the soul.

Rationally, Larry must put off his old foolish mindset by saying, "I repent of the insane idols of my heart." *Relationally,* he must put off his old false lovers by saying, "I divorce the adulterous false lovers of my soul."

He annuls his attachment to alluring false lovers through repentance, which is relational return—returning home to Father. The following trialogues are effective in promoting such return.

- *What would it look like for you to return home as the Prodigal did?*
- *Jesus commanded the lukewarm Laodiceans to open the door of their hearts so they could return home to eat with him. What would that look like for you?*
- *When the floundering Ephesians left their first love, Jesus told them to remember, repent, and return.*
  - *Can you remember your first love for Christ?*
  - *How does that first love motivate you to repent of your current love for false lovers?*
  - *How does it compel you to return home?*
- *Desperate, despairing, and depressed, David repented and then pleaded for rest in the presence of his forgiving God (Psalms 32 and 51). What would your prayer of repentance and return sound like?*

- ◆ *Hosea 14 provides a classic biblical picture of relational return. Building upon the imagery of Gomer's unfaithfulness to Hosea as a symbol of Israel's spiritual unfaithfulness to Jehovah, Hosea concludes with the words, "Return, O Israel, to the LORD your God. Your sins have been your downfall" (14:1). Hosea uses this same word "return" sixteen times in fourteen chapters beginning with Hosea 2:7a, "She will chase after her lovers but not catch them; she will look for them but not find them."*
  - ◆ *How has your sin been like spiritual adultery? Like spiritual unfaithfulness to your Spouse? Like chasing after false lovers?*
  - ◆ *What do you want to say to Jesus, the Lover of your soul, as you return home to his heart?*
  - ◆ *What will renewed relational faithfulness look like for you?*
- ◆ *Something else in Hosea 2:7 and 14:1 may not be quite so obvious. Both passages present a recognition of our false lovers' inability to satisfy. Our sinful lovers are our "downfall;" a word suggesting weakness, lack of strength, inability, and insufficiency. Gomer says it even more clearly when she realizes that she was better off with her true husband than with her false lovers. "I will go back to my husband as at first, for then I was better off than now" (Hosea 2:7b). Relational repentance is always relational return and relational dissatisfaction. The Prodigal came to his senses realizing that even his father's hired servants were better fed than he. Jehovah urged Israel to recognize the futility of her false lovers and to acknowledge that they could neither save her nor fulfill her (Jeremiah 2).*
  - ◆ *How has your false lover dissatisfied your soul?*
  - ◆ *How has your false lover been your downfall?*
  - ◆ *How has your false lover been as despicable as eating pig slop?*
  - ◆ *Given the horrid nature of your false lover, what do you want to say to Christ, the true Lover of your soul?*
- ◆ *We mortify our false lovers through relational contentment in God our true Lover. Returning to Jehovah, Hosea offers us words to say to him, "Forgive all our sins and receive us graciously, that we may offer the fruit of our lips . . . For in you the fatherless find compassion" (Hosea 14:2a, 3b). We return content and amazed by Father's grace and compassion.*
  - ◆ *Have you asked God to forgive your sins of spiritual adultery?*
  - ◆ *Have you asked Father to receive you back home again graciously?*
  - ◆ *How could you offer the fruit of your lips in praise to your forgiving Groom?*
  - ◆ *How could you offer the fruit of your lips in praise to your Father, in whom the fatherless find compassion?*

Trialogues like these may prepare spiritual friends like Larry to pray a prayer of relational, spiritual repentance that might sound something like this.

Father, I come home to you. I confess as sin my false lovers. I confess as sin living like the old person that I used to be. I confess as sin my spiritual adultery and whoredom. I acknowledge to you and to myself that my false lovers are horrible lovers and that my pursuit of them is ugly and putrid. How foolish of me to ever believe that anyone but you could ever satisfy the longings of my soul. How shameful. How disrespectful. Forgive me my relational sin. I acknowledge that you alone are my Supreme Good. I acknowledge that you alone are gracious and compassionate. I return to you as my Forgiving Father. I return to your Son as my Worthy Groom. I return to your Holy Spirit as my Inspiring Mentor. I love you, Lord. Renew my vision of you as a totally competent and totally good God—boundless in holy love.

Spiritual Conversations Putting Off Old Self-Aware Disordered Affections: Relational, Self-Aware Mortification

The putting off process is both logical and theological. Larry follows foolish mindsets fanned into flame by Satan and his lies about God as a shalt-not God. Believing these, Larry chooses to love any lover other than Christ (false spiritual lovers). Doubting God while still being designed to trust someone or something, he trusts himself (false self-aware lovers). Turning from God's love while still being designed to receive infinite love, he craves love in all the wrong places (false social lovers).

Augustine defined abnormality as a soul caved in on itself. That perfectly describes Larry's old self-aware false lovers. He lives fleshly in this area to the degree that he is ruled by internal dispositions toward radical self-centeredness, self-sufficiency, self-protection, self-hatred, selfishness, and self-beautification.

Luther, like Augustine, acutely understood the flesh-oriented conscience. An evil conscience replaces the sacred identity in Christ with a shame identity in self. It rejects grace in favor of works. Larry sees himself as shameful since he's failed to reckon on who he is in Christ. He's refused to live by grace, choosing instead to live his life and see himself according to Satan's lying narrative of works. His shame leads to self-hatred, which he foolishly attempts to deal with through self-sufficiency.

Like Adam and Eve after they sinned, Larry plays games with God. He tries playing *dress up* with God, foolishly and self-sufficiently covering himself with fig leaves of works righteousness. Then he plays *hide-and-seek* with God, defensively running from him, fearing him, and hiding in the bushes.

Larry needs to shed his self-sufficient, defensive identities by repenting of his core self-beautification and of his specific self-sufficient identities. Trialogues such as the following assist in the process.

- *Adam and Eve, in their shame, attempted to run, hide, and cover. Where have you done the same? What would it look like for you to confess your sinful running? Your sinful hiding? Your sinful covering?*
- *In what ways have you repented of your core self-beautification? How have you taken to Christ the fig leaves that you use in your attempts to cover your sin and shame?*
- *Sinners sin by self-sufficiently attempting to cover their sin and shame. How have you been doing this? How could you repent of your self-beautification?*
- *How have you repented to Father of the bent in your heart toward taking care of yourself by yourself?*
- *What are the specific cover-ups you use to try to beautify yourself? To try to deal with the shame of your sin apart from Christ's grace?*
- *What fig leaves are you using to try to deal with your shame apart from Christ?*
- *How are you blocking the real you from coming forth? What are you afraid of? Who do you really think you are deep down inside? If you showed this person to others, what do you think would happen? If you showed this person to God, how do you think he would respond?*
- *What defensive layers are you using to protect your sense of self?*
- *What specific fig leaves do you put on to make others happy with you?*
- *What way of relating to others do you use in order to impress people?*

Spiritual conversations like these may prepare spiritual friends like Larry to pray a prayer of relational, self-aware repentance that might sound something like this.

Father, I've been so like Adam and Eve. Running. Hiding. Defensive. Playing dress up. All because I don't believe you are who you say you are—Forgiving Father. What sin! I put off my shame identity.

I reject my sense of abandonment, ruin, rejection, and condemnation. I put off my futile attempts to quiet my inner restlessness. Instead, I rest in you. I rest in who I am in Christ and to Christ. It is ugly of me to try to beautify myself. It's a slap in the face to your Son, my Savior. Forgive me. Cleanse me. Enlighten me by your Holy Spirit to grasp how much you love me and how loving you are.

Spiritual Conversations Putting Off Old Social Disordered Affections: Relational, Social Mortification

Adam rejects God's sufficiency and satisfaction (foolish mindsets), follows Satan (spiritual false lovers), hides and covers up (self-aware false lovers), then shames and blames his wife (social false lovers). Like father, like son. Cain jealously hates his brother, refusing to be his keeper/shepherd, instead being his judge, jury, and executioner.

Old social disordered affections epitomize the opposite of the radically other-centered Trinity. Adam, Cain, Larry, and all of the rest of us, when we live according to the flesh, are radically self-centered. More than that, we are fueled by a drive that uses others for our own well-being.

In mortification, Larry must uproot his jealous hatred of others (1 John 3:7-15). He needs to put off his old flesh-oriented way of relating. Caved in upon himself because he's rejected God as his Fountain of Life, he desperately craves, and therefore demands, that others fulfill longings and thirsts that only his infinite God can fill.

Finding himself in this hopeless state, James explains that Larry frenetically races between manipulation and retaliation (James 4:1-4). Battling unmet desires, he first attempts to manipulate others to meet his needs. "I want what I want and I want it now and I want it from you!" When they don't come through for him, he retaliates. "If you won't make me feel better about me, then I will make you feel worse about you!"

Reconciling spiritual direction empowers Larry to dislodge his narcissistic, demanding relationships. Thus, true repentance before God is not only relational return to him, it is also relational return to others. It will involve confession, requesting forgiveness, restoration, restitution, and reconciliation.

Trialogues in this life category must identify specific characteristic styles of sinning against others, should lead to repentance of those specific characteristic sinful styles of relating, and ought to produce a longing to see justice done. They might include:

- *In what ways are you demanding that others come through for you?*
- *In what ways are you demanding that others meet your needs?*
- *How do you typically go about manipulating others?*
- *What do you typically do to retaliate against others when they don't seem to come through for you?*
- *What would it be like to be in a relationship with you?*
- *Do you live to feed, nourish, shepherd, and care for others or do you live to get others to take care of you?*
- *It's not enough to say, "Father forgive me for my sins." You need to pray specifically. What would it be like for you to pray prayers like this? "Father, forgive me for my sin of typically and specifically manipulating my wife by pouting every time she brings up another viewpoint." "Father, forgive me for my sin of characteristically and specifically blowing up in an angry rage every time one of my employees misses a deadline."*
- *What trusted friends could offer you honest, constructive feedback concerning how they see you relating to others?*
- *What open, caring, insightful small group are you in or could you become involved in to receive helpful feedback about how you relate to others?*

- *Given your specific pattern of sin, what would reconciliation look like for you and your wife? Your employees?*
- *Specifically, what longing for restoration are you praying for?*
- *Who do you need to ask to forgive you? Specifically, for what?*
- *Who do you need to confess your specific sin to and what would you say?*
- *How do you plan to make this right?*
- *What will restitution look like in this?*

Such trialogues may be just the gentle instruction necessary to lead spiritual friends like Larry to a spirit of relational, social repentance.

Father, I confess as sin my living for self, loving self, and caressing self. I put off shepherding myself and I will now focus on shepherding others. I reject all the self sins: self-sufficiency, self-promotion, self-protection, selfishness, and self-centeredness. I confess as sin my cruel, harsh, manipulative, demanding, shaming, blaming, and maiming way of treating others. Most of all, I confess as sin how far I've moved from reflecting you and your radically other-centered Trinitarian existence. I am putting off the flesh, the characteristic ways I used to relate, and I'm putting on the Spirit, the new me created to relate like you.

Spiritual Conversations Putting Off Old Self-Centered Purposes: Volitional Mortification

Pathways (purposes) are products of the will and the will is the ability to choose, to decide, and to create. "Will is the ability to originate or refrain from originating something: an act or a thing" (Dallas Willard, *Renovation of the Heart*, p. 144). Decisions and actions flow from the will. Pathways are patterned and purposeful behaviors, actions, and interactions in response to the world.

When Larry doubts God's goodness and turns away from him as the Lover of his soul, then his will becomes enslaved to the flesh and he lives to indulge his own needs, cravings, desires, and wants (Galatians 5:13-21). Because he follows spiritual false lovers, he lives an empty life from an empty spiritual reservoir (Ephesians 4:17-19). In his felt emptiness, he lives to protect himself from any additional pain or damage. As he looks to others, he tries to siphon them, stealing "gasoline" from them to fuel his empty tank (James 4:1-3).

Spiritual friendship assists in the process of putting to death these enslaved acts of the flesh. Acts of the flesh are characteristic ways Larry responds to life based upon his foolish mindsets about his false lovers. They're the enslaved strategies that Larry follows and the engrained purposes that he pursues by his actions and through his interactions. They reflect the compulsive choices that Larry follows to fuel himself, rather than the courageous choices that he could follow to fuel others.

God calls Larry to discard his chosen style of destructive self-gratification. Helpful sample trialogues in this process include:

- *When it comes to behavior patterns, we're quick to blame our actions, and even our character, on our temperament, our basic constitution, our upbringing, our mood, or our basic proneness. Where do you find yourself guilty of such excuse making? In what ways has that been blocking the work God wants to do in your life?*
- *Rather than saying, "that's just me," I'd like to see you begin to say, "that's me allowing the fleshly me to break free again. I need to put it off. I need to watch and avoid whatever feeds my characteristic style of sinning. I must practice spiritual disciplines that reorient me to self-control."*
  - *What do you think of these approaches?*

- *How could you apply them to your patterns?*
- *Rather than excusing your patterns, you must recognize them, labeling them accordingly and accurately.*
  - *What would it be like for you to take time to reflect on your characteristic ways of responding to life?*
  - *Tell me about your journaling, praying for God to reveal secret sins, asking God to break sin's deceitfulness and hardness in your life, and seeking feedback from others.*
  - *What personal inventory have you taken to discover sinful patterns in your life?*
- *You need to detect and root out the reasons (not excuses) for this sinful pattern having such dominance and sway in your lifestyle. Since your interactions are guided by your characteristic idols that are created by your characteristic fleshly imagination, you should ask yourself some pointed questions such as:*
  - *What lies am I believing that are leading me to surrender repeatedly to the pathway of envy?*
  - *What false images of God are captivating my mind and leading me to yield to my characteristic, habitual sin of pride?*
- *You must follow recognition with surrender.*
  - *How can God empower you to will God to be God?*
  - *You may still struggle to do his will, but at least you're willing to will it. That's surrender. What's it like for you to put off your will and put on Christ's will?*
- *Engagement is the next "step" in loosening your entangled will.*
  - *Like Jesus, how can you say, "Not my will, but thine be done"?*
  - *How can you avail yourself of Christ's resurrection power?*

Trialogues like these can soften spiritual friends like Larry to pray a volitional prayer of repentance such as the following.

Father, I've sinned against you by walking in the way of the sinner, by following the self-centered pathway of _____. I must put off choosing compulsively and put on choosing courageously. I must put off the old enslaved pathways and put on my new free, empowered pathways. Help me to quit coddling, cuddling, pampering, and spoiling my flesh. Empower me to be ruthlessly fierce in rejecting it and nailing it to the Cross. Reveal my secret sins, show me the patterns that I'm blind to, help me to detect my fleshly pathways. I reject my fleshly inclinations, patterns, and character. I put on the new characteristic of _____. I reject my characteristic approach to life of _____. By Christ's resurrection power, I replace it with my new manner of life.

Spiritual Conversations Putting Off Old Ungoverned Mood States: Emotional Mortification

Feelings, as Willard teaches, "are a primary blessing and a primary problem for human life. We cannot live without them and we can hardly live with them" (Willard, *Renovation of the Heart*, p. 117). Nonetheless, feelings were and are God's idea.

Created to be emotionally alive, sin transformed Larry into a moody anger addict, while salvation restores him to emotional maturity. He is a saint returned to emotional integrity by Christ, enlivened to honestly experience life in all its grief and hope.

Yet the battle continues. The flesh attempts to rule Larry's emotionality through ungoverned mood states. "Feelings live on the front row of our lives like unruly children clamoring for attention" (Willard, *Renovation of the Heart*, p. 117). Emotions are hauntingly present, like a ghostly power possessing

Larry. He requires an "emotional exorcist," not to eradicate all feelings, but to put off his old ungoverned mood states and to put on his new managed mood states.

> **He requires an "emotional exorcist," not to eradicate all feelings,**
> **but to put off his old ungoverned mood states**
> **and to put on his new managed mood states.**

Larry must crucify his addictive passions that seek to make his belly god. His mood states are bound to his volitionality (purposes/pathways of the will), rationality (mindsets of the heart), and relationality (lovers/affections of the soul). In the flesh, Larry surrenders to Satan's lie that "God is not good," and he solicits false lovers who seem better. Then he develops characteristic strategies that he pursues to deal with his starving soul. Given such a state of affairs, is it any wonder that emotionally he obeys addictive passions that seek to make his belly god? Casting off any hope of true soul satisfaction, of course Larry settles for a semblance of sensual satisfaction. He deadens his spiritual pain through feeling sensual pleasure.

Larry must jettison his emotional duplicity, deadening, and denial. The process involves spiritual conversations such as the following.

- *The Apostle Paul highlights two concepts in his description of fleshly emotionality: the loss of sensitivity and the presence of lasciviousness (Ephesians 4:19). Loss of sensitivity signifies ceasing to feel, being callous, past feeling. Faced with excruciatingly painful feelings, we try to deaden, deny and repress them. So tired of feeling pain, we try to live without feelings. We become apathetic (without passion) toward God, others, and ourselves. We end up with emotional duplicity rather than emotional integrity. In emotional integrity, we feel and face whatever we are currently experiencing. We then bring rationality to our emotionality by understanding why we feel what we feel. Subsequently we can bring spirituality to our emotionality by taking our feelings to God and soothing our souls in him. Emotional duplicity is emotional hypocrisy. We fake it. Pretend. We deceive ourselves by being dishonest about what we are really feeling, by refusing to face what we feel. We live a lie, a life of emotional pretense. We are double-minded, or, if you will, we are double-emotive. We feel one thing but pretend to ourselves and others that we are feeling nothing or something entirely different.*
  - *Where have you ceased to feel? Become callous?*
  - *Faced with excruciating pain, where have you tried to deaden, deny, and repress your feelings?*
  - *Where have you become apathetic toward God, others, and yourself?*
  - *Where do you detect emotional duplicity? Emotional hypocrisy? Faking it? Pretending?*
  - *Where do you deceive yourself by being dishonest about what you are really feeling? By refusing to face what you feel?*
  - *Where do you live a lie, a life of emotional pretense?*
  - *Where are you double-emotive, feeling one thing but pretending to yourself and others that you are feeling nothing or something different?*
- *We try to deaden our emotions. We can't. They seep out. Ooze out. Explode out. Lasciviousness is the explosion of ungoverned emotions that we have tried to deaden. Lasciviousness is the duplicitous me sneaking out and hurting you. My stuffed passions running wild. I live without*

restraint, without regard for anything but my own mood states. My mood becomes my god. I must feel good or at least not feel so revolting. I become sensually triggered to indulge in every possible pleasure. This is addiction. The result is damage. Damage to God's reputation, damage that I inflict upon others during my emotional binges, and damage to my own emotional health.

- *Where are your emotions seeping out?*
- *Where are your ungoverned emotions exploding like shrapnel onto others?*
- *Where are your stuffed passions running wild?*
- *How are you living without restraint, without regard for anything but your own moods?*
- *In what ways are your moods becoming your god?*
- *How are you becoming sensually triggered to indulge in pleasure?*
- *What addictions are you battling?*
- *What damage are your ungoverned emotions causing to God's reputation? To others? To your own emotional health?*

- *Logically, you must counter emotional duplicity with emotional integrity. You must put off your refusal to face your feelings. You need to see repression of your feelings as a sin and confess it as such. "Father, I've been denying my emotionality and in doing so I've been denying your creativity." Once you've faced what you're feeling, you need to bring biblical truth to bear on your emotions, rather than practicing emotional denial. You need to ask yourself questions such as:*

- *Is this emotion governed or ungoverned?*
- *Is this a sign of emotional order or disorder?*
- *What does my mood state reveal about my pathways/purposes, mindsets, and lovers/affections?*
- *How do I need to repent of making my belly god?*
- *What confession do I need to make to God about the false lovers of my soul that leave me so desperately empty that I worship feeling states?*

Spiritual conversations such as these empower spiritual friends like Larry to pray prayers of emotional repentance such as the following.

Father, I've sinned against you by worshipping feelings instead of worshipping you. My current mood state of _____ exposes how desperately I'm trying to live without you. My failure to face my feelings exposes my distrust in your ability to care for me. My refusal to soothe my soul in you exposes my doubts about your goodness. I put off my emotional duplicity, replacing it, in the power of your Spirit, with emotional integrity. I will face whatever I feel and bring it to you. I put off my emotional lasciviousness. I put off indulging my fleshly passions. I confess as sin my addiction of/to _____ . I recognize it for what it is: a symptom of the deeper disorder within me, a spiritual, relational, mental, and willful disorder. Forgive me. Empower me to manage my moods. Empower me to put on grace lovers/purified affections, wise mindsets, and other-centered purposes/pathways so that I can put on managed mood states.

Exploring Your Spiritual Journey

- We all struggle with besetting sins. Some call these "addictions," some "bondage," and some "enslavement." By whatever name you label your habitual battle against certain sins, do yourself a favor and face your sins using the "mortification process."
- Due to the personal nature of this exercise, feel free to use this page as a guide, while actually writing your notes "in a secret place." At the same time, I encourage you to share your battle with a loving brother or sister.
- With your "besetting sin" in mind, respond to the following interactions.

1. How will you find victory over your besetting sin by using the principles in this chapter about putting off old foolish mindsets?

2. How will you find victory over your besetting sin by using the principles in this chapter about putting off old spiritual disordered affections?

3. How will you find victory over your besetting sin by using the principles in this chapter about putting off old self-aware disordered affections?

4. How will you find victory over your besetting sin by using the principles in this chapter about putting off old social disordered affections?

5. How will you find victory over your besetting sin by using the principles in this chapter about putting off old self-centered purposes?

6. How will you find victory over your besetting sin by using the principles in this chapter about putting off old ungoverned mood states?

Maturing Your Spiritual Friendship Competency
Enlightening Spiritual Conversations: Repentance

♦ Respond to the following questions using the scenario of Larry and his struggle with anger.

1. Write your own spiritual conversations to help Larry put off old foolish mindsets.

2. Write your own spiritual conversations to help Larry put off old spiritual disordered affections.

3. Write your own spiritual conversations to help Larry put off old self-aware disordered affections.

4. Write your own spiritual conversations to help Larry put off old social disordered affections.

5. Write your own spiritual conversations to help Larry put off old self-centered purposes.

6. Write your own spiritual conversations to help Larry put off old ungoverned mood states.

Spiritual Conversations and the Nature of Grace: "It's Wonderful to Be Forgiven"

You've just explored an intense model of sin and repentance that deals with patterns of the heart. Imagine the agony were you to leave Larry convicted of such sin, but uncomforted by Christ's grace. Terms you've heard for hundreds of pages should now leap across the pages of your mind: "lightening the conscience with grace," "dispensers of grace," and "it's wonderful to be forgiven."

Having been enlightened to the nature of repentance, Larry needs to be enlightened to the nature of grace. Three categories summarize the types of trialogues to master in order to help Larry to grasp the wonders of forgiveness:

- Calm the Conscience
- Assure the Conscience
- Comfort the Conscience

Calm the Conscience

Since little counsel can be received when the conscience is in intense turmoil, spiritual directors *refuse to let sin overwhelm the conscience.* The worst sin of all is denying grace. Therefore, the worst thing that you can do is to allow Satan to overwhelm Larry so that he despairs of grace in the midst of his sin. Sin can be forgiven, but believing that sin can't be forgiven leaves Larry hopelessly despairing. Satan tempts Larry to deny Christ's claims, claiming instead that his sin is greater than Christ's forgiveness. To calm Larry's conscience, help him to distinguish between law and gospel, as Martin Luther did:

It is the supreme art of the devil that he can make the law out of the gospel. If I can hold on to the distinction between law and gospel, I can say to him any and every time that he should kiss my backside. Even if I sinned, I would say, "Should I deny the gospel on this account?" (Luther, *Luther's Works*, Vol. 54, p. 106).

Luther's days were not unlike ours. In his time, almost every conscience had been seduced by human teaching into a false trust in its own righteousness and works. Luther emphasized the need to learn about trust and faith in God, because such teaching had nearly ceased (Luther, *Luther's Works*, Vol. 39, p. 28).

To counter Satan's lies, you might engage Larry in the following spiritual conversations:

- *Where were you recruited into the idea that God is angry with you and rejects you when you sin? Who modeled this idea for you? Does it seem to square with your understanding of the Bible? Of grace? Of Christ?*
- *In the Scriptures (Psalm 1, Psalm 32, Psalm 51, and Romans 8) and throughout Church history, Christians have meditated on images of God and Christ. What images could you meditate on to increase your conviction that God is gracious to you even when you fail him?*
- *Christ always loves you and accepts you. What mental pictures have you used to keep this truth in the forefront of your mind?*
- *What do you think a person should do when they feel overcome and overwhelmed by sin?*
- *What does the Bible suggest that you do when you feel overwhelmed by sin?*
- *What does your pastor suggest that you do when you feel overwhelmed by sin?*
- *What do your Christian friends suggest that you do when you feel overwhelmed by sin?*
- *What do you tell others to do when they are overwhelmed by sin and crushed by guilt?*

Assure the Conscience

The *spirit of bondage* enslaves the fleshly conscience, causing it to feel that it's still under the weight of the law and the condemnation of God who it views as a harsh Judge. The *Spirit of sonship* liberates the spiritual conscience, causing it to understand that it's now under the freedom of grace and the forgiveness of God who it correctly views as a merciful heavenly Father. The Spirit of sonship frees the conscience from fear, releasing it to trust. Knowing these truths, Larry would benefit from the following spiritual conversations:

♦ *Throughout the Scriptures (Romans 5:1-11; 8:1-39; Galatians 3:1-29; 5:1-26) God tells us that we have peace with him through Jesus Christ. When do you experience his peace to the greatest extent? What are you doing differently when you experience his peace?*
♦ *Tell me about your experience of God's peace. What is it like for you?*
♦ *I'm wondering how peace with God motivates you to love God and others.*
♦ *The Bible assures us that we're no longer under condemnation. The spirit of bondage to guilt has been defeated. We've been set free to experience the Spirit of sonship—forgiveness, acceptance, and liberty. How are you allowing the Spirit of sonship to reign in your heart? By faith, how can you accept your acceptance in Christ?*
♦ *According to the Scriptures, who are you in Christ? Who are you to Christ?*

Comfort the Conscience

The Bible teaches that believers are priests (1 Peter 2:1-8) and that God commands Christians to confess their sins one to another (James 5). Throughout Church history, believers knew mutual confession as *consolatio fratrum*—the mutual consolation of the brethren through private confession.

When we have laid bare our conscience to our brother and privately make known to him the evil that lurked within, we receive from our brother's lips the word of comfort spoken by God himself. And if we accept this in faith, we find peace in the mercy of God speaking to us through our brother (Luther, *Bondage of the Will*, 1531/1947, p. 201).

I especially love the phrase, "we receive from our brother's lips the word of comfort spoken by God himself." Allow Larry to confess his hidden sins, and, speaking on behalf of Christ and based on the Word of God, urge him to accept his acceptance in Christ. You can help Larry to experience a comforted conscience through trialogues like:

♦ *Tell me about times when you've experienced God's forgiveness. What was it like? How did it happen?*
♦ *What Scriptures have you turned to, to find Christ's forgiveness? Grace? Love? Friendship?*
♦ *The Bible talks so much about God's grace, forgiveness, and acceptance of us based on our faith in Christ's death for our sins. When are you most aware of and impacted by these truths? What does God seem to do to bring you to these points of awareness? How do you tend to be cooperating with God as he brings you to these points of awareness?*
♦ *How are you allowing other Christians to help you to enjoy and appreciate God's grace?*
♦ *Let's talk about ways that you're using the spiritual disciplines to appreciate God's grace.*
♦ *What passages are you meditating on and memorizing to help you to cling to Father's forgiveness?*
♦ *Who offers you human tastes of grace that somehow mirror God's infinite grace?*

Exploring Your Spiritual Journey

1. Think about a time in your life, perhaps now, when you were/are having a hard time believing that God really forgives, loves, accepts, wants, and likes you. Go through some of the questions, trialogues, and passages on the previous two pages to gain a more biblical and personal grasp of Christ's grace. Then write some personal reflections.

2. Spend some time praying. Focus on receiving Christ's grace and on praising God for his forgiveness. Then write a personal "Psalm of Gratitude for Grace."

Maturing Your Spiritual Friendship Competency
Enlightening Spiritual Conversations: Grace

♦ Imagine that Larry, in his struggle with anger, has come to a point of repentance. However, he's struggling to receive God's forgiveness and to accept Christ's acceptance. Using his battle, respond to the following exercises:

1. Write your own sample spiritual conversations that *calm* his conscience.

2. Write your own sample spiritual conversations that *assure* his conscience.

3. Write your own sample spiritual conversations that *comfort* his conscience.

Empowering Scriptural Explorations: Reconciling Biblical Trialogues—Hebrews 4:12-16

Humble boldness is needed to effectively explore the Word in reconciling. Working with Larry, you need the humility to examine your own life first and the boldness to share how God's Word relates to his life. Since reconciling focuses upon helping Larry to know that it's horrible to sin, but wonderful to be forgiven, scriptural exploration will do likewise.

Scriptural Explorations Communicating, "It's Horrible to Sin"

♦ *What Scriptures could we look at that might clarify God's position on the "rightness" or "wrongness" of this issue?*

♦ *What does God's Word say concerning your current: Situation? Way of relating? Thinking? Goals? Choices? Actions? Emotions?*

♦ *On what biblical basis are you evaluating your: Situation? Way of relating? Thinking? Goals? Choices? Actions? Emotions?*

♦ *What passages have you found helpful in: Gaining God's perspective on this sin? Strengthening you to overcome this sin? Deepening your relationship to Christ even as you do battle with the flesh?*

Scriptural Explorations Communicating, "It's Wonderful to Be Forgiven"

You can use biblical stories, images, and parables to help Larry to weave new grace-oriented stories.

Exploring Luke 15

♦ *How would you compare and contrast yourself with the prodigal son? With the elder brother?*

♦ *In the parable, God presents himself as a Father who longs for his son, rushes out to meet him, embraces him, and celebrates with him. How is this image of God similar to your image of God? Dissimilar? What do you suppose accounts for the difference?*

♦ *What difference would it make in your life if you saw God as a Father willing to forgive and longing to celebrate with you?*

Exploring Additional Passages

♦ *If you were to write your own Psalm 32 or Psalm 51, what words would you use to express your gratitude to God for his forgiveness? What words and images would you use to describe how God had totally wiped your slate clean?*

♦ *Let's look at 1 John 1:9. What does this promise mean to you?*

♦ *What Scriptures could you turn to in order to find Christ's grace, forgiveness, acceptance, love?*

♦ *Where were you recruited into the idea that God is angry with you and rejects you when you sin? Where was this idea modeled for you? Does it square with Scripture?*

♦ *What do you think Paul means in Romans 8:31-39?*

♦ *What Scriptures could we turn to in order to understand the love, grace, and forgiveness of Christ (Luke 15; 1 John 1:9; Romans 5, 6, 8; Colossians 1:21-23; Ephesians 1:15-23; Ephesians 3:14-21; Galatians 5; Hebrews 2:14-18; Hebrews 4:14-16; Hebrews 7; Hebrews 9; Hebrews 10:19-25; etc.)?*

Scriptural Explorations Communicating, "It's Horrible to Sin, but Wonderful to Be Forgiven"

Many passages focus on both of these themes.

Exploring Hebrews 10:10-25

♦ *How are you trying to make yourself acceptable to God? Others? Self?*
♦ *How do you act differently when you rest in Christ's work instead of yours? Relate differently to God? Others? Self? Your past? Think differently? Feel differently?*
   ♦ *How are you resting in Christ's holiness?*
   ♦ *How are you working to make yourself perfect?*
   ♦ *How are you working to make yourself forgiven/forgivable?*
   ♦ *How are you working to make yourself holy?*
   ♦ *How are you demonstrating your confidence in Christ?*
   ♦ *How are you demonstrating your acceptance of your acceptance?*
   ♦ *Tell me about deepening relationships that are helping you to draw nearer to Christ.*
   ♦ *Tell me what it is like when you come to him boldly.*

Scriptural Explorations Contrasting Worldly and Godly Sorrow

2 Corinthians 7:8-13 is an excellent passage to use to explore the true nature of true repentance.

♦ *What do you think Paul means by "worldly sorrow"?*
♦ *Worldly sorrow seems to bring death, and separation—a sense of condemnation. What might you do to battle against this false sorrow?*
♦ *How would you summarize Paul's descriptions of godly sorrow in this passage?*
♦ *Which of these signs of true godly sorrow do you sense growing in your heart? Earnestness/sincerity? Eagerness to clean your slate with God? Indignation and holy anger at your sin? Alarm that you could have done this? Longing to be holy? Concern for those you hurt? Readiness to make restitution?*

Where We've Been and Where We're Headed

That's it, right? What's left? Your spiritual friend has experienced sustaining and healing from hurt and suffering. Your spiritual friend has repented and received grace. Now you send your spiritual friend away to live the Christian life.

Well, yes and no. Certainly, you send your spiritual friend away after every meeting to live the Christian life. However, even the sustained, healed, and reconciled spiritual friend still wants and needs ongoing spiritual direction in the form of biblical guiding.

Biblical guiding (Section Five: Maturing the Art of Guiding Spiritual Friendship) enlightens your spiritual friend to the truth that it's supernatural to mature. It also empowers your spiritual friend to live supernaturally by connecting to Christ's resurrection power. Chapters Fourteen through Sixteen explain the biblical and historical process.

Maturing Your Spiritual Friendship Competency
Empowering Scriptural Explorations

♦ Imagine that Larry, in his struggle with anger, has come to a point of repentance. However, he's struggling to receive God's forgiveness and to accept Christ's acceptance. Using his battle, respond to the following exercises:

1. Write your own sample trialogues using Luke 15.

2. Write your own sample trialogues using other passages about forgiveness.

3. Write your own sample trialogues using Hebrews 10:10-25.

4. Write your own sample trialogues using 2 Corinthians 7:8-13.

Chapter Fourteen

Guiding Diagnosis
Compassionate Discernment in Guiding

"My hope is that I will stimulate you to further concern, thought, and practice in this area, so that together we may reclaim the classic strengths of spiritual friendship for the communities to which we belong and adapt them to our historical moment" (Tilden Edwards, *Spiritual Friend*, p. 2).

Retraining Ingrained Habits

Some models of counseling start and end at guiding. In secular circles, solution-focused therapy (SFT) has become popular in the past few decades. SFT claims to be non-theoretical (beholden to no school of therapeutic thought) while pursuing the goal of guiding clients to clarify and reach their goals.

In Christian circles, especially in many pastoral offices, directive guiding is in vogue. A parishioner has a problem, often conceptualized *only* as a sin problem. The pastor has an answer, often dispensed in the form of direct advice from the Bible. Even with non-sin problems, such as grieving the loss of a loved one, pastors often see their role *only* as teaching how to grieve biblically.

For many trained to preach and teach, it can be almost torture, at first, to wade through the intimate relational processes of sustaining and healing. "Biting my tongue" is a phrase often overheard as pastors learn to listen before speaking and empathize before enlightening. Frank Lake describes his experience attempting to train clergy in methods other than guiding.

Time and again, in clergy groups, even when the whole purpose of a short interview has been to elicit the personal history of a "parishioner" with a problem, the interviewing parson has found himself, in spite of himself, tittering out his usual jocular reassuring prescriptions, minimizing the problem, and thumping in optimism or the need for further effort. Clergy have described how powerless they felt, in the face of their own anxieties, to halt this clerical Coueism (compulsion, habitual response, automatic suggestion), firstly because they couldn't stand the silence, secondly because they could not think of anything further to ask, and thirdly because of an ingrained professional habit of filling every unforgiving minute with sixty seconds' worth of good advice (Lake, *Clinical Theology* p. 58, parenthesis added).

Misuse not withstanding, I obviously value guiding, as does Church history. How is guiding, as presented in the next three chapters, different from these misapplications of the spiritual friendship art?

Exploring Your Spiritual Journey

1. Who has really believed in you; who has been able to stir up and fan into flame the gifts of God within you? Describe what this person is like.

2. How has this person stirred you up to love and good deeds?

3. What impact has this person had on your life; how has he/she made a difference in you?

4. Who have you believed in; who have you stirred up to love and good deeds?

5. How have you fanned into flame the gift of God in this person?

First, guiding is not the totality of the model presented in *Spiritual Friends*. It is one aspect of the spiritual friendship process.

Second, biblical guiding is theory-laden, focusing upon a biblical theology of sanctification. It asks questions like, "What does the Bible teach about how people grow in Christ? What scriptural models do we find concerning how to interact with perplexed people about their life decisions? What are biblical goals when faced with suffering and when fighting against sin?" Though clients' goals are important, counselors always assist clients to examine whether their goals align with biblical ones. Further, solving external problems is not the core agenda. Becoming more like Christ in the midst of problems in a fallen world is the primary goal of guiding.

Third, biblical guiding is not strictly directive. Rather, as with the other aspects of spiritual friendship, it is collaborative. Biblical counselors help their spiritual friends to explore biblical wisdom principles, assisting them to think through how to apply truth to their life situations and relationships.

The Biblical Focus of Guiding: "It's Supernatural to Mature"

In sustaining, you empathize with your suffering spiritual friends, helping them to grasp the truth that it's normal to hurt. In healing, you encourage your seeking spiritual friends, assisting them to see that it's possible to hope. In reconciling, you expose and enlighten your sinning spiritual friends, enabling them to see that it's horrible to sin, but wonderful to be forgiven. In guiding, you empower your spiritual friends with the truth that it's supernatural to mature.

Through guiding, you help people to believe that it's possible to love, possible to fulfill the greatest commandment to love God and others. You long for them to understand that maturity is a "God thing." They're not saved by works nor sanctified by works. Rather, they're sanctified as they commune with God, connect to Christ's resurrection power, and cooperate with the Holy Spirit's grace for daily living.

The Biblical Theology of Guiding: "I Believe in the New Covenant"

By virtue of Christ's marriage covenant, we not only have a new relationship with him; we have a new heart. He's won our heart *and* cleansed our heart. We have a new nurture *and* a new nature. Therefore, we can love God and people. Therefore, we have peace with God, others, and ourselves.

> **New covenant counseling counsels Christians as Christians, not as if they were still old creations.**

New covenant counseling counsels Christians as Christians, not as if they were still old creations. New covenant counseling believes what the Bible teaches—we have all things necessary for godly living. We have already been changed from the inside out. Not perfected, but changed and empowered. (For a detailed biblical explanation of the implications of the new covenant, see pages 307-479 of *Soul Physicians*, revised edition.)

Biblical Sanctification in Guiding: Transformation by Grace

What's the point of life? The point of life is love (Romans 13:8-10). Jesus chooses love as his one word to summarize all of Scripture (Matthew 22:35-40) and all of life (John 17:1-26).

What's the point of the Church? The author of Hebrews summarizes the point of the Church for us:

> And let us consider how we may spur one another on toward love and good deeds. Let us not give up meeting together as some are in the habit of doing, but let us encourage one another—and all the more as we see the Day approaching (Hebrews 10:24-25).

We are to connect for the express purpose of motivating one another toward mature love.

Jesus also encapsulates the point of the Church (Matthew 16:13-20). His grace narrative applied through our grace relationships conquers Satan's works narrative. Paul receives the same commission from Jesus:

> I am sending you to them (the Gentiles) to open their eyes and turn them from darkness to light, and from the power of Satan to God, so that they may receive forgiveness of sins and a place among those who are sanctified by faith in me (Acts 26:17-18, parenthesis added).

Christ's commission is clear. He calls us to share his Gospel of grace through grace relationships so all people can come home, receive forgiveness, and live sanctified (beautiful, powerful, holy, and loving) lives.

Where's the power for living? Here's the not-so-secret secret that Satan wishes he could keep secret: "the power's in us!" The Holy Spirit dwells within us filling us with living water. His springs of living water overflow out of us into others' lives through love, connection, and relationship (John 7:37-39).

We don't have to dig a cistern to find relationships. We don't have to do penance to find forgiveness. We don't have to work in our own self-effort to love. In Christ, we're already loving. More than that, we're already lovely, wise, and strong.

> For this reason I remind you to fan into flame the gift of God, *which is in you* through the laying on of my hands. For God did not *give* us a spirit of timidity, but a spirit of *power, love* and of self-discipline (*wisdom*) (2 Timothy 1:6-7, emphasis and parenthesis added).

Where's the power? It's in there! It's in our new covenant hearts through the Spirit. That's why, "It's supernatural to mature." And why, "You're capable of love."

The curse is reversed. Immediately after fanning into flame Timothy's gifts, Paul reminds his son in the faith that he never needs to be ashamed (2 Timothy 1:8). Shame is a thing of the past, of the old covenant, of the law, and of works. Rejection is over. Condemnation ended. Acceptance arrived. Justification has appeared. We are eternally accepted in the Beloved. No more walking around like a neglected stepsister. No more feeling like the ugly frog waiting to be a handsome prince. No more living the life of the pauper. We are Princes and Princesses, Kings and Queens, Royalty—a royal priesthood. We're more than conquerors through him who loves us so. No more hanging our heads low. We're main characters in the eternal love affair during the endless grand adventure.

What's the power for living? The same power that raised Christ from the dead is active within us (Ephesians 1:15-23). Christ's resurrection power is what we "tap into" to supernaturally mature (Philippians 3:7-10). We connect to supernatural power through *RPMs*—Resurrection Power Multipliers—the Spirit of God, the Word of God, and the people of God (see Box 14:1 at the end of this chapter).

What's the process for living well? How do we help one another to live out what's inside? By meeting together for the express purpose of provoking (stirring, prompting, motivating) one another to live out our faith active in love. By fanning into flame each other's gifts. By nurturing, nourishing, and cultivating each other's spiritual fruit. During the process, we share grace narratives as we love one another in grace relationships. We maintain God's larger vision, God's larger story of who we are *in* and *to* Christ. We say to one another, "Even through your worst suffering, you're capable of love." "Even though you battle against besetting sin, it's supernatural to mature."

What's the problem in this life? With all of this good news, why is Christianity sometimes so difficult? Loving is so hard because we're called to be shepherds in a jungle.

Originally, God called us to be shepherds in the Garden. Adam and Eve obliterated that even though they each had a face-to-face relationship with God in a perfect world with bodies habituated to God. Now we live in a jungle—our fallen world. We must deal with Satan's constant sniping and lying while our new hearts dwell in old bodies habituated to live in independence from God.

Through Christ, we've overcome the world, the flesh, and the Devil. Faith is the victory that overcomes the world—our faith in our grace relationship with God, our faith in Christ's Gospel narrative of grace. Walking in the Spirit, we defeat the flesh. Resisting Satan, he flees from us for he is a defanged foe, a declawed lion.

Still, life is constant warfare with the world (Romans 12:1-2; Ephesians 2:1-3), the flesh (Galatians 5:13-26), and the Devil (Ephesians 6:10-18). That's why we need one another. Together with all the saints, we grasp God's love and connect to Christ's resurrection power (Ephesians 3:15-21). We ponder together how to experience mutual discipleship. We learn communally how to disciple one another to know and live the truth that it's possible to love in an unloving world. We meet together to guide one another during spiritual *perplexity* by aiding each other to make wise and loving decisions based upon our spiritual *priorities*.

What's the point of life and the Church? The point is always loving God and others. *Where's the power and what's the power?* Christ's resurrection power resides in our new covenant hearts. *What's the process?* The process involves enlightening one another to the truth that we already have a new heart empowered by the Spirit to love God and others. It involves equipping and empowering one another toward faith active in love, empowered by grace, and directed by wisdom.

Biblical Diagnosis in Sanctification

Picture your reconciled spiritual friends. If they've truly received grace, how will they live? What will they "look like"? Jonathan Edwards, following in the Puritan tradition of examining the true fruits of regeneration, wrote *Religious Affections* to address this question. How do we recognize the fruits of repentance?

Before you can guide your spiritual friends, you need to diagnose the condition of their souls. Having had their sins exposed, are they clinging by faith to Christ's grace that cleanses (the new nature of the new covenant) and forgives them (the new nurture of the new covenant)? Or, are they working desperately to cleanse themselves (the fleshly nature of the old covenant) and doing penance to somehow earn God's renewed favor (the fleshly nurture of the old covenant)?

Having had their sins forgiven, are they now living holy lives out of gratitude for grace? Or, are they "sinning so that grace may increase" (Romans 6:1)? That is, are they flaunting grace, not knowing that they have died to sin and can no longer live habitually in it (Romans 6:2)?

Chapter Fourteen addresses these diagnostic questions by pondering Hebrews 10-13. The author of Hebrews helps us to discern whether a person is trying to live the Christian life under the old covenant of *law* or through the new covenant of *grace*. He aids us in detecting the signs that identify whether a person is striving to mature in the Christian life by their own *works* or by *faith* in Christ's finished work. He enables us to perceive whether a person is attempting to live out salvation with a *temporal focus* or based upon *future hope*. He equips us to distinguish between the person endeavoring to relate to others through *selfish motivation* and the person endeavoring to relate to others with *sacrificial love*.

Exploring Your Spiritual Journey

1. What is your church already doing to fulfill 2 Timothy 1:6-7 and Hebrews 10:19-25?

2. What could your church do to better fulfill 2 Timothy 1:6-7 and Hebrews 10:19-25?

3. Have you ever been among a group of believers who consistently lived out 2 Timothy 1:6-7 and Hebrews 10:24-25?

    a. If so, what was it like? How did it happen? What kept it going?

    b. If not, write about your longings for such a family.

As a spiritual director in guiding, you compassionately discern whether your directees are trying to live the Christian life by the flesh or by the Spirit. You seek to discern between grace, faith, hope, and love *versus* law, works, temporal focus, and selfish motivation.

In guiding, you long for your spiritual friends to embody faith, hope, and love through grace. You want to move with them from law to grace, from works to faith, from temporal focus to future hope, and from selfish motivation to sacrificial love.

Stage	Fleshly Sanctification Strategy	Spiritual Sanctification Strategy
Stage One	Law	Grace
Stage Two	Works	Faith
Stage Three	Temporal Focus	Future Hope
Stage Four	Selfish Motivation	Sacrificial Love

Stage One: Sanctification by Grace Rather Than by Law

Your first diagnostic indicator asks, "Is my spiritual friend trying to live the Christian life by law *or* by grace?" As Paul contrasts:

You foolish Galatians! Who has bewitched you? Before your very eyes Jesus Christ was clearly portrayed as crucified. I would like to learn just one thing from you: Did you receive the Spirit by observing the law, or by believing what you heard? Are you so foolish? After beginning with the Spirit, are you now trying to attain your goal (sanctification) by human effort (works)? (Galatians 3:1-3, parenthesis added).

The author of Hebrews also emphasizes sanctification by grace:

By one sacrifice he has made perfect forever those who are being made holy. The Holy Spirit also testifies to us about this. First he says: "This is the covenant I will make with them after that time, says the Lord. I will put my laws in their hearts, and I will write them on their minds." Then he adds: "Their sins and lawless acts I will remember no more." And where these have been forgiven, there is no longer any sacrifice for sin (Hebrews 10:14-18).

What a fascinating and important phrase: "he has made perfect forever those who are being made holy." In other words, we're Christ's virgin brides who do not need to work *to* beautify ourselves, but we do need to work *out* our salvation beautifully. We're to reveal what is already in us—our new actions exposing our new attitude, our new behavior expressing our new heart.

God's law written on our hearts, we have a new nature. God's forgiveness granted in Christ, we have a new nurture. Because of these new covenant blessings, we have confidence to live *coram Deo* with Yahweh. No hiding behind veils or waiting nervously in the outer temple area; we boldly enter the very Holy of Holies. Better yet, *the very Holy of Holies has entered us!* Our hearts are sprinkled clean and our guilty consciences purified. No longer ashamed, we draw near to God by grace (Hebrews 10:19-23).

What diagnostic markers indicate that your spiritual friends are living by grace? You'll see them as *rest-takers*—resting in Christ's gracious arms. Having been confronted about their sins, they've draw near to God with a sincere heart in full assurance of faith, having their hearts sprinkled to cleanse them from a guilty conscience (Hebrews 10:22). Knowing that God is faithful, they hold unswervingly to him (Hebrews 10:23). Their conscience is clear before God, others, and themselves. Peace reigns. Shalom rules.

You'll also notice that they're *risk-takers*—leaping off ledges to express gratitude to their Groom by serving others. Rather than a navel-gazing, self-centered focus, they consider how they may spur others on to love and good deeds (Hebrews 10:24). In other words, once reconciled, they don't wallow in their sin; they worship Christ's grace and share it with others. Having received encouragement, they encourage others (Hebrews 10:25). Right with the most righteous Being in the universe, they take risks to intimately love the down-and-outers and dirty-and-sinful of this fallen world.

Additionally, you'll note that they're *respect-givers*. Knowing that grace is costly, not cheap, they refuse to deliberately keep on sinning (Hebrews 10:26). They treat as holy the blood of the new covenant, refusing to trample the Son of God under foot or insult the Spirit of grace (Hebrews 10:29). Their cleared conscience remains a sensitive conscience longing to honor the One who made them perfect forever by living holy now.

Stage Two: Sanctification by Faith Rather Than by Works

Your second diagnostic indicator asks, "Is my spiritual friend trying to live the Christian life by works *or* by faith?" In the past, we lived under the law covenant of works (Hebrews 10:1). With good reason, we doubted our acceptance since we could never believe that by works we would become as pure as Christ (Hebrews 10:2-4). Not knowing any other way of acceptance, we *compulsively lived either to earn God's favor or suppress God's displeasure* (Hebrews 10:11). Either way we were wracked with doubt.

In Christ, we no longer suppress our awareness of God's existence nor do we attempt to earn his favor. Instead, we rest in the favor he's already favored us with (Hebrews 10:12-18).

Now we live by faith (Hebrews 11:1-4) knowing that God is pleased with us in Christ and that only faith pleases God (Hebrews 11:5). We know that God is, and that he's a rewarder of those who diligently seek him (Hebrews 11:6).

Given these truths, what diagnostic indicators mark your spiritual friends who live by faith rather than by works? You'll see *wild obedience*. By faith Noah, when warned, built the ark in holy fear. (Hebrews 11:7). By faith Abraham obeyed and went although he did not know where he was going (Hebrews 11:8). He made his home in the promised land, a stranger in a strange land (Hebrews 11:9). A truly reconciled heart is a fearful heart—fearful of God, not of people.

Therefore, the decisions that they make during perplexing times will perplex the less mature. Wild at heart, they'll live like Abraham.

By faith Abraham, when God tested him, offered Isaac as a sacrifice. He who had received the promises was about to sacrifice his one and only son, even though God had said to him, "It is through Isaac that your offspring will be reckoned." Abraham reasoned that God could raise the dead, and figuratively speaking, he did receive Isaac back from death (Hebrews 11:17-19).

You'll see them as shepherds in a jungle clinging to faith while remembering that God can and has raised the dead. Death experiences won't terminate them and shattered dreams won't break them.

Imagine a spiritual director less mature than Abraham seeking to guide Abraham. "Um, you want to do what? Kill your son! Sacrifice your only begotten! You think you're God or something!" Spiritual directors can't guide a disciple in the jungle of wild obedience if they've chosen to live in the safety of domesticated Christianity.

You'll also detect *promise seeking*. Abraham looked forward to a city (Hebrews 11:10). He considered him faithful who had made the promise (Hebrews 11:11).

All these people were still living by faith when they died. They did not receive the things promised; they only saw them and welcomed them from a distance. And they admitted that they were aliens and strangers on earth. People who say such things show that they are looking for a country of their own. If they had been thinking of the country they had left, they would have had opportunity to return. Instead, they were longing for a better country—a heavenly one. Therefore God is not ashamed to be called their God, for he has prepared a city for them (Hebrews 11:13-16).

Think about that. "They did not receive the things promised." "They only saw them and welcomed them from a distance." That's why "faith is being sure of what we hope for and certain of what we do not see" (Hebrews 11:1). Your truly reconciled, grace-impacted spiritual friends know that they've already received the greatest promise of all—eternal life. Therefore, they can wait for all other promises, believing in and satisfied by the Promiser.

> **When Christians are still pursuing the promises more than the Promiser, they know nothing of Calvary love.**

If your spiritual friends are not here yet, forget about guiding. Return to reconciling. When Christians are still pursuing the promises more than the Promiser, they know nothing of Calvary love.

Stage Three: Sanctification by Future Hope Rather Than by Temporal Focus

The author of Hebrews continues to provide diagnostic indicators. His words provide answers to the question, "Is my spiritual friend living by future hope *or* temporal focus?"

By faith Isaac blessed Jacob and Esau *in regard to their future*. By faith Jacob, when he was dying, blessed each of Joseph's sons, and worshiped as he leaned on the top of his staff. By faith Joseph, when his end was near, spoke about the exodus of the Israelites from Egypt (*400 hundred years into the future*) and gave instructions about his bones (Hebrews 11:20-22, emphasis and parenthesis added).

Your spiritual friends living by future hope *remember to remember the future*. They factor the future into the equation. Death is not final, not their physical death nor their mini, daily deaths, discouragements, and disappointments. Rather than living for today, giving into despair, and choosing to quench their emptiness with sinful pleasures, they look ahead to their eternal rewards (Hebrews 11:24-26).

Your spiritual friends also *think generationally*. They're long-term thinkers building dreams, companies, and ministries built to last beyond them, rather than building empires dependent upon them and glorifying them. They're other-centered and kingdom-focused.

Such spiritual friends *envision predictively*. Isaac blessed Jacob and Esau *with regard to the future*. Terminally ill and barely able to stand, Jacob followed in his father's footsteps by blessing his grandchildren. Joseph, his end near, spoke about events almost half a millennium into the future. Moses' parents, looking at their infant, "saw he was no ordinary child" (Hebrews 11:23). Mature spiritual friends have spiritual eyes to see eternally and internally—seeing God's future plans and sensing human potential in Christ.

Future-focused spiritual friends are *resilient*. Having done the will of God, they persevere (Hebrews 10:35-36). Life knocks them down; they get up. They pull weeds that grow back, and they return to the backbreaking work of pulling more weeds without surrendering to a broken spirit. Some win great earthly victories in the smaller story (Hebrews 11:27-35a). Others lose painful battles in the earthly story (Hebrews 11:35b-38). Either way, they keep looking ahead (Hebrews 11:35-40).

They're amazed by God's estimation of them. "The world was not worthy of them!" (Hebrews 11:38). Remembering the future, they hope. "These were all commended for their faith, yet none of them received what had been promised. God had planned something better for us so that only together with us would they be made perfect" (Hebrews 11:39-40).

They bounce back, not because they pull themselves up by their bootstraps, but because they fix their eyes on Jesus (Hebrews 12:1-2). Since the Author and Finisher of their faith endured such opposition and did not grow weary and lose heart, they struggle against sin and resist the weeds of fallen life with persistence powered by hope (Hebrews 12:3-4). They endure hardship as discipline because they know their Father is treating them as beloved and respected children (Hebrews 12:5-11). Through Christ's resurrection power, they strengthen their feeble arms and weak knees so the lame may be healed (Hebrews 12:12-13). In other words, they press on, not for self, but for others.

Stage Four: Sanctification by Sacrificial Love Rather Than by Selfish Motivation

The author of Hebrews provides a fourth diagnostic indicator answering the question, "Is my spiritual friend living by sacrificial love *or* selfish motivation?" In the past, we spent every second compulsively avoiding or placating God. Now, our relationship with God settled forever, we can spend every second loving.

Mature spiritual friends *make every effort to live in peace*, not because they lack peace, but because they have peace and want to share it (Hebrews 12:14). Having been reconciled, they're Christ's ambassadors of reconciliation.

You'll notice them *dispensing grace*. "See to it that no one misses the grace of God and that no bitter root grows up to cause trouble and defile many" (Hebrews 12:15). Having been recipients of God's medicine of grace for their disgrace, they become soul physicians distributing grace.

You'll also notice their *victorious living*. Though not perfect, they do find increasing victory over sins of the flesh and of the spirit (Hebrews 12:16-17). Why? How? Because they live in awe of their God of holy love (Hebrews 12:18-23) and of "Jesus the mediator of a new covenant" (Hebrews 12:24).

Additionally, you'll detect a *heart of worship*. "Therefore, since we are receiving a kingdom that cannot be shaken, let us be thankful, and so worship God acceptably with reverence and awe, for our God is a consuming fire" (Hebrews 12:28-29).

Finally, you'll rejoice over their *heart of love*. "Keep on loving each other as brothers" (Hebrews 13:1). In fact, it's beyond time to "release" them to the ministry of spiritual friendship. Having had their faith sustained, healed, reconciled, and guided, they're able to connect with and minister to others. "Remember those in prison *as if you were their fellow prisoners*, and those who are mistreated *as if you yourselves were suffering*" (Hebrews 13:3, emphasis added). Send them off to serve with words like these. "It is good for our hearts to be strengthened by grace" (Hebrews. 13:9). Commission them to shepherd for the Good Shepherd.

May the God of peace, who through the blood of the eternal covenant brought back from the dead our Lord Jesus, that great Shepherd of the sheep, equip you with everything good for doing his will, and may he work in us what is pleasing to him, through Jesus Christ, to whom be glory for ever and ever. Amen. (Hebrews 13:20-21).

Maturing Your Spiritual Friendship Competency
Diagnosis in Guiding

♦ You're meeting with Bill for guiding. Having walked through the steps of reconciling, now he wants to lovingly shepherd his wife. However, he feels ill-equipped. Use Hebrews 10-13 plus the diagnostic indicators of law/grace, works/faith, temporal focus/future hope, and selfish motivation/sacrificial love to:

1. Write a scenario where Bill remains stuck in law, works, temporal focus, and selfish motivation. In other words, write sample comments and attitudes indicative of Bill remaining under law, works, temporal focus, and selfish motivation, even as he struggles to mature.

2. Write a scenario where Bill is filled with grace, faith, future hope, and sacrificial love. In other words, write sample comments and attitudes indicative of Bill being controlled by grace, faith, hope, and love as he clings to God for growth in Christ.

3. Describe how you would move with Bill from law to grace, works to faith, temporal focus to future hope, and selfish motivation to sacrificial love.

Guiding Interventions

In guiding, you're asking, "What actions rhyme with Christian faith and love? How do I empower my spiritual friend to live out the faith active in love?" Spiritual directors advise individuals, in areas of ethical and daily living involving struggles of the conscience, to know how to lovingly relate and serve.

Picture Bill again, this time at the beginning of guiding. He's growing because of repentance and forgiveness, yet still required to face a foolish, fallen world, including the consequences of his own sin. In guiding, you address his perplexed conscience (self-aware being) in relationship to his loving God (spiritual being) who calls him to lovingly shepherd others in a jungle (social being). In guiding, God calls you to liberate Bill's conscience so it's free, confident, and flourishing—able to discern how to entrust himself to God and how to love others. For this to occur, Bill needs:

- Grace: Sanctified by Grace
- Wisdom: Christian Living by Thinking Imaginatively
- Power: Christian Living by Choosing Courageously
- Love: Christian Living by Relating Passionately

Grace: Sanctified by Grace

What is necessary for Bill's faith to be strengthened and his conscience liberated to love wisely and powerfully? He needs the medicine of grace with the nourishment of wisdom, power, and love.

Sanctification means living the Christian faith in the world by discerning how to do Christ's work of love and grace in a world of hate and works. Spiritual maturity involves loving out of a pure heart, a good conscience, and a sincere faith (1 Timothy 1:5). Bill grows in grace through grace relationships that share grace perspectives. (Chapters Fifteen and Sixteen use the acrostic *FAITHH* to explain how to exercise the guiding relational competencies necessary to help Christians to grow in grace.)

In Romans 5, Paul describes links in God's chain of grace-growth. Using the bullets below, picture it as an inverted pyramid with the final bullet (grace) the foundation or cornerstone. Or, imagine it as bookends with the *grace* of justification on one end and the *grace* of reconciliation on the other.

- Justification by *grace* through faith results in peace with God.
- Peace with God leads to free access to God.
- Access to God causes joyful celebration in anticipation of the future hope of glorification.
- Future hope provides the endurance to rejoice even during present sufferings.
- Rejoicing in suffering leads to perseverance.
- Perseverance precedes character—inner maturity.
- Character results in being unashamed because of being accepted by God's lavish *grace*-love.

Grace is God's catalyst creating new life. Bill "enters" guiding captivated by grace and you nurture his grace mindset by relating with grace and exploring the Gospel of grace. Then you help him to grow in wisdom (a Dreamer who thinks imaginatively), power (a Creator who chooses courageously), and love (a Romancer who relates passionately).

Wisdom: Christian Living by Thinking Imaginatively

As Bill faces *perplexities*, he needs biblical wisdom principles to guide him in making decisions based upon spiritual *priorities*. Historic Christian guiding employed the metaphor of a journey with a guide who carried a roadmap with three "laws of guiding."

- ♦ The Law of Faith (Spiritual Being): Will doing this evidence faith in God? In my relationships, am I doing what reflects trust in God's grace? What is the faith-oriented thing to do?
- ♦ The Law of Love (Social Being): Will doing this evidence love for my neighbor? In my relationships, am I doing what reflects love for others? What is the loving thing to do?
- ♦ The Law of Conscience (Self-Aware Being): Will doing this enslave or free my conscience? In my relationships, am I doing anything contrary to my conscience? What is the wise action to take?

The guide's ultimate guide is God's Word applied by God's Spirit. Earthly guides can't always be with their spiritual friends, so they strive to teach their spiritual friends how to use God's guidebook with its three roadmaps or laws of guiding.

Spiritual Beings and Guidance: The Law of Faith—"Only Do What Reflects Faith in Christ's Grace"

As Bill moves toward his family, friends, church, and co-workers, he'll need help discerning what he's doing that might be according to the works narrative (acts of penance, people-pleasing, "behaving because he's been caught"). Instead, he needs to live out faith active in love. You'll help him to explore questions like: "What does faith look like? What sort of risks does faith require? How will I evidence my trust in God? If I really believe that I'm forgiven and truly trust Christ's power in my life, then do I continue to supervise Becky, or would that be naïve testing of God?" In Chapters Fifteen and Sixteen, you'll learn how to artfully trialogue about these issues with Bill and other spiritual friends.

Social Beings and Guidance: The Law of Love—"Only Do What Is Indicative of Love for Others"

Part of the discipleship process includes helping your spiritual friends to gain the practical wisdom that answers the question, "What does it look like to love?" Bill needs wisdom to know what love would look like toward Susan, Becky, Jim, Vanita, and Steve. "How do I love them with sincere love? How do I relate to them with mature love, like Christ would? Would my wife prefer that I no longer supervise Becky? Do we no longer socialize with Jim and Becky as a couple?"

Self-Aware Beings and Guidance: The Law of Conscience—"Never Do What Is Contrary to the Conscience Even in Areas of Freedom"

As a believer, Bill's conscience is free, but tender. It's susceptible to Satan's temptation to condemnation. Therefore, a basic wisdom principle states: "Don't exercise freedom while you are still doubting, while your conscience is in turmoil." Instead, guide Bill to make decisions out of freedom. Help him to act out of forgiveness, peace, and joy, not from guilt, remorse, and fear. Bill needs practical wisdom. "Can I, in good conscience, continue as Becky's supervisor? Can I trust myself in situations alone with her? What about the appearance of evil? What about my reputation? Can I handle the false gossip or would it destroy me mentally?"

Power: Christian Living by Choosing Courageously

As a redeemed person, Bill has the grace to want to please God. He's growing in the wisdom to know what pleases God. How does he find the strength he needs to do what he knows to do? Now you're asking the question, "What is necessary for Bill's active faith to be strengthened?"

Paul asked a similar question, "Who will rescue me from this body of death?" (Romans 7:24). In Romans 7:14-23, Paul describes how futile it is to try to be holy through the meager power of the flesh.

The flesh is his small reservoir of independent power. Depending upon the flesh for victory is like a 98-pound-weakling taking on a heavyweight champion. It's no contest. Paul is overmatched.

The power to live a godly life comes from God's Spirit energizing our spirit. As Paul says, "So then, I myself in my mind (the inner spiritual aspect of my being) am a slave to God's law, but in the sinful nature (the flesh—the physical brain, bones, belly, and body) a slave to the law of sin" (Romans 7:25, parenthesis added).

Soul Physicians explains that power for living comes from communion with the Trinity: trusting in the Father (faith through grace), abiding in the Son (union with Christ), and being filled with the Spirit (empowered by the Spirit). Christians derive their power to live for Christ from Christ's resurrection power (Philippians 3). Box 14:1 summarizes God-given sources of resurrection power: RPMs—Resurrection Power Multipliers. Chapters Fifteen and Sixteen explain how to empower your spiritual friends to tap into Christ's RPMs.

Therefore, in biblical guiding, you want to enlighten Bill to the historic spiritual disciplines that believers have used for two millenniums to become conformed to the image of Christ. You want to help him to develop his own unique "spiritual workout routine" fit exactly for him and his personal spiritual needs.

Love: Christian Living by Relating Passionately

Bill has the grace to want to please God, he's discovering the discernment to determine what pleases God, and he's connecting to the spiritual power to do what pleases God. Now you unleash him to love God and others because the result of grace plus wisdom plus power is love.

Grace Relationships	Grace	New Heart to Want to Please God
+ Grace Perspectives	Wisdom	Dreamers Who Think Imaginatively
+ Grace RPMs	Power	Creators Who Choose Courageously
= Passionate Sacrifice	Love	Romancers Who Relate Passionately

Grace relationships instill the motivation to love. Grace perspectives offer the imagination to discern the specifics of how to offer love. Grace RPMs provide the power to courageously love. Together, they result in faith active in love—passionate, Christlike relating.

While Chapters Fifteen and Sixteen explain how to guide your spiritual friends to love, I mention love now to emphasize again that love is the point. When guiding says, "It's supernatural to mature," translate that to mean, "It's supernatural to *love*. You're capable of *love*." Maturity equals loving God and others (Matthew 22:35-40). Maturity results from grace, wisdom, and power leading to faith active in love.

Where We've Been and Where We're Headed

Diagnosis complete, or at least outlined, now you're ready for guiding treatment planning and intervention. *FAITHH* provides the acrostic for the six guiding relational competencies you'll need.

- *F*   Faith-Based Interventions: 2 Timothy 1:5-7
- *A*   Activating Envisioned Maturity: John 21:1-25
- *I*   Insight-Oriented Treatment Planning: Colossians 3:1-25
- *T*   Taking Action: Ephesians 4:17-32
- *H*   Holiness Spiritual Conversations: Romans 5:1-8:39
- *H*   Heroic Scriptural Explorations: Hebrews 10:1-11:40

Box 14:1
RPMs: Resurrection Power Multipliers

Spiritual Foundation: Change through Christ's Word

Spiritual Theology: Preaching, Teaching, Bible Study, and Personal Study

Spiritual Formation: Communion with Christ/Conformity to Christ

Spiritual Disciplines: The Individual and Corporate Disciplines

Spiritual Friendship: Compassionate Discernment from Christ's Ministers

Spiritual Counseling: Individual Soul Care and Spiritual Direction

Spiritual Fellowship: Connection with Christ's Body

Spiritual Discipleship: Small Group Soul Care and Spiritual Direction
Large Group Fellowship and Worship

Spiritual Filling: Control by the Holy Spirit

Spiritual Empowerment: The Filling of the Spirit

Spiritual Fruit: Character and Competence in Christ

Spiritual Ministry/Maturity: Discipleship, Stewardship, and Ambassadorship (Evangelism)

Spiritual Family: Completing One Another in Christ

Spiritual Homes: Godly Marriages and Shepherding Parents

Spiritual Fighting: Conquering Christ's Enemies (The World, the Flesh, and the Devil)

Spiritual Warfare/Victory: The Whole Armor of God

Maturing Your Spiritual Friendship Competency

Intervention in Guiding

◆ You're meeting again with Bill for guiding. You've diagnosed where he is concerning law/grace, works/faith, temporal focus/future hope, and selfish motivation/sacrificial love. You're helping him to move toward grace, faith, hope, and love. Now he needs to leave your office and enter "the real world." He has difficult decisions to make in a confusing world.

1. How would you motivate Bill to love using his grace relationship to Christ, Christians, and you?

2. Bill says, "Should I continue to supervise Becky?" How would you use the laws of faith, love, and conscience to help him to discern God's will?

   a. The Law of Faith (Spiritual Being):

   b. The Law of Love (Social Being):

   c. The Law of Conscience (Self-Aware Being):

3. How could you use the RPMs to help Bill to develop an ongoing plan of personal discipleship?

Chapter Fifteen

Guiding Treatment and Intervention
FAITHH Relational Competencies, Part I

> *"A well-guided life by the rules of Christ stands with the strongest and highest of reason of all, and therefore holy men are called 'wisdom's children' (Luke 7:35), and are able to justify, both by reason and experience, all the ways of wisdom"* (Richard Sibbes, *The Bruised Reed*, p. 81).

Fanning the Flames

In the spiritual friendship process, you've provided soul care to sustain and heal your spiritual friends during times of suffering and offered reconciling during times of sin. Faith has been crucial:

- Sustaining faith that Christ cares: cast your cares upon him for he cares for you (1 Peter 5:7).
- Healing faith that Christ restores: humble yourself under his mighty hand for in due time he will lift you up (1 Peter 5:6).
- Reconciling faith that Christ defeats sin and Satan: resist Satan, standing firm in the faith (1 Peter 5:8-9).

Is there anything left to do? Yes. Live! Guiding empowers your sustained, healed, and reconciled spiritual friends to live out their faith active in love. Faith is still crucial:

- Guiding faith that Christ strengthens: entrust yourself to the God of all grace who calls you to his eternal glory in Christ and will himself make you strong, firm, and steadfast (1 Peter 5:10-11).

To assist your spiritual friends to remain strong for God's glory through Christ's resurrection power, you can implement six guiding relational competencies aptly identified by the acrostic *FAITHH*:

- *F*   Faith-Based Interventions: 2 Timothy 1:5-7
- *A*   Activating Envisioned Maturity: John 21:1-25
- *I*   Insight-Oriented Treatment Planning: Colossians 3:1-25
- *T*   Taking Action: Ephesians 4:17-32
- *H*   Holiness Spiritual Conversations: Romans 5:1-8:39
- *H*   Heroic Scriptural Explorations: Hebrews 10:1-11:40

Exploring Your Spiritual Journey

1. Share some beginning thoughts about the eulogy that you want written for yourself.

2. Share a time when you've experienced real spiritual victory and growth.

3. What led to your spiritual victory and what produced your spiritual growth?

4. Share about some spiritual gifts and abilities that God has blessed you with.

5. How have you been using your God-given gifts and abilities to serve God and others?

Soul Physicians clarifies the results and benefits of salvation, of the new covenant. Among these, you can *know* that your *saved* spiritual friends are:

- Regenerated: Victorious over the presence of sin.
- Reconciled: Victorious over the partition of sin.
- Redeemed: Victorious over the power of sin.
- Justified: Victorious over the penalty of sin.
- Dead with Christ to Sin: Their "old man" is dead, crucified.
- Alive with Christ to God: Their "new man" is alive, resurrected.
- New Creations in Christ: New relationally, rationally, volitionally, and emotionally.
- Saints: New Nature—Enjoying and expressing who they are *in* Christ.
- Sons and Daughters: New Nurture—Enjoying and expressing who they are *to* Christ.
- *Nikao* Saints: More than conquerors over the world, the flesh, and the Devil.
- Neo-Natal Saints: Growing in grace through mortification (putting off the old ways of the flesh) and vivification (putting on the implanted new ways of the new person in Christ).

Therefore, don't counsel your Christian counselees as if they are still unregenerate. Instead, guide them based upon their newness in Christ. *FAITHH* summarizes the relational competencies that you need to disciple your spiritual friends to live out the new covenant that God has already implanted within them.

Faith-Based Interventions: New Covenant Living—2 Timothy 1:5-7

Faith-based interventions practice spiritual direction at its purest. Through it, you enlighten and empower your spiritual friends to live out their new nature and new nurture. You disciple them to release the new covenant heart that already exists within them.

I have been reminded of your sincere *faith*, which first lived in your grandmother Lois and in your mother Eunice and, I am persuaded, *now lives in you* also. For this reason I remind you to fan into flame the gift of God, *which is in you* through the laying on of my hands. For God did not give us a spirit of timidity, but a spirit of power, of love and of self-discipline (wisdom) (2 Timothy 1:6-7, parenthesis and emphasis added).

Sanctification has a dual aspect. Its negative side is mortification—the weakening, defeating, and killing of the flesh. Its positive side is vivification—the growing, maturing, and enlivening of the regenerate person.

Paul urges believers to "put on" the new self, using a common clothing metaphor. "Putting on" pictures literally wrapping a tunic around the chest. Figuratively it speaks of taking on, acting like, and putting on behaviorally what is already true internally. In essence, Paul says, "Take on the characteristics of the new person you already are. Clothe yourself with the virtues Christ implanted in your new nature."

Paul explains the process in Colossians 3. You're already dead, so crucify the remnants of that old dead you (3:1-5). More than that, you've been raised with Christ (3:1). You've already put on the new self that is daily being renewed in knowledge in the image of Christ (3:10). "Therefore, as God's chosen people, holy and dearly loved, clothe yourselves with compassion, kindness, humility, gentleness and patience . . . And over all these virtues put on love, which binds them all together in perfect unity" (3:12, 14). Put your new position into practice through continually clothing yourself with new affections, mindsets, purposes, and mood states so that you're increasingly transformed into the image of Christ.

Having helped your spiritual friends to put off their "old man" through the six steps of the mortification process, it's now time to empower them to put on their "new man" through the six steps of the vivification process. Box 15:1 outlines the "process." It starts with "Step Seven" since vivification follows the six steps of mortification.

Faith-Based Rational Vivification: Putting On New Wise Mindsets

If rational mortification stops the madness, then mental vivification returns to sanity. In light of the Cross, it is insane to doubt God's goodness. Paul's words become our motto. "If *God is for us*, who can be against us? He who *did not spare his own Son*, but *gave him up for us all*—how will he not also, along with him, *graciously give us all things*?" (Romans 8:31b-32, emphasis added).

What is a new mindset? It is the larger story, the eternal, heavenly perspective on life that says, "Trust God and live!" Our new mindsets come complete with new vision. Our Divine Physician performed totally successful laser surgery on our eyes so that we no longer look at life with eyeballs only, but with faith eyes. Our perspective is captivated by Worthy Groom's worth. Our mindset is captured by spiritual imaginations that declare, "Forgiving Father is your Spring of Living Water. Worthy Groom is the Lover of your soul. Inspiring Mentor is your strong Best Friend. Trust them with your heart."

Listen to Paul's explanation of the mental sanctification process. "Be transformed by the renewing of your mind" (Romans 12:2). Paul's telling us to experience a metamorphosis. Be like the caterpillar shedding its outer garment and displaying its true inner nature—the beautiful, free, flying butterfly. Transformation draws out our true inner condition and displays it outwardly so that we become what we are. Paul's also informing us of the central source of our transformation—mind renewal.

In biblical mindset renewal, you assist your spiritual friends to:

- Prepare Their New Mindset: Gird Up the Loins of the Mind
- Aim Their New Mindset: Set the Mind on Things Above
- Reckon on Their New Mindset: Calculate according to Spiritual Reality
- Rest in Their New Mindset: Lighten the Conscience with Grace

Intervention Interactions to Gird Up the Loins of the Mind

Return in your thinking to Becky. You've worked with her for weeks. She's faithfully walked through the sustaining, healing, and reconciling process. Her husband and her boss, for very different reasons, need her forgiveness. She needs to re-enter life triumphantly at home, work, and church.

You can assist her through intervention interactions. They typically start with teaching applied to her life. They then continue with trialogues designed to help her to relate God's truth to her relationships.

When you begin the process, you'll find it helpful to give Becky a copy of the six steps in the biblical process of vivification. Explain them to her in her language. Help her to understand her role in growth in grace. Begin by discussing the process of mind renewal.

- *Becky, Paul teaches that renewing our minds is the first step in the process of growth in grace (Romans 12:1-2). Let's talk practically about what that process looks like in your life, situation, and relationships.*
  - *Paul teaches that we have to cast off the old, dead, caterpillar thoughts about life. What are some of your old ways of thinking about this whole situation with your boss? What would it look like to throw them out like the ugly skin of a dead cicada?*

Box 15:1
The Six Steps of Vivification
Putting On the New Covenant Lifestyle

7. Step Seven: Rational Vivification—Putting On New Wise Mindsets

    "I consent to the truth of Christ's grace narrative."
    "I allow myself to be transformed by the renewing of my mind."

8. Step Eight: Relational Vivification—Putting On New Spiritual Purified Affections

    "I enjoy and exalt Christ as my Supreme Good."
    "I commune deeply with God my Spring of Living Water."

9. Step Nine: Relational Vivification—Putting On New Self-Aware Purified Affections

    "I reckon on the truth of who Christ is to me and who I am in and to Christ."
    "I view myself according to Christ-sufficient, sacred thematic identities."

10. Step Ten: Relational Vivification—Putting On New Social Purified Affections

    "I stir up my new connecting love for others."
    "I nourish my new sacrificial relationships toward others."

11. Step Eleven: Volitional Vivification—Putting On New Other-Centered Purposes/Pathways

    "I fan into flame my new freed will empowered to empower others."
    "I provoke my new chosen style of shepherding through other-centered interactions."

12. Step Twelve: Emotional Vivification—Putting On New Managed Mood States

    "I cooperate with God in enlivening my new managed mood states."
    "I collaborate with God in living according to my new emotional integrity."

- *Paul also teaches that we have to put on Christ's new, beautiful, butterfly thoughts about life. What metamorphosis in your mind needs to take place regarding how you view your situation? Yourself? Your husband? Bill? God?*
- *After sharing about our glorious, grace-based regeneration, Peter says, "Prepare your minds for action" (1 Peter 1:13). The King James Version says it so picturesquely: "Gird up the loins of your mind." Grab your flowing robe, pull it up tight, and get ready to rumble. Take your mental belt and pull it taut. Since you have the capacity to choose what you set your mind on, the first step in your mental renewal process is to take personal responsibility for your thought life.*
  - *When you think about your husband, what are you thinking? When you ponder his failures to be there for you, what comes to mind?*
  - *When you think about Bill, what are your thoughts? When you remember the two incidences where he sexually abused you, what do you allow yourself to think?*
- *Becky, Paul commands us saying, "Let the peace of God rule in your hearts" (Colossians 3:15). You're to make sure that in your thought life God's truth acts as umpire. You're responsible for making Christ's grace narrative the final arbiter for interpreting every life event. Paul explains how. "Let the word of Christ dwell in you richly as you teach and admonish one another with all wisdom, and as you sing psalms, hymns, and spiritual songs with gratitude in your hearts to God" (Colossians 3:16). Putting on your new mindset begins when you allow God's truth about life to govern your thought life. You make a mental decision to allow God's version of reality to take up residence in your mind as you feed on and meditate upon his wisdom.*
  - *How are you letting Christ's peace umpire in your heart as you reflect on all that has happened over the past weeks and months?*
  - *Whose words are dwelling in you richly?*
  - *In what ways are you allowing God's truth about life to govern your thought life?*
  - *How have you been making conscious mental decisions to allow God's version of reality to take up residence in your mind?*

Intervention Interactions to Set the Mind on Things Above

- *Becky, now you must aim your mind. Set your mindset and direct your thinking toward things above where Christ is seated at the right hand of God, not on earthly things (Colossians 3:1-2).*
  - *What would be different if every morning you arose with a clear mental picture of Christ seated victoriously at the right hand of God, ruling over every event of your life, graciously giving you everything you need for life and godliness?*
  - *How would your perspective change if every incident you encountered, you filtered through the heavenly narrative of Christ your Victor?*
  - *What would it be like for you, as you reflect on these events, to remain characteristically, habitually mindful of God-reality as you perceive and interpret life?*
  - *Let's be specific. A sinful thought enters your mind about your husband. First, you put it off, rooting out every corrupt imagination. Second, you reflect on godly thoughts. You gather up all your experiences of God and call to mind God's truth. Then you ask yourself:*
    - *How would Jesus view my thoughts about my husband?*
    - *How am I to view this thought about Jim in light of Christ being seated at the right hand of God?*
    - *How can I take on the mind of Christ?*
    - *How can I have the attitude Christ had?*
    - *What would Jesus think (WWJT)?*

Intervention Interactions to Calculate According to Spiritual Reality

♦ *Becky, you're also to live based upon your new mindset in Christ (Romans 6:11). You're to reckon on or continually calculate life using Divine mathematics. When you're trying to make sense of your life, trying to figure life out, count and take into account spiritual math.*

   ♦ *What would it be like in your recent situation to consider and evaluate your earthly life based upon heavenly reality?*

   ♦ *What would it be like to reckon on (picture, imagine, see, view) your whole situation from God's perspective?*

Intervention Interactions to Lighten the Conscience with Grace

♦ *Becky, mind renewal also requires resting in your new mindset. Recall that mortification of your old mindset required loading your conscience with guilt by seeing how horrible it is to sin. We never want to stop there. We also need to lighten your conscience with grace by recognizing how wonderful it is to be forgiven.*

   ♦ *A moment ago we read about Christ umpiring or ruling in your heart (Colossians 3:15). Specifically, Christ is to rule in your heart. Since Satan's insidious scheme emphasizes condemning accusations; mind renewal counters his agenda by highlighting acceptance in Christ. You rest serenely in your new mindset filled with gospel truth that says, "Once you were alienated from God and were enemies in your minds because of your evil behavior. But now he has reconciled you by Christ's physical body through death to present you holy in his sight, without blemish and free from accusation" (Colossians 1:21-22).*

      ♦ *What would it be like for you to live free from accusation? Free from the Accuser of the brethren?*

      ♦ *What would it look like for you to see yourself as without blemish? As reconciled? As no longer enemy, but family?*

   ♦ *John Owen, in* **The Mortification of Sin,** *not only spoke of loading the conscience with guilt, but also of lightening the conscience with grace. Among his suggestions were:*

      ♦ *Consider the infinite patience and forbearance of God toward you (p. 123). Becky, what would that look like for you?*

      ♦ *Fill your thoughts with thoughts of the excellency of God's mercy and majesty (p. 131). How can you do this?*

      ♦ *Reckon on Christ's victory over sin (p. 161). Tell me about times when you've done this.*

      ♦ *By faith, fill your soul with consideration of the provision that's laid up in Christ (p. 162). Tell me what this would mean for you.*

      ♦ *Focus your faith upon the death, blood, and cross of Christ; that is, on Christ as crucified and slain for the forgiveness of your sins (p. 170-176). How could you do this, Becky?*

   ♦ *Becky, Bill needs the same forgiveness. Paul tells us in 2 Corinthians 2:5-11 that if you don't grant Bill forgiveness, Satan will win the day by overwhelming Bill with guilt. Of course, that doesn't mean being naïve as you relate to Bill. It doesn't mean "letting him off the hook." But, as you know, he has asked for your forgiveness. He is working through the restoration process biblically.*

      ♦ *What would it be like for you to see Bill as free from accusation? As without blemish? No longer your enemy? How can you grant him forgiveness? How can you offer him God's peace and Christ's grace?*

      ♦ *What would it be like for you to see Christ crucified for Bill's sin of sexually abusing you? How would it help you to hear Jesus saying, "Father, forgive Bill"?*

Because of such intervention interactions, spiritual friends like Becky could pray a prayer of rational renewal something like this.

Father, I surrender my mind to you. I consent to the truth of Christ's grace narrative. I allow you to transform me by the renewing of my mindset. Moment by moment fill my thought life with images of God-reality. Enlighten me to know you and the power of your resurrection and the fellowship of your suffering. Enlighten me together with all the saints to grasp how high and deep and wide and long is your love. I commit to being a spiritual mathematician, adding life up from your perspective. When I face suffering, I promise to believe that though life is bad, you are my Supreme Good. When struggling against sin, I promise to believe that even when I am sinful, you are gracious. I promise not to take your grace for granted, for though I know that it is wonderful to be forgiven, I understand that it is horrible to sin. Empower me to gird up the loins of my mind, to aim my mind toward heavenly things, to reckon on my new mindset, and to rest in my new mindset in Christ.

Faith-Based Relational Spiritual Vivification: Putting On New Spiritual Purified Affections

Spiritual vivification builds upon a basic premise of *Soul Physicians. We pursue what we perceive to be pleasing.* "Objects are actually desired in virtue of the goodness, real or illusory, which is attributed to them. One who truly appreciates God's goodness, therefore, cannot but desire him" (J. I. Packer, *A Quest for Godliness*, p. 194).

Through the ongoing process of rational vivification, you've helped Becky to put on the truth that God is her Supreme Good. Based on this realization, this conviction, she's drawn toward God. Made to know good with her mind, she's also created to pursue good with her soul. Recreated to know Worthy Groom's supreme worth, she puts on her new spiritual purified affections. That is, she puts on loving God supremely out of recognition of his supreme good and flowing from gratitude for his amazing grace.

Relationally, Becky puts on her new spiritual purified affection by saying, "I enjoy and exalt God as my Supreme Good." Her chief end is to glorify God and enjoy him forever as her Chief Good. God is most highly exalted when Becky enjoys him as the most enjoyable Being in the universe.

To disciple Becky in this area, the guiding process involves vivifying her spiritual affections—stirring up and fanning into flame the love that her renewed soul has for Christ.

Spiritual renewal involves an "affection set" just as rational renewal involves a "mind set." "*Set* your *hearts* on things above" (Colossians 3:1, emphasis added). "Set" means to seek with desire, to pursue passionately, to desperately desire. "Heart" is a comprehensive biblical term for the inner person, including all the aspects of personhood—affection, cognition, volition, and emotion. Used as it is here with a word of affection, "heart" especially highlights the relational aspect that longs, thirsts, hungers, and desires—the affection set.

How do you vivify, fan into flame, and stir up Becky's spiritual appetite for and adoration of God? You vivify her religious affection for God her Spring of Living Water by helping her to:

- Taste Thirsts: Dare to Desire
- Gaze Upon the Groom: Fix Spiritual Eyes on Jesus
- Feed the Soul: Pursue Spiritual Formation

Intervention Interactions to Dare to Desire

- *Becky, tasting your thirsts is rarer and scarier than you might ever imagine. It's rare because modern/post-modern Christianity seems to believe that holiness is the elimination of desire.*

However, as J. I. Packer notes, holiness is: "the redirecting of desire so that it focuses on fellowship with the Father and the Son, and the strengthening of desire so redirected, is the real essence of holiness. All mature forms of Christian holiness teaching down the centuries have started here, seeing this as the true foundation to everything else in the Christian life, and insisting that the only truly holy people are those with a passion for God" (Packer, **Rediscovering Holiness***, p. 101).*

♦ *Let's talk about your passion for God.*

♦ *How have the events of the past months invigorated your passion for Christ?*

♦ *How have the events of the past months reminded you that the only person you can truly count on is Jesus?*

♦ *Following Jesus never means killing the new you with all your new desires, longings, loves, affections, delights, and passions. The grace of God comes to us teaching us to say, "No!" to worldly passions, but "Yes!" to God and godly passions (Titus 2:11-14).*

   ♦ *What worldly passions is Christ crucifying in you?*

   ♦ *How is God's grace teaching you to say, "Yes!" to him?*

♦ *Only those who admit that they're spiritually sick ever turn to the Divine Physician of the Soul (Luke 5:31-32). Likewise, only those who acknowledge that they are thirsty ever drink from the Spring of Living Water (John 4:1-42; 6:25-71; 7:25-44; Revelation 21:6; 22:17). The invitation to dine with Jesus goes to those who are hungry. The invitation to come to Jesus is sent to those who are thirsty.*

   ♦ *Becky, are you hungry? Are you thirsty? Starving? Parched? For what?*

♦ *Tasting our thirsts is scary because so few of us dare to experience the liberating power of holy pleasure.*

   ♦ *Becky, taste your thirsts by admitting that you're thirsty. Tap into your hunger by asking yourself, "Why do I feel so empty so often? What is it that my soul craves but goes without? Why do worldly pleasures seem so enticing but offer so little and satisfy so briefly?"*

   ♦ *Don't run from your wants. Identify them. Label them. Ask yourself, "What do I want? What do I really want? Deep down in my soul, what do I long for?"*

Intervention Interactions to Fix Spiritual Eyes on Jesus

♦ *Becky, we pant after God by gazing on our Groom. By fixing our eyes on the Author and Finisher of our faith. Our gaze should never be far removed from his scars. "Let us fix our eyes on Jesus, the author and perfecter of our faith, who for the joy set before him endured the cross, scorning its shame, and sat down at the right hand of the throne of God" (Hebrews 12:2).*

   ♦ *What is it like for you, Becky, when you pant after God?*

   ♦ *What do Christ's scars stir up in your soul?*

♦ *Becky, our gaze should never be far removed from God's grace. "Therefore, brothers, since we have confidence to enter the Most Holy Place by the blood of Jesus . . . and since we have a great priest over the house of God, let us draw near to God with a sincere heart in full assurance of faith" (Hebrews 10:19, 21-22a). Calvin explains the necessity of grace gazing: "The basis of this confidence is that the throne of God is not marked by a naked majesty which overpowers us, but is adored with a new name, that of grace. This is the name that we ought always to keep in mind when we avoid the sight of God . . . In order to help our lack of confidence, and to free our minds of all fears, the apostle clothes it with grace and gives it a name which will encourage us by its sweetness. It is as if he were saying, 'Since God has fixed on His throne . . . a banner of grace and fatherly love towards us, there is no reason why His majesty should ward us off from approaching Him'" (Calvin,* **Hebrews***, p. 181).*

♦ *Tell me about your gazing upon God's grace.*

♦ *What is it like for you to draw near to your gracious God?*

♦ *How does God's grace attract you? How does it encourage you by its sweetness?*

Intervention Interactions to Pursue Spiritual Formation

♦ *Becky, to vivify your spiritual affections, you taste your thirsts, gaze upon your Groom, and feed your soul. Feeding your soul involves pursuing spiritual formation through the practice of the classic spiritual disciplines of the faith.*

   ♦ *Let's talk about your practice of the spiritual disciplines.*

   ♦ *Let's talk about RPMs: Resurrection Power Multipliers.*

   ♦ *What personal spiritual workout routine are you following to grow in grace?*

   ♦ *It's through prayer, meditation, fasting, silence, solitude, worship, fellowship, secrecy, and the like, that we connect with Christ, commune with Christ, and become conformed to the image of Christ. Tell me about your practice of any of these. Tell me about any of these that you would like to learn more about.*

Intervention interactions like these can help spiritual friends like Becky to pray a prayer of relational spiritual renewal that might sound something like this.

Father, I long for you more than gold or silver. Nothing else could ever satisfy. Reorient my affections toward you and what you choose to provide. May my nearness to you be my Chief Good. Allure me. Entice me. Invite me. Captivate me. Capture me. Show me your beauty so that in worshipping your loveliness, I exalt you. Empower me to enjoy you so that the universe marvels in amazement at how fulfilling you are. Silence all the clamoring of other lovers who would seek my attention. I want to love you with everything I am. With undivided adoration. Give me a heart for you. A constant longing and breathing after you. Incite within me passion for you.

Faith-Based Relational Self-Aware Vivification: Putting On New Self-Aware Purified Affections

The putting on process is both logical and theological. We follow wise mindsets fanned into flame by Christ's grace narrative about God as the Rewarder not a Hoarder. Convinced by Christ, we pursue our soul's sole Lover. Entrusting ourselves to our good God, we rest knowing who we are *in* Christ and who we are *to* Christ. Therefore, our renewed self-awareness is grace-based and Christ-focused. By grace, we gain Christ-esteem. Christ-shalom.

If abnormality, as Augustine reminded us, is a soul caved in upon itself, then normality is a soul covered by Christ. Spiritual health is a soul at peace with itself *in Christ*. We live spiritually in this area to the degree that we are ruled by internal dispositions toward radical Christ-sufficiency.

In Romans 12, Paul begins to apply all the truth that he has taught in Romans 1-11 concerning our salvation in Christ. His first two points of application are about *rational renewal* (being transformed by the renewing of our minds) and about *relational spiritual renewal* (offering ourselves to God in a spiritual act of worship). His third application highlights our *relational self-aware renewal*. "For by the grace given me I say to every one of you: Do not think of yourself more highly than you ought, but rather think of yourself with sober judgment, in accordance with the measure of faith God has given you" (Romans 12:3).

Paul's a realist. We're going to think about ourselves, in fact, God designed us with this very capacity. Paul also understands that we can either distort that capacity or fulfill its original function. One way we distort our capacity for self-awareness occurs when we think more highly of ourselves than we ought. "More highly" means hyper thoughts, haughty thoughts, assuming we're superior to others, being cocky, arrogant, high-minded, and over proud. Instead, we're to think of ourselves according to sober judgment. "Sober judgment" means clear thinking, wise thinking, accurate self-awareness. Be wise-minded about yourself, be in your right mind about yourself, about who you are in Christ.

What does this look like? How are we to evaluate ourselves? Paul begins and ends the verse with the answer: "for by the grace given me . . . in accordance with the measure of faith God has given you." Our sense of self must be grace-based. "I am who I am because of the great I Am." "I am who I am by Christ's grace."

Our personal holiness includes personal wholeness—the ongoing reintegration of our disintegrated and disordered sense of self.

Biblical self-acceptance equals Christ-acceptance. Healthy self-esteem is Christ-esteem. Robust self-image corresponds to Christ-image. In our renewed self-shalom, we're comfortable with and confident in who we are in Christ. Our personal holiness includes personal wholeness—the ongoing reintegration of our disintegrated and disordered sense of self.

The guiding process involves helping spiritual friends like Becky to view themselves according to Christ-sufficient, sacred thematic identities through:

- Reckoning on the New Universal Identity
- Reckoning on the New Unique Identity
- Reckoning on the New Reconciled Conscience

Intervention Interactions to Reckon on the New Universal Identity

- *Becky, you must begin with a firm grasp on the new you in Jesus. Remind yourself daily of who you are to Christ and in Christ.*
  - *How do you think it would impact you to read, ponder, probe, study, meditate on, and memorize verses that speak about your identity in Christ?*
  - *What would it do to your sense of self as you recover from your sexual abuse, to claim images of yourself as daughter, saint, more than conqueror, athlete, bride, etc.?*
  - *How could you bring the old you into mind and resolutely and consciously disassociate yourself from her?*
  - *How could you bring the new you into mind and consciously accept your acceptance in Christ? Consciously rest in the new you in Christ? Move from shame to shalom as you understand and apply God's Word to your sense of self?*
  - *Becky, what impact might it have on you if you were to meditate on the following concepts that assist you to put on your new self-awareness?*
    - *Reckon on your new relationship to God as your forgiving Father: Romans 8:14-17; Galatians 3:26-4:7.*
    - *Reckon on your new relationship to Christ as your loving Groom: Ephesians 5:22-33.*
    - *Reckon on your new relationship to the Spirit as your encouraging best Friend: John 14-16; 2 Timothy 1:6-7.*
    - *Reckon on your new heart: Ephesians 4:20-24.*

- *Reckon on your new peace: Romans 5:1-11.*
- *Reckon on your new purpose: Matthew 22:35-40; 28:18-20.*
- *Reckon on your new power: Romans 8:1-13.*
- *Reckon on your new future: Romans 8:17-39.*
- *Reckon on your new acceptance: Hebrews 10:19-23.*

Intervention Interactions to Reckon on the New Unique Identity

- *Becky, you can build upon your new universal identity by gaining insight into your new unique identity in Christ.*
  - *Who are you?*
  - *What is the "shape" of your unique soul?*
    - *Spiritual Gifts: What spiritual gifts do you have? What ministries are you drawn to? Successful in? Excited about? What is the most thrilling thing you've ever done for God? For others?*
    - *Hopes: What are your dreams? Your desires? What eulogy would you want spoken at your funeral? What epitaph do you want written on your gravestone?*
    - *Abilities: What talents do you have? If time, talent, and money were no issue, what would you devote your life to? What equipping do you have for God's kingdom? What experiences do you have in ministry? What education do you have for service?*
    - *Personality: What is unique about you? What images of yourself stand out to you? To others? How are you different from others? What one word summarizes what makes you, you? What one picture captures who you are?*
    - *Enjoyment: What are you passionate about? What do you sense God calling you to do for his kingdom? What energizes you? What do you get excited about?*

Intervention Interactions to Reckon on the New Reconciled Conscience

- *Becky, you also need to reckon on your new reconciled conscience. Satan longs to leave you with an evil conscience that doubts your standing before and relationship to God. Father offers you clear scriptural principles for resting in him. What impact would it have on you if you meditated on and applied the following principles and passages?*
  - *Reckon on your shalom conscience: Ephesians 3:17-19; 6:14.*
  - *Calm your changed conscience: Ephesians 6:14-15.*
  - *Assure your tender conscience: Romans 8:14-16.*
  - *Liberate your clear conscience: Galatians 5:1.*
  - *Accept your forgiven conscience: 2 Corinthians 2:5-11; James 5:15-16; 1 John 1:9.*
  - *Live according to your empowered conscience: John 17:17.*
  - *Enjoy your restored conscience: Romans 12:1-8.*

Intervention interactions like these can assist spiritual friends like Becky to pray a prayer of relational self-aware renewal such as the following.

Father, I choose to live according to the peace that I have with you in Christ. I recall that one of Satan's primary tools is the power of his false accusation that you are not generously accepting and that, therefore, I am your enemy. The power of the gospel renews my mind to the assurance that I am your son/daughter, Christ's bride, and the Spirit's best friend! I put on wholeness, consciously reflecting on and resting in who I am in Christ. I put on my thematic sacred identity. I enjoy who I am in Christ and who I am becoming through Christ as I become like Christ. I renew my mind to my new core sacred identity in Christ. I reckon on this, and I re-ignite and fan it into flame. I clothe myself in my new regenerative peace. I cover myself in my new cleared, cleansed, and good conscience. I envelop myself in contentment with who I am in Christ.

Faith-Based Relational Social Vivification: Putting On New Social Purified Affections

As relational beings, we are *spiritual* beings designed to relate to God, *self-aware* beings designed to relate to ourselves, and *social* beings designed to relate to others. In our renewal, we love God because he first loved us. Our renewed communion with Christ allows us to experience a new contentment with who we are in and to Christ. Communing with Christ and content in Christ, now we're free to connect to others. We're energized by a godly passion to epitomize Trinitarian relationships that are radically other-centered.

Vivification is the process of putting on in our daily relationships our new capacity to experience and enjoy mutual one anothering. Unlike fallen Adam, we no longer have to hide, cover up, shame, and blame. Unlike fallen Adam and Eve, we no longer have to live competitively. Unlike fallen Cain, we no longer have to jealously hate our brother, no longer have to refuse to be our brother's keeper.

Like the Second Adam (Christ), we're free to experience open, vulnerable, honest, and transparent relationships. Like the Second Adam, we encourage, edify, live cooperatively, and complete one another. Like the Second Adam, we live as servants loving our brothers and sisters, happily, sacrificially choosing to be our brother's keeper, our sister's shepherd.

Our new love for others is a *grace* love. Having received grace from God, having accepted our grace-based acceptance in Christ, now we view and relate to others from a grace perspective. We love others "warts and all." We love others when they hurt us. We value others even when they feel worthless. We esteem others even when the world spits on them.

When we put on our new social grace love, we involve ourselves in the process of stirring up new cooperative love for others. We fan into flame the spirit of power, *love*, and wisdom implanted in us at salvation (2 Timothy 1:6-7). We love others with authenticity that flows from our newness in Christ.

Returned to purity by Christ, we're motivated by gratitude to love God wholeheartedly and our neighbor sacrificially. As Packer says, "we pursue our goal of single-minded Jesus-likeness; the increasing mastery of life that comes as we learn to give it back to God and away to others" (Packer, *Rediscovering Holiness*, p. 93).

The guiding process involves nourishing your spiritual friends' new sacrificial relationships toward others through:

♦ Remaining in Christ's Grace Love
♦ Imitating Christ's Grace Love
♦ Engaging in Spiritual Friendship
♦ Engaging in Spiritual Fellowship

Intervention Interactions to Remain in Christ's Grace

♦ *Becky, to love like Jesus, you must remain in his love. To connect to others, you must commune with Christ. Jesus doesn't leave us to guess how it's done. He tells us to follow his example of remaining in his Father's love (John 15:10). Then he shows us how through his intimate, unbroken communion (John 17:1-26). The courage to be intimate with others has a prerequisite—your choice to be intimate with God.*
♦ *Tell me about how you abide in Christ.*

- *How are you communing with Christ?*
- *How is your communion with Christ deepening your desire to connect with others?*
- *Tell me about your choice to be intimate with God.*

Intervention Interactions to Imitate Christ's Grace Love

- *Becky, filled with God's grace love, now you're empowered to imitate Christ's grace love. His love is not sentimental, syrupy sweet, or sappy. Certainly not easy. His love stoops to wash filthy feet. Hangs on a cursed cross. His love is servant love. His love lays down his life for his friends. And for his enemies.*
  - *How can your love for Jim imitate Christ's love?*
  - *How can your love for Bill imitate Christ's love?*

Intervention Interactions to Engage in Spiritual Friendship

- *Becky, where in the world does this relational power come from? It should not be surprising that the power to relate like Christ comes from relating to Christ and Christians. If you're to grow in your capacity to express Christ-like love, then you must choose to engage in spiritual friendship.*
  - *Besides me, what spiritual friend or two are you connecting with deeply enough that they know you intimately enough to be able to encourage you daily so you're not hardened by sin's deceitfulness?*
  - *After our "official" meetings end, who will you turn to for spiritual friendship?*

Intervention Interactions to Engage in Spiritual Fellowship

- *Becky, you also must choose to engage in spiritual fellowship. Hebrews 3:12-15 suggests the spiritual friendship of one other person who knows you through and through. Hebrews 10:24-25 recommends the spiritual fellowship of a small group of kindred spirits willing to provoke, prod, needle, incite, nudge, push, entice, exhort, and encourage you toward love and good deeds.*
  - *What small group are you meeting with for these purposes?*
  - *What group of people could you meet with for purposes like these?*

Intervention interactions like these can assist spiritual friends like Becky to pray a prayer of relational social renewal that might sound something like this.

Father, Oh to be like you, Oh to be like you. Oh to be like the Trinitarian community. Mold me and make me, scour and shape me. Though I don't feel it, I believe it—I believe that I have what it takes to love like Jesus. Wow! I can't believe I just prayed those words. I'm scared. Scared because I've been scarred. Every time I try to love like Jesus, I face what you faced. Maybe that's what you mean by the "fellowship of Christ's suffering." Speaking of scars, Jesus, you know scars. And you did not shrink from them. Spirit, empower me to shrink not from the scars of death-to-self relating. I'll be honest (may as well, you know everything!), the pain of entering another person's pain overwhelms me. The hurt of being hurt when I try to help—that terrifies me. Through my communion with you, through my connection with my spiritual friend and with my small group—please enable me to give others a taste of grace love. More than anything in my being, I want to give. You made me, re-created me, to give. I feel strong, powerful, and purposeful when I give grace. I want it. I will. Thank you!

Faith-Based Volitional Vivification: Putting On New Other-Centered Purposes/Pathways

We are purposeful beings with a will that chooses to follow certain characteristic pathways and patterns as we engage life. Our renewed wills are freed and empowered to courageously create good for God's glory and to sacrificially empower others.

Other-centered pathways or patterns are the supernatural outflow of our new grace-based social relationships to others. It is in our actual behaviors and interactions that we live out our new passion to connect with others. As Packer reminds us, "holiness means not only desiring God, but also loving and practicing righteousness, out of a constant exercise of conscience to discern right from wrong and an ardent purpose of doing all that one can to please God" (Packer, *Rediscovering Holiness*, p. 101).

But what does it mean, what does it look like, to move from putting off self-centered pathways to putting on new other-centered pathways? And what resources has God provided to empower us to fulfill this calling?

Volitional maturity starts as we fan into flame a new answer to the age-old question, "Why am I here?" In Adam, we're here to *survive*. To take care of ourselves. At best, we're here to build a tower of power that boosts our ego. At worst, we're here to huddle in the corner of our domicile hoping we'll be safe from the storms of life.

In Christ, we are here to *thrive*. We're not here for ourselves. We're here for God. We're here to fulfill his Creation Mandate. Here to be our brother's keeper. Here to be a shepherd in a jungle.

Thus, volitional wholeness pursues a whole new *purpose*. We put off the futility of trying to make life work on our own for ourselves. We put on the vitality of working for God through Christ. We put off dominating others and put on empowering them.

Wholeness also pursues a whole new *pattern*. We put off cowardice and put on courage. Life is terrifying when this is all there is. We are of all people most miserable if there is no resurrection of the dead. But since there is, this life does not have to overwhelm, does not have to terrorize us. We can live confidently, putting on our new power for holy living, our new inclination to lovingly obey Father and sacrificially serve our brothers and sisters. With courage we live out our new *telos*, our new reason for being.

The guiding process involves provoking your spiritual friends' new chosen styles of shepherding through other-centered interactions by:

- Yielding to the Spirit
- Walking in the Spirit
- Cultivating the Fruit of the Spirit

Intervention Interactions to Yield to the Spirit

- *Becky, we're to put on in our purposes, practices, and behavior what Christ has already resurrected in our wills. We find this power, paradoxically, by admitting that we are powerless. The Bible calls it yielding to the Spirit. Yieldedness to the Spirit begins with our conscious conviction that without God we can do nothing, but that with God we can do all things through Christ who strengthens us. When we yield to the Spirit, we place ourselves in a "greenhouse environment" where the soil of our soul is so soft that we become ready recipients of the nourishing love, power, and wisdom of God. That soil is our confession of our neediness.*
  - *Have you come to the place in your spiritual walk, Becky, that you've admitted that you are powerless?*
  - *Have you come to the place in your spiritual life, Becky, where you're consciously aware that without God you can do nothing?*

♦ *What is it like for you when you confess your neediness and absolute dependence?*

♦ *Various biblical terms such as "present" and "yield" come from a Greek word meaning to offer, to bring, to place beside. It was used for a bride presenting herself to her groom. Picture the vulnerability, trust, and intimacy.*

♦ *Let's discuss what it would be like to say to Jesus, "I'm yours. I need you. I want you. Take me. Fill me. Nourish and cherish me. I'm responsive to you. Submitted to you. Open to you."*

♦ *How would you rate your level of intimacy with Jesus?*

Intervention Interactions to Walk in the Spirit

♦ *Becky, Paul speaks of walking in the Spirit, being led by the Spirit, and keeping in step with the Spirit. While each of these terms maintains a distinctive emphasis, the essence is the same. We're to actively appropriate the Spirit's power in our lives. We're to "allow" the Spirit to guide our walk, our way, our pathway—to direct our steps and lead our interactions with others.*

♦ *What would it be like for you to be involved in a continual conversation where you're always asking, "Spirit, what would other-centered living look like in this situation? What are you calling me to be and to do right now? How would you want me to respond? What way of relating would please you? Help them?"*

♦ *Tell me about times when you've walked in the Spirit.*

♦ *Tell me about times when you've been led by the Spirit.*

♦ *Tell me about times when you've kept in step with the Spirit.*

Intervention Interactions to Cultivate the Fruit of the Spirit

♦ *Becky, the supernatural result of yielding to the Spirit and walking in the Spirit is the cultivation of the fruit of the Spirit. The fruit of the Spirit are relational traits (characteristic pathways, disciplined styles of relating, interactional patterns) that evidence love for our neighbor. Packer describes the fruit of the Spirit as the nine-fold pattern of habitual reaction to life's pressures (Packer, **Rediscovering Holiness**, p. 106). In Galatians, Paul commands us to replace the vices of the flesh with the fruit of the Spirit. Being fruit, connection to the vine is vital for volitional maturity. We must deliberately and regularly practice the spiritual disciplines that connect us to the vine, using the means of grace to promote spiritual health. "Spiritual health, like bodily health, is God's gift. But, like bodily health, it is a gift that must be carefully cherished, for careless habits can squander it" (Packer, **Rediscovering Holiness**, p. 149).*

♦ *How are you connecting to the vine?*

♦ *What are you doing in cooperation with Christ to produce the Spirit's fruit?*

♦ *Which fruit of the Spirit seems most necessary as you relate to Jim? To Bill?*

♦ *What vices of the flesh do you need to replace with what fruit of the Spirit?*

♦ *What are you doing to cultivate the fruit of the Spirit in your life?*

Interaction interventions like these can assist spiritual friends like Becky to pray a prayer of volitional renewal something like the following.

Holy Spirit, I yield to you. I consciously choose to admit that I'm a coward without you. With you, I can do all things. With you, no purpose of yours can be thwarted. I put on choosing to depend upon you. I put on choosing to live for you. I put on seeking not only your power to do right, but also your guidance to know what is right. Step by step please lead me, all of the days of my life. In each relational interaction, empower and enlighten me to know what other-centered living looks like.

Flow through me so that the disciplined, habitual passion and energy of my soul reflects your fruit. Show me how to connect to you, how to depend upon you, how to be nourished by you. Then let my greatest purpose be being like you, like Jesus.

Faith-Based Emotional Vivification: Putting On New Managed Mood States

We can, with integrity, face our feelings and experience life with all its joys and sorrows. God has given us all that we need for emotional life and emotional maturity so that we can put off unmanaged moods and put on new managed mood states.

The guiding process with emotions involves helping your spiritual friends toward emotional maturity as image bearers (relational, rational, volitional, and emotional beings). It includes intervention interactions to:

- Soothe the Soul in the Savior (Relational Spiritual)
- Accept Mood States (Relational Self-Aware)
- Empathize with Others (Relational Social)
- Bring Rationality to Emotionality (Rational)
- Courageously Respond to Emotions (Volitional)
- Openly Experience Emotions (Emotional)

Intervention Interactions to Soothe the Soul in the Savior (Relational Spiritual)

- *Becky, as a spiritual being experiencing intense emotions, you can soothe your soul in your Savior.*
  - *What's it been like for you to take your feelings to God in this situation?*
  - *How have you found your Savior's solace during these trying times?*
  - *What is different about those times when you do go to God for solace?*

Intervention Interactions to Accept Mood States (Relational Self-Aware)

- *Becky, as a self-aware being sensing profound moods, you can admit, understand, label, and accept your mood states.*
  - *How would you rate yourself in these areas?*
  - *Which of these do you find hardest? Easiest? Why?*
  - *Let's talk about your emotional quotient.*

Intervention Interactions to Empathize with Others (Relational Social)

- *Becky, as a social being sensing emotions in others, you can empathize with others, sustaining and healing them.*
  - *How has your suffering increased your ability to empathize with others who are suffering?*
  - *Tell me about some people you have sustained and healed over the past few months.*
  - *How are you allowing the comfort you're receiving from God to comfort others?*

Intervention Interactions to Bring Rationality to Emotionality (Rational)

- ◆ *Becky, as a rational being, you can bring rationality to your emotionality. You can gain the wisdom to understand the causes and nature of your feelings. You can envision with spiritual eyes imaginative ways to handle your moods.*
    - ◆ *How well are you bringing rationality to your emotionality?*
    - ◆ *How well are you able to feel your feelings and understand your feelings?*
    - ◆ *Tell me about times during all this that you've been able to imaginatively manage your moods.*

Intervention Interactions to Courageously Respond to Emotions (Volitional)

- ◆ *Becky, as a volitional being, you can consciously and courageously choose to creatively respond to your emotional states.*
    - ◆ *Tell me about some times when you've done that as you related to Jim. To Bill.*
    - ◆ *What are some of the conscious creative and courageous choices you're making as you respond to your moods?*
    - ◆ *What conscious, creative, courageous choices do you sense Christ leading you to make?*

Intervention Interactions to Openly Experience Emotions (Emotional)

- ◆ *Becky, as an emotional being, you can openly experience whatever you're feeling, being responsive to God and God's world. Thus cooperating with God, the Creator of emotions, you put on emotional integrity, harmony, and honesty.*
    - ◆ *Tell me about your emotional honesty and openness with yourself.*
    - ◆ *Tell me about your emotional honesty and openness with God.*
    - ◆ *Tell me about how you've faced your feelings in all this with emotional integrity, harmony, and honesty.*

Interactions such as these can assist spiritual friends like Becky to pray a prayer of emotional renewal that might sound something like the following.

Father, thank you for feelings. Thank you that you have them. Thank you that I have them. Sometimes, many times, I feel like wishing them away. But then I would be such a shell of a person. A Stoic, not a Poet. I don't want that. What I want is heaven—no more cryin' there. No more tears. No more looking in the eyes of a hurting loved one and feeling more pain than I ever thought possible. But until heaven, I want to be real. Raw. Honest. I want emotional integrity. I want emotional maturity. Help me to bring spirituality, rationality, and volitionality to my emotionality. Help me to be as emotional as King David, as Jeremiah, as Job, as Asaph, as Jesus, as you, as the great saints throughout Church history. Help me to feel life fully. Fortify me to feel the feelings of others. Deeply. Sincerely. Accurately. Help me to feel your pain—the fellowship of your suffering.

Exploring Your Spiritual Journey

♦ Select a sanctification issue that you're facing in your spiritual life. Use the six steps in the vivification process to guide yourself toward growth in grace and victory in Christ.

1. How will you grow in grace by using the principles in this chapter about faith-based rational vivification—putting on new wise mindsets?

2. How will you grow in grace by using the principles in this chapter about faith-based relational spiritual vivification—putting on new spiritual purified affections?

3. How will you grow in grace by using the principles in this chapter about faith-based relational self-aware vivification—putting on new self-aware purified affections?

4. How will you grow in grace by using the principles in this chapter about faith-based relational social vivification—putting on new social purified affections?

5. How will you grow in grace by using the principles in this chapter about faith-based volitional vivification—putting on new other-centered purposes/pathways?

6. How will you grow in grace by using the principles in this chapter about faith-based emotional vivification—putting on new managed mood states?

Activating Envisioned Maturity: Stirring Up God's Gifts—John 21

The Apostle Peter had regained his vision of the resurrected Christ, but now he needed to reclaim his vision of resurrection power in his life (John 21). As with so many areas of life, Peter first needed someone else to envision his maturity before he could gain a vision of ministry.

Principles from his life, found in John 21, teach spiritual friends how to activate envisioned maturity in others. By God's grace, you envision your spiritual friends walking in maturity. You then stimulate the maturity you envision by stirring up God's gifts.

Realize That Vision Comes from God

Start by envisioning what God has seen from all eternity. Visionary words that excite simply echo what God has been whispering to your spiritual friends their entire lives.

Mr. Dahlene, my fifth grade teacher, made me a "Playground Patrol" and said, "You'll be a great leader. You care about people." When I heard those words, for the first time in my life a human being spoke words that God had been speaking into my soul. What do I love doing now? Leading with love.

Visionary words sound strangely familiar to your spiritual friends. Your visionary words reach, touch, and call forth something that is already there, arousing possibilities.

Since visionary words come from God, as you interact, pray for God's vision. Ask God's Spirit to reveal the uniqueness of your spiritual friends.

Thrill at the Prospect of What People Will Become

Visionaries penetrate people's senseless, ceaseless chatter to see terrific potential. Peter is the poster boy for senseless chatter. He's the original carrier of foot-in-mouth disease. Yet through all Peter's senseless chatter, Christ senses and conveys Peter's heart and Peter's future. "Feed my sheep."

With Becky, delight in the integrity you see in place. Joyfully celebrate the unique shape of her heart. Sort through the inane and absurd to uncover the shrewd and the astute. Peer into the future to imagine what God might do in and through her.

Think Vision

To see vision, you must think vision. Be asking yourself, pondering curiously, thinking imaginatively:

- *How has God built my spiritual friend?*
- *What is God wanting to release through all the joys and heartaches of her life?*
- *What is being released right now in his life?*
- *What do I already see her offering others, which if stirred up, could grow mightily?*
- *What strengths does he have, that if surrendered to God, could powerfully advance the kingdom?*
- *What potential remains unrealized because of undealt-with weaknesses?*
- *How does she uniquely bless me? Uniquely bless others? What does this tell me about the character strengths that God is specially weaving into the fabric of her soul?*
- *How is he uniquely designed to reflect the Father's character?*
- *What aspects of Father's goodness does she wonderfully reflect?*
- *What passions do I see flowing from his life already?*
- *Where does she seem to find great joy in life?*
- *What ministry seems most easy for him?*

Connect with the uniqueness already stamped into Becky's makeup by the Holy Spirit. Then envision what the Spirit has designed her to become. Catch a glimpse of what she could be.

Remember that redemption is God's restoration of lost beauty, the restoration of the lost glory of the image of God within (glorious ruins). Spiritual friendship is the recognition and re-ignition of that lost glory.

Listen for and evoke the unfolding image of God. Display Becky's fullest, called out, renewed humanity.

Think about Peter and Jesus. What was Peter's occupation before he met Jesus? Fisherman. What does Peter do after Jesus' resurrection? "I'm going out to fish" (John 21:3). We're not talking here about a weekend wader fly-fishing in Montana to get away from it all. This is Peter's job. His livelihood. Peter lives to feed others.

Jesus taps into Peter's natural bent. "Feed my sheep" (John 21:16). Jesus crafts Peter's natural bent into a supernatural mission. Peter, like everyone, needs more than a job. His soul longs for a mission. Jesus links Peter's mission to the God-given skills, talents, gifts, and deep joys he already has.

Link Vision to God's Resurrection Power

Three times Peter denied Christ. Three times Christ asks, "Do you love me?" The third time Peter grieves, remembering his failure. No. He could never forget his failure. He sees the link between his three failures and Christ's three questions. Then he answers, "Lord, you know all things; you know that I love you" (John 21:17). As with God and Adam in the Garden, Jesus doesn't need Peter's answer. Peter needs Peter's answer.

God's strength is made perfect in our weakness. God's greatest calling often flows from our greatest failures. With vision, you can empower Becky by reminding her of God's power—Christ's resurrection power—in her weakness.

> **God's strength is made perfect in our weakness.**
> **God's greatest calling often flows from our greatest failures.**

Peter's greatest sense of shame came from his failure to fulfill his pledge to Jesus. "I will lay down my life for you" (John 13:37). Peter's greatest joy will come not only in feeding Christ's sheep, but in keeping his promise. "I tell you the truth. When you were younger you dressed yourself and went where you wanted; but when you are old you will stretch out your hands, and someone else will dress you and lead you where you do not want to go. Jesus said this to indicate the kind of death by which Peter would glorify God. Then he said to him, 'Follow me.'" (John 21:18-19).

Jesus is not envisioning Peter's geriatric days. He's envisioning Peter's fulfillment of his promise. It's as if Jesus says, "You failed me. Yes. But failure is not final, nor fatal, with Father. You will keep your pledge. You will feed my sheep. You will lay down your life for me, as I laid down mine for you."

Rejoice That Vision That Comes from God Is Relayed through God's People

You're an "en-courager"—a companion giving your spiritual friends the courage to persevere when they're on the brink of surrender. You facilitate the grace you see by acting as an "awakener" of what is already there. You draw out and stir up by "affirmingly" exposing the supernatural integrity already residing within.

Draw Out by Recognizing and Verbalizing the Spirit's Craftsmanship

- *If there were no time, talent, or financial restraints, what would you do with your life?*
  - *How could you start pursuing a little of that now?*
- *Maybe you're built to think about this kind of stuff.*
- *Perhaps God designed you to do this kind of thing.*
- *Tell me about the unique gifts that you have allowed to lay dormant that you can fan into flame and stir up into action.*

Draw Out by Exploring Narratives of Past Exploits

- *Tell me about some similar situations where you've cooperated with God's grace to make a difference in someone's life.*
- *When faced with similar situations in the past, what's helped to stir up the gift of God within you?*
- *What weaknesses has God been using to show you how much you need him?*
- *God tells us that he has given us his Spirit of power, love, and wisdom. Tell me about times when you've utilized God's spiritual power, love, and wisdom.*
- *Tell me about some of the spiritual resources that you've previously used.*
- *Share with me some of the scriptural resources you've used.*
- *I'd love to hear about some of the church resources you've used. Group resources. Personal resources.*

Draw Out by Exploring Narratives of Current Resources

- *Tell me about the spiritual gifts God has blessed you with.*
- *How are you using your gifts and talents to serve others?*
- *What strong points has God built into your life?*
  - *How are you using these to minister to others?*

Draw Out by Exploring Narratives of Future Exploits

- *As you leave here today filled with the Spirit, what will you be doing differently? How will you be loving others? How will you be making wise biblical decisions?*
- *In addition to personal spiritual resources, God gives us his Spirit, his people, and his Word to empower us. Tell me about how you will be using his resources to impact others for Christ.*
- *Imagine that over the next six months, God does a mighty work within you. How will your home life be different? Your work life? Church life? Relationships? Impact on your community?*
- *Dream with me. More than anything else, what do you long to do for God?*
  - *What legacy do you long to leave?*
  - *What impact do you hope to make?*
  - *Who would you most want to impact?*
- *How will you be cooperating with God to bring these dreams to fruition?*

Maturing Your Spiritual Friendship Competency
Activating Envisioned Maturity

♦ With a partner, use the following trialogues to begin to activate envisioned maturity in each other.
♦ If you're working through this material individually, then use this page to activate God's vision in your own life.

1. What is God wanting to release through all the joys and heartaches of your life?

2. Where do you seem to find great joy in life? What ministry seems most easy for you?

3. If there were no time, talent, or financial restraints, what would you do with your life? How could you start pursuing a little of that now?

4. Tell me about the unique gifts that you've allowed to lay dormant that you can fan into flame and stir up into action.

5. Tell me about some situations where you've cooperated with God's grace to make a difference in someone's life.

6. As you leave here today filled with the Spirit, what will you be doing differently? How will you be loving others? How will you be making wise biblical decisions?

7. Dream. More than anything else, what do you long to do for God? What legacy do you long to leave? What impact do you hope to make? Who would you most want to impact?

Insight-Oriented Treatment Planning: Collaborative Spiritual Direction
Colossians 3:1-25

Chapter Nine explored overall spiritual friendship treatment planning and soul care (sustaining and healing) treatment planning. The current section examines spiritual direction (reconciling and guiding) treatment planning.

In spiritual direction treatment planning, you focus on how your spiritual friends are facing the sins they have committed. Through reconciling and guiding, you expose their sins and God's grace as you empower them to grow in grace.

What process do you follow to spiritually direct your believing spiritual friends away from following the old ways of sin and toward following the new way of sanctification? Combining reconciling and guiding, you have two primary modes of spiritual direction treatment planning at your disposal.

- Spiritual Direction Treatment Planning and the Process of Sin and Sanctification
- Spiritual Direction Treatment Planning and the Process of Mortification/Vivification

Spiritual Direction Treatment Planning and the Process of Sin and Sanctification

In reconciling diagnosis, you compared and contrasted unhealthy and healthy responses to sin. You explored typical ways that people try to resist sin and how they try to manage sin when forced to face it. Additionally, you examined biblical ways to come to an awareness of sin and to find grace and forgiveness for sin. You saw blindness, stubbornness, works, and stagnation contrasted with awareness, acknowledgement, acceptance, and advance.

Under guiding diagnosis, you compared and contrasted fleshly and spiritual sanctification strategies. You probed the way of law, works, temporal focus, and selfish motivation versus the way of grace, faith, future hope, and sacrificial love.

Together, these eight stages provide a "sancticology" (biblical theology of sanctification or growth in grace) treatment plan. As you move through the spiritual direction process, you should be asking yourself the following *sanctification diagnostic questions*:

- Reconciling Stage One: Is my spiritual friend blind to guilt or aware of guilt?
- Reconciling Stage Two: Is my spiritual friend stubborn toward sin or acknowledging sin?
- Reconciling Stage Three: Is my spiritual friend working to find forgiveness or accepting grace?
- Reconciling Stage Four: Is my spiritual friend stagnating spiritually or advancing in growth?
- Guiding Stage One: Is my spiritual friend practicing sanctification by law or by grace?
- Guiding Stage Two: Is my spiritual friend practicing sanctification by works or by faith?
- Guiding Stage Three: Is my spiritual friend practicing sanctification by temporal focus or by future hope?
- Guiding Stage Four: Is my spiritual friend practicing sanctification by selfish motivation or by sacrificial love?

You should also be asking *sanctification treatment planning questions*:

- Reconciling Stage One: How can I reconcile my spiritual friend away from blindness to guilt toward awareness of guilt? How well am I doing so?
- Reconciling Stage Two: How can I reconcile my spiritual friend away from stubbornness regarding sin toward acknowledging sin? How well am I doing so?

- ◆ Reconciling Stage Three: How can I reconcile my spiritual friend away from working to find forgiveness toward accepting grace? How well am I doing so?
- ◆ Reconciling Stage Four: How can I reconcile my spiritual friend away from spiritual stagnation toward advancement in growth? How well am I doing so?
- ◆ Guiding Stage One: How can I guide my spiritual friend away from practicing sanctification by law toward practicing sanctification by grace? How well am I doing so?
- ◆ Guiding Stage Two: How can I guide my spiritual friend away from practicing sanctification by works toward sanctification by faith? How well am I doing so?
- ◆ Guiding Stage Three: How can I guide my spiritual friend away from practicing sanctification by temporal focus toward practicing sanctification by future hope? How well am I doing so?
- ◆ Guiding Stage Four: How can I guide my spiritual friend away from practicing sanctification by selfish motivation toward sanctification by sacrificial love? How well am I doing so?

The *Sancticology Spiritual Direction Treatment Plan Sheet* (see pages 325-326) integrates these issues. You can use this two-sided form to track your spiritual friends' progress, evaluate your effectiveness, and plan your interventions.

Spiritual Direction Treatment Planning and the Process of Mortification/Vivification

The second spiritual direction treatment plan uses the twelve steps of the mortification and vivification process. The *Mortification/Vivification Treatment Plan Sheet* (see pages 327-328) integrates these concepts. With this form and format, you're asking yourself where you are in the twelve steps of the putting off and putting on process. You're also asking how effectively you're moving through these "steps" and what you can do in future meetings to continue the process.

Insight Facilitation

Insight-oriented treatment planning leads naturally into insight facilitation. Once you've accurately diagnosed where your spiritual friends are in the sanctification process and how you can assist them toward growth, then you need to consider the most effective ways to communicate with them. What methods for facilitating insight might best direct them to develop the patterns of life and practice of spiritual disciplines that will empower them toward maturity? How can you guide them toward growth in grace? How can you help them to find ongoing victory over sin?

Both biblically and historically, facilitation of insight has taken many forms. Facilitating insight is more than confronting wrongs, telling what is right, and then exhorting to do what one now knows to do. Many biblical injunctions teach the spiritual director the importance of nuanced, appropriate responding and guiding: Proverbs 9:7-9; 10:31; 15:1, 23; 25:11; Ephesians 4:29; Colossians 4:6.

Church history has defined facilitating insight as leading perplexed people toward a set of values through which they can make decisions. You help your spiritual friends during spiritual *perplexity* to make wise decisions based upon spiritual *priorities* so they can live out their spiritual *victory*.

God's Word is the authoritative source of wisdom for forging decision-making principles in the midst of specific troubles. Historically, guiding used the resources of the helper and the helped to discern these principles. It assumed that the one being helped would grow in wisdom through the ongoing practical application of the Word. "Solid food is for the mature, who by constant use have trained themselves to distinguish good from evil" (Hebrews 5:14). Thus, the historical practice favored collaborative guidance over either strictly non-directive or directive means.

Sancticology Spiritual Direction Treatment Plan Sheet
Part I: Reconciling Treatment Planning

Reconciling and Sanctification: "It's Wonderful to Receive Forgiveness by Grace."

Stages	Unhealthy Responses to Sin	Healthy Responses to Sin
Stage One	Blindness	Awareness: Guilt
Stage Two	Stubbornness	Acknowledgement: Grief/Repentance
Stage Three	Works	Acceptance: Grace
Stage Four	Stagnation	Advancement: Growth

Sanctification Diagnostic Indicators: Reconciling

♦ Reconciling Stage One: Is my spiritual friend blind to guilt or aware of guilt?

♦ Reconciling Stage Two: Is my spiritual friend stubborn toward sin or acknowledging sin?

♦ Reconciling Stage Three: Is my spiritual friend working to find forgiveness or accepting grace?

♦ Reconciling Stage Four: Is my spiritual friend stagnating spiritually or advancing in growth?

Sanctification Treatment Plan Evaluators: Reconciling

♦ Reconciling Stage One: How can I reconcile my spiritual friend away from blindness to guilt toward awareness of guilt? How well am I doing so?

♦ Reconciling Stage Two: How can I reconcile my spiritual friend away from stubbornness regarding sin toward acknowledging sin? How well am I doing so?

♦ Reconciling Stage Three: How can I reconcile my spiritual friend away from working to find forgiveness toward accepting grace? How well am I doing so?

♦ Reconciling Stage Four: How can I reconcile my spiritual friend away from spiritual stagnation toward advancement in growth? How well am I doing so?

Sancticology Spiritual Direction Treatment Plan Sheet
Part II: Guiding Treatment Planning

Guiding and Sanctification: "It's Supernatural to Grow in Grace."

Stages	Fleshly Sanctification Strategy	Spiritual Sanctification Strategy
Stage One	Law	Grace
Stage Two	Works	Faith
Stage Three	Temporal Focus	Future Hope
Stage Four	Selfish Motivation	Sacrificial Love

Sanctification Diagnostic Indicators: Guiding

◆ Guiding Stage One: Is my spiritual friend practicing sanctification by law or by grace?

◆ Guiding Stage Two: Is my spiritual friend practicing sanctification by works or by faith?

◆ Guiding Stage Three: Is my spiritual friend practicing sanctification by temporal focus or by future hope?

◆ Guiding Stage Four: Is my spiritual friend practicing sanctification by selfish motivation or by sacrificial love?

Sanctification Treatment Plan Evaluators: Guiding

◆ Guiding Stage One: How can I guide my spiritual friend away from practicing sanctification by law toward practicing sanctification by grace? How well am I doing so?

◆ Guiding Stage Two: How can I guide my spiritual friend away from practicing sanctification by works toward sanctification by faith? How well am I doing so?

◆ Guiding Stage Three: How can I guide my spiritual friend away from practicing sanctification by temporal focus toward practicing sanctification by future hope? How well am I doing so?

◆ Guiding Stage Four: How can I guide my spiritual friend away from practicing sanctification by selfish motivation toward sanctification by sacrificial love? How well am I doing so?

Mortification/Vivification Treatment Plan Sheet
Part I: Mortification/Putting Off

1. Step One: Rational Mortification—Putting Off Old Foolish Mindsets

   ♦ How well is my spiritual friend repenting of the insane idols of his/her heart?

   ♦ How can I help my spiritual friend break the stranglehold of strongholds?

2. Step Two: Relational Mortification—Putting Off Old Spiritual Disordered/Impure Affections

   ♦ How well is my spiritual friend divorcing the adulterous false lovers of his/her soul?

   ♦ How can I help my spiritual friend annul attachment to alluring lovers?

3. Step Three: Relational Mortification—Putting Off Old Self-Aware Disordered/Impure Affections

   ♦ How well is my spiritual friend rejecting the ugliness of his/her self-beautification?

   ♦ How can I help my spiritual friend shed self-sufficient, defensive thematic identities?

4. Step Four: Relational Mortification—Putting Off Old Social Disordered/Impure Affections

   ♦ How well is my spiritual friend uprooting his/her jealous hatred of others?

   ♦ How can I help my spiritual friend dislodge his/her narcissistic, demanding relationships toward others?

5. Step Five: Volitional Mortification—Putting Off Old Self-Centered Purposes/Pathways

   ♦ How well is my spiritual friend putting to death his/her enslaved acts of the flesh?

   ♦ How can I help my spiritual friend discard chosen styles of destructive self-gratification?

6. Step Six: Emotional Mortification—Putting Off Old Ungoverned Mood States

   ♦ How well is my spiritual friend crucifying addictive passions that seek to make his/her belly god?

   ♦ How can I help my spiritual friend jettison emotional duplicity, deadening, and denial?

Mortification/Vivification Treatment Plan Sheet
Part II: Vivification/Putting On

7. Step Seven: Rational Vivification—Putting On New Wise Mindsets

    ◆ How well is my spiritual friend consenting to the truth of Christ's grace narrative?

    ◆ How can I help my spiritual friend to be transformed by the renewing of his/her mind?

8. Step Eight: Relational Vivification—Putting On New Spiritual Purified Affections

    ◆ How well is my spiritual friend enjoying and exalting Christ as his/her Supreme Good?

    ◆ How can I help my spiritual friend to commune deeply with God the Spring of Living Water?

9. Step Nine: Relational Vivification—Putting On New Self-Aware Purified Affections

    ◆ How well is my spiritual friend reckoning on the truth of who Christ is and who he/she is in and to Christ?

    ◆ How can I help my spiritual friend view himself/herself according to Christ-sufficient, sacred identities?

10. Step Ten: Relational Vivification—Putting On New Social Purified Affections

    ◆ How well is my spiritual friend stirring up his/her new connecting love for others?

    ◆ How can I help my spiritual friend nourish his/her new sacrificial relationships toward others?

11. Step Eleven: Volitional Vivification—Putting On New Other-Centered Purposes/Pathways

    ◆ How well is my spiritual friend stirring up his/her new freed will empowered to empower others?

    ◆ How can I help my spiritual friend provoke his/her new chosen style of shepherding through other-centered interactions?

12. Step Twelve: Emotional Vivification—Putting On New Managed Mood States

    ◆ How well is my spiritual friend cooperating with God in enlivening new managed mood states?

    ◆ How can I help my spiritual friend collaborate with God to experience new emotional integrity?

Consider some common insight facilitation mistakes that spiritual friends should avoid.

- *Premature Empathy*: Expressing empathy before you've truly heard your spiritual friend's story of suffering and before you've entered the casket.
- *Premature Teaching*: Moving to guiding before listening, sustaining, healing, and reconciling.
- *Monologue*: Failure to engage your spiritual friend in dialogue and trialogue, using personal counseling as a pulpit/preaching time. Only directive guiding instead of collaborative interacting.
- *Denial of Emotions*: Conveying that your spiritual friend's emotions are out of proportion or illegitimate, without truly allowing your friend candor, complaint, cry, communion, wailing, waiting, weaving, and worshipping.
- *Denial of Longings*: Acting as if the pains of desert living are illegitimate, shaming your spiritual friend for groaning for heaven, minimizing desires, thirsts, and affections.
- *Patronizing*: Pitying your spiritual friend, pretending to care, acting as if your spiritual friend is a child to be rescued or a car to be fixed.
- *Rejection*: Condemning your spiritual friend, haughtiness, and holier-than-thou attitudes.
- *Long-windedness*: Dominating the conversation, turning the tables so you become the counselee, and story-sharing that tells too many details.
- *Entering Power Struggles*: "You must see it as I do." "You need to change for me."
- *Presenting Truth Academically*: Using cliches, using the Bible as a lucky charm, teaching without passion, teaching unrelated to real life, and teaching disconnected from your spiritual friend.
- *Using Dogmatism*: "There are two ways. My way or the highway!"
- *Expressing Judgmentalism*: Exhorting change while communicating superiority.

Ponder some general principles for facilitating insight.

- *Present the Truth in the Context of Relationship*: Connect, empathize, engage, and enter.
- *Embody the Truth*: Have the integrity to live the truth you are sharing. Be able to share examples of how you've struggled to grow in that particular area—by God's grace.
- *Present the Truth from as Many Different Angles as Possible*: Use trialogues, spiritual conversations, scriptural explorations, stories, images, pictures, quotes, and questions.
- *Use Imagery*: Ask God to give you a creative mind to offer summarizing pictures of life.
- *Use Your Spiritual Friend's Frame of Reference/Language*: Listen and speak the language of your spiritual friend's soul, world, education, and experience.
- *Explain How the Truth Relates to the Issue*: Make connections, discuss implications, and co-derive applications.
- *Involve Your Spiritual Friend in the Truth-Learning and Truth-Applying Process*: Seek to activate insight into scriptural principles, give homework, and ask your spiritual friend to develop his or her own homework assignments.

Where We've Been and Where We're Headed

So far in guiding, you've helped your spiritual friends put on their new person in Christ, fanned into flame their giftedness, and collaborated with them in discerning God's will and applying God's Word. Through the final three guiding relational competencies that you'll learn in Chapter Sixteen, you'll help your spiritual friends to take action through homework that works, explore what holiness looks like in their lives, and heroically apply God's truth to their relationships.

Maturing Your Spiritual Friendship Competency
Insight-Oriented Treatment Planning

1. Using the *Sancticology Spiritual Direction Treatment Plan Sheet* (see pages 325-326), assess someone you're currently ministering to through spiritual friendship (professional counseling, pastoral counseling, biblical counseling, or lay counseling).

   a. Summarize your sense of how he or she is progressing.

   b. Summarize your plan for how you can continue to help him or her.

2. Using the *Mortification/Vivification Treatment Plan Sheet* (see pages 327-328), assess someone you're currently ministering to through spiritual friendship (professional counseling, pastoral counseling, biblical counseling, or lay counseling).

   a. Summarize your sense of how he or she is progressing.

   b. Summarize your plan for how you can continue to help him or her.

3. Which of the common responding mistakes tend to be a problem for you? How might you replace those mistakes with more healthy responses?

4. Which of the principles for facilitating insight do you use the most? How have you learned to use these healthy principles in such a good way?

Chapter Sixteen

Guiding Treatment and Intervention
FAITHH Relational Competencies, Part II

"Every vital Christian testifies that the instinctive passions and desires of the flesh can be replaced with the new priorities of the Spirit. This reorientation is not instant and complete, but it is genuine and progressive" (David Powlison, *Seeing with New Eyes*, p. 161).

Discipling Disciple-Makers

As you head toward "the homestretch" in guiding, you want to teach your spiritual friends to fish, instead of simply giving them a fish. That is, you want them Christ-dependent, not dependent upon you, connected to the Body of Christ, not only connected to you. You want to disciple them so that they can disciple themselves and others.

The six guiding relational competencies focus on helping your spiritual friends to see that it's supernatural to mature. You assist your spiritual friends to grow strong for God's glory through Christ's resurrection power. Through the final three competencies, you help them develop a supernatural lifestyle that lives out the new covenant heart placed within.

- ◆ *F* Faith-Based Interventions: 2 Timothy 1:5-7
- ◆ *A* Activating Envisioned Maturity: John 21:1-25
- ◆ *I* Insight-Oriented Treatment Planning: Colossians 3:1-25
- ◆ *T* Taking Action: Ephesians 4:17-32
- ◆ *H* Holiness Spiritual Conversations: Romans 5:1-8:39
- ◆ *H* Heroic Scriptural Explorations: Hebrews 10:1-11:40

Taking Action: Homework That Works—Ephesians 4:17-32

After explaining to the Ephesians that they are saints with a new nature (Ephesians 4:17-24), Paul exhorts them to make specific application to activate their faith. Taking action, or homework that works, follows his model.

Like Paul, you need to master the art of helping your spiritual friends apply new covenant truth to the specifics of their daily relationships. You help them to learn the art of faith active in love through:

Exploring You Spiritual Journey

1. What are some of the diagnostic concepts that you will take with you from your study of *Spiritual Friends*?

2. What are some of the relational competencies that you will take with you from your study of *Spiritual Friends*?

3. What are some of the major thoughts, phrases, pictures, ideas, etc., that you will take with you from your study of *Spiritual Friends*?

4. How will your *life* be different because of your application of *Spiritual Friends*? Try to be as specific as possible.

5. How will your *ministry* to people be different because of your application of *Spiritual Friends*? Try to be as specific as possible.

6. If you've studied *Spiritual Friends* in a group context, what has been most meaningful about your time together?

7. Dream. How do you want God to use you as a spiritual friend?

- User-Friendly Action Plans
- User-Focused Action Plans
- Commencement Summaries

User-Friendly Action Plans

Out of the abundance of the heart, the mouth speaks. When you truly believe that your spiritual friends are new creations, saints with a new nature, new covenant believers who have all they need to live godly, and are supernaturally enabled to mature through Christ's resurrection power, then how will you speak? How will you word your interactions? You'll shape your trialogues to communicate your faith in their supernatural ability to live a life of faith active in love. You'll frame your guiding interactions:

- In a Positive Form
- In a Continuous Process Form
- With a Here-and-Now Focus
- In a Specific Form
- With a Responsibility Focus

In a Positive Form

- *What renewed longings will **replace** your old ones?*
- *What will you be thinking **differently**?*
- *What do you want to be doing **instead**?*
- *What new managed moods will you **put on**?*

In a Continuous Process Form

- Continuous Past Tense: *How **were** you putting off and putting on those new longings?*
- Continuous Present Tense: *How **are** you renewing your mind?*
- Continuous Future Tense: *How **will** you be living out your new nature in Christ?*

With a Here-and-Now Focus

- *As you apply what we've been discussing, how **will you be progressing** toward victory?*
- *As you leave today's meeting and **you're on track** toward applying this truth, how will you be relating differently?*

In a Specific Form

- *Can you tell me more **specifically** how you will be listening to your son?*
- ***Exactly** what will you be doing differently?*

With a Responsibility Focus

- *How will **you** cooperate with Christ to make this happen?*
- *How will **you** choose to respond?*
- *What will **you** be doing when that happens?*

User-Focused Action Plans

Albert Einstein surmised, "You cannot solve problems with the same kind of thinking that created those problems." Problems tend to create myopia—shortsighted, non-creative, black-and-white, inside-the-box thinking. Everything looks bleak. Black. Futile. Resources remain unrecognized. People feel stuck and stunted.

Confused, your spiritual friends need focus—twenty/twenty spiritual vision, spiritual eyes, faith eyes. You need to enlighten the eyes of their hearts to see possibilities and to implement those possibilities practically and powerfully. User-focused action plans shine the light of new covenant spiritual theology by:

- Developing Clarity
- Encouraging Responsibility
- Drawing Out Spiritual Resources
- Keeping Accountable
- Turning Setbacks into Comebacks

Developing Clarity

Help your spiritual friends clearly see what the issues are, what decisions they need to make, what actions they need to take, what they want, and what God wants in and from them.

- *What would you like us to focus on today?*
- *What would you like to change about your situation? Your relationship? Your problem?*
- *What do you see as the problem?*
  - *Give me a recent example of it.*
  - *Who is present when the problem occurs?*
  - *What does each person say or do? Then what happens?*
  - *When does the problem most frequently occur?*
- *What is your goal in sharing about this?*
- *So, what brings you in today?*

Encouraging Responsibility

Once you've helped your spiritual friends to clarify and focus, motivate them to act responsibly.

- Probe What They Will Be Doing Differently When the Problem Is Solved:

  - *When God answers your prayers for empowerment, what will you be doing differently?*
  - *If a miracle happened, and you were acting that way now, how would you be acting?*
  - *If as you leave here today, you were on track to acting more maturely, what would you be doing differently?*
  - *When your husband is acting more the way you pray that he will, what will you be doing differently?*
  - *What would your wife say you would be doing differently?*
  - *If I were a fly on the wall, what would I see you doing differently?*
  - *What will be the very first signs that things are moving in the right direction?*
    - *Who will be the first to notice? What will he/she say or do? How will you respond?*

- *After the problem is resolved, what might your family be doing differently?*
- *If we think of this step as the beginning of a trend, what do you think the next step will be?*

- Urge Them to Do a Small Piece of That Now:

  - *Since you know how you want to relate to your husband, and since you know you have the power to do that, how 'bout doing part of that this week?*
  - *You've done a great job clarifying the issues biblically and practically. So, what would it look like for you to do a small piece of that starting today?*

Drawing Out Spiritual Resources

Evoke spiritual resources, solutions, and strengths. Cooperate with God to organize the chaos of life into beautiful shapes and patterns.

- Explore How Growth Is Happening Some Now:

  - *Tell me about some times when you're acting a little that way now.*
  - *How are you specifically doing that?*
  - *When are you acting a little more maturely?*
  - *Where are you already experiencing some spiritual victory in this area?*

- Explore When the Problem Isn't Happening:

  - *Are there some times when the problem isn't happening?*
  - *Tell me about some times when you're having victory over this.*

- Find Out How Growth Is Happening:

  - *What is different about these victorious times?*
  - *What are you doing differently when you see God at work?*
  - *How did you do that!*
  - *How do you do that?*
  - *How do you get that to happen?*
  - *How were you able to take this step?*
    - *What led up to it?*
    - *Just before taking this step, did you nearly back down? How did you stop yourself from backing down?*

- Do More of It:

  - *How will you and God keep this victory going?*
  - *How do you predict that you and Christ will keep these successes going?*
  - *How will others know that you're keeping this fruit growing?*
  - *So, how will you continue to make these choices?*
  - *How will you continue to commune with God, connect with Christ, and cooperate with the Holy Spirit?*

- Cheerleading/Encouraging:

    - *That's great!*
    - *Awesome!*
    - *Wow!*
    - *That's so cool!*
    - *How did you do that!*
    - *How do you explain that?*
    - *How did you decide to do that?*
    - *What does that say about your surrender to Christ? Your love for Christ? Your dependence upon Christ?*
    - *What does that say about Christ's grace at work in your life? His power? His love? His wisdom?*
    - *Of all the people you know, who would be the least surprised by your recent spiritual growth?*

- Complimenting:

    - *I'm really impressed by how you're cooperating with Christ to experience his power.*
    - *I'm truly impressed with your dependence upon the Spirit.*
    - *I'm struck by your tenacity. Dedication. Perseverance. Forgiving spirit. Love.*

Keeping Accountable

Accountability is vital to all spiritual friendships. Maintain accountability by giving and following up on homework assignments.

- Giving Responsibility Tasks/Homework Assignments:

    - *Of everything we've discussed today, what strikes you as most central to the change process God is working out in your life?*
        - *What do you think it would look like for you to change in these ways?*
        - *Specifically, how could you apply these changes in your life and relationships this next week?*
    - *How could you apply all that we've discussed today?*
    - *What homework assignment will you give yourself this week?*
    - *What are you going to do differently because of our meeting today?*
    - *Let's talk about how you could apply the insights you've gained today.*
    - *How will you be putting off your old affections and putting on your new? Your mindsets? Your purposes? Your mood states? Your habituated tendencies?*
    - *Keep track of what you're doing this week that gives you victory over this.*
    - *Between now and the next time we meet, I would like you to observe, so that you can report back to me, what happens in your marriage that you want to continue to have happen.*
    - *Do at least one or two things that will surprise your spouse.*

Note that these assignments not only give tasks to do, but place responsibility on your spiritual friends for thinking about what to do, why to do it, and how doing it will be helpful. Other categories of helpful responsibility tasks (homework) include: memorizing Scripture, meditating on Scripture, studying relevant Scripture passages, applying specific passages, putting into practice specific biblical principles, journaling, and "psalming."

- Following-Up on Responsibility Tasks/Homework Assignments:

Once they've started taking responsibility, keep the ball rolling. Do so by amplifying and helping to maintain change and growth. Motivate your spiritual friends by catching them doing well.

- *So, give me an update. How did things go with last week's assignment?*
- *I'm eager to hear about how you implemented last week's homework.*
- *What's your report today? Tell me how you were able to apply what you learned last week.*
- *So, tell me what is different or better?*
- *I'm interested to hear how you were able to offer yourself to others last week.*
- *I'm interested to hear how your time of silence and solitude with God went.*
- *I'm curious about what it was like for you when you talked honestly and openly with God.*
- *I'd love to hear how it went when you wrote your own Psalm 13.*
- *I'd love to hear your journal to God.*
- *So, what was happening this past week that you want to continue doing? Thinking?*
- *Tell me about your progress in putting off _____ and in putting on _____.*

Turning Setbacks into Comebacks

Sometimes you'll open a meeting eagerly expecting a positive report on the past week only to hear negatives. What do you do then? How do you turn setbacks, apparent or real, into comebacks?

- When They Say, "No Change in the Situation," Then Reply:

  - *Hmm. How have you been able to continue to cope with this?*
  - *I'm sorry to hear that it feels like the "same old, same old." How have you managed to stay on top of things through all of this?*
  - *That's gotta' be hard.*
    - *How have you managed your moods?*
    - *How have you continued to make godly choices?*
    - *How have you renewed your mind even in the middle of old circumstances?*
    - *How have you kept longing for Christ even when your human longings go unmet?*

- When They Say, "No Change in Themselves," Then Explore before You Exhort/Confront:

  - *No? Not even a little?*
  - *Was there one time when you were able to experience a bit more victory than previously?*
  - *How did you keep matters from getting worse?*

- If They Still Share No Positive Report:

  - Implement Previous Reconciling Relational Competencies:

    - Confronting Discrepancies
    - Softening Stubbornness

- Connecting Intimately
- Sharing Scripture (Trialogues, Spiritual Conversations, and Scriptural Explorations)

- Impart Grace While Encouraging Confession:

  - *Have you talked to the Lord about your failure?*
  - *Talk to me about any battles with guilt.*
  - *Tell me about the forgiveness you received when you confessed that to the Lord.*

- Explore What They Wish They Had Done Differently:

  - *What would you do with a "do over"?*
  - *Are there actions, attitudes, or words that you would do differently if you had the week to do over again?*
  - *What do you think kept you from drawing on God's power to do this?*

- Promote Resilience:

  - *What can you learn from last week's setback?*
  - *How can you persevere through these trying times?*
  - *What would you like to do differently this week?*

- Be a Bit Predictive:

  - *Are there times when you can imagine it will be tempting to go back to the old ways?*
  - *How will you get through those times?*

Commencement Summaries

As a counselor, pastor, or spiritual friend, you can take action, also. At the end of your spiritual friendship meetings, a *Spiritual Friendship Commencement Summary* (see page 339) allows you to review the initial goals for your meetings, overview the progress that has actually been made, summarize unresolved areas that yet need work, and record reasons for concluding official spiritual friendship meetings. Such information is helpful for you in assessing how well you're using God's gifts. It's also quite beneficial should your spiritual friend decide to return later for additional meetings.

"Commencement" pictures positive images of graduation, accomplishments, goals met, and moving on to the next, higher stage.

I label this a *Commencement Summary* as opposed to a *Termination Summary*. "Commencement" pictures positive images of graduation, accomplishments, goals met, and moving on to the next, higher stage.

Spiritual Friendship Commencement Summary

Spiritual Friend's Name: _____

Date First Seen: _____ **Date Last Seen:** _____

Today's Date: _____ **Your Name:** _____

Summary of Initial Issue(s), Major Goal(s), Diagnosis, and Treatment Plans:

Summary of Growth/Maturity Resulting from Spiritual Friendship Meetings:

Insight Concerning Any Unresolved Areas and Suggestions for Growth:

Reason(s) for Commencement:

Maturing Your Spiritual Friendship Competency
Taking Action: Homework That Works

1. Using the scenario with Bill, write dialogues/trialogues using user-friendly action plans:

    a. In a Positive Form:

    b. In a Continuous Process Form:

    c. With a Here-and-Now Focus:

    d. In a Specific Form:

    e. With a Responsibility Focus:

2. Using the scenario with Becky, write dialogues/trialogues using user-focused action plans that:

    a. Develop Clarity:

    b. Encourage Responsibility:

    c. Draw Out Spiritual Resources:

    d. Keep Accountable:

    e. Turn Setbacks into Comebacks:

Holiness Spiritual Conversations: Guiding Theological Trialogues—Romans 5:1-8:39

According to 2 Timothy 1:6-7 and 2 Peter 1:3-4, your redeemed spiritual friends have all the power, wisdom, and love they need to live godly Christian lives. According to Romans 5:1-8:39; Ephesians 4:17-32; and Colossians 3:1-25, your redeemed spiritual friends have a new nature empowered to love God and others. According to Hebrews 7:1-10:39, your redeemed spiritual friends enjoy a new covenant heart enabled by God and indwelt by the Holy Spirit to produce the fruit of righteousness. According to 2 Corinthians 5:17 and 1 Peter 1:15-16, your redeemed spiritual friends are new creations commanded to be holy as God is holy.

Soul Physicians commits nearly 200 pages to explaining the biblical truths of who your spiritual friends are *to* and *in* Christ. What can you do to help them to live out the new person residing within? The following trialogue categories offer sample interactions designed to fan into flame new covenant hearts.

Spiritual Conversations Enlightening Your Spiritual Friends to Their Worthy Groom's Love for Them as His Virgin Bride

Christ, the Worthy Groom, pursues, woos, wins, and renews your spiritual friends. They are his virgin brides. Victory in Christ requires the awareness, enjoyment, and application of their new intimacy.

- *How does Christ's tenacious, pursuing love influence you?*
- *Knowing that Christ woos you tenderly, how will you be relating to him?*
- *God stops at nothing to cause you to crave him more than anything. What is he doing in your life to stimulate your craving for him? How are you responding?*
- *How are the kindness, goodness, forbearance, and longsuffering of God leading you to repentance and renewal?*
- *What impact does the passion of the Christ have on you? How is his precious sacrifice of his life infiltrating your soul?*
- *How does seeing Christ as your Lover affect your life?*
- *How does seeing Christ as your Hero affect your life?*

Spiritual Conversations Enlightening Your Spiritual Friends to Their Salvation Gowns

At salvation, Christ dressed your spiritual friends in four virginal gowns: regeneration, reconciliation, redemption, and justification. Unfortunately, many believers are unaware of their new attire, and many more are unable to apply their new attire. The following sample trialogues can help your spiritual friends to put on their new clothing in Christ.

Regeneration Trialogues

- *Through regeneration, you're a new creation in Christ. How will you be living differently based upon your newness in Christ?*
- *Through regeneration, you have a new nature. You're a saint. Ever realized that before? How saintly do you feel? Even when you don't feel the least bit saintly, what would it be like to live out your sainthood?*

♦ *Through regeneration, you have new capacities to live purely. You have a new want to and a new can do to live for Christ. What new want to is God stirring in you? What new can do is the Spirit empowering within you?*

♦ *Through regeneration, you have new propensities. You're restored in your affections, mindsets, purposes, and mood states. How would knowing and applying these truths influence your longings? Your thinking? Your choices? Your actions? Your emotions?*

♦ *Through regeneration, you have new life. You're resurrected with Christ. How does it hit you when you realize that you're a partaker of the Divine nature? How does Christ's resurrection power change you daily?*

Reconciliation Trialogues

♦ *Through reconciliation, you're a son/daughter of God the Father. How does this change your thinking about yourself? Your life? Your responsibilities? You're also Christ's virgin bride. How does that image impact you?*

♦ *Through reconciliation, you're the repentant Prodigal returned home, forgiven, and loved with Father's lavish, ravishing love. If you kept that image in mind constantly, how would you live?*

♦ *Through reconciliation, God adopted you into his forever family. You're his adult child. How do you want to please Father?*

Redemption Trialogues

♦ *Through redemption, Christ has freed you from the power of sin. What sins do you want liberation from?*

♦ *Through redemption, God grants you a new purpose in life, a new reason for living. You're empowered and called to be a shepherd in a jungle, serving God by serving others. Who is God calling you to serve? How?*

♦ *Through redemption, you have the power to not let sin reign. In what areas do you want to apply your new power?*

♦ *Through redemption, you have freedom from sin and victory over sin. You're more than a conqueror through Christ. What sins do you want to conquer? What victories do you long for? What battles do you want to win?*

Justification Trialogues

♦ *Through justification, Christ cancels the penalty of sin. He declares you, "Not guilty!" because he took your guilt, your punishment. What does this awareness prompt in you? What does this knowledge incite in you?*

♦ *Through justification, you share Savior's salvation and shalom. Acceptance reigns in your heart. When do you most deeply experience your acceptance in Christ? How does it affect how you relate to others?*

♦ *Through justification, God has given you new peace. He hushes the voices of condemnation in your mind. How could you enjoy and experience your new peace with God through Christ?*

♦ *Through justification, God declares you righteous. Tell me how you will live like the righteous person you already are.*

♦ *Through justification, you enjoy a new boldness—confidence in your victory in Christ. Tell me about the victories you've been winning for Christ. Tell me about the victories you'll continue to win through Christ.*

Spiritual Conversations Enlightening Your Spiritual Friends to Who They Are *to* Christ: New Nurture

Believers have a new nurture—a new forgiven, reconciled, intimate relationship with the God of the universe. You can enlighten your spiritual friends to enjoy who they are to Christ. One way is to copy for them Box 22:1 from *Soul Physicians* (first edition, revised edition, and at www.rpmbooks.org) which summarizes over 100 verses about who they are to Christ. You can then ask:

♦ *Did you realize that the Bible has so much to say about who you are to Christ? If not, why do you suppose that is? If so, has it been having the impact it could?*

♦ *Which of these verses stand out to you? Why? What difference will they make in your life?*

♦ *Which of these verses do you want to commit to memory? How will memorizing them impact you?*

♦ *Which of these verses do you want to meditate upon this week? How will meditating upon these images of who you are to Christ impact you? Your relationships? Your current situation?*

♦ *Let's talk about some of the biblical images of who you are to Christ. Which ones grab you, jolt you, delight you? How? Why? What are you doing with these new truths?*

Your spiritual friends need to learn how to reckon on their new nurture. They need to live out their core identities as Beloved Virgin Bride, Celebrated Son/Daughter, and Best Friend. You can help them with trialogues such as these:

♦ *Your primary identities in Christ are: Beloved Virgin Bride, Celebrated Son/Daughter, and Best Friend. Wow. What difference could it make in your daily life if you kept these images in the forefront of your mind?*

♦ *Let's talk about renewing your mind by memorizing, meditating upon, and applying your new nurture in Christ.*

♦ *Nothing you do can ever cause God to love you more or less. Tell me how that truth hits you.*

♦ *What spiritual disciplines are you practicing to help you to renew your mind with the truth of your new nurture in Christ?*

♦ *Paul teaches that we grasp God's love for us in community, in connection with other believers. How can you connect with others in order to grasp together the height, depth, breadth, and width of Christ's love for you?*

♦ *Who are you to your Forgiving Father? When has he celebrated with you? How do you sense him delighting in you? What would it be like to see him jumping for joy when he "sees" you? When have you deeply sensed his love before? How did that happen? How can you cooperate with Father to experience more of the same? How can you fan into flame your friends' awareness of how much Father delights in them?*

♦ *Who are you to your Worthy Groom? How is he showing you that he loves you? When have you experienced his love? What is it like when you sense intimacy with Christ? In what ways does Jesus nourish and cherish you? How can you magnify Christ's love for you? How can you cooperate with him to stir up and live out your acceptance? How can you help others to sense and stir up their acceptance in Christ?*

♦ *Who are you to your Inspiring Mentor (Holy Spirit)? When has the Holy Spirit helped you to apply the truth that he is your strong Best Friend? How did that happen? How did you react? How can you cooperate with him to experience more of the same? How can you re-ignite in others their awareness of how the Spirit is their Best Friend?*

- *If you believed your new nurture, how would you be relating differently? Thinking differently? Choosing and acting differently? Feeling differently?*
- *What poem is God writing in your soul?*
- *What script, role, costume, are you wearing?*
  - *Who cast you in this role?*
  - *What original you is hidden beneath your costume?*
  - *What shame (controlling identity) leads you to hide beneath your costume?*
- *Where have you felt most uniquely valued for you? Wanted? Pursued? Enjoyed? Sought after?*
- *Think back. What are some of the unique contributions you've made?*
- *In one sentence, how would you describe the purpose of your life?*
- *Jonathan Edwards taught that God is most glorified when he is most cherished and enjoyed. How can you exalt God by enjoying him?*

Spiritual Conversations Enlightening Your Spiritual Friends to Who They Are *in* Christ: New Nature

Believers have a new nature—new sainthood, new heart, new power from the God of the universe. You can enlighten your spiritual friends to enjoy who they are in Christ. One way is to copy for them Box 23:1 from *Soul Physicians* (first edition, revised edition, and at www.rpmbooks.org) which summarizes over 150 verses about who they are in Christ. You can then ask:

- *Did you realize that the Bible has so much to say about who you are in Christ? If not, why do you suppose that is? If so, has it been having the impact it could?*
- *Which of these verses stand out to you? Why? What difference will they make in your life?*
- *Which of these verses do you want to commit to memory? How will memorizing them impact you?*
- *Which of these verses do you want to meditate upon this week? How will meditating upon these images of who you are to Christ impact you? Your relationships? Your current situation?*
- *Lets talk about some of the biblical images of who you are in Christ. Which ones grab you, jolt you, delight you? How? Why? What are you doing with these new truths?*

Your spiritual friends need to learn how to reckon on their new nature. They need to live out their core identities as neonatal saints and *nikao* saints (see *Soul Physicians* for a full explanation). Neonatal saints are born again, healthy saints given all the spiritual nourishment necessary to grow in grace. *Nikao* saints are born again, hearty saints provided all the "spiritual vitamins" necessary to experience victory in Christ. You can help your spiritual friends to reckon on their new nature with trialogues such as these:

- *At the moment of salvation, something real and amazing actually occurred in you. A real change took place in you. God implanted a new, healthy spiritual heart inside you. Your regeneration is more than having something taken away. It is more than having something added. Something new was birthed. You're a new creation in Christ empowered to live powerfully for God.*
  - *Have you heard these truths before? Are they new to you?*
  - *What impact can these truths have on how you live? Relate? Think? Act? Feel?*
- *At the moment of salvation, your old self died, crucified with Christ. Your new self was born, resurrected with Christ. Therefore, you no longer have to let sin reign. You rule over sin.*
  - *Have you heard these truths before? Are they new to you?*
  - *What impact can these truths have on how you live? Relate? Think? Act? Feel?*

- *At the moment of salvation, your "old man" died with Christ and your "new man" came to life with Christ.*
  - *Have you heard these truths before? Are they new to you?*
  - *What impact can these truths have on how you live? Relate? Think? Act? Feel?*
  - *What old ways of relating, thinking, choosing, acting, and feeling do you want to put off?*
  - *What new ways of relating, thinking, choosing, acting, and feeling do you want to put on?*
- *At the moment of salvation, Christ freed you from sin's power, liberating you to live a holy and loving life for his glory.*
  - *Have you heard these truths before? Are they new to you?*
  - *What impact can these truths have on how you live? Relate? Think? Act? Feel?*

Spiritual Conversations Enlightening Your Spiritual Friends to Their Redeemed Personality Structure

Believers have a new personality structure—new relationally, rationally, volitionally, and emotionally. You can enlighten your spiritual friends to enjoy and experience their newness. One way is to copy for them Box 24:1 from *Soul Physicians* (first edition and revised edition) which summarizes their redeemed personality structure. You can then ask:

- *Did you realize that you became like this at the moment of salvation? If not, why do you suppose that is? If so, has it been having the impact it could?*
- *Which of these aspects of the new you stand out to you? Why? What difference will they make in your life?*

After instructing your spiritual friends in the nature of their new nature, including relational, rational, volitional, and emotional implications, you can use the following *Redeemed Personality Inventory* to help them evaluate their current progress toward Christlikeness.

- *How well are you clinging to God/running home to Father, like a faithful son or daughter?*
- *To what extent are you enjoying your Worthy Groom more than any other joy in life?*
- *To what extent are you depending upon the Holy Spirit to beautify you?*
- *How well are you loving others deeply from the heart?*
- *To what extent are you resting confidently and comfortably in who you are in Christ?*
- *To what extent are you valuing what God values?*
- *To what extent do you see God as your chief good?*
- *How well are you allowing the eternal story to invade your earthly story?*
- *How well are you stirring up wholesome thinking in your mindsets?*
- *To what extent are you finding life by dying to yourself, taking up your cross, and following Christ?*
- *How well are you living to empower others?*
- *To what extent are you asking, "What would courageous trust in Christ look like in my relationships?"*
- *How well are you practicing emotional self-awareness—admitting, experiencing, and labeling your feelings?*
- *How well are you practicing emotional self-mastery—soothing your soul in your Savior?*
- *How well are you practicing emotional maturity—managing your moods?*
- *How well are you practicing emotional empathy—recognizing emotions in others?*
- *How well are you practicing emotional savvy—handling your relationships maturely?*

♦ *To what extent are you admitting your absolute need, body and soul, for God?*
♦ *To what extent are you allowing physical frailties to remind you of your need for God?*

Spiritual Conversations Enlightening Your Spiritual Friends to Progressive Sanctification: Growth in Grace

God commands and enables believers to grow in grace. You can enlighten your spiritual friends about growth in grace. One way is to copy for them Box 25:1 from *Soul Physicians* (first edition and at www.rpmbooks.org) which summarizes over 200 verses about growing in grace. You can then ask:

♦ *Did you realize that the Bible has so much to say about growth in grace? If not, why do you suppose that is? If so, has it been having the impact it could?*
♦ *Which of these verses stand out to you? Why? What difference will they make in your life?*
♦ *Which of these verses do you want to commit to memory? How will memorizing them impact you?*
♦ *Which of these verses do you want to meditate upon this week? How will meditating upon them impact you? Your relationships? Your current situation?*
♦ *Let's talk about some of the biblical images of growth in grace. Which ones grab you, jolt you, delight you? How? Why? What are you doing with these new truths?*

The Bible teaches about the believer's battle against sin. You can enlighten your spiritual friends concerning these warfare descriptions. One way is to copy for them Box 25:2 from *Soul Physicians* (first edition and at www.rpmbooks.org) which summarizes over 150 warfare verses. You can then ask:

♦ *Did you realize that the Bible has so much to say about your battle against sin? If not, why do you suppose that is? If so, has it been having the impact it could?*
♦ *Which of these verses stand out to you? Why? What difference will they make in your life?*
♦ *Which of these verses do you want to commit to memory? How will memorizing them impact you?*
♦ *Which of these verses do you want to meditate upon this week? How will meditating upon them impact you? Your relationships? Your current situation?*
♦ *Let's talk about some of the biblical warfare images. Which ones grab you, jolt you, delight you? How? Why? What are you doing with these new truths?*

The Bible teaches about Resurrection Power Multipliers. You can enlighten your spiritual friends concerning their RPMs. One way is to copy for them Box 14:1 from *Spiritual Friends* which summarizes eight resurrection power mutlipliers. You can then ask:

♦ *Did you realize that the Bible has so much to say about Christ's resurrection power and how we tap into it? If not, why do you suppose that is? If so, has it been having the impact it could?*
♦ *Which of these RPMs stand out to you? Why? What difference will they make in your life?*
♦ *Which of these RPMs do you want to commit to? How will doing so influence you? Your relationships? Your current situation?*

The Bible teaches about mortification (putting off) and vivification (putting on). You can enlighten your spiritual friends concerning biblical victory principles. One way is to copy for them Box 26:1 from *Soul Physicians* (first edition and at www.rpmbooks.org) which summarizes nearly 100 putting off/putting on verses. You can then ask:

- *Did you realize that the Bible has so much to say about mortification and vivification? If not, why do you suppose that is? If so, has it been having the impact it could?*
- *Which of these verses stand out to you? Why? What difference will they make in your life?*
- *Which of these verses do you want to commit to memory? How will memorizing them impact you?*
- *Which of these verses do you want to meditate upon this week? How will meditating upon them impact you? Your relationships? Your current situation?*
- *Let's talk about some of the mortification/vivification images. Which ones grab you, jolt you, delight you? How? Why? What are you doing with these new truths?*

Your spiritual friends need to learn how to apply biblical truth about growth in grace. You can help your spiritual friends with trialogues such as these:

- *God associates sin with the world, the flesh, and the Devil.*
  - *How is the world influencing you? The flesh? The Devil?*
  - *When you give into their influences, what are the results in your life?*
  - *Would you like to work cooperatively toward negating these effects in your life?*
  - *In refusing to cooperate with sin (the world, the flesh, and the Devil) are you supporting or undermining it? How so?*
  - *What difference will knowing what you now know about the flesh, yourself, and God make to your future relationship to the flesh?*
- *How have you managed to tap into God's spiritual resources to be effective against the flesh?*
  - *How does this victory reflect on you as a Christian?*
  - *How does it reflect on God's power, grace, and forgiveness at work in your life?*
  - *What spiritual gifts, resources, and attitudes were you tapping into and relying upon in these victorious times?*
  - *What ideas about further steps to reclaim spiritual control over the flesh do these victories suggest?*
- *When you do not give into sin/temptation, what is different about these times? How are you relating differently? Thinking differently? Choosing and acting differently? Feeling differently?*
- *As you leave here today on track toward victory over the flesh, what will you be doing differently?*
  - *Specifically, how will you be doing this?*
  - *How will you keep this victory going?*
- *If you were convinced that Satan had no hold over you, what would you be doing differently?*
- *If you were convinced that this sin had no power over you, what would you be doing instead? (Not just not sinning, but yielding to holiness).*
- *So instead of giving into sin, what will you be doing?*
- *You're in a prisoner of war camp. The guards have dropped their weapons. You are armed to the teeth. I'm curious about what motivates you to stay a prisoner.*
- *How have you worked through similar struggles with sin before in order to come to a point of victory? How did you manage to resist the influence of sin on those occasions?*
  - *What does your success at resisting sin say about God's power in your life? Your love for God? The spiritual resources God has given you? Your cooperation with the work of God? Your commitment to serving and loving God?*
  - *How does your victory reflect on you as a believer?*
- *How might you find the strength to overcome this sin?*

♦ *What impact does Christ's suffering and death have upon you as you attempt to overcome this sin?*

♦ *What unique gifts have you allowed to lay dormant that you can now fan into flame and stir into action in order to prevail in your Christian walk?*

♦ *How 'bout we talk about the spiritual gifts, resources, attitudes, and spiritual identity you were tapping into and relying on during these victorious times.*

♦ *What spiritual (personal, group, church, or scriptural) resources have you previously used in order to prevail in your relationships?*

♦ *Tell me about how you've managed to tap into God's spiritual resources to defeat this ungodly trinity of the world, the flesh, and the Devil.*

♦ *What does God provide that you might use to overcome the ways of relating that are destructive to those you love?*

♦ *If you were experiencing Christ's resurrection power in this, how would you be living? Relating? Thinking? Acting? Feeling?*

♦ *What difference might it make in your struggle with sin to see yourself as the Father's beloved child? Christ's forgiven friend? Inspiring Mentor's best friend?*

♦ *What difference will biblical views of yourself and God make during your next encounter with these temptations?*

　　♦ *In what ways do you think these discoveries might alter your attitude toward God? Yourself? Others?*

　　♦ *How might this new discovery influence your relationship with God?*

Spiritual Conversations Enlightening Your Spiritual Friends to Biblical Decision-Making

Even when your spiritual friends become aware of their victories, they still need to make difficult decisions. You can guide them toward discerning God's will through trialogues such as these:

♦ *What Scriptures are you turning to in order to find God's guidance in this situation?*

♦ *Tell me what you have found to be helpful in past decisions like this.*

♦ *What role is your relationship to Christ playing in how you will make this decision?*

♦ *Do you sense that you have the freedom to participate in this?*

♦ *Would anything about participating in this produce guilt, doubt, or turmoil for you?*

♦ *How would this serve others in love?*

♦ *How 'bout we talk about ways this would indicate love for others.*

♦ *In what way would this indicate faith in God's grace?*

♦ *Are you doing anything contrary to your conscience?*

♦ *What sort of things are you doing that are indicative of love for others? Indicative of faith in God?*

♦ *Tell me about biblical principles you could turn to for perspective and direction concerning this decision.*

Exploring Your Spiritual Journey

♦ Use the following holiness spiritual conversations (guiding theological trialogues) to work through a sanctification issue in your life.

1. What unique gifts have you allowed to lay dormant that you can now fan into flame and stir into action in order to prevail in your Christian walk?

2. How have you managed to tap into God's spiritual resources to be effective against the world, the flesh, and the Devil?

3. How have you worked through similar struggles with sin before in order to come to a point of victory? How did you manage to resist the influence of sin on those occasions?

4. What does your success at resisting sin say about God's power in your life? Your love for God? The spiritual resources God has given you? Your cooperation with the work of God? Your commitment to serving and loving God?

5. What difference will new biblical views of yourself and God make during your next encounter with this sin? In what ways do you think these discoveries might alter your attitude toward God? Yourself? Others?

6. So instead of giving into sin, what will you be doing?

7. As you leave here today on track toward victory over the flesh, what will you be doing differently? Specifically, how will you be doing this? How will you keep this victory going? How will you be thinking and relating differently?

8. When you do not give into sin, what is different about these times? How are you relating, thinking, choosing, acting, and feeling differently?

Heroic Scriptural Explorations: Guiding Biblical Trialogues—Hebrews 10:1-11:40

Faith active in love involves trusting God while risking deep relationships with others. In heroic scriptural explorations, you empower your spiritual friends to be God's heroes.

Holiness spiritual conversations referred to hundreds of verses about progressive sanctification. In heroic scriptural explorations, you'll want to select from among those verses to help your spiritual friends courageously apply God's truth to their relationships. Here are just a few sample trialogues from a few sample passages.

Scriptural Explorations Based Upon Romans 6-8

- *Since you died to sin, how can you continue to live in it?*
- *Do you realize the implications of your baptism into Christ's death?*
- *What are the implications of your co-crucifixion with Christ?*
- *What are the personal implications of your resurrection with Christ?*
- *Since your old self was crucified, you're no longer a slave to sin. How will this impact your sanctification?*
- *Since you are dead, you are freed from sin. Tell me about your freedom.*
- *What does it mean in your life to count yourself dead to sin, but alive to God in Christ?*
- *You do not need to let sin reign in your mortal body. Tell me about God's reign in your life.*
- *Tell me how you are offering yourself as a servant of righteousness.*
- *Are you trying to live the Christian life by works?*
- *What can you learn from Paul's failures when he tried to live his Christian life by self-effort?*
- *Those who live according to the flesh set their minds on the flesh. Let's talk about your mindsets.*
- *Those who live according to the spirit/Spirit set their minds on the things of the spirit/Spirit. Tell me about your spiritual mindsets.*
- *As a believer, the Spirit controls you. What difference is his control making in your life?*
- *The Spirit of God leads you. What is that like? How is he leading? Where?*
- *Celebrate the Spirit of Sonship, of Adoption!*
- *You are more than a conqueror. Live like one!*

Scriptural Explorations Based Upon Romans 12-15

- *Paul urges us to live for Christ in view of God's mercies. Tell me about your understanding of and appreciation for God's mercies.*
- *What does it mean in your life to present your body as a living sacrifice, holy and pleasing to God as your reasonable act of worship?*
- *How have you ceased being conformed to the world?*
- *How are you being transformed by the renewing of your mind?*
- *Let's discuss how you're using your gifts to serve others.*
- *What does sincere love look like in your relationships?*
- *How are you blessing those who persecute you? Weeping with those who weep? Rejoicing with those who rejoice?*
- *Love is the royal law of Scripture. To what extent is it the royal law of your life?*
- *How are you accepting those whose faith is weak?*
- *How are you bearing with the failings of the weak?*
- *How are you living to please God and others rather than yourself?*
- *How are you accepting others just as Christ has accepted you?*

Scriptural Explorations Based Upon Galatians 5

- *Are you depending on your strength or Christ's?*
- *How are you depending on your strength instead of the Spirit's?*
- *How are you depending on the Spirit's power rather than your own?*
- *Tell me about a recent time when you relied upon God's strength to defeat temptation.*
- *What are you doing differently in those times when you are depending on the Spirit? How are you relating differently? Thinking differently? Behaving differently? Feeling differently?*
- *What are you depending on? What do you expect these things to do for you?*
- *Who are you depending on? What do you expect these people to do for you?*

Scriptural Explorations Based Upon Ephesians 3:15-21

- *How is Christ's amazing love for you motivating you to love others?*
- *Tell me about how you and a few other Christians are connecting so that you grasp the depth of Christ's love.*
- *Have you surrendered to the Spirit's enlightenment so you can grasp the depth of Christ's love for you?*
- *Tell me about your enjoyment of God.*

Scriptural Explorations Based Upon Ephesians 4:17-24

- *What will it look like to put off _____ and put on _____?*
  - *How will you do that?*
  - *What joy will it bring God? Others? You?*
- *How would the "old unregenerate you" have related? Thought? Chosen? Acted? Felt?*
- *How will the "new regenerate you" relate? Think? Choose? Act? Feel?*

Scriptural Explorations Based Upon Ephesians 4:25-32

- *What will it look like to no longer let the sun go down upon your wrath?*
- *What will it look like to forgive like Christ forgives you?*
- *Let's role-play the conversation where you ask your wife for forgiveness.*
- *Let's role-play the conversation where you approach your husband to reconcile.*

Scriptural Explorations Based Upon Ephesians 5:18

- *Have you told the Spirit that you surrender to his control? To his empowerment? His filling? His fruit-cultivation in you?*
  - *What influences you most when you make this decision?*
  - *What results when you make this decision?*

Scriptural Explorations Based Upon Colossians 1

- *Who are you thanking God for?*
- *Who are you praying for?*
- *Tell me about your faith, hope, and love as you face this situation.*
- *How is Christ's Gospel of grace bearing fruit in your life?*

♦ *In what ways are you filled with the knowledge of God's will?*

♦ *To what extent are you living worthy of the Lord and pleasing him?*

♦ *How are you being strengthened with might according to his glorious power?*

♦ *If Christ truly had supremacy in your life, how would you be relating? Thinking? Acting? Feeling?*

♦ *What is it like to realize that you've been reconciled to God, freed from accusation, and seen as holy and without blemish in his sight?*

♦ *Are you rejoicing in your suffering for others? How?*

♦ *Let's talk about how you are laboring, struggling with all Christ's energy which so powerfully works in you.*

Scriptural Explorations Based Upon Colossians 2

♦ *How are you being encouraged in heart and united in love?*

♦ *If you really believed that in Christ are hidden all the treasures of wisdom and knowledge, how would this impact your decision-making process?*

♦ *You received Christ by faith. How can you live in him by faith?*

♦ *What hollow and deceptive human philosophies attempt to take you captive?*

♦ *God made you alive with Christ. What difference is this making in your life?*

Scriptural Explorations Based Upon Colossians 3

♦ *Since you have been raised with Christ, set your heart on things above. What does it mean for you to set your affections on Christ?*

♦ *Paul commands us to set our minds on things above. What does this mean in your life?*

♦ *How do you put to death the things that belong to your old, earthly nature?*

♦ *Of the list of vices to rid yourself of in Colossians 3:7-8, which do you need to eradicate? How?*

♦ *Your new self is being renewed in Christ. How are you cooperating with your renewal?*

♦ *Of the list of virtues in Colossians 3:12-14, which do you need to implement? How?*

Scriptural Explorations Based Upon Hebrews 11

♦ *How would you define faith?*

♦ *Share some examples of God as your Rewarder.*

♦ *Tell about times when you've delayed your gratification in order to please God.*

♦ *What temporary pleasure would giving into this sin provide?*

   ♦ *What is it like when you reject temporary pleasure to please God?*

♦ *Of the various heroes of the faith, which ones do you relate to? Why? How could you follow their examples? In what ways are you already following their examples?*

Where We've Been and Where We're Headed

Congratulations! You made it. Now the journey continues, ever onward. By God's grace, continue to develop your character, content, and competence in community.

You were a spiritual friend before you began reading *Spiritual Friends*. I know that. My hope and my prayer is that God has and will use your reading and engagement with *Spiritual Friends* to nudge you a little further along the path.

Above all else, keep connected to your ultimate Spiritual Friend.

Maturing Your Spiritual Friendship Competency
Heroic Scriptural Explorations/Guiding Biblical Trialogues

♦ For each of the passages listed below, develop at least five of your own heroic scriptural explorations/guiding biblical trialogues.

1. Matthew 5:1-7:29

2. Acts 2:42-47

3. 2 Corinthians 5:11-21

4. James 4:1-17

5. 1 Peter 1:1-25

6. 2 Peter 1:3-11

7. 1 John 3:1-24

Appendix

Conducting a Spiritual Friendship Meeting

> *"Let the church, then, assume her counseling duty, and let Christians of all sorts encourage her to do so. Let no one stand in her way, lest he be found opposing her Head and King Himself!"* (Jay Adams, *More Than Redemption: A Theology of Christian Counseling*, p. 280).

Organizing the Organism

You may wonder why conducting a meeting appears last and why it's in the Appendix. Shouldn't the "how to" of conducting a spiritual friendship meeting come first? Shouldn't the details concerning facilitating a counseling session be placed in the Introduction? Not when we view spiritual friendship primarily as a life-style. Spiritual friendship is not simply something we do during an official appointment lasting fifty minutes. It is who we are—*spiritual friends*.

However, I'm a realist. At times, friends will meet in formal settings for spiritual friendship. Pastors will arrange counseling appointments with parishioners. Professional counselors will schedule sessions with clients. *Conducting a Spiritual Friendship Meeting* assumes a more formal setting than chatting over the backyard fence or talking at the local Country Kitchen diner. Of course, spiritual friendship should and does take place in these informal settings. However, I'm now focusing on how to conduct a spiritual friendship meeting in more formal settings.

More than just a realist, I want to be a biblicist. The Bible does teach how to *organize the organism*. Though the Church is a living organism, Jesus, Peter, Paul, and John offer organizational prescriptions. Though spiritual friendship is a living relationship, the Scriptures insist upon doing all things decently and in order. They do offer insight into how to implement personal ministry.

Consider the Appendix my endeavor to organize the organism—to provide prescriptions for spiritual friendship meetings. Consider also the key word in the title: *Conducting*. Picture an orchestra conductor artistically facilitating the harmonious interplay of many talented musicians. Even organizing the organism requires art, heart, emotional intelligence, and relational competency.

Spiritual friends (whether lay encouragers, pastoral soul physicians, or professional Christian counselors) blend beautiful spiritual conversations, integrating grace relationships and grace narratives so that disciples can listen to the voice of God composing the music of their lives. Spiritual friends compose a symphony of truth and love.

Spiritual friendship orchestra conductors follow a few basic principles in their preparation to create a beautiful symphony of form and function. Those principles include:

Exploring Your Spiritual Journey

1. As the *provider* of spiritual friendship, which spiritual friendship settings do you prefer: the more informal settings such as sipping coffee at the local diner or the more formal settings such as scheduling an office appointment? Why?

2. As the *recipient* of spiritual friendship, which spiritual friendship settings do you prefer: the more informal settings such as sipping coffee at the local diner or the more formal settings such as scheduling an office appointment? Why?

3. Concerning the more formal settings:

   a. What are the benefits of more formal spiritual friendship?

   b. What are the disadvantages of more formal spiritual friendship?

4. Concerning the more informal settings:

   a. What are the benefits of more informal spiritual friendship?

   b. What are the disadvantages of more informal spiritual friendship?

- The Physical Setting
- The Personal Setting
- Connecting with Spiritual Friends
- The Initial Spiritual Friendship Meeting
- In-Between Spiritual Friendship Meetings
- Ongoing Spiritual Friendship Meetings
- Referring a Spiritual Friend
- Commencing with Hope

The Physical Setting

Assuming a more formal setting, a few basic principles guide the physical setting for spiritual friendship.

Standard Equipment

You need at least two comfortable chairs arranged, if possible, at a slight angle. A box of soft tissues and a wastebasket are important. Position a clock above your spiritual friends so that you can glance at it without interrupting the process. Depending upon your "style," perhaps you'll want a notepad and pen and a small end table, for jotting down occasional quick notes or important information. Additionally, an uncluttered room communicates, "I have time for you. You're the most important concern for me right now. You have my focused, prepared, undivided attention."

Privacy

Do everything in your power to minimize the possibility of distractions. Take the phone off the hook, turn the ringer off, or put it on "Do Not Disturb." Turn off all beepers, pagers, and cell phones. Make entrance to your meeting place as convenient as possible—passing through as few people as possible. Also, use a well-insulated, soundproof room, or use ambient noise (soft music playing in the background so others cannot hear your voices).

Propriety

Horror stories abound concerning inappropriate relationships developing during the intimate sharing in counseling/spiritual friendship. Therefore, take great care, especially in counseling members of the opposite sex. Never counsel someone in a building or home alone. Always use a door that has a glass window.

The Personal Setting

By "personal setting" I mean who you are and how you act and relate. Someone has said that professional counseling is the most intimate relationship in the least intimate of settings. Therefore, it's important to be yourself. Be comfortable and help your spiritual friends to feel comfortable.

For some, that may mean loosening their ties, dressing in jeans, or putting their feet up. For others, the posture and attire may be formal, but the interactions are caring, open, and comfortable. Regardless of the physical setting, remind yourself that the personal setting emphasizes friendship that focuses upon helping your friends to be healthier people—people who love God and others more. Love is caught and taught through speaking the truth in love.

Connecting with Spiritual Friends

Depending upon your setting, how will you "get clients"? What are the ways in which people come to you for formal spiritual friendship, pastoral care, or professional Christian counseling?

By Referral

Someone may request that you see someone else. A parent may say, "Please talk to my son." A spouse may ask, "Would you meet with my spouse?"

With adults, respond, "Could you have your spouse call me so that we could arrange a meeting?" This puts the responsibility on the person being counseled, as well as on the person requesting the referral. It also helps you to determine whether the person being referred *wants* to meet with you.

When you are contacted by the referred person, with permission, share the information you've been given. Ascertain if the person wants to meet with you and why. Arrange the meeting and use principles from earlier chapters for infusing hope and helping your new "counselee" to begin thinking through issues and goals.

By Request

Someone may seek you out. He or she knows that you've been trained as a lay counselor, that you're a professional counselor, or that as a pastor you offer pastoral care and counseling. First, communicate concern and interest. If in public, see if you can step to the side for a little privacy. As you talk, assess the urgency of the issue. Clarify what he or she desires. A chat? A gripe session? A quick fix? Short-term counseling? Long-term therapy? Also, assess whether you're able to handle the issue—do you have the time and training?

By Recognition of Need

At other times, especially in the Christian community, you will hear the hurts and struggles of fellow church members. Listening attentively, you sustain, empathize, and draw out. Then you might suggest, "Would you care to schedule a time when we could talk about your concerns more fully?" Or, they might say, "I feel so good talking with you. Do you think that we could arrange a time to meet?"

The Initial Spiritual Friendship Meeting

One way or another, you have your first spiritual friendship meeting. Now what?

The following principles assume that you have already collected some initial contact information using the various methods shared in previous chapters. Depending upon the nature of the setting and your own "policies," you may want to ask your spiritual friends to arrive fifteen or thirty minutes early for your first meeting so that they can complete any additional information forms.

Or, you may prefer to complete the information forms together during the beginning of the first meeting. If this is the case, I've found it helpful to caution my spiritual friends that our initial time together may feel a bit more "clinical" because of our need to collect necessary information.

Getting Started

Nervousness (your nervousness) is normal during your first meeting. Pray. Trust. Care. Especially care. Remember that your "job" is not to cure, it's to care. Nothing can prevent you from caring.

Be friendly. Help your spiritual friends relax. They're nervous also.

At the same time, be a bit to the point. Excessive "chit-chat" may communicate that you really don't want to deal with the issues. After some moments of friendly "settling," ask, "Could I pray for us as we begin?"

After prayer, share any previous information that you have so that both of you are "on the same page." This may mean following up on the brief conversation you had in the foyer after church last week. It may mean sharing what the referring person has shared with you. It may mean reviewing together the *Spiritual Friendship Information Form* or the *Personal Information Form*.

Setting Goals

If you've discussed your *Welcome Form*, then your spiritual friends should begin to understand the broad goal of Christian counseling/spiritual friendship—growing more in love with Christ and more loving like Christ. If you've used and discussed various *Personal Information Forms*, then you and your spiritual friends should be able to state a few specific goals concerning what will be different or better because of meeting.

Specific Objectives of the First Meeting

By the end of the first meeting, you want to accomplish the following basic objectives:

- A clear understanding of the presenting problem, including when it started, when it's better, when it's worse, what has already been done to deal with it, and what will be different when it is cared for.
- A mutual understanding of your goals.
- A commitment obtained to work toward those goals, stressing the work that needs to be done both in and outside the meetings.
- Some initial sustaining—empathizing with your spiritual friends as they seek victory.
- Some initial infusion of hope.

In-Between Spiritual Friendship Meetings

Your actual meetings "prime the pump." They invigorate a process that stirs your spiritual friends to more deeply connect with Christ's resurrection power. Constantly remind yourself and your spiritual friends that the bulk of progress will occur *between* meetings as they take the risks to apply what you're experiencing together.

Think of the process as similar to a church service. There believers experience worship, fellowship, and discipleship. However, that hour must not be the beginning and ending of spiritual nurture and training. That hour is not the only place, or even the primary place, where believers grow in grace. Believers engage in worship, fellowship, discipleship, stewardship, and ambassadorship the entire week by applying what they've experienced during the "Worship Service."

Also, think of the spiritual friendship "hour" like a sports practice. It's where athletes become prepared and equipped to actually "play the game" and be victorious. So it is with a counseling session. The time that you spend together better prepares and equips your spiritual friends to live victorious lives in Christ.

Forms

You can implement this "pump-priming-attitude" through the use of carefully crafted and specifically assigned forms such as the sample ones you've seen throughout *Spiritual Friends*. Focus on that word *sample*. Create *your own* information forms, meeting forms, and homework forms that fit for you and your spiritual friends. Create *your own* record keeping forms that work for you and your ministry.

You will need a simple appointment slip so that you and your spiritual friends know the next scheduled meeting. Create a basic wallet-size slip that includes a place for a name, the date and time of your next meeting, and a small space for homework assignments.

Counselee Homework

Review the guiding section for many ideas about taking action and homework that works. From the very beginning of your meetings, emphasize the idea that you expect your spiritual friends to work even harder than you will be working. Inform them that you work between meetings planning and praying and that they should be working between meetings praying and growing.

Mutually develop homework assignments specifically related to your spiritual friends and their unique issues. Homework might involve reading, praying, Bible study, spiritual disciplines, journaling, managing moods, changing behaviors, renewing the mind, reconciling relationships, and hundreds of other possibilities.

Counselor Homework: Treatment Planning and Praying

Immediately after the conclusion of a meeting, plan at least ten minutes between appointments so that you can complete your *Spiritual Friendship Treatment Plan Sheet*. Use the front side, if you're using the sample form from *Spiritual Friends*, to summarize key elements of the meeting, to remind yourself of homework assignments, and to prayerfully consider future goals.

At some point during the week, take at least fifteen minutes to use the backside for your treatment planning. Assess what progress is being made in sustaining, healing, reconciling, and guiding as a relational, rational, volitional, and emotional being. Diagnose what the issues are in each of those areas. Prayerfully plan interventions and interactions designed to continue the soul care and/or spiritual direction process.

During this time, do *your* homework. Study the Scriptures related to this issue. Read other materials about this area. Pray. This also may be the time when you write a spiritual friendship letter.

Ongoing Spiritual Friendship Meetings

You've had your first meeting. You've prepared in-between. Now what?

The Heart of the Spiritual Friendship Meeting

"But what do I do for an entire meeting?" Initially, we all ask this. Soon we're saying, "I wish I had more time. There's so much to do and so little time during our meetings!"

To make the most of the time that you have, remember that grace is the heart of spiritual friendship: grace relationships and grace narratives. Together, explore God's truth in love as it relates to your spiritual friends.

There is no straightjacket that tells you exactly what to do during each meeting. Based upon your growing spiritual character, your increasing biblical convictions, and your deepening relational competencies, enjoy connecting with your spiritual friends and helping them to commune with Christ.

Of course, this book provides a myriad of principles and practices explaining how to sustain, heal, reconcile, and guide while describing various relational competencies and hundreds of sample trialogues to implement during your spiritual friendship meetings. You've learned how to engage your spiritual friends as relational, rational, volitional, and emotional beings in deserts, thirsts, cisterns, and springs.

Consider some additional basic guidelines. When your spiritual friends return, seek feedback on how they're doing. This allows them to introduce new attitudes and events that you would have no way of knowing about. Also, seek specific input on how their homework assignments progressed.

You can summarize your insights from your between meeting work. Be sure to do so in an attitude of, "Here's what I've been thinking, how does that hit you?"

Together you can then discuss the focus and goals for your current meeting. "Where do we go from here? What do we focus on, why, and how?"

Then flexibly, wisely, and relationally be a spiritual friend. "Do" what you've been equipped to do.

Stages of Spiritual Friendship

Spiritual Friends offers you a detailed, historic, biblical approach to spiritual friendship: sustaining, healing, reconciling, and guiding. These concepts and their accompanying content and competencies provide a roadmap to follow.

However, life is never a nice, neat package. Spiritual friendship is "spaghetti relationships." Everything is intertwined, interrelated. It's messy but delicious and worth the effort.

As you listen to yourself on tape, you'll note how you moved from sustaining, to reconciling, back to healing, to guiding, back to reconciling. This is fine, as long as you're aware of where you are and why you are there.

Concluding a Spiritual Friendship Meeting

Ending a meeting is much harder than you might think. Like it or not, you're a time-bound being. You're finite. If you spend endless hours with one person, then the rest of your ministry will suffer.

Typically "counseling sessions" last a "fifty-minute-hour." You schedule an appointment from 1:00 to 1:50, then from 1:50-2:00 you do your preliminary record keeping.

Obviously, the strictness of this structure depends upon your setting. Professional counselors scheduling appointment after appointment, need to keep pretty firmly on task. Pastoral counselors may have a little more flexibility and lay spiritual friends perhaps even more. However, everyone has limits.

Lay spiritual friends, in particular, may find it difficult to end meetings. They feel guilty. They may not have an appointment to follow. However, they do have lives and they do have finite personal resources.

Whatever amount of time you've allotted, be aware. Face the clock. As you come within five-to-ten minutes of the end of your time, be careful about opening new issues. You may want to comment, "That's a very important point. I notice that we're close to our ending time. Let me jot that down so that we can be sure to focus on it next week."

Even without the issue of new material, a similar statement can also help. "Unfortunately, we're about five minutes from needing to wrap up things. Let's try to summarize where we've been and where we might need to head."

Length of Spiritual Friendship Meetings

I've already addressed length issues relative to how long an individual session lasts. Here I'm speaking about how many sessions you have and over what length of time. Numerous factors influence your decision.

I've found that regardless of the setting, some common principles hold. First, during the first meeting be sure to discuss mutual expectations about how often you can meet, how long each meeting will be, and over what period/length of time you will meet.

Second, during the very first meeting, mention that not every counselor and counselee always match. "Sometimes there's not a good fit. That's all right. Don't feel a compulsion to continue to meet so that my feelings are not hurt."

Third, after about every five meetings, you will find it helpful to review together. "What type of progress are we making? Are we meeting the goals we mutually set? Where do we need to go from here?"

Referring Spiritual Friends

No one can do everything or help everyone. There are times where wisdom and love dictate that you refer your spiritual friends to see someone else. Perhaps it will be someone else *in addition* to meeting with you. Perhaps someone else *instead* of meeting with you.

Sometimes you refer when you sense that there's not a good match or good fit between the two of you. Other times, the fit may be fine, but for some reason progress is not being made.

Sometimes you will sense that you are "in too deep." Perhaps you're over your level of experience, training, and competencies. Perhaps you have become too emotionally attached. Perhaps you simply need a break for your own health.

At other times, your spiritual friends may be refusing to work. You are working in sessions and between meetings, but you do not sense that they are. You've shared your concern. Still no change. You may need to make the suggestion of referral.

Whatever the issue, supervision is vital. Meet with someone who can be an objective listening ear to provide feedback.

Once you've come to a tentative decision to refer, discuss your thoughts and reasons with your spiritual friends. Integrate their thoughts into your decision-making process.

Commencing with Hope

I've noted my preference for "commencing" over "terminating." Regarding commencing, ponder a few helpful mindsets.

- Maturity is a life-long process. You desire to be an encourager who helps with whatever current issue may be blocking the path to maturity.
- God does not work on every problem at every moment. You are working on personal maturity regarding some specific changes in some limited areas of greatest struggle.
- There is a biblical strategy to follow in responding to every life situation.
- God can and will use you to help others to grow. Nothing happens by chance, including your meetings with your spiritual friends.
- When you feel lost, never give up. With Jesus, you are never hopeless. He is the way, the truth, and the life.

"But how do I know when to commence, when to end?" Much, of course, depends on the nature of your relationship. This Appendix assumes more of a formal process. Some spiritual friendship relationships, in the informal Body of Christ model, equate to ongoing discipleship. Those, in a sense, may never end.

However, with formal spiritual friendship, pastoral counseling, and professional Christian counseling, you normally experience a beginning, middle, and an ending. Many times you and your spiritual friends will simply "sense" that it's about time. Issues are resolved or resolving. Growth continues to take place. Talking and relating are enjoyable but no longer "necessary."

Prayerfully seek the leading of the Holy Spirit. Review your goals, objectives, and reasons for meeting.

Sometimes you commence because your spiritual friends want to, but you do not sense that the goals have been met. Discuss this humbly and openly, always leaving an opening to return.

Sometimes you need to suggest commencement in conjunction with referral when you do not sense progress occurring. Together reexamine your goals. Process honestly how you are relating. Seek help from your supervisor. Review and update your treatment plans. Pray.

Thankfully, most times you are commencing for the more positive reasons noted above. How do you commence with hope in those situations?

Link your spiritual friends to the Body of Christ. Be sure that they're connected to ongoing fellowship, worship, ambassadorship, discipleship, and stewardship.

Link your spiritual friends to Christ. Remind them that Jesus is the answer—the way, the truth, and the life.

Celebrate. Use the materials from guiding to stir up, affirm, encourage, empower, and equip your spiritual friends to commence with hope.

Where We've Been and Where We're Headed

Do you want to learn how to apply what you've read in *Spiritual Friends*? Of course you do. Here's the best way. *Do it*.

That's right. After a quarter-century training lay spiritual friends, pastoral soul physicians, and professional Christian counselors, "just do it" remains my best advice.

I guarantee you that "doing" spiritual friendship will drive you back to prayer, back to God's Word, and back to books like *Spiritual Friends*. Whatever your role, whatever your setting, start being a spiritual friend. As you do, your hunger will swell for character, content, and competence in the context of community.

You're a *Nikao* saint—victorious in Christ. So, *Nike*—"just do it"—empowered by Christ, your ultimate Spiritual Friend.

Maturing Your Spiritual Friendship Competency
Conducting a Spiritual Friendship Meeting

1. What was the physical setting like in some situations where you felt encouraged and helped by another person?

2. How do you feel about conducting your first formal spiritual friendship meeting?

3. What aspects of a spiritual friendship meeting do you think will be:

    a. Hardest for you? Why?

    b. Easiest for you? Why?

4. What do you think runs through the typical spiritual friend's mind:

    a. Just before his or her first time of being counseled?

    b. In-between meetings?

    c. Just after the final meeting?

5. Rate your personal level of confidence as a spiritual friend. Explain your rating. What will you do to increase your level of confidence and competence in Christ?

Bibliography

Works Cited and Consulted

Adams, Jay. *The Christian Counselor's Manual*. Grand Rapids: Zondervan, 1973.

———. *Competent to Counsel*. Phillipsburg, NJ: Presbyterian & Reformed Publishing, 1970.

———. *How to Help People Change: The Four-Step Biblical Process*. Grand Rapids: Zondervan, 1988.

———. *More Than Redemption: Theology of Christian Counseling*. Grand Rapids: Zondervan, 1979.

Aden, L. "Comfort/Sustaining." Pages 193-195 in *The Dictionary of Pastoral Care and Counseling*. Edited by R. J. Hunter. Nashville: Abingdon Press, 1990.

Ahlskog, Gary, and Harry Sands, eds. *The Guide to Pastoral Care and Counseling*. Madison, CT: Psychological Press, 2000.

Allender, Dan. *Bold Love*. Colorado Springs: NavPress, 1992.

———. *The Healing Path*. Colorado Springs: WaterBrook Press, 1999.

———. *The Wounded Heart: Hope for Adult Victims of Childhood Sexual Abuse*. Second edition. Colorado Springs: NavPress, 1996.

Allender, Dan, and Tremper Longman. *The Cry of the Soul: How Our Emotions Reveal Our Deepest Questions About God*. Colorado Springs: NavPress, 1994.

Almy, Gary. *How Christian Is Christian Counseling?* Wheaton, IL: Crossway Books, 2000.

American Association of Christian Counselors. *AACC Christian Counseling Code of Ethics*. Forest, VA: AACC, 2001.

American Psychiatric Association. *Diagnostic and Statistical Manual of Mental Disorders*. Fourth edition. Text revision. Washington, DC: APA, 2000.

Anderson, Neil, Julianne Zuehlke, and Terry Zuehlke. *Christ-Centered Therapy: The Practical Integration of Theology and Psychology*. Grand Rapids: Zondervan, 2000.

Baker, Howard. *Soul Keeping: Ancient Paths of Spiritual Direction*. Colorado Springs: NavPress, 1998.

Barnes, Dorothy, and Ralph Earle. *Healing Conversations: Therapy and Spiritual Growth*. Downers Grove, IL: InterVarsity, 1998.

Barry, W., and W. Connolly. *The Practice of Spiritual Direction*. New York: Seabury Press, 1982.

Bauer, Walter. *A Greek-English Lexicon of the New Testament and Other Early Christian Literature*. Second edition revised and augmented by F. Gingrich and F. Danker. Chicago: University of Chicago Press, 1979.

Baxter, Richard. *A Christian Directory*. Philadelphia: Soli Deo Gloria Publications, 1997.

———. *The Reformed Pastor*. Carlisle, PA: Banner of Truth Trust, 1999.

Beamer, Lisa. *Let's Roll!* Wheaton, IL: Tyndale House, 2002.

Becker, A. H. "Luther as *Seelsorger*: The Unexamined Role." Pages 136-150 in *Interpreting Luther's Legacy*. Edited by F. W. Meuser and S. D. Schneider. Minneapolis: Augsburg, 1969.

Begalke, M. V. "An Introduction to Luther's Theology of Pastoral Care." Ph.D. Dissertation, University of Ottawa, 1980.

———. "Luther's *Anfechtungen*: An Important Clue to His Pastoral Theology." *Consensus* 8 (1982): 3-17.

Behm, J. "*noeo.*" Pages 636-646 in *The Theological Dictionary of the New Testament.* Abridged edition. Edited by G. Bromiley. Grand Rapids: Eerdmans, 1992.

———. "*parakletos.*" Pages 782-784 in *The Theological Dictionary of the New Testament.* Abridged edition. Edited by G. Bromiley. Grand Rapids: Eerdmans, 1992.

Benjamin, Alfred. *The Helping Interview.* Third edition. Dallas: Houghton Mifflin, 1981.

Benner, David, ed. *Baker Encyclopedia of Psychology.* Grand Rapids: Baker, 1985.

———. *Care of Souls: Revisioning Christian Nurture and Counsel.* Grand Rapids: Baker, 1998.

———. *Sacred Companions: The Gift of Spiritual Friendship and Direction.* Downers Grove, IL: InterVarsity, 2002.

Berman, J. S., and N. C. Norton. "Does Professional Training Make a Therapist More Effective?" *Psychology Bulletin* 98, no. 2 (1985): 401-407.

Bissler, Jane. "Counseling for Loss and Life Changes." http://www.counselingforloss.com (accessed August 1, 2004).

Blanchette, Melvin, John Compton, and Barry Estadt, eds. *Pastoral Counseling.* Second edition. Englewood Cliffs, NJ: Prentice Hall, 1991.

Boisen, A. *The Exploration of the Inner World.* San Francisco: Harper, 1937.

Broger, John. *Self-Confrontation: A Manual for In-Depth Discipleship.* Nashville: Thomas Nelson, 1994.

Bromiley, Geoffrey, ed. *Theological Dictionary of the New Testament.* Abridged edition. Grand Rapids: Eerdmans, 1992.

Brown, Francis, S. Driver, and C. Briggs. *The New Brown, Driver, and Briggs Hebrew and English Lexicon of the Old Testament.* Lafayette, IN: Associated Publishers, 1981.

Bucer, Martin. *On the True Cure of Souls.* Translated by R. Johnson. Grand Rapids: Baker, 1538/1950.

Bulkey, Ed. *Why Christians Can't Trust Psychology.* Eugene, OR: Harvest House, 1993.

Burck, J. R. "Reconciliation." Pages 1047-1048 in *The Dictionary of Pastoral Care and Counseling.* Edited by R. J. Hunter. Nashville: Abingdon Press, 1990.

Burck, J. R., and R. J. Hunter. "Pastoral Theology: Protestant." Pages 867-872 in *The Dictionary of Pastoral Care and Counseling.* Edited by R. J. Hunter. Nashville: Abingdon Press, 1990.

Burke, Mary, and Judith Miranti, eds. *Counseling: The Spiritual Dimension.* Alexandria, VA: American Counseling Association, 1995.

Butman, R. "Where's the Beef?: Evaluating Counseling Trends." *Christian Counseling Today* (October 1993): 20-24.

Calvin, John. *Calvin's Commentaries.* 22 Vols. Grand Rapids: Eerdmans, 1981.

———. *Commentary on Hebrews.* Grand Rapids: Eerdmans, 1994.

———. *The Institutes of the Christian Religion.* Vols. 20-21 of *The Library of Christian Classics.* Edited by John T. McNeil. Translated by Ford Lewis Battles. London: Westminster Press, 1559/1960.

Carkhuff, Robert. *The Art of Helping.* Eighth edition. Amherst, MA: Human Resource Development Press, 2001.

Carson, David. *How Long, O Lord? Reflections on Suffering and Evil.* Leicester, UK: InterVarsity, 1990.

Chandler, C. K., J. M. Holden, and C. A. Kolander. "Counseling for Spiritual Wellness: Theory and Practice." *Journal of Counseling and Development* 71 (1992): 168-175.

Cheston, Sharon E. *Making Effective Referrals: The Therapeutic Process.* Lake Worth, FL: Gardner, 1991.

Ciarrocchi, Joseph. *The Doubting Disease: Help for Scrupulosity and Religious Compulsions.* New York: Paulist Press, 1995.

———. *A Minister's Handbook of Mental Disorders*. New York: Paulist Press, 1993.

Clebsch, William, and Charles Jaekle. *Pastoral Care in Historical Perspective*. New York: Harper, 1964.

Clinton, Timothy, and George Ohlschlager. *Competent Christian Counseling*. Vol. 1 of *Foundations and Practice of Compassionate Soul Care*. Colorado Springs: WaterBrook Press, 2002.

Cloud, Henry, and John Townsend. *How People Grow: What the Bible Says About Personal Growth*. Grand Rapids: Zondervan, 2001.

Collins, Gary. *The Biblical Basis of Christian Counseling for People Helpers*. Colorado Springs: NavPress, 1993.

———. *Christian Counseling: A Comprehensive Guide*. Revised edition. Dallas: Word Publishing, 1998.

———. "Evangelical Pastoral Care." Pages 372-374 in *The Dictionary of Pastoral Care and Counseling*. Edited by R. J. Hunter. Nashville: Abingdon Press, 1990.

———. *How to Be a People Helper*. Revised edition. Wheaton, IL: Tyndale House, 1995.

———. *The Soul Search: A Spiritual Journey to Authentic Intimacy with God*. Nashville: Thomas Nelson, 1998.

Collins, Gary, and Craig Ellison, eds. *From Stress to Well-Being: Contemporary Christian Counseling*. Eugene, OR: Wipf & Stock Publishers, 2003.

Crabb, Larry. *Connecting*. Nashville: Word Publishing, 1997.

———. *The Safest Place on Earth*. Nashville: Word Publishing, 1999.

———. *Shattered Dreams: God's Unexpected Pathway to Joy*. Colorado Springs: WaterBrook Press, 2001.

———. *Soul Talk: The Language God Longs for Us to Speak*. Nashville: Integrity Publishing, 2003.

Crabb, Larry, and Dan Allender. *Encouragement: The Key to Caring*. Grand Rapids: Zondervan, 1984.

Curtis, Brent, and John Eldredge. *The Sacred Romance*. Nashville: Thomas Nelson, 1997.

Davies, Gaius. *Genius, Grief, and Grace*. Ross-Shire, Scotland: Christian Focus Publications, 1992.

Davison, R. *The Courage to Doubt: Exploring an Old Testament Theme*. London: SCM Press, 1983.

Delitszch, Franz. *A System of Biblical Psychology*. Second edition. Translated by Robert Wallis. Eugene, Oregon: Wipf & Stock Publishers, 1861/2003.

DePree, Max. *Leadership Jazz*. New York: Bantam Dell Publishing, 1992.

Didascalia Apostolorum. Translated by M. N. Dunlop. London: Cambridge University Press, c. 225/1903.

Donne, John. *Devotions upon Emergent Occasions*. New York: Vintage, 1999.

Driskill, Joseph. *Protestant Spiritual Exercises: Theology, History, and Practice*. Harrisburg, PA: Moorehouse, 1999.

Durlak, J. "Comparative Effectiveness of Paraprofessional and Professional Helpers." *Psychological Bulletin* 86, no. 1 (1979): 80-92.

Earle, Ralph. *Word Meanings in the New Testament*. Peabody, MA: Hendricksen, 2000.

Edwards, Jonathan. "The Christian Pilgrim." In *The Works of Jonathan Edwards*. 2 vols. Revised by Edward Hackman. Peabody, MA: Hendricksen Publishing, 1998.

———. "The End for Which God Created the World." In *The Works of Jonathan Edwards*. 2 vols. Revised by Edward Hackman. Peabody, MA: Hendricksen Publishing, 1998.

———. *Freedom of the Will*. Philadelphia: Soli Deo Gloria Publications, 1998.

———. *Religious Affections: How Man's Will Affects His Character Before God*. Portland, OR: Multnomah, 1984.

———. *The Works of Jonathan Edwards*. 2 vols. Revised by Edward Hackman. Peabody, MA: Hendricksen Publishing, 1998.

Edwards, Tilden. *Spiritual Friend: Reclaiming the Gift of Spiritual Direction*. New York: Paulist Press, 1980.

Egan, Gerald. *The Skilled Helper: A Problem Management Approach to Helping.* Sixth edition. Pacific Grove, CA: Brooks & Cole, 1998.

Eldredge, John. *Dare to Desire: An Invitation to Fulfill Your Deepest Dreams.* Nashville: Thomas Nelson, 2002.

———. *Waking the Dead: The Glory of a Heart Fully Alive.* Nashville: Thomas Nelson, 2003.

Engles, Dennis, and Joseph Dameron, eds. *The Professional Counselor: Competencies, Performance Guidelines, and Assessment.* Alexandria, VA: American Counseling Association, 1993.

Eyrich, Howard, and William Hines. *Curing the Heart: A Model for Biblical Counseling.* Ross-Shire, Scotland: Christian Focus Publications, 2002.

Fitzpatrick, Elyse. *Idols of the Heart: Learning to Long for God Alone.* Phillipsburg, NJ: Presbyterian & Reformed Publishing, 2001.

Foster, Richard. *Celebration of Discipline: The Path to Spiritual Growth.* Revised edition. San Francisco: Harper, 1998.

———. *Streams of Living Water: Celebrating the Great Traditions of the Christian Faith.* San Francisco: Harper, 1998.

Foster, Richard, and Emile Griffin, eds. *Spiritual Classics.* San Francisco: Harper. 2000.

Foster, Richard, and James Smith, eds. *Devotional Classics.* San Francisco: Harper. 1993.

Frame, M. W., and C. B. Williams. "Counseling African-Americans: Integrating Spirituality in Therapy." *Counseling and Values* 41, no. 1 (1991): 27-45.

Ganz, Richard. *PsychoBabble: The Failure of Modern Psychology and the Biblical Alternative.* Wheaton: Crossway Books, 1993.

Gibson, J. C. "The Book of Job and the Cure of Souls." *Scottish Journal of Theology* 42 (1990): 303-317.

Gilbert, Marvin, and Raymond Brock, eds. *The Holy Spirit and Counseling.* 2 vols. Peabody, MA: Hendricksen, 1985.

Gilligan, S., and R. Reese, eds. *Therapeutic Conversations.* New York: W. W. Norton, 1993.

Goleman, Daniel. *Emotional Intelligence.* New York: Bantam, 1997.

Goleman, Daniel, Richard Boyatzis, and Annie McKee. *Primal Leadership: Realizing the Power of Emotional Intelligence.* Boston: Harvard Business School Press, 2002.

Graham, L. K. "Healing." Pages 497-501 in *The Dictionary of Pastoral Care and Counseling.* Edited by R. J. Hunter. Nashville: Abingdon Press, 1990.

Griffin, Emilie. *Wilderness Time: A Guide for Spiritual Retreat.* San Francisco: Harper Collins, 1997.

Guenther, Margaret. *Holy Listening: The Art of Spiritual Direction.* Boston: Cowley, 1992.

Gundmann, Walter. "*agathos.*" Pages 3-4 in *The Theological Dictionary of the New Testament.* Abridged edition. Edited by G. Bromiley. Grand Rapids: Eerdmans, 1992.

Habermas, G. R. "A House Divided?" *Christian Counseling Today* (October 1993): 32-35.

Hackney, Harold, ed. *Changing Context for Counselor Preparation in the 1990s.* Alexandria, VA: American Counseling Association, 1990.

Harris, Laird, Gleason Archer, and Bruce Waltke, eds. *Theological Wordbook of the Old Testament.* 2 vols. Chicago: Moody Press, 1981.

Hart, Archibald. *The Anxiety Cure: You Can Find Emotional Tranquility and Wholeness.* Nashville: Word Publishing, 1999.

Hart, Archibald, Gary Gulbranson, and Jim Smith, eds. *Mastering Pastoral Counseling.* Portland, OR: Multnomah, 1992.

Hattie, J. A., C. F. Sharpley, and H. J. Rogers. "Comparative Effectiveness of Professional and Paraprofessional Helpers." *Psychological Bulletin* 95, no. 3 (1984): 534-541.

Hendriksen, William. *Galatians and Ephesians.* Grand Rapids: Baker, 1968.

Herman, Keith. "Reassessing Predictors of Therapist Competence." *Journal of Counseling and Development* 72 (September/October 1993): 29-32.

Hersen, Michel, and Samuel Turner, eds. *Diagnostic Interviewing*. New York: Plenum, 1985.

Hiltner, Seward. *Preface to Pastoral Theology*. New York: Abingdon Press, 1954.

Hindson, Edward, and Howard Eyrich. *Totally Sufficient: The Bible and Christian Counseling*. Grand Rapids: Baker, 1997.

Holifield, E. Brooks. *A History of Pastoral Care in America: From Salvation to Self-Realization*. Nashville: Abingdon Press, 1983.

Huggins, Kevin. *Friendship Counseling*. Colorado Springs: NavPress, 2003.

Hulme, William. *Pastoral Care and Counseling: Using the Unique Resources of the Christian Tradition*. Minneapolis: Augsburg, 1981.

Hunter, Rodney, ed. *The Dictionary of Pastoral Care and Counseling*. Nashville: Abingdon Press, 1990.

Ice, Thomas, and Robert Dean. *A Holy Rebellion: Strategies for Spiritual Warfare*. Eugene, OR: Wipf & Stock Publishers, 1999.

Ivarsson, H. "The Principles of Pastoral Care According to Martin Luther." *Pastoral Psychology* 13 (February 1962): 19-25.

Ivey, Allen. *Intentional Interviewing and Counseling: Facilitating Client Development in a Multicultural Society*. Third edition. Pacific Grove, CA: Brooks, 1994.

Johnson, Eric, and Stanton Jones, eds. *Psychology and Christianity: Four Views*. Downers Grove, IL: InterVarsity, 2000.

Jones, Alan. *Exploring Spiritual Direction: An Essay on Christian Friendship*. San Francisco: Harper, 1982.

———. "Spiritual Direction and Pastoral Care." Pages 1213-1215 in *The Dictionary of Pastoral Care and Counseling*. Edited by R. J. Hunter. Nashville: Abingdon Press, 1990.

Jones, Cheslyn, ed. *The Study of Spirituality*. New York: Oxford University Press, 1986.

Jones, Stanton, and Richard Butman. eds. *Modern Psychotherapies: A Comprehensive Christian Appraisal*. Downers Grove, IL: InterVarsity, 1991.

Kennedy, Eugene and Victor Heckler, *The Catholic Priest in the United States: Psychological Investigations*. Washington, DC: U.S. Catholic Conference, 1972.

Kellemen, Robert. "Hebrew Anthropological Terms as a Foundation for a Biblical Counseling Model of Humanity." Master's Thesis, Grace Theological Seminary, 1985.

———. *Sacred Companions: A History of Soul Care and Spiritual Direction*. Taneytown, MD: RPM Books, forthcoming.

———. *Soul Physicians: A Theology of Soul Care and Spiritual Direction*. Revised edition. Taneytown, MD: RPM Books, 2005.

———. "Spiritual Care in Historical Perspective: Martin Luther as a Case Study in Christian Sustaining, Healing, Reconciling, and Guiding." Ph.D. Dissertation, Kent State University, 1997.

Keller, Timothy. "Puritan Resources for Pastoral Counseling." *Journal of Pastoral Practice* 9, no. 3 (1988): 11-44.

Kelly, Eugene W. *Spirituality and Religion in Counseling and Psychotherapy*. Alexandria, VA: American Counseling Association, 1995.

Kemp, Charles. *Physicians of the Soul*. New York: MacMillan, 1947.

Kolb, R. "God Calling: 'Take Care of My People': Luther's Concept of Vocation in the Augsburg Confession and Its Apology." *Concordia Journal* 8 (1982): 4-11.

———. "Luther: The Master Pastor." *Concordia Journal* 9 (1983): 179-187.

———. "Luther as *Seelsorger*." *Concordia Journal* 11 (1985): 2-9.

Kollar, Charles. *Solution-Focused Pastoral Counseling: An Effective Short-Term Approach for Getting People Back on Track*. Grand Rapids: Zondervan, 1997.

Kottler, Jeffrey. *The Complete Therapist*. San Francisco: Jossey Bass, 1991.

———. *On Being a Therapist*. San Francisco: Jossey Bass, 1993.

Kraus, G. "Luther as *Seelsorger*." *Concordia Theological Journal* 98 (1984): 153-163.

Kruis, John. *Quick Scripture Reference for Counseling*. Second edition. Grand Rapids: Baker, 1994.

Kubler-Ross, Elisabeth. *On Death and Dying*. Reprint edition. San Francisco: Scribner, 1997.

Lake, Frank. *Clinical Theology*. London: Darton, Longman & Todd, 1966.

Lane, G. *Christian Spirituality: An Historical Sketch*. Chicago: Loyola University Press, 1984.

Langberg, Diane. *On the Threshold of Hope*. Wheaton, IL: Tyndale House, 1999.

Leech, Kenneth. *Experiencing God: Theology as Spirituality*. San Francisco: Harper, 1985.

———. *Soul Friend: The Practice of Christian Spirituality*. San Francisco: Harper, 1977.

Levicoff, Steve. *Christian Counseling and the Law*. Chicago: Moody Press, 1991.

Luther, Martin. *The Bondage of the Will*. Translated by O. R. Johnston and J. I. Packer. Grand Rapids: Revell. 1525/1957.

———. *Career of the Reformer I*. Vol. 31 of *Luther's Works*. Edited and translated by H. T. Lehmann. Philadelphia: Fortress Press, 1957.

———. *Career of the Reformer II*. Vol. 32 of *Luther's Works*. Edited and translated by G. W. Forell. Philadelphia: Fortress Press, 1958.

———. *Commentary on Galatians*. Translated by P. S. Watson. Grand Rapids: Revell, 1535/1988.

———. *Commentary on Romans*. Translated by J. T. Mueller. Grand Rapids: Kregel, 1516/1947.

———. *Devotional Writings I*. Vol. 42 of *Luther's Works*. Edited and translated by M. O. Deitrich. Philadelphia: Fortress Press, 1969.

———. *Devotional Writings II*. Vol. 43 of *Luther's Works*. Edited and translated by G. Wiencke. Philadelphia: Fortress Press, 1968.

———. *The Holy and Blessed Sacrament of Baptism*. Vol. 35 of *Luther's Works*. Edited by A. Wents. Translated by A. Steinhauser. Philadelphia: Fortress Press, 1959.

———. *Large Catechism*. Translated by Robert Fischer. Philadelphia: Fortress Press, 1981.

———. *Lectures on Genesis Chapters 6-14*. Vol. 2 of *Luther's Works*. Edited by J. Pelikan. Translated by V. Schick. Saint Louis: Concordia, 1960.

———. *Lectures on Genesis: Chapters 21-25*. Vol. 4 of *Luther's Works*. Edited by J. Pelikan and W. Hansen. Translated by G. Schick. Saint Louis: Concordia, 1964.

———. *Lectures on Isaiah: Chapters 1-39*. Vol. 16 of *Luther's Works*. Edited by J. Pelikan and H. Oswald. Translated by H. Bouman. Saint Louis: Concordia, 1970.

———. *Letters I*. Vol. 48 of *Luther's Works*. Edited and translated by G. G. Krodel. Philadelphia: Fortress Press, 1963.

———. *Letters II*. Vol. 49 of *Luther's Works*. Edited and translated by G. Krodel. Philadelphia: Fortress Press, 1972.

———. *Letters III*. Vol. 50 of *Luther's Works*. Edited and translated by G. Krodel. Philadelphia: Fortress Press, 1975.

———. "Sermon on John 18:28." In *What Luther Says*. 3 vols. Edited by E. Plass. St. Louis: Concordia, 1959.

———. *The Sermon on the Mount*. Vol. 21 of *Luther's Works*. Edited and translated by J. Pelikan. St. Louis: Concordia, 1953.

———. *Table Talks*. Vol. 54 of *Luther's Works*. Edited and translated by G. Tappert. Philadelphia: Fortress Press, 1967.

MacArthur, John, and Wayne Mack, eds. *Introduction to Biblical Counseling: A Basic Guide to the Principles and Practice of Counseling*. Dallas: Word Publishing, 1994.

Mack, Wayne. *A Homework Manual for Biblical Living*. Vol. 1. Phillipsburg, NJ: Presbyterian & Reformed Publishing, 1979.

Matzat, Don. *Christ Esteem: Where the Search for Self-Esteem Ends*. Eugene, OR: Harvest House, 1990.

McGrath, Alister. *Christian Spirituality*. Malden, MA: Blackwell, 1999.

———. *Historical Theology: An Introduction to the History of Christian Thought*. London: Blackwell, 1998.

———. *The Journey: A Pilgrim in the Lands of the Spirit*. New York: Doubleday, 2000.

———. *Luther's Theology of the Cross*. Grand Rapids: Baker, 1990.

McMinn, Mark. *Psychology, Theology, and Spirituality in Christian Counseling*. Wheaton, IL: Tyndale House, 1996.

McMinn, Mark, and Timothy Phillips. *Care for the Soul: Exploring the Intersection of Psychology and Theology*. Downers Grove, IL: InterVarsity, 2001.

McNeil, John. *A History of the Cure of Souls*. New York: Harper, 1951.

Meiburg, A. "Care of Souls." Page 122 in *The Dictionary of Pastoral Care and Counseling*. Edited by R. J. Hunter. Nashville: Abingdon Press, 1990.

Michaelis, W. "*pascho*." Pages 798-803 in *The Theological Dictionary of the New Testament*. Abridged edition. Edited by G. Bromiley. Grand Rapids: Eerdmans, 1992.

Mills, L. "Pastoral Care." Pages 832-844 in *The Dictionary of Pastoral Care and Counseling*. Edited by R. J. Hunter. Nashville: Abingdon Press, 1990.

Minirth, Frank. *The Minirth Guide for Christian Counselors*. Nashville: Broadman & Holman, 2003.

Moessner, Jeanne, ed. *Through the Eyes of Women: Insights for Pastoral Care*. Minneapolis: Fortress Press, 1996.

Moline, Mary, George Williams, and Kenneth Austin. *Documenting Psychotherapy: Essentials for Mental Health Practitioners*. London: Sage Publications, 1998.

Moon, Gary. "Spiritual Directors and Christian Counselors: Where Do They Overlap?" *Christian Counseling Today*. (Winter 1994): 29-33.

Moon, Gary, and David Benner, eds. *Spiritual Direction and the Care of Souls: A Guide to Christian Approaches and Practices*. Downers Grove, IL: InterVarsity, 2004.

Muller, R. "Soul." Pages 1201-1203 in *The Dictionary of Pastoral Care and Counseling*. Edited by R. J. Hunter. Nashville: Abingdon Press, 1990.

Nebe, A. *Luther as Spiritual Advisor*. Translated by C. H. Hays and C. E. Hays. Philadelphia: Lutheran Publication Society, 1894.

Nouwen, Henri. *The Return of the Prodigal: A Story of Homecoming*. New York: Doubleday, 1992.

———. *The Way of the Heart: Desert Spirituality and Contemporary Ministry*. San Francisco: Harper, 1981.

———. *The Wounded Healer*. New York: Doubleday, 1972.

Oates, Wayne. *The Presence of God in Pastoral Counseling*. Waco, TX: Word Publishing, 1986.

———. *Protestant Pastoral Care*. Louisville: Westminster John Knox Press, 1982.

Oberman, Heiko. *Luther: Man Between God and the Devil*. New York: Doubleday, 1992.

Oden, Thomas C. *Care of Souls in the Classic Tradition*. Philadelphia: Fortress Press, 1983.

———. *Classical Pastoral Care*. 4 Vols. Grand Rapids: Baker, 1987.

———. *Pastoral Theology*. San Francisco: Harper, 1983.

———. *Systematic Theology*. 3 Vols. San Francisco: Harper, 2001.

———. "Whatever Happened to History?" *Good News* (January-February 1993): 8-10.

O'Hanlon, William, and Michele Weiner-Davis. *In Search of Solutions: A New Direction in Psychotherapy*. New York, W. W. Norton, 1989.

Oliver, Gary. *Promoting Change Through Brief Therapy in Christian Counseling*. Wheaton, IL: Tyndale House, 1997.

Olson, Roger. *The Story of Christian Theology*. Downers Grove, IL: InterVarsity, 1999.

Ortlund, Raymond C. *Whoredom: God's Unfaithful Wife in Biblical Theology*. Grand Rapids: Eerdmans, 1996.

Owen, John. *The Death of Death*. London: Banner of Truth Trust, 1963.

———. *The Mortification of Sin*. Ross-Shire, Scotland: Christian Focus Publications, 1656/1996.

———. *Sin and Temptation*. Minneapolis: Bethany House, 1658/1996.

Packer, J. I. *A Grief Sanctified*. Ann Arbor, MI: Servant Publications, 1997.

———. *A Quest for Godliness: The Puritan Vision of the Christian Life*. Wheaton, IL: Crossway Books, 1990.

———. *Rediscovering Holiness*. Ann Arbor, MI: Servant Publications, 1992.

Pascal, Blaise. *Pensees*. New York: Penguin, 1995.

Passantino, Bob, and Gretchen Passantino. *Witch Hunt*. Nashville: Thomas Nelson, 1990.

Peterson, Eugene. *The Contemplative Pastor: Returning to the Art of Spiritual Direction*. Grand Rapids: Eerdmans, 1989.

———. *The Message: The Bible in Contemporary Language*. Colorado Springs: NavPress, 2002.

———. *Subversive Spirituality*. Grand Rapids: Eerdmans, 1997.

———. *The Wisdom of Each Other: A Conversation Between Spiritual Friends*. Grand Rapids: Zondervan, 1998.

Petty, James. *Step by Step: Divine Guidance for Ordinary Christians*. Phillipsburg, NJ: Presbyterian & Reformed Publishing, 1999.

Piper, John. *Desiring God: Meditations of a Christian Hedonist*. Revised and expanded edition. Sisters, OR: Multnomah, 2003.

———. *The Legacy of Sovereign Joy*. Wheaton, IL: Crossway Books, 2000.

———. *The Pleasures of God: Meditations on God's Delight in Being God*. Revised and expanded edition. Sisters, OR: Multnomah, 2000.

Plantinga, Cornelius. *Not the Way It's Supposed to Be: A Breviary of Sin*. Grand Rapids: Eerdmans, 1995.

Powlison, David. "Crucial Issues in Contemporary Biblical Counseling." *Journal of Pastoral Practice* 9, no. 3 (1988): 53-78.

———. "Questions at the Crossroads: The Care of Souls and Modern Psychotherapies." Pages 23-61 in *Care for the Soul*. Edited by Mark McMinn and Timothy Phillips. Downers Grove, IL: InterVarsity, 2001.

———. "Needs and Idols." *Christianity Today* (May 1994): 21.

———. *Seeing with New Eyes: Counseling and the Human Condition Through the Lens of Scripture*. Phillipsburg, NJ: Presbyterian & Reformed Publishing, 2003.

Pyne, Robert. *Humanity and Sin: The Creation, Fall, and Redemption of Humanity*. Nashville: Word Publishing, 1999.

Rea, Jane. *A Spiritual Formation Journal*. San Francisco: Harper Collins, 1996.

Roberts, Robert, and Mark Talbot, eds. *Limning the Psyche: Explorations in Christian Psychology*. Grand Rapids: Eerdmans, 1997.

Robertson, A. T. *Word Pictures in the New Testament*. Concise edition. Nashville: Holman, 2000.

Rollins, Wayne. *Soul and Psyche: The Bible in Psychological Perspective*. Minneapolis: Fortress Press, 1999.

Ruffing, Janet. *Spiritual Direction: Beyond the Beginnings*. New York: Paulist Press, 2000.

Ryken, Leland. *Worldly Saints: The Puritans as They Really Were*. Grand Rapids: Zondervan, 1986.

Sawyer, Joy. *The Art of the Soul: Meditations for the Christian Spirit*. Nashville: Broadman & Holman, 2000.

———. *Dancing to the Heartbeat of Redemption: The Creative Process of Spiritual Growth*. Downers Grove, IL: InterVarsity, 2000.

Scaer, D. "The Concept of *Anfechtungen* in Luther's Thought." *Concordia Theological Quarterly* 47 (1983): 15-30.

———. "Sanctification in Lutheran Theology." *Concordia Theological Quarterly* 49, no. 2 (1985): 15-30.

Schaumburg, Harry. *False Intimacy: Understanding the Struggle of Sexual Addiction.* Colorado Springs: NavPress, 1992.

Scheldrake, Philip. *Spirituality and History.* New York: Orbis Books, 1995.

Schieler, C. *Theory and Practice of the Confessional.* Second edition. New York: Benziger Brothers, 1905.

Schleiner, W. "Renaissance Exampla of Schizophrenia: The Cure by Charity in Luther and Cervantes." *Renaissance and Reformation* 9, no. 3 (1985): 157-176.

Schon, David. *The Reflective Practitioner: How Professionals Think in Action.* New York: SCM Press, 1974.

Seligman, Linda. *Diagnosis and Treatment Planning in Counseling.* New York: Human Science Press, 1986.

———. *Selecting Effective Treatments.* San Francisco: Jossey Bass, 1990.

Shaw, Luci. *Polishing the Petoskey Stone.* Wheaton, IL: Harold Shaw, 1990.

———. *Water My Soul: Cultivating the Interior Life.* Grand Rapids: Zondervan, 1998.

Sheilds, Harry, and Gary Bredfeldt. *Caring for Souls: Counseling Under the Authority of Scripture.* Chicago: Moody Press, 2001.

Shive, David. *Night Shift: God Works in the Dark Hours of Life.* Lincoln, NB: Back to the Bible Publishing, 2001.

Sibbes, Richard. *The Bruised Reed.* Revised edition. Carlisle, PA: Banner of Truth Trust, 1998.

Smith, David. *With Willful Intent: A Theology of Sin.* Wheaton, IL: Victor Books, 1994.

Smith, James. *A Spiritual Formation Workbook.* San Francisco: Harper Collins, 1993.

Smith, P., ed. *The Life and Letters of Martin Luther.* New York: Barnes & Noble, 1911.

Smith, P., and C. Jacobs, eds. *Luther's Correspondence and Other Contemporary Letters.* 2 vols. Philadelphia: Lutheran Publication Society, 1918.

Smith, Robert. *The Christian Counselor's Medical Desk Reference.* Stanley, NC: Timeless Texts, 2000.

Southard, Samuel. *Theology and Therapy: The Wisdom of God in the Context of Friendship.* Dallas: Word Publishing, 1989.

Sproul, R. C. *The Soul's Quest for God: Satisfying the Hunger for Spiritual Communion with God.* Wheaton, IL: Tyndale House, 1992.

Stafford, Tim. "The Therapeutic Revolution: How Christian Counseling Is Changing the Church." *Christianity Today* (May 13, 1993): 24-32.

Stahlin, G., and O. Schmitz. "*parakaleo*." Pages 778-782 in *The Theological Dictionary of the New Testament.* Abridged edition. Edited by G. Bromiley. Grand Rapids: Eerdmans, 1992.

Stott, John. *The Cross of Christ.* Downers Grove, IL: InterVarsity, 1986.

Strohl, J. E. "Luther's Fourteen Consolations." *Lutheran Quarterly* 3 (1989): 169-182.

Sue, D. W., and D. Sue. *Counseling the Culturally Different: Theory and Practice.* New York: Wiley, 1999.

Tan, Siang-Yang. *Lay Counseling: Equipping Christians for a Helping Ministry.* Grand Rapids: Zondervan, 1991.

Tan, Siang-Yang, and John Ortberg. *Understanding Depression: A Short-Term Structured Model.* Grand Rapids: Baker, 1995.

Tappert, G. *Luther: Letters of Spiritual Counsel.* Vol. 18 in *The Library of Christian Classics.* Edited by J. Baillie, J. McNeil, and H. van Dusen. Philadelphia: Westminster Press, 1955.

Taylor, John. *The Go-Between God.* Oxford: Oxford University Press, 1979.

Thomas, Gary. *The Glorious Pursuit: Embracing the Virtues of Christ*. Colorado Springs: NavPress, 1998.

Thompson, Marjorie. *Soul Feast: An Invitation to the Christian Spiritual Life*. Louisville: Westminster John Knox Press, 1995.

Tournier, Paul. *Creative Suffering*. San Francisco: Harper, 1981.

———. *Guilt and Grace*. Translated by Arthur Heathcote. San Francisco: Harper, 1983.

Tripp, David Paul. *Instruments in the Redeemer's Hands: People in Need of Change Helping People in Need of Change*. Phillipsburg, NJ: Presbyterian & Reformed Publishing, 2002.

———. *War of Words: Getting to the Heart of Your Communication Struggles*. Phillipsburg, NJ: Presbyterian & Reformed Publishing, 2000.

Waite, Terry. *Taken on Trust*. New York: Harcourt, Brace & Co., 1993.

Wakefield, Gordon S., ed. *The Westminster Dictionary of Christian Spirituality*. Philadelphia: Westminster Press, 1983.

Walker, Clarence. *Biblical Counseling with African-Americans*. Grand Rapids: Zondervan, 1992.

Walter, John, and Jane Peller. *Becoming Solution-Focused in Brief Therapy*. New York: Brunner/Mazel Publishers, 1992.

Wangerin, Walter. *Mourning Into Dancing*. Grand Rapids: Zondervan, 1992.

Watson, Jeffrey. *Biblical Counseling for Today: A Handbook for Those Who Counsel from Scripture*. Nashville: Word Publishing, 2000.

Weber, Carl. "*hazaq*." Pages 276-277 in Vol. 1 of *The Theological Wordbook of the Old Testament*. 2 vols. Edited by Laird Harris, Gleason Archer, and Bruce Waltke. Chicago: Moody Press, 1981.

Weiner-Davis, Michele. *Divorce Busting*. New York: Simon & Schuster, 1992.

Welch, Ed. *Addictions—A Banquet in the Grave: Finding Hope in the Power of the Gospel*. Phillipsburg, NJ: Presbyterian & Reform Publishing, 2001.

———. *Blame It on the Brain?: Distinguishing Chemical Imbalances, Brain Disorders, and Disobedience*. Phillipsburg, NJ: Presbyterian & Reformed Publishing, 1998.

———. *When People Are Big and God Is Small*. Phillipsburg, NJ: Presbyterian & Reformed Publishing, 1997.

Westberg, Granger. *Good Grief*. Philadelphia: Fortress Press, 1971.

White, M., and D. Epston. *Narrative Means to Therapeutic Ends*. New York: W. W. Norton, 1990.

Whitney, Donald. *Spiritual Disciplines for the Christian Life*. Colorado Springs: NavPress, 1991.

Wicks, Robert, and Richard Parsons. *Clinical Handbook of Pastoral Counseling*. 2 vols. New York: Paulist Press, 1993.

Wicks, Robert, and Thomas Rodgerson. *Companions in Hope: The Art of Christian Caring*. New York: Paulist Press, 1998.

Willard, Dallas. *The Divine Conspiracy: Rediscovering Our Hidden Life in God*. San Francisco: Harper, 1998.

———. *Renovation of the Heart: Putting on the Character of Christ*. Colorado Springs: NavPress, 2002.

———. *The Spirit of the Disciplines: Understanding How God Changes Lives*. San Francisco: Harper, 1991.

Wolff, Hans. *Anthropology of the Old Testament*. Translated by Margaret Kohl. London: SCM Press, 1974.

Worthington, Everett. *Hope-Focused Marriage Counseling: A Guide to Brief Therapy*. Downers Grove, IL: InterVarsity, 1999.

Zuckerman, Edward. *Clinicians Thesaurus: The Guidebook for Writing Psychological Reports*. Fourth edition. London: Guilford Press, 1995.

You've Grown from the *Methodology* of *Spiritual Friends*
Now Learn from the *Theology* of *Soul Physicians*

Soul Physicians: A Theology of Soul Care and Spiritual Direction

Join the growing number of lay people, pastors, professional counselors, and students who are using *Soul Physicians* as their twenty-first century theology manual for Christian counseling and spiritual friendship. Learn our Great Physician's authoritative truth about:

- Nourishing the Hunger of the Soul: Preventative Medicine—God's Word
- Knowing the Creator of the Soul: The Great Physician—The Trinity
- Examining the Spiritual Anatomy of the Soul: People—Creation
- Diagnosing the Fallen Condition of the Soul: Problems—Fall
- Prescribing God's Cure for the Soul: Solutions—Redemption
- Envisioning the Final Healing of the Soul: Home—Glorification
- Dispensing God's Care for the Soul: Spiritual Friends—Sanctification

To order *Soul Physicians*, or our other products, visit us at: www.rpmbooks.org, or e-mail us at: orders@rpmbooks.org.

About *RPM Ministries* and *RPM Books*

Dr. Bob Kellemen founded *RPM Ministries* in 2000 and established *RPM Books* in 2003. *RPM* is Bob's acronym for *Resurrection Power Multipliers* which takes its name from Paul's longing in Philippians 3:10 to know the power of Christ's resurrection.

RPM Ministries exists to empower Christians toward Christlikeness by relating God's truth to human relationships. Through *RPM Ministries*, Bob and others offer conferences and seminars on Spiritual Friendship, Soul Care and Spiritual Direction, Marriage, and Parenting.

RPM Books is the publishing arm of *RPM Ministries*. It exists to change lives with Christ's changeless truth.

To learn more about *RPM Ministries* and *RPM Books*, visit us at: www.rpmbooks.org.

To discuss scheduling a conference, e-mail us at: bookings@rpmministries.org.

About Dr. Kellemen

Dr. Robert W. Kellemen is Chairman of the Master of Arts in Christian Counseling and Discipleship Department at Capital Bible Seminary where he has field-tested *Spiritual Friends* for a decade. In his three pastoral ministries, Bob has trained hundreds of lay people in the art of spiritual friendship. As a Licensed Clinical Professional Counselor, he brings a practitioner's sensitivity to his writing. Bob and his wife, Shirley, have been married for twenty-four years. They have two children, Josh, who is twenty, and Marie, who is seventeen.